Bottom Line's
HEALTH
BREAKTHROUGHS
2009

Bottom Line
Books
www.BottomLineSecrets.com

Articles in this book were written by reporters for HealthDay, an award-winning international daily
consumer health news service, headquartered in Norwalk, Connecticut.

Bottom Line Books® publishes the opinions of expert authorities in many fields.

The use of this book is not a substitute for health or other professional service. Consult a physician
or other health-care practitioner for answers to your specific questions and before you make
any decision regarding your health.

Addresses, telephone numbers and Web sites listed in this book are accurate
at the time of publication, but they are subject to frequent change.

Bottom Line Books® is a registered trademark of Boardroom® Inc.

281 Tresser Boulevard, Stamford, CT 06901

Printed in the United States of America

Contents

1

Aging & Senior Health

The Vitamin That May Lengthen Life

Supplementing with vitamin D could prolong your life, according to a new European study. "The intake of usual doses of vitamin D seems to decrease mortality from any cause of death," said lead researcher Philippe Autier, MD, from the International Agency for Research on Cancer in Lyon, France.

The new finding is somewhat of an anomaly, because the benefits of vitamin supplements remains uncertain at best. While they are often touted as a means of reducing risks for cancer and heart disease, some studies have found supplements have no effect on these conditions.

But vitamin D may be the exception, according to the results of this new study.

"This is the first study that shows that taking one vitamin has an impact on mortality," Dr. Autier said. "If you want to increase your vitamin D intake by taking supplements, it looks like a great idea."

THE STUDY

Dr. Autier and colleagues looked at data from 18 trials involving more than 57,000 people. Doses of vitamin D in the trials varied from 300 international units (IU) to 2,000 IU, with an average dose of 528 IU.

Over a follow-up of almost six years, 4,777 of the study participants died. Those who took vitamin D supplements had a 7% lower risk of death compared with those who didn't take the supplement, according to the researchers.

Nine of the trials had collected blood samples. Participants who took the supplements had a 1.4- to 5.2-fold higher level of vitamin D in their blood compared to those who did not, the researchers noted.

Philippe Autier, MD, International Agency for Research on Cancer, Lyon, France.

Michael F. Holick, MD, PhD, director, Vitamin D, Skin and Bone Research Laboratory, Boston University Medical Center.

Archives of Internal Medicine.

IMPLICATION

This finding could lead to new drugs to fight cancer and other diseases, Dr. Autier said. "Vitamin D can reduce the proliferation of cells and the proliferation of cells is something you see in cancer," he said.

RECOMMENDATION

Dr. Autier believes people should take between 400 IU and 600 IU of vitamin D daily. "There is no need to take more—that's crazy," he said. "You have to be careful not to take a dose that's too high," he added.

Another way to make sure you get vitamin D is to get a moderate amount of sun exposure each day, since the skin uses sunlight to produce its own vitamin D.

info For more information on vitamin D, visit the National Institutes of Health Web site at *http://ods.od.nih.gov/factsheets/vitamind.asp.*

Zinc Fights Pneumonia And More in Those Over 50

Tufts University, news release.

Maintaining normal zinc concentrations in the blood may help prevent pneumonia in nursing home residents, a new study shows.

THE STUDY

Researchers at Tufts University looked at 617 people ages 65 and older in 33 nursing homes in the Boston area. All the study participants received daily supplements containing 50% of the recommended dietary allowance of several vitamins and minerals, including zinc, for one year. Blood samples were taken from the residents at the start and conclusion of the one-year study.

STUDY FINDINGS

Study participants with normal blood zinc concentrations were about 50% less likely to develop pneumonia than those with low concentrations of the mineral.

The study, published in the *American Journal of Clinical Nutrition*, also found that people with normal zinc concentrations had a 39% lower rate of death from all causes.

MORE ZINC BENEFITS

"Not only did (people with lower zinc concentrations) have a higher risk of developing pneumonia, when they did become sick, they did not recover as quickly and required a longer course of antibiotics," said corresponding author Simin Nikbin Meydani, PhD, director of the nutritional immunology laboratory at the US Department of Agriculture's Human Nutrition Research Center on Aging at Tufts.

"Zinc is already known to strengthen the immune system. However, there needs to be further investigation of zinc and its effect on pneumonia development and prevention in nursing homes. The next step would be a clinical trial," Dr. Meydani said.

SOURCES OF ZINC

Red meat, poultry, whole grains, beans, dairy products, and oysters are examples of foods that provide zinc.

info The American Lung Association has more information about pneumonia at their Web site at *www.lungusa.org.* Click on "Diseases A to Z."

Important Supplement Info for Seniors

Nutritionist Alan H. Pressman, DC, PhD, CCN, host of the daily radio show *Healthline with Dr. Pressman* on WWRL 1600 in New York City and syndicated nationally on Air America, *www.drpressman.com.* He is author of numerous books on nutrition and health, including, with coauthor Sheila Buff, *The Complete Idiot's Guide to Vitamins and Minerals.* Alpha.

Many older adults regularly take vitamins, minerals and other dietary supplements. But just because something is "natural" or "drug free" doesn't mean that it's always safe. As a senior, if you take any sort of supplement, you need to be aware of the risks and be sure to take the right dosage.

YOUR DAILY MULTIVITAMIN

Most doctors agree that taking a daily multivitamin with minerals is good insurance against those times when you can't eat as well as you should. Doctors often also recommend daily multis to people older than age 50 because the ability to absorb some nutrients in food, such as the B vitamins, declines as people get older. Your doctor may also recommend specific B vitamins, such as B-12, in addition to a multivitamin, if he/she thinks you need it. Check for a good brand on ConsumerLab.com or ask your pharmacist.

Also look for a formulation designed for the nutritional needs of older adults. These multis generally contain the same amounts of vitamins A, C, D, E and K as those formulated for younger adults, but may contain higher amounts of the B vitamins. Multis made for seniors may also contain some ingredients that are helpful for older adults, such as lutein and zeaxanthin (they can help prevent sight-robbing age-related macular degeneration) and lycopene (which may be helpful for preventing prostate cancer).

Important: Your multivitamin *should* not contain iron. Even without taking supplements, older adults can start to build up higher than normal levels of iron in their bodies. This isn't an issue for most people. But, if you have the hereditary disease *hemochromatosis* (iron overload disease), iron builds up in the body to dangerously high levels. You may not find that you have this disease until you start to exhibit serious symptoms, such as liver problems or diabetes, because there is no direct test for it.

Bottom line: Take an iron supplement only if your doctor tells you to for a specific reason.

Dosage: Doubling up on your daily multivitamin probably won't hurt—but it probably won't give you any extra benefit. Get more of the vitamins and minerals that are in your daily supplement, as well as extra fiber, antioxidants and other valuable nutrients, by adding more whole grains, fresh fruits and vegetables to your diet.

CALCIUM

Most daily multivitamin supplements contain from 100 milligrams (mg) to 300 mg of calcium —considerably less than the recommended daily intake of 1,200 mg for men and women older than age 50. If you can't get the additional calcium from your diet (dairy products, sardines and spinach are good sources), consider taking calcium and vitamins D and K—all nutrients you need to maintain strong bones.

One good choice: Viactiv, which combines all three nutrients.

Interaction caution: If you're taking a cycline antibiotic (*tetracycline, doxycycline,* etc.) or the antibiotic *ciprofloxacin* (Cipro), skip the calcium supplements until you finish the course of antibiotics—calcium blocks your absorption of the drug. You can continue taking a daily multivitamin while on a course of antibiotics, but take the drug and the multi several hours apart.

Dosage: 1,000 to 1,500 mg a day of calcium is safe for most people. More than that can cause constipation and could interfere with prescription medications. Calcium in the form of calcium carbonate is effective—and inexpensive. When taking calcium, take a total of 500 mg of magnesium daily for proper calcium absorption. And, be sure to get the recommended dietary allowance of vitamin D (400 IU) and the daily adequate intake of vitamin K (90 mcg for women, 120 mcg for men).

HERB CAUTIONS

Herbal supplements should be used with caution at any age, but there are some herbs that can be especially dangerous for older adults...

• **St.-John's-wort.** Also called hypericum, this herb is usually taken at a dosage of 900 mg to 1,800 mg daily, and can help mild depression.

Problem: It can interact badly with a number of drugs commonly prescribed for older adults, including blood thinners and medications for depression, epilepsy, Parkinson's disease, heart disease—even heartburn.

What to do: Because the list of drugs that interact with St.-John's-wort keeps growing, don't take it if you take any prescription drug. If you think you might benefit from treatment for depression, ask your doctor what will be the best course of action.

• **Ginkgo biloba** can help age-related memory problems by improving blood flow to the brain.

Beware: Ginkgo biloba is a mild blood thinner. Don't use it at all if you take a prescription blood thinner, such as *warfarin* (Coumadin). If you take a daily low-dose aspirin, you can use ginkgo, but take it 12 hours apart from the aspirin. If you take a daily regular-dose aspirin, ask your doctor about taking ginkgo.

Dosage: All reputable brands are standardized to contain 24% of flavonoids (chemical compounds with antioxidant properties). The usual dose is 60 mg, taken one to three times a day. Take with meals to avoid stomach upset.

•**Ginseng.** Ginseng is an adaptogen, a naturally occurring substance found in plants that helps strengthen your body's ability to handle stress and fight off illness. Ginseng is especially helpful as you grow older. Studies have shown that ginseng can improve thinking and learning.

Side effects: Ginseng can lower blood sugar, which could be a problem if you take medication for diabetes. Ginseng can also cause headaches—stop taking it if that happens.

Quality caution: Be sure to use only American ginseng root (*Panax quinquefolius*), which is the species that has been most thoroughly studied and is believed by herbal practitioners to be most effective, and select a product from a well-known, brand-name manufacturer.

Dosage: Ginseng is traditionally made into a tea—have no more than one cup a day. If you prefer capsules, stick to no more than 100 mg a day. Start with a low dose—half a cup of tea or 50 mg in capsule form. If you don't notice any negative effects, such as itching, skin rash, diarrhea or insomnia, gradually increase the daily dose to one full cup or 100 mg over a week's time.

•**Saw palmetto** helps relieve symptoms of benign prostatic hyperplasia (BPH), also called enlarged prostate. Check with your doctor to be sure that your symptoms (frequent urination or difficulty urinating) aren't caused by something more serious.

Interaction cautions: Do not take saw palmetto if you're taking any prescription drug to relieve the symptoms of BPH, such as *finasteride* (Proscar) or *tamsulosin* (Flomax). Saw palmetto lowers levels of testosterone, as do the drugs, and levels may get lowered too much. Don't use saw palmetto if you take a blood-thinning drug such as warfarin. (Saw palmetto is safe to take with a daily aspirin.)

Quality caution: Saw palmetto products vary in quality, so look for a product from a well-known manufacturer.

Dosage: 320 mg daily.

Two Supplements That Boost Muscle, Cut Fat in Seniors

Mark A. Stengler, ND, naturopathic physician in private practice, La Jolla, California…adjunct associate clinical professor at the National College of Natural Medicine, Portland, Oregon…author of many books, including *The Natural Physician's Healing Therapies* and coauthor of *Prescription for Natural Cures* (both from Bottom Line Books)…and author of the *Bottom Line/Natural Healing* newsletter.

Canadian researchers examined the effects of two supplements—*creatine monohydrate* (CrM), a compound found in meat, and *conjugated linoleic acid* (CLA), a fatty acid in dairy products and plant oils—believed to have a synergistic effect. For six months, 39 men and women, ages 65 to 85, did two hours of muscle-building resistance exercises twice weekly and took either placebos or 5 g of CrM plus 6 g of CLA daily.

Results: On average, supplement users lost 4.2 pounds of body fat, compared with a loss of 0.88 pounds of body fat for placebo users. Supplement users also showed greater increases in muscle mass, strength and endurance.

My view: Strong muscles make it easier to perform tasks of daily living, maintain balance and avoid falls. Reducing body fat lowers blood pressure and improves blood sugar regulation. Seniors should ask their doctors about incorporating resistance training, such as weight lifting, into their exercise program.

Recommended: Adults over age 65 who are overweight or who have muscle weakness should take 5 g of CrM plus 6 g of CLA daily for six months, continuing indefinitely if strength improves. Both are sold at health food stores. Do not take CrM if you have kidney or liver disease—you may have problems metabolizing it.

■ ■ ■ ■

Foods That Fight Macular Degeneration

Vitamin-rich foods reduce risk of macular degeneration, the leading cause of severe vision loss in Americans age 60 and over. A diet rich in vitamins C and E, beta-carotene and zinc lowers risk for the disease. Vitamin E and zinc are especially effective. Vitamin E is found in whole grains, eggs, nuts and vegetable oil…zinc in meat, poultry, fish, whole grains and dairy… vitamin C in citrus fruits and juices, broccoli, green pepper and potatoes…beta-carotene in carrots, spinach and kale.

Redmer van Leeuwen, MD, PhD, Erasmus Medical Center, Rotterdam, the Netherlands, and leader of an eight-year study of more than 4,000 residents of Rotterdam, published in *The Journal of the American Medical Association.*

■ ■ ■ ■

Better Therapy for Hip Fractures

In a study of 2,127 adults undergoing hip fracture surgery, half received annual intravenous (IV) infusions of *zoledronic acid* (Reclast) within 90 days of the surgery, and half were given a placebo.

Result: Those who received zoledronic acid had a 35% lower risk, on average, for a second hip fracture than the placebo group.

Theory: Zoledronic acid works to reduce bone breakdown.

If you have recently broken your hip: Ask your doctor if this therapy is right for you.

Kenneth W. Lyles, MD, professor of medicine, Duke University Medical Center, Durham, North Carolina.

■ ■ ■ ■

DHEA Doesn't Work to Fight Aging

An extensive two-year study conducted on the popular antiaging supplement DHEA (*dehydroepiandrosterone*) found that it provided "no beneficial effects" for either men or women. The study findings are expected to be controversial because DHEA is a very big seller in the health food supplements industry.

K. Sreekumaran Nair, MD, division of endocrinology, lead author of the study, Mayo Clinic, Rochester, Minnesota, *www.mayoclinic.com.*

Dr. Oz's Seven Simple Ways to Live to 100

Mehmet C. Oz, MD, professor of cardiac surgery at Columbia University, New York City. He is medical director of the integrative medicine program and director of the Cardiovascular Institute at New York–Presbyterian Hospital/Columbia University Medical Center. Dr. Oz is coauthor, with Michael F. Roizen, MD, of four books, including *YOU…Staying Young: The Owner's Manual for Extending Your Warranty.* Free Press. He also is the health expert for *The Oprah Winfrey Show.*

Today's life expectancy is 75 years for men and 80 years for women. That's better than it was in 1970—when life expectancy was 69 for men and 74 for women—but people still could be living much longer. Many of us can increase life expectancy and have a good chance of reaching 100. *Here's how…*

FIGHT FREE RADICALS

Every cell has hundreds of *mitochondria*, which convert nutrients into energy. During this conversion process, mitochondria create waste—particularly *free radicals*, molecules that cause inflammation and cell damage. The mitochondria in someone over age 60 are 40% less efficient than the mitochondria in someone age 40.

Result: More inflammation…more damaged cells…and more age-related diseases.

Solution 1: Eat colorful produce. Fruits and vegetables with bright colors—red grapes, blueberries, tomatoes, etc.—are high in flavonoids and carotenoids, antioxidants that inhibit free radicals and reduce inflammation.

Solution 2: Take coenzyme Q10 (CoQ10). If you don't eat lots of produce—and most people don't—consider this supplement, which can improve the efficiency of mitochondria. It also is a potent antioxidant that helps neutralize free radicals. I usually recommend that people start taking CoQ10 after age 35.

Dose: 200 milligrams (mg) daily (100 mg in the morning and 100 mg in the afternoon). The gel-cap form is easier for the body to absorb than the tablets.

EAT FISH INSTEAD OF MEAT

Americans eat a lot of red meat, one of the main sources of saturated fat. Saturated fat increases LDL "bad" cholesterol, one of the main risk factors for heart disease, and stimulates the body's production of inflammatory proteins, believed to be an underlying cause of most age-related diseases, including cancer.

Solution 1: Eat fish three times a week. The omega-3 fatty acids in fish reduce inflammation…increase joint lubrication…decrease risk for atherosclerosis (hardening of the arteries) and arterial clots…improve immunity…reduce menopausal discomfort…and improve memory and other cognitive functions.

Solution 2: Take DHA if you don't eat fish regularly. Fish oil supplements contain the omega-3s *docosahexaenoic acid* (DHA) and *eicosapentaenoic acid* (EPA)—but humans need only the DHA.

Daily dose: 400 mg of DHA for women, and 600 mg for men. Buy the algae form. It doesn't have the fishy taste—or the undesirable additives that prolong shelf life—found in many fish oil supplements.

TAKE ASPIRIN

It's estimated that about 50 million Americans should be taking aspirin daily, but only about 20 million are doing so.

Reasons: Some people don't know that they should be taking aspirin. Others experience stomach upset when using it. And some tend to think that a drug that's so cheap and readily available isn't likely to be effective.

Fact: In studies, taking 162 mg of aspirin daily reduces the risk for a heart attack by about 36% and the risk for colon, esophageal, throat and stomach cancers by about 45%. Serious side effects from aspirin are rare.

Solution: Take one-half of a regular aspirin or two 81-mg (baby) aspirins daily (162 mg total)—but check with your doctor first. Buy the cheapest tablets. These usually are unbuffered and dissolve more quickly in the stomach.

Also helpful: Drink half a glass of warm water before and after taking aspirin. It causes the aspirin to dissolve more rapidly, so it doesn't stick to the stomach wall—the main cause of discomfort.

BOOST NITRIC OXIDE

Nitric oxide is a naturally occurring, short-lived gas that is produced mainly in the lining of blood vessels. It plays a critical role in *vasodilation*—the expansion of blood vessels that allows blood to circulate with less force. Nitric oxide is thought to lower blood pressure, reduce the buildup of plaque in atherosclerosis and foster better lung function. The traditional American diet, which promotes the accumulation of fat-laden deposits on artery walls, lowers nitric oxide in the blood.

Solution: Eat less saturated fat. Limit foods that are high in saturated fat, such as meats, butter and whole-milk dairy products. Studies show that the body's production of nitric oxide declines immediately after people eat a meal that is high in saturated fat—and nitric oxide levels stay depressed for about four hours after such a meal.

REDUCE STRESS

Researchers have found that chronic stress prematurely shortens *telomeres*, the tips of chromosomes that control the ability of cells to divide and repair damaged tissues. Impaired cell division is among the main causes of age-related diseases. Research has shown that people who achieve control over daily stress have lower levels of harmful stress hormones, lower blood pressure and better immunity.

Solution: Meditate for five minutes daily. Sit silently, and try to clear your mind of thoughts. To help do this, pick a word (it doesn't matter what it is), and repeat it to yourself over and over. Focusing on the one word helps prevent other thoughts from entering your mind. Another stress reducer is exercise, such as yoga or walking.

LIMIT SUGAR

Sugar consumption in the US has increased almost every year since the early 1980s. The average American eats 20 teaspoons of added sugar a day—from sweets, soft drinks, table sugar, etc.

Because sugary foods often replace more healthful foods in the diet, they're a primary cause of heart disease, cancer and osteoporosis.

Of course, a high-sugar diet contributes to obesity, a main cause of diabetes. Excessive sugar (glucose) in the blood can result in nerve damage, kidney failure, memory problems, eye disease and arthritis.

Solution: Avoid sugar. Also avoid other white carbohydrates, such as white rice, white potatoes and white flour. These "simple sugars" have few nutrients and cause blood sugar to spike.

Diabetes indicator: If you have to urinate more than 12 times a day, or more than three times in a three-hour period, ask your doctor to test your urine for sugar, an early indicator of diabetes.

STRENGTHEN BONES

Falls—and the resulting broken bones and complications—are among the top five causes of death.

Solution: A regular exercise regimen—particularly weight-bearing exercise, including lifting weights and using exercise bands—increases muscle strength and bone density. Taking a daily walk strengthens leg bones, but you also need exercises that target the upper body.

Self-test: Stand on one foot with your arms out to the sides. Close your eyes, and count the seconds until you fall off balance. If you can't stay balanced for 15 seconds at age 40 or seven seconds at age 60 or older, your balance and/or strength aren't optimal. Ask your doctor about balancing exercises, etc.

Study Reveals More Drugs for Dementia

Bruce Pollock, MD, department of psychiatry, University of Toronto, Canada.

Ralph A. Nixon, MD, PhD, professor, psychiatry and cell biology, New York University School of Medicine, New York City, and member, Alzheimer's Association's medical and scientific advisory council.

American Journal of Geriatric Psychiatry, online.

The antidepressant *citalopram* (Celexa) may be as effective as often-prescribed antipsychotic drugs to control the agitation and psychotic symptoms associated with dementia, a new study suggests.

BACKGROUND

Agitation and psychotic symptoms are often more disturbing than the memory loss associated with Alzheimer's and other forms of dementia. They are also the most difficult challenge for family members caring for an elderly person. Currently, antipsychotic drugs such as *risperidone* (Risperdal) are used to control these symptoms. But the side effects, including sedation, tension and apathy, can be debilitating, the study authors said.

"We found that an antidepressant worked as well in severely agitated patients suffering from Alzheimer's disease as an antipsychotic," said lead researcher Bruce Pollock, MD, of the University of Toronto's department of psychiatry. "And citalopram had fewer side effects."

The surprise was that citalopram worked as well for psychotic symptoms such as delusion and visual hallucinations, he said.

THE STUDY

Dr. Pollock's team randomly assigned 103 patients who were hospitalized at the University of Pittsburgh Medical Center with psychiatric disturbances related to dementia to receive either citalopram or risperidone.

After 12 weeks, the researchers found that both drugs had a similar effect in relieving psychotic symptoms, such as hallucinations, delusions and suspicious thoughts. There was a 32% reduction in symptoms among patients receiving citalopram, compared to a 35% reduction among those receiving risperidone.

However, there was a significant 19% *increase* in side effects among patients taking risperidone, compared with a 4% decrease with citalopram, the researchers reported.

IMPLICATIONS

If further studies replicate these findings, Dr. Pollock thinks antidepressants could be a viable alternative to antipsychotic drugs for Alzheimer's patients.

"Behavioral disturbances are the most terrible thing that patients and caregivers have to cope with in dementia," he said. "And 90% of Alzheimer's patients will experience them. It's the phenomenon that results in patients going to nursing homes and requiring higher levels of care."

Pollock also said that antipsychotic drugs have an increased risk for death associated with their use. "But, for the first time, it has been shown that an antidepressant may work as well for psychotic symptoms as an antipsychotic," he said.

One expert thinks these findings are promising but need to be confirmed before they can be put into clinical practice.

"This is an interesting direction for further research," said Ralph A. Nixon, MD, PhD, a professor of psychiatry and cell biology at New York University School of Medicine and a member of the Alzheimer's Association's medical and scientific advisory council. "It is a preliminary indication of a new class of medications to treat something that has been a very vexing problem to treat."

Dr. Nixon thinks these drugs need to be compared with placebos to gauge the true effect of antidepressants on the psychotic symptoms associated with Alzheimer's.

info For more information on Alzheimer's disease, visit the Alzheimer's Association Web site at *www.alz.org*.

Nine New Ways to Fight Alzheimer's

Dharma Singh Khalsa, MD, president and medical director of the Alzheimer's Research and Prevention Foundation, based in Tucson, Arizona. He is associate fellow at the University of Pennsylvania's Center for Spirituality and the Mind, Philadelphia, and author of *Brain Longevity*. Warner.

More than five million Americans have Alzheimer's disease, and the number is expected to triple by the year 2050 as the population ages.

New finding: A study in the journal *Neurology* reports that mild cognitive impairment, once thought to be a normal part of aging, might be an early sign of Alzheimer's—a finding that could double the total number of people who are known to have Alzheimer's.

Medications can slow the disease's progression, but they can't cure it. A vaccine has been developed that reduces the deposits in the brain that occur with Alzheimer's, but a trial of the vaccine was halted because of dangerous side effects, including brain inflammation.

The good news is that lifestyle approaches can significantly decrease disease progression and may even play a role in prevention. All the supplements listed here are safe for most people, but always check with your doctor first.

STOP INFLAMMATION

In patients suffering from Alzheimer's disease, a normally harmless protein, called *beta amyloid*, accumulates in the brain and blocks the connections between neurons. In addition, many of the neurons that produce *acetylcholine*, a neurotransmitter that carries signals from one neuron to the next, die off. The result is problems with memory, abstract thinking and other cognitive functions, along with personality changes, such as increased aggressiveness and/or anxiousness.

The drugs that are currently available increase the levels of neurotransmitters in the brain—an approach that's only marginally effective for many patients. It now seems likely that reducing brain inflammation may be more effective.

Alzheimer's patients have higher levels of *oxidative stress* in the brain. Oxidation, caused by free radicals (harmful molecules that damage cells), leads to inflammation and is believed to be one of the main causes of heart disease as well as Alzheimer's. A diet high in fruits and vegetables—particularly brightly colored produce—is ideal because it provides the highest amounts of antioxidant nutrients. Also important...

• **Combine vitamins C and E.** Vitamin C reduces oxidation in the watery portions of cells, while fat-soluble vitamin E works in the fatty portions.

Dose: As a preventive measure, 1,000 mg of vitamin C daily and 400 IU of vitamin E. Alzheimer's patients may need 2,000 mg of vitamin C daily and 2,000 IU of vitamin E.

• **Take acetyl L-carnitine.** L-carnitine is a substance that's particularly active in brain cells, where it stimulates *mitochondrial efficiency*—

the ability of structures inside cells to produce energy while releasing fewer free radicals.

Dose: 100 mg daily of the acetylated form, which is easier for the body to utilize. Take it with 100 mg each of alpha lipoic acid and co-enzyme Q10 (CoQ10). The combination reduces free radicals and improves mitochondrial efficiency more than acetyl L-carnitine alone.

• **Reduce saturated fat.** Saturated fat is a *proinflammatory nutrient* that increases brain inflammation. Meat, butter and whole milk are high in saturated fat. The best diet for the brain is one that includes no more than 20% of calories from total fat—with most of it coming from healthful nonsaturated fats, such as olive oil and the fats in nuts, avocados and fish.

• **Eat fish at least twice weekly.** Cold-water fish, including salmon and sardines, are especially high in omega-3 fatty acids, which are potent antioxidants. One of the omega-3 fatty acids, *docosahexaenoic acid* (DHA), appears to reduce brain plaques.

IMPROVE BLOOD FLOW

The same factors that increase the risk for cardiovascular disease—high blood pressure, smoking, high cholesterol, etc.—also have been linked to Alzheimer's disease. People who control these factors and maintain healthy circulation are less likely to experience later-life dementia.

• **Exercise most days of the week.** It increases brain circulation along with levels of growth factors, substances needed to repair damaged neurons. Exercise also stimulates the migration of stem cells to the *hippocampus* (the region of the brain that controls memory)—important for increasing neurons.

• **Consider ginkgo.** This extract that comes from the leaf of the ginkgo biloba tree is an antioxidant that promotes brain circulation. A 2006 study published in *European Journal of Neurology* followed patients with mild-to-moderate dementia for 24 weeks. Those given ginkgo supplements did as well overall as those given the Alzheimer's drug *donepezil* (Aricept).

Dose: 240 mg of ginkgo daily.

Caution: Because ginkgo has a blood-thinning effect, check with your doctor if you're on aspirin therapy or taking a blood thinner, such as *warfarin* (Coumadin).

New finding: Contrary to earlier reports, statin drugs, used to reduce cholesterol, offer no protection against Alzheimer's disease, according to research published in *Neurology.*

ASK ABOUT HUPERZINE A

This moss extract used in Chinese medicine is a natural *cholinesterase inhibitor*—the same mechanism involved in some Alzheimer's drugs. The chemical compounds in huperzine A may turn out to be superior to current drugs because they work more directly to increase brain levels of acetylcholine.

Dose: 50 micrograms (mcg) to 100 mcg daily.

REDUCE STRESS

People who experience excessive, chronic stress—from job pressures, marital difficulties, etc.—experience an abnormal deactivation of the frontal lobe, the part of the brain associated with cognitive functions. Stress also triggers the release of *cortisol*, a hormone that in high concentrations kills brain cells in the hippocampus.

Physical exercise is among the best ways to reduce chronic stress. Daily meditation also is helpful. Our research shows that just 12 minutes a day of meditation can reduce stress.

BE MENTALLY DIFFERENT

The famous Nun Study, a study of aging and Alzheimer's in 678 nuns, found that cloistered nuns with the highest levels of education and vocabulary were the ones least likely to develop cognitive impairment, even when their brains were later found to have signs of Alzheimer's.

Reason: They had higher cognitive reserves, increased levels of neurons and connections between neurons.

People who stay mentally active experience *neurogenesis*, the growth of new brain cells. Even if these people develop Alzheimer's disease in later life, the additional neurons and neuronal connections can help them stay mentally sharp longer.

Best: Do activities that stimulate the *opposite* side of the brain from the one you normally use. A "left-brain" person, for example, is more likely to work in fields that require analytical thinking. He/she would benefit from creative or intuitive right-brain activities—art, spirituality, etc. An artist, on the other hand, might want to focus more on left-brain stimulation, such as crossword puzzles or learning a language.

■ **More from Dharma Singh Khalsa, MD…**

Delay Alzheimer's Onset

Delay the onset of Alzheimer's by drinking fresh vegetable juice. It has a concentrated array of anti-inflammatory vitamins, minerals and trace elements that promote cognitive health. Try juicing broccoli, celery, carrots and peeled cucumber with apples for sweetness to enhance day-to-day brain performance.

Best: Drink eight to 12 ounces per day, preferably using organic produce to avoid harmful chemicals.

■ ■ ■ ■

Alzheimer's May Be Linked to Lead Poisoning

Alzheimer's may be linked to lead poisoning during infancy.

Recent finding: After 23 years, monkeys that had been given a lead-laced baby formula had higher levels of Alzheimer's-related proteins and DNA damage than monkeys given ordinary formula.

Nasser Zawia, PhD, associate professor of pharmacology and toxicology, University of Rhode Island, Kingston, and lead author of a study published in *The Journal of Neuroscience.*

Alzheimer's Update— New Treatments on The Horizon…

David Knopman, MD, professor of neurology at the Mayo Clinic College of Medicine, Rochester, Minnesota, *www.mayoclinic.com.* Dr. Knopman has been an Alzheimer's disease researcher for more than 25 years.

There are four drugs currently on the market that can delay the progression of Alzheimer's symptoms for up to a year.

And researchers are investigating dozens of new medications that attack Alzheimer's underlying disease mechanism. Hopefully, at least several will be found effective and approved for use over the next few years.

Here are the drugs currently available for treating Alzheimer's and the experimental drugs that may work better…

CURRENT MEDICATIONS

Four FDA-approved medications are currently used to treat Alzheimer's disease.

Three drugs—*donepezil* (Aricept), *rivastigmine* (Exelon) and *galantamine* (Razadyne)—are cholinesterase inhibitors, which boost levels of *acetylcholine*, a chemical in the brain known as a neurotransmitter that is involved in attention and memory. The FDA recently approved an Exelon skin patch. Applied just once a day and worn for 24 hours (as opposed to the pill form, which is taken twice a day), it decreases the likelihood of forgetting a dose, while minimizing the gastrointestinal side effects of nausea and diarrhea sometimes caused by these medications.

The fourth medication, *memantine* (Namenda), reduces brain levels of glutamate, a chemical linked to brain cell degeneration. Namenda may be taken alone or with a cholinesterase inhibitor.

All four drugs are equally effective and can be useful in the appropriate circumstances—with mildly affected patients who are otherwise in good health. However, they're basically plugging a leaky dike—improving symptoms temporarily, but doing nothing to prevent the continued destruction of brain cells. They typically delay onset of further Alzheimer's symptoms by six months to a year, after which patients begin to deteriorate. Continuing on these medications will still keep them functioning at a higher level than they would otherwise, delaying the onset of severe symptoms, such as loss of ability to carry out basic daily living activities (bathing, dressing, etc.).

EXPERIMENTAL MEDICATIONS

What's desperately needed are drugs that intervene in the Alzheimer's disease process to halt, or even reverse, its progression.

About a dozen candidates are now in middle-to-late stages (Phase II or III) of human trials, while many others are in earlier stages (Phase I) of study.*

To find out more about clinical trials that you or a loved one may be eligible for, visit the National Institute of Aging's Web site (*www.nia.nih.gov/Alzheimers*) and click on "Search the AD Clinical Trials database."

Many of these new drugs focus on reducing brain levels of beta amyloid, a protein that forms plaque deposits inside the brains of people with Alzheimer's. Many researchers think beta amyloid is the disease's primary cause. These experimental medications either speed removal of beta amyloid particles from the brain, block their production or immunize the brain against them. *For Phase II, they include...*

•*Compound LY450139,* from Eli Lilly.

Action: Deactivates gamma-secretase, an enzyme involved in beta amyloid production. Phase II trials are completed.

Phase III trials include...

•*Tramiprosate* (**Alzhemed**), an amyloid-reducing therapy from Neurochem.

Action: Binds with beta amyloid, preventing it from forming brain deposits. Recently completed its Phase III trials. The results of the trials were inconclusive.

•*Tarenflurbil* (**Flurizan**), from Myriad Pharmaceuticals.

Action: Modulates gamma-secretase activity to reduce levels of a particularly toxic amyloid sub-type.

Status: Recently completed its Phase III trials.

•*Bapineuzumab,* from Wyeth and Elan.

Action: An Alzheimer's "vaccine," containing antibodies that bind with amyloids and remove them from the brain.

Other experimental medications focus on the fact that the brains of Alzheimer's patients show reduced glucose metabolism, which could be

*In Phase I of a clinical trial, the drug or treatment is tested for the first time with a small group (20 to 30 people) to evaluate its safety, determine dosage ranges and identify side effects. In Phase II, it is tested with a larger group (100 to 300 people) to evaluate effectiveness, as well as to further evaluate its safety. In Phase III, large groups (1,000 to 3,000 people) are given the drug or treatment to confirm effectiveness, monitor side effects, compare it with other commonly used treatments and collect other data that will allow the drug to be used safely.

damaging brain cells by depriving them of sustenance. *Phase II trials include...*

•*Compound AC-1202* (**Ketasyn**), a drug from Accera.

Action: Provides brain cells with an alternative energy source to glucose.

Phase III trials include...

•*Rosiglitazone* (**Avandia**), from GlaxoSmithKline, a drug already used to treat type 2 diabetes.

Action: Enhances glucose metabolism by increasing insulin sensitivity. Now in Phase III trials for mild to moderate Alzheimer's in a subset of patients with one genetic marker. Questions have been raised about its safety.

A number of other studies are looking at potential benefits of familiar medications for Alzheimer's disease, including...

•**A variety of statins.** Studies have found that people taking statins tend to have lower Alzheimer's rates.

Possible reasons: Statins may modify beta amyloid production processes and/or reduce inflammation. Improved cardiovascular health in general also has been linked to reduced Alzheimer's risk.

•**Dimebon,** a drug used for decades in Russia as an antihistamine, has shown promise in delaying the onset of Alzheimer's symptoms in ongoing Phase II trials.

ALTERNATIVE TREATMENTS

There is some evidence that several nutritional supplements may have a modest preventive effect against Alzheimer's. *Several large studies of these supplements are now under way, including...*

•**A Phase III trial in which subjects are taking 2,000 mg/day of DHA**—an omega-3 fatty acid shown to reduce beta amyloid levels and slow the accumulation of tau, a protein linked to the development of neurofibrillary tangles—another signature brain lesion associated with Alzheimer's.

•**Another study in which 10,000 people are taking daily supplements of the antioxidants vitamin E** (400 IU/day) and selenium (200 micrograms/day), which are thought to have neuroprotective properties.

•**A 10-year study—nearly concluded—of ginkgo biloba,** an herb with antioxidant and anti-inflammatory properties, long reputed to improve mental function.

Although these supplements are readily available, they are not yet proven to a reasonable scientific standard to have any effect on Alzheimer's. Use as a preventive or for symptomatic therapy is not recommended.

STAYING MENTALLY ACTIVE

Finally, there's a very interesting and extensive line of research showing that people who are mentally active have a lower risk of developing Alzheimer's. It's not clear whether this mental activity actually forestalls the disease, or if those who are mentally active have healthier brains to start with—brains that allow them to be more active. That said, it's clear that staying mentally engaged—whether by continuing to work, reading and discussing books, doing challenging crossword puzzles, volunteering or belonging to a group or organization in which you take an active role—is an important factor in maintaining health and vitality as you get older.

ALZHEIMER'S WARNING SIGNS

Alzheimer's is a degenerative brain disease that starts with occasional memory lapses and eventually progresses to the point where much of one's memory and reasoning power is lost. Ordinary tasks, such as dressing and eating, become difficult or impossible. *Early warning signs include…*

•**Decreased ability to recognize common odors.**

•**Forgetting recently learned information** or the names of common objects.

•**Difficulty performing the steps involved in familiar tasks,** such as preparing a meal or making a phone call.

•**Dressing inappropriately**.

•**Inability to perform even simple mental tasks,** such as basic arithmetic.

•**Chronically misplacing objects.**

•**Rapid mood swings.**

•**A dramatic personality shift,** such as becoming extremely confused, suspicious or fearful, or becoming very dependent on another family member.

•**Loss of interest in daily activities.**

If someone exhibits any of these signs, he/she should see a neurologist. While there's no single brain scan or lab test that can definitively identify Alzheimer's, an experienced doctor can usually recognize its early stages.

■ ■ ■ ■

High Blood Pressure May Raise Alzheimer's Risk

High blood pressure may raise Alzheimer's risk, warns researcher Cyrus Raji. High blood pressure reduces blood flow to the part of the brain that controls memory and learning.

Self-defense: Exercise and proper diet are very effective at keeping blood pressure down. Ask your doctor what is best for you.

Cyrus Raji, MD/PhD candidate at University of Pittsburgh School of Medicine and coauthor of a study of blood flow in the brains of older adults, presented at a meeting of the Radiological Society of North America.

■ ■ ■ ■

Drugs That Slow Alzheimer's

Drugs that slow Alzheimer's disease work best when taken early on, says geriatric psychiatrist Richard Powers, MD.

Problem: Many Alzheimer's patients have symptoms years before being diagnosed. Warning signs include short-term memory loss, confusion about time and place, and changes in mood or personality. If you detect symptoms, consult a geriatrician who can do an evaluation.

Richard Powers, MD, chair of the medical advisory board, Alzheimer's Foundation of America (*alzfdn.org*), and senior scientist/associate director, Alzheimer's Disease Research Center, University of Alabama, Birmingham.

■ ■ ■ ■

Drug Boosts Memory for Alzheimer's Patients

A commonly used drug can help patients with severe Alzheimer's, according to Sandra E. Black, MD. Many patients with *mild-to-moderate* Alzheimer's disease take *donepezil* (Aricept) to help memory and functioning in everyday life.

New study: Aricept stabilized and sometimes even improved memory, thinking skills and certain other functions in 63% of patients with the advanced stage of Alzheimer's. The comparable figure for patients given a placebo was 39%.

Sandra E. Black, MD, Brill Chair of Neurology, University of Toronto, and research director of the neurosciences research program, Sunnybrook Research Institute, Toronto. She was lead author of a study of 343 patients, published in *Neurology*.

■ ■ ■ ■

Warning Sign of Alzheimer's

Older people with mild difficulty recognizing scents, such as cinnamon and lemon, are 50% more likely to develop cognitive impairment within five years, compared with people whose odor recognition is intact. This impairment often precedes the development of Alzheimer's.

Robert S. Wilson, PhD, senior neuropsychologist, Rush Alzheimer's Disease Center, Rush University Medical Center, Chicago, and author of a study of 589 people, ages 55 to 100, published in the journal *Archives of General Psychiatry*.

■ ■ ■ ■

Overweight Women Are More Likely to Develop Alzheimer's

Overweight women are more likely to develop Alzheimer's than women who are a healthy weight. On average, Alzheimer's risk increases by 36% for every five to eight pounds over your ideal weight (based on your height). If your body mass index (BMI)—a ratio relating weight to height—is 25 or above, you are considered overweight. A BMI in the range of 19 to 24.9 is healthy. For an on-line BMI calculator, go to the National Heart, Lung and Blood Institute's Web site, *www.nhlbisupport.com/bmi*.

Deborah Gustafson, PhD, associate professor, unit for neuropsychiatric epidemiology, Gothenburg University, Sweden, and leader of a study of 392 people, published in *Archives of Internal Medicine*.

■ ■ ■ ■

Estrogen Linked to Alzheimer's Disease in Older Men

Men typically have lower levels of the hormone estrogen than women. However, after menopause women have lower estrogen levels than men of the same age.

In a recent study, researchers evaluated hormone levels and cognitive function in 2,974 men ages 71 to 93 over an average of six years.

Result: The risk for Alzheimer's rose with increasing levels of estrogen.

Theory: The production of estrogen involves *aromatase*, an enzyme that, in some cases, may serve as a marker for Alzheimer's. Previous research found a similar link in women. More studies are needed.

Mirjam I. Geerlings, PhD, associate professor, University Medical Center Utrecht, The Netherlands.

■ ■ ■ ■

Low Testosterone May Be Hazardous to Your Health

Low testosterone may be hazardous, warns Molly Shores, MD. According to a recent study, which followed men over age 40 for an average of four years, those with low testosterone were up to 88% more likely to die during the study period than men with normal levels.

Self-defense: Men with symptoms of testosterone deficiency—decreased sexual interest, fatigue, irritability, hot flashes and increased abdominal fat—should have their testosterone level checked.

Molly Shores, MD, associate professor of psychiatry, University of Washington, and a physician for the Veterans Administration Puget Sound Health Care System, both in Seattle. She led a study of 858 veterans, published in *Archives of Internal Medicine*.

■ ■ ■ ■

Testosterone Danger

Testosterone levels decline naturally as men age. Despite some advertising claims, supplemental testosterone products—including creams, gels, patches and oral supplements—have no proven age-reversing abilities, and they may increase risk for heart disease and prostate cancer.

Best: Testosterone supplements should be used only by men who have been diagnosed with a significant deficiency and under a doctor's supervision.

Victor M. Montori, MD, associate professor, Mayo Clinic College of Medicine, Rochester, Minnesota, and leader of a series of studies that summarized all available clinical trials of testosterone use on humans, published in *Mayo Clinic Proceedings*.

■ ■ ■ ■

Helping the Older HIV Patient

More than 10% of new HIV patients in the US are 50 or older, reports Barbara Bartlik, MD. Safe-sex messages are not aimed at this age group, but practicing safe sex is as important for older people as it is for younger. Unfortunately, older men, especially those with erectile problems, may be resistant to condom use and women may not insist.

Another issue: As women age, lack of estrogen thins vaginal tissue and genital lesions become common, increasing susceptibility to HIV infection.

Barbara Bartlik, MD, medical sex therapist, psychiatrist, and assistant professor of psychiatry, Weill Cornell Medical College, New York City.

■ ■ ■ ■

Weight Loss? It Could Be an Early Sign of Dementia

Unintended weight loss may occur up to 20 years before dementia is diagnosed.

Recent finding: On average, women with dementia weighed 12 pounds less than women without the condition.

Possible reason: In early dementia, women may develop apathy and lose some sense of smell, so food is less appealing. No correlation was found in men—and the study, unlike others, did not find obesity in middle age to be a risk factor for dementia. Women who have unintentionally lost weight should ask their doctors to check for diseases that might cause weight loss, such as cancer and heart or lung

disease. If none are found, consider a dementia connection.

David S. Knopman, MD, neurologist, Mayo Clinic, Rochester, Minnesota, and leader of a study of 962 people, published in *Neurology*.

Dementia— What to Do If It's Not Alzheimer's

Muriel R. Gillick, MD, an associate professor in the department of ambulatory care and prevention at Harvard Medical School/Harvard Pilgrim Health Care, and staff geriatrician at Harvard Vanguard Medical Associates, all in Boston. She is the author of several books, including *Tangled Minds: Understanding Alzheimer's Disease and Other Dementias*. Penguin.

Memory-robbing Alzheimer's disease is the most common form of dementia. The condition affects more than five million Americans.

What you may not know: One-third to one-half of patients with dementia suffer from a non-Alzheimer's neurological disease that typically starts with symptoms other than memory loss.

In advanced stages, the symptoms of these other dementias resemble those of Alzheimer's disease. Besides suffering from memory loss, patients eventually have minimal ability to speak and/or limited ability to move.

Anyone who has problems with walking, planning activities or mood (such as apathy or depression) should be evaluated by a neurologist or geriatrician, who may suggest treatments that can help improve symptoms.

Non-Alzheimer's dementias…

VASCULAR DEMENTIA

It's the second most common form of dementia in older adults, and the one that's potentially the most preventable.

Key symptoms: Difficulty performing mental tasks, such as balancing a checkbook or planning an activity, and problems with walking, bladder control and/or vision. Although memory loss is one of the first symptoms experienced by people with Alzheimer's disease, it typically occurs later in most patients with vascular dementia.

Vascular dementia can be caused by a single large stroke, multiple small strokes or narrowing of small blood vessels to the brain due to plaque formation (atherosclerosis).

Some patients experience symptoms of vascular dementia abruptly—for example, immediately after a stroke. More often, damage to the brain occurs over a period of years. A magnetic resonance imaging (MRI) scan of the brain often shows abnormalities in people with vascular dementia.

The same conditions that increase the risk for stroke—elevated blood pressure, diabetes and high cholesterol—also increase the risk for vascular dementia. Treating these conditions won't reverse cognitive changes but can play a significant role in prevention.

Recent finding: European researchers followed a group of patients age 60 and older for four years. All had hypertension, but none had signs of dementia. Those who were given the drug *nitrendipine*—a calcium channel blocker similar to the US drug *nifedipine* (Procardia)—to control hypertension were half as likely to develop vascular dementia over a four-year period as those who weren't given the drug.

Treatment: Alzheimer's drugs known as cholinesterase inhibitors, such as *donepezil* (Aricept) and *rivastigmine* (Exelon), may reduce symptoms of vascular dementia in some patients.

LEWY BODY DEMENTIA

Lewy body dementia, which typically occurs in adults age 65 and older, is named for Dr. Friederich H. Lewy, the scientist who discovered the disease's characteristic abnormal protein deposits that form inside nerve cells in the brain.

Key symptoms: Some are typical of Alzheimer's disease, such as memory loss and confusion...others resemble those caused by Parkinson's disease, such as muscle rigidity. Lewy body dementia also causes visual hallucinations (seeing objects or people that are not really there)...delusions (a false belief that cannot be altered by a rational argument)...and fluctuations in alertness.

No one knows exactly what causes Lewy body dementia. The protein deposits are often present in patients with Alzheimer's and Parkinson's diseases, suggesting that the conditions may be linked in some way.

To diagnose Lewy body dementia, doctors look for a progressive decline in cognitive abilities, along with intermittent episodes of hallucinations, a lack of alertness and Parkinson's-like symptoms.

Treatment: Parkinson's disease drugs, such as *carbidopa* and *levadopa* (Sinemet), to improve motor symptoms.

Warning: In some Lewy body patients, Sinemet may worsen hallucinations.

For hallucinations and delusions, low doses of antipsychotics, such as *quetiapine* (Seroquel) or *olanzapine* (Zyprexa), if necessary.

Warning: The antipsychotic drugs *haloperidol* (Haldol) and *risperidone* (Risperdal) worsen Parkinson's-like symptoms in patients with Lewy body dementia.

FRONTOTEMPORAL DEMENTIA

This is a rare form of dementia in which portions of the brain shrink, causing extreme changes in personality. Unlike other forms of dementia, which are most common in older adults, frontotemporal dementia typically appears between ages 40 and 60.

Key symptoms: Inappropriate public behavior, such as getting undressed in public...rude comments...lack of inhibition...apathy or a loss of interest in everyday life...short-term memory loss...and compulsive behavior, such as constantly shutting doors.

No one test can diagnose frontotemporal dementia. Imaging studies of the brain, such as MRI, will sometimes show shrinkage of the frontal or temporal lobes. There are no treatments that can stop frontotemporal dementia or slow its progression. Most patients die within two to 10 years after the initial diagnosis.

Treatment for symptoms: Antipsychotic drugs (preferably low-dose) may be used to reduce agitation or compulsive behavior. However, research shows that these drugs are not very effective for this purpose and may even hasten death in older dementia patients.

IS IT DEMENTIA?

Dementia potentially is reversible if it is caused by medication reactions, decreased thyroid function, a vitamin B-12 deficiency and/or depression.

True dementia typically progresses slowly over time—sometimes over decades—and current treatments are generally not very effective. Medication can sometimes improve cognitive function in people with Alzheimer's or vascular dementia, but it does not affect the outcome of these diseases.

Research shows that healthy lifestyle factors, such as not smoking, getting regular exercise and staying mentally active and socially engaged, can possibly delay the onset of dementia in some people by one to two years.

■ ■ ■ ■

Eating Fish Improves Memory

In a recent study of men and women between the ages of 70 and 74, those who ate an average of more than 10 grams (0.35 ounces) of fish daily scored better on several tests that measure cognitive skills, including memory, visual conception, attention, orientation and verbal fluency.

The effect was stronger as fish consumption increased to as high as 80 grams (2.8 ounces) per day.

A. David Smith, PhD, professor emeritus of pharmacology, University of Oxford, England.

■ ■ ■ ■

Caffeine Zaps Memory Problems

Caffeine may keep memory problems at bay in women, according to new research. Women age 65 and older who drank three cups of coffee per day had 30% less risk for memory decline than women who drank one cup or less.

Female coffee drinkers over age 80 had 70% less risk.

Karen Ritchie, PhD, director of nervous system pathologies and epidemiological and clinical research, French National Institute for Health and Medical Research, Montpellier, France.

Attention Men: You May Not Need Prostate Surgery

J. Stephen Jones, MD, chair of the Glickman Urological and Kidney Institute at the Cleveland Clinic Foundation. He is the author of *The Complete Prostate Book: What Every Man Needs to Know* (Prometheus) and many scientific papers on prostate and bladder diseases.

If you're a man over age 50, chances are you find yourself running to the bathroom more often than you once did.

Until recently, doctors were quick to attribute these symptoms to an enlarged prostate—a noncancerous condition known as *benign prostatic hyperplasia* (BPH)—and prescribe drugs to shrink or relax the gland, or surgery to reduce its size.

The prostate is a walnut-sized gland that lies just below the bladder. It produces the fluid in semen that helps nourish sperm. As a man ages, the prostate usually enlarges—perhaps due to normal hormonal changes—sometimes leading to such symptoms as trouble urinating.

Latest development: Researchers now strongly suspect that the prostate may be only partially responsible for the symptoms usually blamed on BPH—or, in some cases, not at all. This means that many men may be able to avoid prostate surgery altogether if the problem is properly diagnosed.

THE HIDDEN CULPRIT

Because the prostate is located next to the *urethra* (the tube that carries urine from the bladder), the flow of urine can become partially obstructed when the gland enlarges. As a result, the urinary stream becomes weaker. Other "obstructive" symptoms include *hesitancy* (it takes longer to start urination) and *intermittency* (the flow stops and starts repeatedly during urination).

What's new: Other urinary problems, called "irritative" symptoms—*urgency* (a strong, sudden need to urinate)...*frequency* (repeated trips to the bathroom)...and *nocturia* (excessive need to urinate at night)—are now believed, in some cases, to be only indirectly related to an enlargement of the prostate and/or may have more to do with the bladder.

One possible reason: When the prostate compresses the urethra and obstructs urinary flow, the bladder may not empty completely. Bladder muscles grow stronger to overcome the obstruction, possibly making the bladder harder to control.

DIAGNOSING THE PROBLEM

Prostate enlargement can be diagnosed with a *digital rectal examination* (the doctor inserts a gloved finger into the rectum and feels the prostate). But prostate size alone can be misleading—it's only when the gland grows *inward* that the urethra becomes compressed and urinary problems develop.

Although other tests are available to check urinary and bladder function, the majority of doctors simply suggest a trial of prostate medication. If a prostate drug relieves the symptoms, the diagnosis can be safely assumed to be BPH.

THE CONVENTIONAL APPROACH

The majority of men with obstructive symptoms (slow start, slow stream and/or incomplete emptying) get relief from two types of medication commonly used for BPH. The drugs work in different ways—one type may help when the other fails, and both types used together may be more effective than either alone.

•**Alpha blockers,** such as *terazosin* (Hytrin), *alfuzosin* (Uroxatral), *doxazosin* (Cardura) and *tamsulosin* (Flomax), relax the smooth (involuntary) muscles in the prostate and the neck of the bladder, loosening their grip on the urethra. These drugs usually relieve urinary symptoms within one week.

Side effects: Low blood pressure when you stand up and/or dizziness. These side effects typically resolve within three days.

Caution: Alpha blockers can cause complications during cataract surgery. If you take an alpha blocker, tell your doctor before undergoing a cataract operation.

•**5-alpha reductase inhibitors,** such as *finasteride* (Proscar) and *dutasteride* (Avodart), interfere with the conversion of testosterone into *dihydrotestosterone*, the active form of the hormone that stimulates the prostate to grow. These drugs can shrink the gland and are particularly useful when the prostate is very large.

But they can take months to work—and are often less effective than alpha blockers.

Side effects: Decreased libido and impotence in 3% to 10% of cases.

THE NEW APPROACH

In a groundbreaking study recently published in the *Journal of the American Medical Association*, 879 men who had both obstructive and irritative urinary symptoms were divided into groups that were given the prostate drug tamsulosin...*tolterodine* (Detrol), a drug for overactive bladder (a condition that causes urinary frequency, urgency and/or nocturia)...a placebo...or both drugs.

The bladder drug, the prostate drug and the placebo were equally effective in reducing both types of urinary symptoms. The drug *combination*, however, was significantly more effective than either drug alone—symptoms improved in 80% of men who received it.

Self-defense: If you experience urinary frequency, urgency and/or nocturia that has not been adequately relieved by the use of prostate drugs alone, see a urologist to determine whether a combination of prostate and bladder drugs may help.

SURGICAL OPTIONS

If an overactive bladder drug doesn't bring relief within two months, and prostate drugs do not do so within a few months, surgery may be necessary.

Options include...

•**Transurethral resection of the prostate (TURP)** is the most effective for BPH and rarely requires repeat surgery. Instruments inserted through the urethra remove parts of the prostate to widen the path for the flow of urine. It requires general or spinal anesthesia and a hospital stay.

Complications: Rarely, impotence and urinary incontinence occur.

•**Transurethral microwave therapy (TUMT)** uses a microwave antenna that produces heat to shrink the prostate. It does not require anesthesia and can be performed in a doctor's office. TUMT generally is less effective than TURP, and some men require further treatment within several years.

Complications: Similar to those with TURP, though even less common.

•**Photo vaporization prostate (PVP)** is a type of laser therapy that precisely targets the part of the prostate that the surgeon wants to destroy. Like TUMT, repeat treatment can be required. PVP is performed on an inpatient or outpatient basis.

Complications: Similar to those with TURP, though even less common.

■ ■ ■ ■

Shingles More Common Among Healthy Older Adults

The shingles virus—and the complications associated with it—is more common among healthy adults ages 50 to 59 than previously thought, according to a new study. There is a shingles vaccine (Zostavax) approved for those over age 60, but those 50 to 59 should also speak with their physicians about vaccination.

Barbara Yawn, MD, director of research, Olmsted Medical Center, and adjunct professor of family and community health, University of Minnesota, Rochester.

Great Ways to Stay Strong for Life

Timothy Doherty, MD, PhD, Canada research chair in neuromuscular function in health, aging and disease and associate professor of clinical neurological sciences and rehabilitation medicine at the University of Western Ontario in London, Ontario. He is the author or coauthor of more than 60 scientific papers on aging, neuromuscular disease and exercise physiology.

Most people have never heard of *sarcopenia*, but risk for it increases dramatically for those in their 40s, 50s and 60s—and an estimated 50% of adults age 75 and older have the condition.

What is this common—but little-known—health problem?

It's age-related muscle loss, also known as muscle atrophy. Sarcopenia can have several causes, including a lack of physical activity, insufficient dietary protein, diminishing levels of

hormones that affect muscles and the decline in muscle mass that naturally occurs with aging.

Because sarcopenia progresses very gradually—it's common to lose approximately 1% of muscle mass per year from about age 40 to age 65 and about 2% per year thereafter—you're unlikely to notice it until you discover that you can't do something you've always done, whether it's lift your grandchild, swing a golf club or get out of a chair.

Good news: While you can't entirely prevent sarcopenia, you can substantially control the rate of muscle decline—and even reverse previous losses—with strengthening exercises and an appropriate diet. Numerous studies have shown that as little as two months of proper training can boost muscle strength by as much as 40%—and it's never too late to start. Even men and women in their 90s can improve muscle mass and strength with strength training.

WHY YOU NEED STRONG MUSCLES

If you think bodybuilders are the only ones who need strong muscles, consider this: healthy muscles have been shown to help us…

•**Maintain independence into old age.** Muscle strength enables us to perform the tasks of daily living, including getting dressed, bathing and climbing stairs.

•**Avoid falls.** Strong muscles are essential for balance and help safeguard us against hip fractures and other debilitating or life-threatening injuries.

•**Boost metabolism.** Muscle burns more blood sugar (glucose) than fat does, helping us to keep off unwanted pounds and protecting us against diabetes and obesity.

GETTING STARTED

Aerobic exercise is essential for cardiovascular fitness, but it's typically not enough to maintain the strength of all your major muscles. Even if you regularly walk or run, you're susceptible to sarcopenia.

That's because walking or running does not prevent you from losing muscle mass (the amount of muscle you have) and muscle strength (what you can do with that muscle) from your core and upper-body muscles. Your core muscles (abdomen, low back, hip and buttocks) and upper-body muscles (arm, chest, shoulder, upper back and neck) are crucial—they allow you to pick up heavy packages, rise from a low chair and perform most everyday activities.

My advice: Aim to do two or three strength-training workouts weekly, consisting of six to eight exercises.* Appropriate exercises can be performed on weight-training machines, with hand weights (dumbbells) or by using the resistance created by your own body weight. Ideally, your workout will include two sets of 12 to 15 repetitions of each exercise.

Examples: To target your pectoral (chest) muscles, try push-ups...for your back muscles, try a rowing machine...to work your lower body, try leg lifts, squats and lunges (taking

ROWING MACHINE

long steps forward or backward from an upright position).

If you're using hand weights, you'll need to experiment to find the right weight. Select a weight you can lift 12—but no more than 15—times using perfect form. By the last repetition, it should be difficult—but possible—for you to lift the weight without jerking it up or dropping it.

LUNGE

Best: Work with a trainer at your local gym, who can help you devise a routine and demonstrate proper technique. You often can accomplish this in a single training session, which typically costs $50 to $100.

UP YOUR PROTEIN INTAKE

Studies show that up to 27% of older Americans are not getting the recommended daily intake of protein (56 g daily for men...46 g daily for women). Yet we appear to need even *more* protein in later life, as our bodies become less efficient at converting it into muscle.

My advice: To get a better estimate of your protein requirement, divide your body weight

---

*Consult your doctor before beginning any exercise program.

Illustrations by Shawn Banner.

---

in half, and aim for that number daily in grams of protein.

Example: If you weigh 150 pounds, consume about 75 g of protein daily.

Beef, pork, chicken, turkey, tuna and salmon are highly concentrated sources of protein, generally offering more than 20 g of protein per 3.5-ounce serving.

Other good protein sources: Eggs, low-fat milk and yogurt, tofu and legumes (such as black beans, lentils and kidney beans).

Caution: If you want to try protein supplements or shakes (which typically contain high levels of protein per serving), talk to your doctor—especially if you have kidney or liver disease, which can affect your body's ability to break down and excrete large amounts of protein. In addition, high intakes of protein (more than 150 g daily) from food can tax the kidneys and liver.

A SUPPLEMENT THAT HELPS

There is no silver bullet to combat sarcopenia, but that hasn't stopped supplement makers from promising strength in a bottle. *Human growth hormone* (HGH) has been touted as a "fountain of youth," but there have been no reliable clinical trials showing that HGH significantly improves strength or endurance, and the potential side effects include tissue swelling and joint pain.

Dehydroepiandrosterone (DHEA) is a naturally occurring substance that, when metabolized, turns into testosterone, a hormone that contributes to healthy muscle mass in men and women. DHEA and testosterone have been sold as muscle-building supplements, but so far, neither has been proven to deliver a significant strength or endurance benefit. In addition, supplemental testosterone may increase men's risk for prostate cancer. In women, it may cause acne and/or facial hair.

Preliminary evidence suggests that *creatine*, a substance that is produced naturally in the liver and helps to fuel muscle cells, may boost the beneficial effects of strength training.

New finding: Older adults who took a 5-g supplement of creatine daily—and did strength training twice weekly for 60 minutes per session—had 10% to 15% greater gains in muscle mass and strength after six months than those who relied on exercise alone.

If you want to maximize the benefits of your strength training, ask your doctor about taking creatine as an adjunct to a strength-training regimen. Known side effects include muscle cramps and gastrointestinal upset. More studies are needed before creatine can be definitively recommended as a muscle-enhancing supplement for all older adults.

Secrets to Staying Motivated to Exercise From the Father Of Aerobics

Kenneth H. Cooper, MD, MPH, founder and head of the Cooper Aerobics Center in Dallas and CooperLife, a residential healthy-living community, in McKinney, Texas. His latest book, written with his son, Tyler C. Cooper, MD, MPH, is *Start Strong, Finish Strong*. Penguin.

D r. Kenneth Cooper is widely recognized as one of the world's leading authorities on fitness and preventive medicine. His work on the importance of cardiovascular health has led to a worldwide revolution in physical fitness. His first book, the international best seller *Aerobics*, was published in 1968. *He was asked recently about his personal approach to health and fitness…*

At age 76, I'm now in my 47th year of regular, scheduled exercise. What keeps me motivated after all this time? The same thing now as when I first began—better health, improved quality of life and increased happiness.

When I broke my leg a couple of years ago in a skiing accident, for the first time in decades I couldn't have regular activity. I became depressed, I gained weight, I felt my quality of life had gone downhill. As I gradually was able to return to my normal level of activity, I started feeling better and better. I've had to substitute fast walking for running, but that doesn't really make any difference. Once I was moving again, my heart rate went down…I returned to my normal weight…my depression lifted. I felt great again.

What this proved: Even seniors like me can modify their exercise programs to compensate for injuries and other health problems and continue to stay active. I'm still working 50 to 60 hours a week and exercising at least an hour a day. You *can* get healthier as you get older. What's more, to a great extent, *you* control whether this happens—not your doctor, not your insurance company, not the government. This is the underlying concept of CooperLife, a residential community devoted to healthy living that I started with my son, Tyler Cooper, MD, MPH, in McKinney, Texas.

We know from many studies that fitness is the single most important predictor of health and quality of life at any age. In general, people with the highest levels of fitness have the highest quality of life…less-fit people have a lower quality of life…and people with the lowest levels of fitness have an even worse quality of life. That's what motivates my patients. They want to reach and maintain a high level of physical and mental functioning for as long as possible. They want to "square off the curve" that says you get less healthy and have a lower quality of life as you age.

BENEFITS OF FITNESS

Positive things motivate us—and fitness brings a lot of positives. At the Cooper Institute (the research division of Cooper Aerobics Center), we've pinpointed important benefits that go along with increased fitness, no matter how old you are…

•**The longevity benefit.** Being fit can add three years to your life—and you are 65% less likely to die prematurely than someone who is unfit.

•**The mental health benefit.** Exercise more and you'll improve your mental health, with less likelihood of depression.

•**The physical function benefit.** Establish good health habits, and you'll delay by several years the age at which you develop even minimal disability.

•**The cancer protection benefit.** Exercise lowers your risk for most types of cancer.

•**The strong bone benefit.** Weight-bearing exercise, such as walking or running, lowers your risk of excessive bone loss after age 50.

•**The healing benefit.** If you're an older adult who exercises regularly, skin wounds heal faster. It might also help you recover from other ailments.

THE SIX MOTIVATION "NOs"

In my many years of medical practice, I've heard, over and over again, the same six reasons for not exercising, to the point where I've developed an acronym for them—TEMMPF.

TEMMPF stands for six "nos": No time… no energy…no motivation….no money…no place…no fun.

The good news: All these nos can easily be overcome. Let's take the six nos one by one and turn them into "yeses"…

•**No time.** You can easily work exercise into your daily routine, what I call "activity add-ons."

Examples: Take the stairs instead of the elevator…walk or pace while you're talking on the phone…do exercises while watching TV… park farther from a store's entrance than you have to, then don't use a shopping cart for manageable loads.

Smart move: Make a point of spending time with people who have the same health goals as you—you can swap ideas about new activity add-ons.

•**No energy.** Just take the first few steps. It will energize you to take the next steps—and to keep on going. You'll be amazed at how your energy level goes up.

•**No motivation.** A sincere decision on your part that you don't want to lose your quality of life will be a big motivator to get you moving.

Motivation strategy: Think about what makes you feel good. Getting fit and staying fit means that you're more likely to be able to continue doing the things you enjoy as you get older. You might even be able to return to a favorite activity that you gave up because it was too physically demanding.

•**No money.** You don't have to join a gym or health club, or hire a trainer or buy expensive equipment to get fit. All you have to do is get out and go for a 30-minute walk just three times a week.

Stick with it: Walk with a friend or listen to music on headphones—you'll enjoy it and the time will pass quickly.

•**No place.** You can walk anywhere. Try walking in a mall—not just to avoid inclement weather, but also if you don't have safe, lighted places to walk outdoors. Walk in circles in your house or march in place while you watch TV if that's what it takes.

Strategy: Many of my patients enjoy the companionship of a walking group—members motivate each other to keep going. Your local hospital or Y may be able to help you find a group.

•**No fun.** Fitness can be a lot of fun—just ask anyone in a walking group. Saying you're bored by your fitness program is a cop-out. It's easy to vary your routine and find ways to make fitness enjoyable.

Example: Use a pedometer and add steps every day until you reach your target—then see if you can surpass that number.

Bottom line: My real message here is that you can…

•**Start your fitness program at any age.**

•**Continue your program as you age.**

•**Adjust your program to meet changing needs and interests.**

Fitness is a journey, not a destination. If you keep it up for the rest of your life, you'll find that you can build muscle mass and improve your overall fitness at any age, even if you've never exercised before.

■ ■ ■ ■

Walk Your Way to A Better Memory

The brain starts to shrink during middle age, so it processes information more slowly.

Recent finding: As little as three hours a week of walking triggers biochemical changes that increase the volume of brain regions responsible for memory and cognitive function.

Arthur Kramer, PhD, department of neuroscience and psychology, University of Illinois, Urbana-Champaign, and leader of a study, published in *Journal of Gerontology.*

■ ■ ■ ■

Only the Lonely Have Higher Blood Pressure

Lonely middle-aged and older adults have higher blood pressure and higher levels of the stress hormone *epinephrine* than people of the same age who are not lonely. This increases their risk for cardiovascular problems.

Self-defense: Maintain or expand your range of social acquaintances as you age.

John Cacioppo, PhD, professor and director of the Center for Cognitive and Social Neuroscience at the University of Chicago, and coauthor of a study published in *Current Directions in Psychological Science.*

Why So Many Women Are Getting an "Old Man's" Lung Disease

MeiLan Han, MD, assistant professor of internal medicine and medical director of the Women's Respiratory Health Program at the University of Michigan Medical Center in Ann Arbor.

Many physicians think of chronic obstructive pulmonary disease (COPD) as an old man's disease—but that is no longer true.

Facts: COPD is on the rise among women… its severity and symptoms tend to be worse for females…women with COPD seem to experience more anxiety and depression and a lower quality of life than men with the disease do… and more American women than men now die of COPD each year.

Some women who develop COPD may not even have known risk factors for it. What's going on, and how can women protect themselves?

WHAT IS COPD?

COPD is a progressive lung disease that can cause serious, long-term disability. In severe cases, sufferers may become short of breath so easily that they cannot walk half a block. *Patients with COPD have one or both of the following…*

•**Chronic bronchitis,** which involves inflammation of the lining of the bronchial tubes (the two large tubes that carry air from the windpipe into the lungs). The inflammation narrows the airways, making it hard to breathe. Over time, the bronchial tubes become scarred and produce too much mucus, further blocking airflow.

Symptoms: Labored breathing, wheezing and a mucus-producing chronic cough.

•**Emphysema,** which involves damage to the lung's tiny air sacs (alveoli). As these sacs lose elasticity, it is increasingly difficult to draw in air and expel it from the lungs.

Symptoms: Shortness of breath, chronic cough, wheezing and a tendency to exhale through pursed lips to force out trapped air.

COPD is the fourth-leading cause of death in the US and is expected to be third by 2020. More than 12 million Americans have been diagnosed with COPD, and another 12 million may have it but not know it. Symptoms usually appear after age 40. More than one-third of COPD patients are under age 65.

The most common cause of COPD is smoking. Since the disease may take decades to develop, some of the increased incidence in women today is attributed to the rise of smoking among women starting in the 1950s. About 20% of smokers get COPD.

Even after a person quits smoking, his/her lungs may have some permanent damage—so a former smoker also remains at increased risk for COPD.

Long-term exposure to secondhand smoke also can contribute to COPD.

Troubling: From 5% to 12% of COPD patients are not smokers or ex-smokers—and the majority of these patients are women.

THE GENDER BIAS

Theories on why COPD is hitting women harder…

•**Since COPD is still thought of as a man's disease,** women may not be correctly diagnosed in a timely fashion. COPD is commonly mistaken for asthma and treated with the wrong drugs. In general, primary care doctors refer a smaller percentage of female patients to the specialists most likely to order diagnostic tests to make the proper identification.

•**Some evidence suggests that women smokers may be more likely to develop COPD than men smokers**—perhaps women's lungs are more sensitive to toxins.

•**Once addicted to cigarettes,** women have a harder time quitting than men.

Among my patients, women tend to feel more keenly the stigma of using an oxygen tank in public. Embarrassment contributes to the anxiety and depression that often accompany COPD.

HOW TO PROTECT YOURSELF

COPD tends to develop gradually, so you may not notice it for years—yet the longer treatment is delayed, the worse the condition gets. COPD cannot be cured but often can be controlled. The sooner you are diagnosed and treated, the better your outcome is likely to be.

What every woman should do…

•**If you have any symptoms of COPD,** see your doctor or a pulmonologist for a physical, chest X-ray and a spirometry test—a noninvasive breathing test that measures how much and how fast you can blow air out of your lungs.

Referrals: American College of Chest Physicians, 800-343-2227, *www.chestnet.org.*

•**If you smoke, stop now.** Giving up cigarettes leads to even greater improvement in lung function for women than for men. Call 800-QUIT-NOW (784-8669), a free government service that provides trained "quit coaches"…or visit *www.smokefree.gov* for a how-to guide.

If you're diagnosed with COPD…

•**Investigate your health care options.** These may include medication…supplemental oxygen therapy…surgery to remove damaged lung tissue…and in very severe cases, a lung transplant. The American Lung Association offers a personalized on-line guide to the latest research (*www.lungprofiler.nexcura.com*).

•**Use drugs properly.** Bronchodilators relax airway muscles, and corticosteroids suppress inflammation. However, one-third of COPD sufferers do not correctly use a handheld device, called a dry powder inhaler, to administer medication. If your doctor prescribes an inhaler,

get instructions on proper use of the device and follow them precisely.

•**Get vaccinated against flu and pneumonia.** These illnesses can be fatal for COPD patients.

•**Ask your physician about pulmonary rehabilitation.** It combines training in the use of breathing techniques, aerobic and strengthening exercises and nutrition counseling.

•**Call your doctor without delay** if you develop a fever…mucus that is green, yellow or tinged with blood…worsening of your cough… or increased difficulty breathing. These may be signs of an infection, pneumonia or other problem that should be treated immediately.

•**Make sure your doctor monitors your overall health.** COPD patients are at increased risk for cardiovascular disease, muscle problems, brittle bones (a side effect of steroid medication) and depression.

•**Join a COPD support group.** Contact the American Lung Association (800-586-4872, *www.lungusa.org*). Support groups do more than provide information. They also provide the emotional benefits of sharing with others who know what you are dealing with.

■ ■ ■ ■

Holy Cow! Aging Increases Cavity Risk

Receding or damaged gums can expose the roots of teeth, which are susceptible to plaque buildup that causes decay.

Also: Old fillings may weaken, and the seals between them and teeth may be broken, causing cracks in which decay-causing bacteria can build up.

Self-defense: See your dentist regularly, and contact him/her anytime you experience increased tooth sensitivity, swollen or painful gums, or other changes in oral health.

Maxwell Anderson, DDS, MS, national oral-health adviser, Delta Dental Plans Association, Oak Brook, Illinois.

Trouble Swallowing?

JoAnne Robbins, PhD, a specialist in swallowing disorders and professor in the department of medicine at the University of Wisconsin School of Medicine and Public Health in Madison. Dr. Robbins is also associate director for research at the Geriatric Research Education and Clinical Center at the William S. Middleton Memorial Veterans Hospital, also in Madison. She is coauthor of *Easy-to-Swallow, Easy-to-Chew Cookbook*. Wiley.

Eating and drinking are among life's greatest pleasures, yet about 15 million Americans have difficulty swallowing foods and/or liquids, a condition known as *dysphagia*.

Everyone knows what it feels like when a bite of food "gets stuck" or a sip of liquid "goes down the wrong pipe." It's an uncomfortable but rare problem that can be corrected by coughing or drinking a small amount of liquid.

However, when dysphagia begins to occur with greater frequency (generally, more than once per month), you should see your doctor to determine the cause. Prompt treatment will help you avoid serious complications, such as dehydration, malnutrition, choking and aspiration (when food or liquid leaks into the airways), pneumonia and even death.

Caution: If a swallowing problem leads to an obstruction that interferes with your breathing in any way, have someone perform the Heimlich maneuver on you.

What to do: While standing behind you, the person should place the thumb side of his/her fist just above your navel...grasp his fist with his other hand...and give four quick inward thrusts. This should be continued until the obstruction is removed. If this technique does not help, have someone call 911. If you are alone, you can perform the inward thrusts on yourself.

ARE YOU AT RISK?

Aging can affect our ability to swallow. That's because our muscles, including those in the mouth and throat, weaken as we grow older. Even healthy adults may begin to notice subtle swallowing and eating problems, such as difficulty swallowing pills or eating dry or crunchy foods, by age 60. However, serious problems are not a normal sign of aging and should be promptly evaluated by a doctor.

Several medical conditions can cause dysphagia. Chronic heartburn increases risk for dysphagia—stomach acid backs up into the esophagus, sometimes damaging esophageal tissue, which may lead to swallowing difficulties. A stroke or head injury may affect the coordination of the swallowing muscles or limit sensation in the mouth and throat. Neurological disorders, such as Parkinson's disease and multiple sclerosis, also can cause swallowing problems.

A tumor in the esophagus can narrow this passageway, making it difficult to swallow. Surgery, radiation and chemotherapy for head and neck malignancies also can irritate the esophagus and/or lead to a buildup of scar tissue that interferes with swallowing.

Related problem: About 2,000 medications, ranging from diuretics (water-excreting drugs) to drugs used to treat such conditions as insomnia, can cause *xerostomia*, a drying of the mouth that often makes swallowing food difficult.

GET A CORRECT DIAGNOSIS

A primary care physician often is the first health care professional to suspect dysphagia. Depending on the cause of the disorder, you may be referred to an otolaryngologist (ear, nose and throat specialist), a gastroenterologist (specialist in diseases of the digestive system) or a neurologist (specialist in diseases of the nervous system).

A process known as *video fluoroscopy* is the most common and effective way to diagnose dysphagia. This test videotapes the entire swallowing process so the doctor can see how a patient's tongue and throat movements affect the flow of food, fluid and medication.

BEST TREATMENT OPTIONS

Treatment for dysphagia depends on what's causing the disorder. People with heartburn can make lifestyle changes, such as not eating for at least two hours before bedtime, and/or take medications, such as *ranitidine* (Zantac) or *omeprazole* (Prilosec), to reduce stomach acid. People who have suffered a stroke may be asked to perform muscle exercises to strengthen weak facial, tongue and throat muscles.

Dysphagia improves for some people when they follow certain practices while eating, such as turning the head to one side or looking straight ahead with the chin tucked toward the chest. These steps help direct food and fluids away from the airway and into the esophagus.

TIPS ON EATING AND DRINKING

What helps one individual with a swallowing difficulty may not help another. However, there are many basic strategies that allow people to swallow food and drink with greater ease. *For example...*

•**Sit upright in a chair while eating**—do not eat in bed.

•**Swallow a single bite or sip before taking another,** and put eating utensils down between bites.

•**Limit bite sizes** (to one-half inch or less) and limit the amount of liquid taken with each swallow.

•**Eat one type of food texture at a time.** Swallow a bite of mashed potatoes, for example, before chewing and swallowing a piece of chicken.

•**Choose soft foods,** such as cooked cereal, mashed potatoes, soft-cooked eggs, cottage cheese, applesauce, yogurt and soups.

•**Thicken thin fluids,** such as tea, apple juice and water, if necessary. This allows more time for throat muscles to get into position to ensure safe swallowing.

Natural thickeners include many flours (tapioca flour is often used), instant potato flakes and oats. To determine the amount of natural thickener to be added to a liquid, ask your doctor for a referral to a nutritionist or speech and language pathologist (a clinician with expertise in swallowing problems).

■ **More from JoAnne Robbins, PhD...**

Easier Pill Swallowing

Even people who do not have trouble swallowing food or liquid sometimes have difficulty with pills. *In addition to sitting upright or standing when taking a pill...*

•**Take a sip of water before you take a pill.** A moist mouth helps the pill go down easier. Also take a few sips with and after each pill—to prevent the pill from getting stuck in the esophagus.

•**Swallow one pill at a time.** Putting more than one pill at a time in your mouth can cause you to choke.

•**Do not throw your head back when you take your pills.** This can increase your risk for choking.

Clearly a Better Way to Fight Depression for Those Over 55

JAMA/Archives journals, news release.

Correcting nursing home residents' poor vision not only boosts quality of life, it may lower risks for depression, US researchers report.

THE STUDY

A team at the University of Alabama at Birmingham studied 78 nursing home residents, 55 and older, who received eyeglasses one week after having an eye exam and 64 residents who received eyeglasses two months after an eye check-up.

The residents' vision-related quality-of-life and depressive symptoms were assessed at the start of the study and again two months later.

At the start of the study, both groups had similar medical and demographic characteristics and similar vision problems. After two months, those who received eyeglasses at the start of the study showed improvement in distance and near vision, while those who didn't receive eyeglasses showed no change in vision.

Also at two months, residents who received eyeglasses had higher scores for general vision, reading, activities, hobbies, social interaction, and fewer depressive symptoms, than those residents who did not receive glasses. The study was published in the journal *Archives of Ophthalmology.*

IMPLICATIONS

"This study implies that there are significant, short-term quality-of-life and psychological benefits to providing the most basic of eye care services—namely, spectacle correction—to older adults residing in nursing homes," the researchers concluded.

"These findings underscore the need for a systematic evaluation of the factors underlying the pervasive unavailability of eye care to nursing home residents in the United States so that steps can be taken to improve delivery and eye care utilization."

info For more information about aging and eyes, visit the National Institute on Aging Web site, *www.nia.nih.org*. Under "Publications," click on "All Age Pages" and then "Aging and Your Eyes."

Five Myths About Cataracts

David F. Chang, MD, clinical professor of ophthalmology at the University of California, San Francisco. He is chair of the Cataract Clinical Committee of the American Society of Cataract and Refractive Surgery. He is coauthor, with Howard Gimbel, MD, of *Cataracts: A Patient's Guide to Treatment*. Addicus.

Cataract surgery is one of the most common surgical procedures in the US. About half of Americans age 65 and older show significant signs of cataracts, and nearly everyone will develop cataracts—which may or may not be severe enough to interfere with vision—at some time during his/her life.

A cataract is a clouding of the normally clear lens of the eye located behind the pupil. Some cataracts are caused by injuries, but the majority are age-related, due to changes in the proteins that make up the lens.

There are many misconceptions about what cataracts are and how they're treated.

Example: Most people assume that all cataracts need medical attention. Not true. Unless cataracts are causing blurriness, "halos" from bright lights or other vision problems, they don't have to be treated.

Here's what else you may not know about cataracts…

Misconception: You can see a cataract in the eye.

Because the lens is located behind the iris and pupil, cataracts aren't visible to the naked eye. People sometimes confuse other eye changes with cataracts. For example, you might notice pale, yellow thickenings on the surface of the white of the eye. These callus-like growths, called *pterygia*, are due to lifelong irritation from dryness and/or sunlight. They don't affect vision in most people and thus rarely require treatment.

Some people develop a hazy white ring around the edges of the cornea. These rings often are mistaken for cataracts, but they are actually accumulations of cholesterol deposited by nearby blood vessels. Like pterygia, they usually don't cause problems with vision and they don't need to be treated.

Misconception: A cataract is a growth on the lens that is removed during surgery.

A cataract is not a growth on the lens—it *is* the lens. During the most common kind of cataract surgery, the entire lens is broken into pieces with sound waves. The pieces are vacuumed out and replaced with an artificial lens.

Misconception: Cataract surgery is risky.

Complications can occur with any surgery, but the risks with cataract surgery are low. Uncommon but possible complications include inflammation and infection.

Before surgery, patients are given a local anesthetic (often in the form of eyedrops). A tiny incision—usually about one-eighth of an inch long—is made in the cornea. The original lens is removed, and a new lens is inserted through the incision.

Cataract surgery is typically an outpatient procedure. The surgery itself takes less than one-half hour, but preoperative procedures can extend patients' time at the surgery center.

The incision usually closes on its own, without stitches. Most patients notice a major improvement in vision within one week and can resume activities and exercise almost immediately.

Misconception: Cataracts can come back after surgery.

Unlike the original lens of the eye, the new artificial lens implant maintains its transparency forever.

Some patients do require a subsequent treatment, but not for cataracts. The replacement lens is placed within the membrane that held the original natural lens in place.

In fewer than 10% of cases, the normally transparent capsule will get slightly foggy within two to three years after surgery. This fogginess can cause a decline in vision similar to that caused by the cataract.

It's easily cleared with a laser, in a painless onetime office procedure called a *YAG laser capsulotomy.*

Misconception: Surgery should be delayed as long as possible.

In the past, cataract surgery had a much higher rate of complications than it does today. Also, most people had to wear thick, unsightly "Coke bottle" spectacles after the procedure.

Because of these disadvantages, doctors often advised patients to wait until their vision was significantly impaired before having surgery.

Today, the risk of complications is extremely low. Also, patients don't require strong glasses, because the intraocular lenses act like prescription contact lenses.

Important: Some people mistakenly believe that they won't need any glasses after surgery. This usually is not the case, because most intraocular lens implants are monofocal—they're set for a single focus, usually distance. Patients will therefore need reading glasses after the procedure—just as they probably did before it.

New development: *Implantable multifocal lenses.* They act like bifocals and allow patients to see both near and far without glasses.

Drawback: The new lenses are expensive… usually are not covered by insurance…and may not work in patients with other eye problems, such as astigmatism or macular degeneration.

Breakthrough in Glaucoma Treatment

Joel S. Schuman, MD, FACS, Eye and Ear Foundation Professor and chairman of the ophthalmology department at the University of Pittsburgh School of Medicine in Pennsylvania. He is the director of the University of Pittsburgh Medical Center eye center, and a professor of bioengineering at the University of Pittsburgh School of Engineering.

Glaucoma is an eye condition usually caused by increased pressure inside the eyeball, which, if left untreated, can cause irreversible damage to the optic nerve—leading to vision loss, even blindness. It affects 2.4 million Americans older than age 40, *but only half of them know they have it.*

Reason: Early-stage glaucoma has no detectable symptoms and can be discovered only through an eye exam.

Vital: Get an eye exam from an ophthalmologist every two or three years if you are age 61 or older. If glaucoma is detected and treated early, vision loss can usually be prevented. *What you need to know…*

DIAGNOSTIC BREAKTHROUGH

One of the biggest advances in recent years is the development of scanning devices that measure the amount of healthy optic nerve tissue. If glaucoma is suspected, these can be used to evaluate how much nerve damage has occurred as well as allow doctors to monitor how well glaucoma treatments are working over time. *Three types of scans…*

•**Heidleberg retina tomograph** creates a high-resolution, 3-D image of the optic nerve.

•**Optical coherence tomograph** obtains high-resolution cross-sectional images and creates a 3-D image of the retina and optic nerve.

•**GDx nerve fiber analyzer** uses filtered light to measure nerve tissue in the retina.

All three types of scans are equally effective and can be done in-office. If your ophthalmologist doesn't have access to a scanning device, ask him/her to refer you to a clinic that does.

LATEST TREATMENTS

Since vision loss due to optic nerve damage is irreversible, the key in treating glaucoma is early detection and intervention. The three approaches to treatment—medications, laser procedures and surgery—all significantly lower intraocular pressure (IOP) and thereby protect the optic nerve by reducing fluid levels in the eye…

MEDICATIONS

Eyedrop medications are usually the first-line treatment for glaucoma. *Four types…*

•**Prostaglandins**—*travoprost* (Travatan), *bimatoprost* (Lumigan) and *latanoprost* (Xalatan). Typically the first drugs tried, they don't cure glaucoma, so they must be used indefinitely. Prostaglandins increase fluid drainage in the eye, usually lowering IOP 25% to 30%. Possible side effects include gradual change in eye color due to increased brown pigment in the iris, and stinging, redness, itching or burning of the eyes.

If a prostaglandin isn't fully effective, your doctor may try any of the following drugs, either alone or in combination with a prostaglandin.

•**Beta blockers**—*timolol* (Betimol, Istalol, Timoptic), *betaxolol* (Betoptic), *levobunolol* (Betagan) and *metipranolol* (Optipranolol)—reduce IOP by reducing fluid production and slightly increasing the rate of flow through and out of the eye. They're as effective as prostaglandins at lowering IOP but can result in more serious side effects, including low blood pressure, reduced pulse rate, fatigue and shortness of breath.

•**Alpha 2 agonists**—*apraclonidine* (Iopidine) and *brimonidine tartrate* (Alphagan)—decrease fluid production in the eye. While not quite as effective as prostaglandins or beta blockers, their potential side effects are less bothersome, compared with beta blockers, for many patients. These include burning or stinging upon administration of the drops, fatigue, headache and dry mouth.

•**Carbonic anhydrase inhibitors**—*brinzolamide* (Azopt), *dorzolamide* (Trusopt), *acetazolamide* (Diamox) and *methazolamide* (Neptazane)—decrease fluid production. They're available as eyedrops and in pill form. The drops are about as effective as alpha 2 agonists. The pills are somewhat stronger but have more potential side effects, including tingling or weakness in the hands and feet, upset stomach, mental fuzziness, memory problems, depression, kidney stones and frequent urination.

Once the patient's glaucoma stabilizes, treatment continues for life—or until it stops working. Checkups occur every three to six months to monitor IOP and optic nerve condition.

LASER PROCEDURES

If medications stop working, or a patient tires of daily eyedrops, a laser surgical procedure—which takes just minutes and can be done in-office—is an option…

•**Selective laser trabeculoplasty (SLT).** This new technique may be a viable alternative to medications as a first-line treatment for open-angle (the angle between the cornea and the iris) glaucoma, the most common type of glaucoma in the US. SLT uses a low-level laser (which minimizes collateral tissue damage and scarring) to improve the function of the eye's drainage canals, improving fluid flow and reducing IOP, often to the point where medication is no longer needed. Some people will still need to use drops afterward. Like any surgery, SLT can cause complications, including scarring—though this risk is minor.

•**Argon laser trabeculoplasty (ALT).** An older technique more widely available than SLT, ALT uses a high-energy laser (which can cause tissue damage and scarring) to open the eye's drainage system. It's as effective as SLT for open-angle glaucoma, but has more scarring risk, which could result in increased eye pressure and negatively affect vision.

•**Laser peripheral iridotomy is commonly used for closed-angle glaucoma,** which affects mainly people of Asian descent. A laser makes a hole in the iris, removing the blockage and allowing fluid to flow out of the eye normally.

TRADITIONAL SURGERY

If medications and laser surgery don't stop glaucoma progression, a number of effective operations are available. The most common, trabeculectomy, involves building a new drainage system from the patient's own eye tissue. This remains the gold standard in glaucoma surgery, producing significant, lasting reductions in IOP.

Problem: To prevent scarring, at the time of surgery most patients are given medications that can sometimes cause serious eye infection later on. Other complications, such as worsened cataract, severe blurring that can last several weeks and/or bleeding in the eye can occur. Also, a very slight droop in the eyelid is common.

Latest advances: New surgical techniques let patients minimize risks. One still in clinical studies involves implanting a synthetic drain in the eye. Another, newer procedure entails implanting a tiny shunt made out of gold to channel eye fluid to an area where it's more easily absorbed into the bloodstream. If the shunt becomes clogged, a titanium sapphire laser—which selectively targets gold—may be used to reopen it.

Another procedure, canaloplasty, involves inserting a tube into the eye's natural drain. This doesn't require lifelong medication. It's the first operation that works on the eye's own drain, rather than creating an alternate drainage system. Results are promising, but long-term efficacy hasn't been established.

Two other promising advances, but where the long-term effects aren't yet known…

•**Removing the part of the eye's drainage system** that's preventing fluid flow and replacing it with a Trabecutome shunt, a device that slips into the eye drain and allows diseased tissue to be removed using electrical sparks.

•**Going around the clogged section entirely using a Glaukos iStent—**a tube-like device that takes fluid past the clogged portion of the eye's drain, bypassing the diseased tissue and lowering the eye pressure.

Is a Hidden Hernia Causing Your Heartburn?

J. Scott Roth, MD, associate professor of surgery at the University of Maryland School of Medicine, director of the University of Maryland Hernia Center and head of surgical endoscopy at the University of Maryland Medical Center, all in Baltimore.

A hernia is a protusion of an organ or tissue into a part of the body where it does not belong. Most people are familiar with the type that appears as a bulge in the groin. Much more common in men than in women,

this type (known as an *inguinal* hernia) occurs when part of the intestine protrudes into the groin, possibly as a result of pressure caused by lifting heavy objects and/or straining during a bowel movement.

What you may not know: There is another type of hernia, called a *hiatal* hernia, that far fewer people are aware of, even though estimates show that it occurs in up to six out of 10 people over age 60. A hiatal hernia, in which a portion of the stomach protrudes into the chest cavity, usually causes no symptoms. When symptoms do occur, however, they are often misdiagnosed as ordinary heartburn and/or nausea. Such hernias can be detected only with medical tests, such as a barium X-ray.

WHEN THE STOMACH MOVES

The *diaphragm* (a dome-shaped muscle that helps with breathing) separates the abdominal and chest cavities. The esophagus passes from the throat through an opening in the diaphragm (*hiatus*) to the stomach. The diaphragm opening is normally less than one inch across.

In patients with hiatal hernias, the opening is larger—sometimes up to 4.7 inches.

Result: The upper portion of the stomach can poke through the enlarged hole into the chest cavity. As the hernia enlarges, an increasing amount of the stomach may enter the chest. Large hiatal hernias may cause swallowing difficulties, nausea and vomiting.

Very large hiatal hernias, in which a significant portion of the stomach has entered the chest, can sometimes be detected during a physical exam. A doctor may be able to detect bowel sounds inside the chest cavity. In most cases, hiatal hernias can be diagnosed only with a barium X-ray (the patient drinks a chalky liquid that coats—and illuminates—the upper digestive tract) or an endoscopic procedure, in which a doctor uses a lighted tube to view the esophagus and stomach.

RISK FACTORS FOR HERNIAS

Some people have a genetic susceptibility to hernias—they're born with an unusually large hiatus or the opening enlarges due to weakness in the surrounding muscles.

As with inguinal hernias, repeated abdominal pressure—from lifting heavy objects, straining to have bowel movements, being overweight, and/or severe coughing, sneezing or vomiting —may increase risk for hiatal hernias.

Two types of hiatal hernias…

•**Sliding hernias are the most common.** They occur when a small portion of the stomach (typically about an inch) "slides" into the chest cavity, then returns to its normal position. This movement reduces pressure on the lower esophageal sphincter (LES), a circular band of muscle at the base of the esophagus, allowing reflux (backing up) of stomach acid.

•**Paraesophageal hernias,** though quite rare, are potentially more serious. The upper part of the stomach rises until it's next to the LES. This can restrict (strangulate) blood flow in the stomach, which if untreated, can result in necrosis (death) of the stomach. If the necrosis is not treated, it can be fatal.

If a paraesophageal hernia causes symptoms, such as chest pain, it should be surgically repaired.

CONTROLLING HEARTBURN

Without treatment, the chronic surge of stomach acid that occurs in patients with symptomatic hiatal hernias can cause inflammation of the esophagus…iron-deficiency anemia from esophageal bleeding…or premalignant changes (Barrett's esophagus) that can lead to esophageal cancer. Some patients experience difficulty breathing or even severe chest pain that resembles a heart attack.

Most people with hiatal hernias don't require surgical repair as long as they can minimize discomfort and damage caused by the reflux of stomach acid. *My advice…*

•**Make lifestyle changes.** *Most patients with hernia-related heartburn require medication, but some improve significantly with lifestyle adjustments…*

•Avoid eating within four to five hours of bedtime. Eating stimulates the production of stomach acid, which is more likely to cause heartburn when patients lie down soon afterward.

•Avoid peppermint and caffeine. Both reduce muscle tension in the LES, the muscular band that helps prevent reflux.

•Raise the head of the bed about six inches. Gravity can prevent stomach acid from moving into your esophagus while you sleep. Use bricks, wood or plastic risers designed to elevate the head of the bed.

•**Consider taking medication.** For most medical conditions, doctors usually prefer to start treatment with the mildest drugs first. *In my experience, the opposite approach—starting strong, then tapering off, if possible—seems to work better for hernia-related heartburn…*

•Proton-pump inhibitors (PPIs) are considered the strongest heartburn medication, so your doctor may advise you to start with one of these drugs. PPIs, such as *omeprazole* (Prilosec) and *esomeprazole* (Nexium), inhibit acid production in the stomach and allow damaged tissues to heal. If a PPI taken twice daily improves symptoms within about six weeks, your doctor may suggest that you cut back to one dose a day.

•Antacids and H2-blockers. If heartburn symptoms continue to improve over roughly a six-week period, you can probably switch to a milder (and less expensive) drug, such as an over-the-counter antacid or H2-blocker, including *famotidine* (Pepcid) or *cimetidine* (Tagamet), for occasional relief.

WHEN TO CONSIDER SURGERY

Most people with hiatal hernias can control heartburn with drugs alone. Therefore, surgery is recommended only if you have a twisted stomach that endangers your stomach's blood supply…complications, such as scarring or bleeding due to reflux…or severe discomfort or reflux of stomach contents (such as bile or digestive enzymes) that isn't relieved by medications. Surgery also is recommended for patients who no longer wish to take reflux medications.

Most hernias, including hiatal hernias, are repaired with laparoscopic "keyhole" surgery, in which the surgeon inserts a camera and instruments through four or five small (less than half an inch) incisions in the abdomen.

About 95% of patients who receive surgery for hiatal hernias will no longer need medication to control symptoms.

2

Asthma & Allergies

Aspirin Lowers Asthma Risk for Older Women

Taking a small dose of aspirin every other day seems to reduce the risk of developing asthma among older women, concludes a study appearing in the on-line issue of *Thorax*.

The new study essentially mirrors a similar one in which men taking aspirin saw the same reduced risk.

BACKGROUND

The incidence of asthma is on the increase, possibly due to obesity, dietary factors, exposure to allergens and environmental factors.

But the trend also coincides with a decreased use of aspirin as people have switched to other over-the-counter pain relievers, or have avoided aspirin use in children due to concerns about Reye's syndrome (a condition characterized by swelling of the liver and brain, typically triggered by using aspirin to treat a virus).

That led some researchers to wonder whether the reduction in aspirin use was contributing to the rise of asthma.

THE STUDY

This study, the first randomized trial in women, looked at nearly 40,000 healthy, female health care professionals, ages 45 and older, who were participating in the Women's Health Study.

Women were randomized to receive 100 milligrams (mg) of aspirin every other day, or a placebo. This dose was much lower than that taken by men in a previous study (325 mg).

Over the next decade, there were 10% fewer new cases of asthma in the women who had been taking aspirin regularly. However, aspirin had no effect in women who were obese, the researchers discovered.

Tobias Kurth, MD, ScD, associate epidemiologist, Brigham and Women's Hospital, and assistant professor, medicine, Harvard Medical School, Boston.

Len Horovitz, MD, pulmonary specialist, Lenox Hill Hospital, New York City.

Thorax.

"It could be due to the low dose, or there may be a biological reason," said Dr. Tobias Kurth, MD, ScD, an associate epidemiologist at Brigham and Women's Hospital and assistant professor of medicine at Harvard Medical School, both in Boston.

"It may be a dose-related issue," added Dr. Len Horovitz, MD, a pulmonary specialist with Lenox Hill Hospital in New York City. "It's basically like a baby aspirin."

According to the researchers, the effect of the regular aspirin dose in non-obese women was smaller than that seen in men (they saw a 22% risk reduction), but that may be at least partly attributable to the lower dose.

POSSIBLE COMPLICATION

Interestingly, aspirin can exacerbate symptoms in 4% to 11% of people who have already been diagnosed with the condition.

"It's not usual for us to encourage people to take aspirin, because you don't know who does or does not have [this sensitivity] until you have a problem," Dr. Horovitz said.

At this point, it's not clear exactly why aspirin has this effect.

IMPLICATIONS

The study authors warned that the research was still not enough to recommend taking aspirin regularly.

"These two studies are not sufficiently strong to make a recommendation for primary prevention of adult-onset asthma," said Dr. Kurth, who was involved in both studies.

For the many older adults already taking aspirin for its salutary effects on heart health, "this could be an added benefit," he added.

info For more information on asthma, visit the Web site of the American Academy of Allergy, Asthma & Immunology at *www.aaaai.org*.

To find out more about the health benefits and risks of aspirin, visit the MayoClinic.com Web site at *www.mayoclinic.com*. Type "daily aspirin therapy" into the search box.

Cleaning Sprays Can Increase Asthma Risk

Jan-Paul Zock, PhD, research fellow, the Centre for Research in Environmental Epidemiology, Municipal Institute of Medical Research, Barcelona, Spain.

David Rosenstreich, MD, director of the division of allergy and immunology, department of medicine, Montefiore Medical Center and Albert Einstein College of Medicine, New York City.

American Journal of Respiratory and Critical Care Medicine.

Using household cleaning sprays and spray air fresheners just once a week can increase your risk for developing asthma, new research suggests.

Using spray cleaners as little as once a week increased the risk of developing the respiratory ailment by nearly 50%, the researchers found.

"Cleaning sprays, especially air fresheners, furniture cleaners and glass cleaners, had a particularly strong effect. The risk of developing asthma increased with the frequency of cleaning and number of different sprays used, but on average was 30% to 50% higher in people regularly exposed to cleaning sprays than in others," said the study's lead author, Dr. Jan-Paul Zock, PhD, a research fellow at the Centre for Research in Environmental Epidemiology at the Municipal Institute of Medical Research in Barcelona, Spain.

BACKGROUND

Previous research found an association between asthma and being employed as a professional cleaner. Other studies have also noted a link between respiratory symptoms and certain cleaning products, but Dr. Zock and his colleagues wanted to learn if typical household exposures to cleaning products would have any effect on the development of asthma.

THE STUDY

Drawing on a 10-country database called the European Community Respiratory Health Survey, the researchers identified more than 3,500 people without any history of asthma or asthma symptoms. All reported being responsible for the cleaning of their homes.

Study participants were followed for nine years. Overall, 42% of the participants reported using a spray cleaner at least once a week. Glass cleaning sprays were the most commonly used sprays, with about 22% reporting using them at least once a week.

Weekly use of a spray cleaner increased the risk for asthma by 45% in women and 76% in men. Among those who used the cleaning sprays at least four days a week, the risk for asthma was more than doubled.

Liquid multi-purpose cleaners were also frequently used—just over 83% said they used such a product at least once a week. However, the researchers didn't find any association between asthma and properly used liquid cleaners.

IMPLICATIONS

Whether or not the cleaning products are a direct cause of asthma, or simply a trigger for people who already have the disease, isn't clear.

However, the research team believes that spray cleaners can be a cause of new-onset asthma, because the people included in this study did not have asthma or asthma symptoms at the start of the study.

WHAT TO DO

Dr. Zock said it's too soon to tell people to swear off spray cleaners altogether, but added, "Nevertheless, from the perspective of precaution, we may recommend to use sprays only when really necessary. In most cases, it is possible to replace the spray by non-spray cleaning liquids and to do the cleaning properly. If [sprays are] used, people can protect themselves by opening windows, avoiding the application near the breathing zone, and by using masks or other types of personal respiratory protection."

"Cleaning compounds are generally just tested to make sure that they don't kill people or cause cancer," noted Dr. David Rosenstreich, MD, director of the division of allergy and immunology in the department of medicine at Montefiore Medical Center and Albert Einstein College of Medicine in New York City.

"But these products may not be safe for asthmatics to breathe in. And, if it's not safe for asthmatics, it's probably not safe for anyone else," he said.

His advice: "Switch to liquid cleaning products rather than aerosols. If there's any difference in cleaning, it's a small sacrifice to be made in terms of protecting your respiratory health. But don't forget that old-fashioned liquid cleaning products can involve risks for respiratory disorders as well. The most notorious example is bleach, particularly when mixed with other cleaners—something that should never be done."

info To learn more about what triggers asthma, visit the Asthma and Allergy Foundation of America's Web site at *www.aafa.org*. Click on "Asthma" and then "What Causes Asthma."

■ ■ ■ ■

Ease Asthma with Acupressure

Acupressure—applying thumbs or fingertips to pressure points on the body—can help people with asthma. One primary acupressure point for the lungs is located at the intersection of the shoulder and shoulder blade on either shoulder. Use mild, consistent pressure and hold for 30 to 60 seconds and repeat twice. This technique can be used up to three times daily, regardless of whether you have symptoms.

Caution: If you experience any sudden change in your breathing, such as difficulty breathing, go to the emergency room.

Richard Firshein, DO, medical director, Firshein Center for Comprehensive Medicine, New York City.

Illustration by Shawn Banner.

■ ■ ■ ■

Amazing Technique Cuts Asthma Symptoms by 33%

The Papworth method, created in the 1960s at Papworth Hospital in Cambridgeshire, England, can help anyone who starts breathing rapidly and shallowly because of anxiety. It had not been studied in asthma patients until recently. It has now been shown to cut asthma symptoms by one-third, but it does not improve lung function or replace medications. This form of physical therapy integrates breathing and relaxation exercises to discourage shallow breaths while focusing on slow nasal expiration using the abdomen and diaphragm. It teaches patients to recognize stress and use breathing to physically manage that stress. Ask your doctor for a referral to a respiratory therapist who teaches the technique.

Martha V. White, MD, director of research, Institute for Asthma and Allergy, Wheaton, Maryland.

Natural Ways to Breathe Better

Mark A. Stengler, ND, naturopathic physician in private practice, La Jolla, California…adjunct associate clinical professor at the National College of Natural Medicine, Portland, Oregon…author of many books, including *The Natural Physician's Healing Therapies* and coauthor of *Prescription for Natural Cures* (both from Bottom Line Books)…and author of the *Bottom Line/Natural Healing* newsletter.

When she spoke, 53-year-old Shelly made a wheezing sound. She'd had chronic asthma since childhood, and several times yearly suffered acute attacks so severe that she could hardly breathe. Her medical doctor prescribed oral steroids to reduce lung inflammation, but since these can have serious side effects—including immune system suppression, weight gain and hair loss—Shelly asked me for a safer alternative.

For some people, asthma attacks are triggered by sensitivities to dairy products, sugar, gluten (in grains and grain products) or other foods. However, Shelly had no major food sensitivities. Certain supplements can ease lung inflammation or reduce the airways' reaction to environmental factors, such as pollen and cold air. Shelly was already taking the supplements that I typically recommend for breathing problems—fish oil, magnesium, lycopene (a plant pigment) and quercetin (a plant compound).

Many asthma patients use a *nebulizer*, a mechanical device that uses pressurized air to turn liquid medication into a fine mist for inhalation, allowing for a more direct healing effect on the lungs. While nebulized steroids are less toxic than oral steroids, they can cause a sore throat and oral yeast infection.

Natural alternative: Nebulized *glutathione* (an amino acid) eases congestion by thinning mucous secretions so that they drain more easily. Glutathione is an antioxidant (nutrient that neutralizes harmful molecules called free radicals), so it also may reduce lung inflammation.

Taking this therapy a step further, I combine glutathione with *N-acetylcysteine* (NAC) and licorice root extract. NAC, an antioxidant amino acid-like substance that thins mucus, is often used in nebulized form (prescription drug name Mucomyst) to treat respiratory conditions. Licorice root, an anti-inflammatory, has been used by herbalists for centuries to ease breathing problems. I believe that these three components, used together, produce a synergistic healing effect.

Over the past two years, I have prescribed this nebulized formula for about 30 patients suffering from bronchitis, sinusitis, emphysema (damaged air sacs in the lungs) and/or asthma. None had an adverse or allergic reaction. Most reported significantly easier breathing—and not one developed pneumonia, a common problem among patients with respiratory ailments.

When Shelly first tried this therapy in my clinic, her wheezing lessened after just five minutes. Thereafter, she used this treatment at home once daily—and within four weeks, her chronic asthma symptoms had improved by 90%. Shelly now uses the nebulizer as needed at the first signs of an acute asthma flare-up, and her asthma attacks are milder and far less frequent.

Important: This prescription formula must be prepared at a compounding pharmacy and used under a doctor's care. To order, your doctor can contact ApothéCure (800-969-6601, *www.apothecure.com*) and ask for stock number 19348. When properly prepared, this treatment is quite safe—I even administered it to my four-year-old son for sinusitis with excellent results.

How Birth Order Could Cause Allergies

Wilfried Karmaus, MD, professor, department of epidemiology and biostatistics, University of South Carolina, Columbia, South Carolina.

Ngoc Ly, MD, assistant professor, pediatrics, University of California at San Francisco.

American Thoracic Society International Conference, Toronto.

At least some of the biological risk for childhood asthma and allergies traces back to the womb, new research suggests.

Both the order of birth and even the way a baby is delivered have a significant impact on the long-term strength of a child's allergic defenses, scientists say.

The findings were presented during the American Thoracic Society's International Conference in Toronto.

At the meeting, one team of scientists said it had evidence indicating that when a specific genetic marker linked to the development of allergies and asthma is present among a first-born child, it appears to raise the risk for allergic conditions as far as ten years down the road. However, when the exact same marker is present in a family's second or third child, the gene seems to have exactly the opposite effect—actually lowering such risk.

"This is the first time it has been demonstrated that birth order can affect the behavior of genes related to asthma and allergies, and that birth order can therefore affect the risk for developing one or the other," said study author Wilfried Karmaus, MD, a professor in the department of epidemiology and biostatistics at the University of South Carolina in Columbia.

On a second front, another team of researchers suggested that regulatory cells associated with proper immune function might be impaired in babies delivered by cesarean section.

"We found a dysfunctional cellular response in the normally protective immune system among C-section babies," observed Ngoc Ly, MD, an assistant professor of pediatrics at the University of California at San Francisco. "And although more work needs to be done to follow how long this response might endure, we think this disrupted immune pathway may influence the development of asthma later on."

BIRTH ORDER STUDY

To explore the relationship between birth order and asthma/allergy risk, Dr. Karmaus and his team tracked more than 1,200 newborns from Great Britain's Isle of Wight.

After recording birth orders, the researchers tested each newborn's allergic status by examining indicators present in umbilical cord blood. They also conducted standard skin prick allergy tests at age 4 and age 10.

The authors found that among firstborn children, the presence of a particular gene strain—known as the IL-13 gene variant—was associated with a higher risk for having

an "allergic response." This link continued to persist a decade later.

By contrast, among second or later-born children, no such association between IL-13 and higher risk was found. In fact, the role of IL-13 seemed to "switch over" to that of a risk protector.

THEORY

"The fetus is, in effect, a foreign body," noted Dr. Karmaus. "And a foreign body can be exposed to a lot of immune arousal or not, depending. So we think that something during pregnancy—it's probably the immune system of the mother—stimulates the IL-13 gene to act differently, depending on birth order. We haven't shown how this works yet, but that's the idea."

IMPLICATIONS

Dr. Karmaus suggested that the finding could theoretically lead to the crafting of interventions—perhaps therapeutic, perhaps simply lifestyle changes—which could reduce the allergic response risk for firstborns.

CESAREAN SECTION STUDY

Meanwhile, Dr. Ly and her colleagues explored similar risks associated with cesarean sections by analyzing the cellular immune regulatory activity present (in the form of so-called treg cells) in the umbilical cord blood of 50 babies born by cesarean and 68 babies delivered vaginally. All the babies had at least one parent with allergies and/or asthma.

The authors found that among C-section babies, treg cells were more likely to fail to operate properly, raising the risk for the early onset of immune system disruption. This, in turn, may increase the likelihood that a child could grow up to develop an allergy or asthma.

THEORY

Dr. Ly and her team said that the suggestion that the manner of delivery could actually influence immune system development, and ultimately asthma/allergy risk, could be due to the fact that vaginal labor provides beneficial exposure to birth canal microbes that simply aren't available to a C-section baby.

IMPLICATIONS

"But still I think it's important to reiterate that while this is interesting research, it is a small study and the first of its kind," noted Dr. Ly. "So there is much more follow-up work that needs to be done to see if these newborns in fact start developing symptoms of asthma or allergies as they grow."

info For details on childhood asthma, visit the Web site of the American Lung Association, *www.lungusa.org*, and search "childhood asthma overview."

Fewer Children Outgrowing Allergies To Milk, Eggs

Johns Hopkins Children's Center, news release.

Childhood milk and egg allergies may be more persistent and harder to outgrow than they were a generation ago, US researchers report.

FINDINGS FROM TWO STUDIES

In two studies from the Johns Hopkins Children's Center, researchers followed more than 800 children with milk allergy and nearly 900 children with egg allergy for more than 13 years.

They found that the allergies often persist well into the school years and beyond.

Earlier research suggested that about 75% of children with milk allergy outgrew the allergy by age 3. But the Hopkins researchers found that only 20% of children with milk allergy outgrew it by age 4, and 42% outgrew it by age 8. By age 16, 79% no longer had the allergy.

There were similar findings among the children with egg allergy. Only 4% outgrew it by age 4, 37% by age 10, and 68% by age 16.

The studies were published in the *Journal of Allergy and Clinical Immunology.*

IMPLICATIONS

"The bad news is that the prognosis for a child with a milk or egg allergy appears to be worse than it was 20 years ago," said lead investigator Robert Wood, MD, head of allergy and immunology at the Johns Hopkins Children's Center. "Not only do more kids have allergies, but fewer of them outgrow their allergies, and those who do, do so later than before."

The findings seem to confirm what many pediatricians have long suspected—that food allergies diagnosed in recent years behave more unpredictably and aggressively than food allergies in the past.

"We may be dealing with a different disease process than we did 20 years ago. Why this is happening we just don't know," Dr. Wood said.

info For more information on food allergy, visit the Web site of the National Institute of Allergy and Infectious Diseases, *www3.niaid.nih.gov/topics/foodallergy/.*

The Digestion Connection— Surprising Causes of Allergic Sniffles

Andrew L. Rubman, ND, director, Southbury Clinic for Traditional Medicines, Southbury, Connecticut.

When you think about controlling allergies or hay fever, you probably think about avoiding pollen, freshly mown grass, your friend's cat or a moldy basement. In many cases, this avoidance strategy is effective. Often, however, the allergy triggers remain elusive and there's a possibility you may be overlooking an important one—what you eat and drink.

EAT, DRINK AND BE MISERABLE?

Since allergic sensitivities may be, in effect, cumulative, certain foods and beverages can make you more vulnerable to allergy symptoms such as sneezing, sniffling, congestion, skin irritations and red, watery eyes, confirms Andrew L. Rubman, ND. In his opinion, it's simplistic to just suppress these symptoms with medication. Instead, he advises looking deeper into dietary connections to potentially "cure" the problem rather than simply mask it. Dr. Rubman shared more of his thoughts on food allergies, along with advice on what can be done about them...

In most cases, what we commonly refer to as food "allergies" would be more accurately described as food "sensitivities." On occasion, a person may experience a true food allergy—in the worst case, a life-threatening allergic reaction (anaphylaxis) to foods such as shellfish or peanuts. Far more commonly, however, a runny nose, sneezing, hives and other sorts of allergy symptoms reflect a sensitivity to certain foods that are difficult for the body to process. The foods that typically are hardest to digest—cow's milk and gluten grains (wheat, barley, rye)—are the most likely to cause problems.

How does a glass of milk and a sandwich on whole-wheat bread—a meal digested in the gut—cause symptoms in the nose? According to Dr. Rubman, the body has several mechanisms for dealing with digestive challenges. Normally, food residues are effectively contained within the intestine, through which nutrients are absorbed while the remainder passes efficiently and completely from the body. However, when factors such as disease, stress, excessive alcohol, medication or foods containing dairy proteins/sugars or gluten cause inflammation, the intestinal wall may "leak," permitting tiny partially digested food particles to escape. This causes the body to produce antibodies that attack the unknown particles (called antigens).

One surprising response to the presence of these microscopic food particles is *rhinitis*—inflammation of the nose's mucous membranes. Nasal defenses normally handle airborne challenges, deftly filtering out and destroying millions of irritating pollutants, particles and chemicals in the air you breathe. But they can also respond to intestinal permeability (or what's called leaky gut). The mucous membranes react by producing extra mucus (hence, the sniffles).

STRATEGY TO REDUCE THE SYMPTOMS

Mainstream medicine generally treats allergy symptoms with antihistamines, decongestants or immunotherapy. Dr. Rubman, however, advises allergy sufferers to examine and change their diet as necessary. Consume more whole foods—such as fresh vegetables and fruits and legumes, deep-water fish like salmon and tuna, and poultry without skin—and fewer processed foods laden with additives, saturated fats and sugar, all of which can worsen allergy symptoms and leaky gut. In particular, limit intake of cow's milk, milk products and products with gluten because these have the greatest capacity to disrupt the gut lining, particularly the large intestine.

Dr. Rubman's recommendations...

•**Leave cow's milk to baby cows.** Every species of mammalian mother produces special milk to feed their young, so it is not surprising that some people are allergic to the specific proteins in cow's milk—they are different from what humans naturally digest. Other people are unable to digest lactose, a milk sugar. Cow's milk can cause digestive disturbances, mucus build-up in the sinuses, immune system reactions and more.

Note: Cultured dairy products like cheese and yogurt are more easily tolerated in the lactose sensitive or intolerant.

Worried about getting enough calcium if giving up your daily glass of milk? Try the many other rich—and more readily digestible—sources of calcium, including broccoli, kale, spinach, turnip greens, salmon and canned sardines with bones.

•**Cut back on products containing gluten.** Gluten—the complex protein in grains like wheat, barley and rye—can cause disturbances in the structural and functional performance of the intestine, explains Dr. Rubman. This can result in both intestinal (gas, bloating, diarrhea, for example) and non-intestinal symptoms (e.g., fatigue, irritability, and bone and joint pain in addition to the allergy symptoms), ranging from mild to severe.

Opt for gluten-free alternatives such as quinoa, amaranth, buckwheat or brown rice. Look for gluten-free labels on processed foods (such as soy sauce, ketchup and salad dressings, products that often contain hidden gluten). Or, better yet, forego the processed foods altogether.

NOT SUCH AN "EXTREME" MAKEOVER

When you've explored the obvious causes—such as pollen and mold—and your allergy symptoms still bother you, it's time to wonder whether your diet might be the real problem. Since dairy and gluten products are naturally challenging to the human digestive tract, says Dr. Rubman, it is likely that everyone is affected to varying degrees by a dairy and/or gluten sensitivity.

In fact, the question may not be "if", but rather "how much" milk or cereal it will take to trigger symptoms. Often, the answer depends on one's overall health. *Dr. Rubman advises taking these factors into account...*

•**How pumped is your immune system?** The healthier you are, the better prepared your body will be to meet the challenge of processing hard-to-digest food and drink.

•**How old are you?** Sometimes, the older you get, the less robust immune protection you have, compared with younger people.

•**Is your body coping with seasonal airborne irritants (pollen, ragweed, etc.)?** If so, on occasion, this will leave you especially vulnerable to the ill effects of digestive challenges, due to systemic inflammation that can affect intestinal permeability.

Natural Way to Relieve Springtime Allergies

University of Michigan Health System, news release.

When you're doing your spring cleaning, don't forget about your nose. Nasal irrigation is a cheap and easy way for people with spring allergies, nasal congestion, stuffy noses and post-nasal drip to get relief, says Melissa Pynnonen, MD, codirector of the Michigan Sinus Center and an assistant professor in the University of Michigan's department of otolaryngology.

HOW TO PERFORM NASAL IRRIGATION

Nasal irrigation involves rinsing the nose and nasal passages with a solution made from a quarter-teaspoon of salt (non-iodized, if possible), eight ounces of warm tap water and a quarter-teaspoon of baking soda.

There are a number of ways to administer the solution. For people who've never done nasal irrigation, Dr. Pynnonen recommended using an eight-ounce squeeze bottle (specially designed to fit the nose and available at drugstores) and squirting four ounces of the solution into each nostril. The solution exits through the opposite nostril. Opening your mouth and making a "K" sound will prevent the solution from coming out of your mouth.

Some people use a neti pot, which looks like a miniature teapot. When using a neti pot, the solution is poured, rather than squeezed, into the nose. Turkey basters or syringes, like those used to suction a baby's nose, also work.

BENEFITS OF NASAL IRRIGATION

"For most patients, the benefit of nasal irrigation is that it does a great job of treating symptoms that otherwise aren't well treated with medicine," said Dr. Pynnonen. "Nasal irrigation can be considered a first-line treatment for common nasal and sinus symptoms. It's often more effective than medications," she concluded.

Nasal irrigation alone may be sufficient to control mild allergy symptoms in some people, but others may need to use medications in addition to nasal irrigation.

So long as children are old enough to cooperate, it's safe to try nasal irrigation with them, using a smaller amount of solution, said Dr. Pynnonen.

info For an instructional video on nasal irrigation, visit the Web site Mayoclinic.com and type "nasal irrigation" into the search box.

■ ■ ■ ■

No Prescription Needed

Newly over-the-counter Zyrtec provides a superior degree of relief from allergy symptoms, such as runny nose and sneezing, and can be helpful for itchy skin rashes as well. It is effective in a larger percentage of patients when compared with Claritin.

Caution: Zyrtec has been shown to cause more drowsiness than Claritin.

Martha V. White, MD, director of research, Institute for Asthma & Allergy, Wheaton, Maryland.

■ ■ ■ ■

Soothing Sinus Relief

Antibiotics aren't always the best treatment for sinusitis, says Donald A. Leopold, MD. Sinusitis can be caused by viruses and/or bacteria, or it can be an ongoing inflammation from viral colds, fungal infections or allergies. Antibiotics fight only bacterial infections. For most cases of sinusitis, *saline lavage*—rinsing saline solution through the nose and sinuses—provides some relief as the body fights the infection. Discuss this procedure with your doctor. Some patients may need oral or topical steroids, antifungal drugs, allergy therapy or even surgery to get relief.

Donald A. Leopold, MD, professor and chair, department of otolaryngology—head and neck surgery, University of Nebraska Medical Center, Omaha.

Christmas Trees Trigger Annoying Allergies

Philip Hemmers, DO, allergist and immunologist, St. Vincent's Medical Center, Bridgeport, Connecticut.

David Khan, MD, associate professor, internal medicine, University of Texas Southwestern Medical Center, Dallas.

James Sublett, MD, clinical professor and section chief, pediatric allergy, University of Louisville School of Medicine, Kentucky.

Dennis Ownby, MD, professor, pediatrics and medicine, Medical College of Georgia, Augusta.

American Academy of Allergy, Asthma & Immunology annual meeting, Dallas.

While bringing home a live Christmas tree marks the beginning of the holiday season for many, the mold that thrives on its branches can trigger weeks of suffering for some, a new study shows.

Connecticut researchers have found that the mold count from a live Christmas tree rose to five times the normal level two weeks after the tree was brought indoors, and that can prove problematic for people with mold allergies.

"Christmas trees are another possible source of mold exposure during the holiday season,"

said study coauthor Philip Hemmers, DO, an allergist and immunologist with St. Vincent's Medical Center in Bridgeport, Connecticut. "Mold allergies peak in the fall, and we see a second peak with a lot of our mold-sensitive patients during the holiday season. Our finding correlates with this second peak of mold sensitivity."

THE STUDY

The researchers studied the mold growth of a live Christmas tree in a house in Connecticut. After the tree was brought inside the house and decorated, the researchers measured mold spore counts 12 times over a two-week period between December 24 and January 6. Mold reproduces by releasing spores into the air. The researchers did not assess the types of mold or whether these molds triggered allergic symptoms in people living in the house.

RESULTS OF THE RESEARCH

The mold spore count was 800 spores per cubic meter (m^3) for the first three days. Normal spore counts are less than 1,000 spores/m^3, said Dr. Hemmers. However, the spore count rose after day four, reaching a maximum of 5,000 spores/m^3 by day 14.

"This mold spore count is five times above normal. These high levels have been correlated with allergic rhinitis and an increased rate of asthma symptoms and asthma-related hospitalization in other studies," said Dr. Hemmers. "So if you don't feel well during the holidays, consider the Christmas tree as a possible source of allergies."

WHAT TO DO

Dr. Hemmers recommended that people with mold sensitivity keep a live Christmas tree in the house for only four to seven days. An artificial tree may be a better option for people with mold allergies, he added, but they carry their own set of problems, especially if they've been stored in the attic or basement where they can collect dust and mold.

According to David Khan, MD, an associate professor of internal medicine at the University of Texas Southwestern Medical Center in Dallas, there are things you can do to minimize a live tree's impact.

"If one is mold-allergic, running an air cleaner in the same room as the tree could theoretically reduce the mold exposure, but this has not been studied," he said. "For some people who are sensitive to odors, the aroma from the tree, which most people like, could irritate their nose and cause symptoms. For these people, avoiding live trees may be best."

FURTHER RESEARCH IS NEEDED

Before people start avoiding live Christmas trees because of their mold growth, more research needs to be done, said Dennis Ownby, MD, a professor of pediatrics and medicine at the Medical College of Georgia, in Augusta. Since this study only looked at a single tree in one home, more homes with trees should be investigated, as well as the types of mold found and whether those molds trigger allergies. He added that the researchers should also measure mold counts outside the home and correlate those to indoor mold counts.

Dr. Hemmers said that the outdoor mold count was likely low, since the study was done during the winter. The research team does plan to do further work by looking at more homes and the types of mold found.

MORE HOLIDAY ALLERGENS

In addition to Christmas trees, there are other potential holiday allergens, said James Sublett, MD, section chief of pediatric allergy at the University of Louisville School of Medicine in Kentucky. These can include foods consumed at holiday parties, such as nuts and shellfish, and Christmas ornaments and lights that have been contaminated with dust or mold.

"Store Christmas decorations in plastic containers that you can wipe off, since cardboard can potentially have mold," he advised. "Also, wear a N95 dust mask when bringing stuff out of storage."

info For more on holiday allergies, visit the Web site of the Asthma and Allergy Foundation of American, *www.aafa.org*, and search "holiday allergies."

Don't Let Allergies Dig Into Gardening Fun

American Academy of Allergy, Asthma & Immunology, news release.

For gardeners with allergies, it can be difficult to enjoy their passion for plants when they have to cope with the misery of sneezing, itchy eyes, congestion and, in some cases, an asthma attack.

"Gardening outside during times of high pollen counts puts patients at risk for severe allergic symptoms," said Dr. Warren Filley, an allergist/immunologist in Oklahoma City.

GUIDELINES FOR AVOIDING ALLERGIES

"Avoidance measures, as well as the use of medications and allergy immunotherapy, can make the difference between having fun in the garden and being miserable," said Filley, a long-time gardener who suffers from allergies.

An allergist/immunologist can help determine which plant species are causing allergies and offer advice on the best time of day or season to work in the garden, according to the American Academy of Allergy, Asthma & Immunology (AAAAI). For example, pollen levels are typically lower on rainy, cloudy and windless days.

Gardeners can also control their allergies by careful selection of plants. Certain flowers, trees and grasses are less likely to produce pollen. These include cacti, cherry, dahlia, daisy, geranium, iris, magnolia, rose, snapdragon and tulip.

Plants that are highly allergenic include ash, cedar, cottonwood, oak, maple, pine, salt grass and timothy.

Skin testing is the best way to determine which plants will trigger allergic reactions in individuals, said the AAAAI.

Additional allergy prevention tips from the AAAAI for gardeners include…

•**Avoid touching your eyes or face** whenever working around plants likely to cause an allergic reaction.

•**Consider wearing a mask** to reduce the amount of pollen grains that you inhale.

•**Wear gloves, long-sleeved shirts and long pants** to minimize skin contact with allergens.

•**Leave gardening tools and clothing,** such as gloves and shoes, outside to avoid bringing allergens indoors.

•**Shower immediately after gardening** or doing other yard work.

info For more information on controlling allergy symptoms, visit the Web site of the American Academy of Family Physicians, *http://familydoctor.org*, and search "allergies: control your symptoms."

Stopping the Itch Of Poison Ivy

University of Michigan, news release.

Each year, 25 million to 40 million Americans suffer severe itchiness caused by an allergic reaction to the oil in poison ivy. The itchy rash appears one to two days after contact and can last from 10 days to three weeks.

"The reaction usually starts with redness and swelling of the skin, which is then followed by either bumps or blisters," said Dr. Lisa Hammer, a pediatrician at the University of Michigan C.S. Mott Children's Hospital.

POISON IVY TIPS

Dr. Hammer offers some tips on how to avoid poison ivy and treatments to use if you do have a brush with it...

•**"If you come into contact with poison ivy,** the best advice is to wash your skin as quickly as possible," Hammer said. Don't scrub too hard or use hot water because that may irritate the skin or open pores too much and make it easier for the poison ivy oil to be absorbed into the skin.

•**Wash the clothing and shoes you were wearing** when you came into contact with poison ivy.

•**Give your dog a bath in order to remove poison ivy oil** and wash garden tools and other items that may have come into contact

with poison ivy. "Oil can stay on these types of (tool/implement) surfaces for up to five years," Hammer said.

•**Poison ivy oil on your skin can be transferred to other people,** but fluid from sores caused by poison ivy is not contagious.

•**Cool baths, cool compresses, or massaging the affected area** with an ice cube can help relieve itchiness. Allow the area to air dry, which will reduce itching and oozing of blisters.

•**Oral and topical antihistamines** can help reduce itchiness.

WHEN TO SEE YOUR DOCTOR

Most cases of poison ivy can be managed at home, but you should seek medical attention if you have a severe reaction.

According to Dr. Hammer, "If individuals are experiencing a more severe poison ivy reaction, specifically involving the face or genital area, or there's a significant swelling pain or irritation that disrupts their sleep or daily activities, they should seek additional help from their health care providers," who can prescribe oral steroids or steroid creams to reduce itching, pain and discomfort.

info For more on poison ivy, visit the Web site of the Poison Ivy, Oak, and Sumac Information Center at *www.poisonivy.com*.

■ ■ ■ ■

Forewarned Is Forearmed

Allergy alerts and pollen counts are available anytime at the American Academy of Allergy, Asthma & Immunology's free Web site, *www.aaaai.org* (click on "Pollen Counts"). Click on your region for a list of all national allergy bureau locations, where measurements of pollen and mold are taken.

Helpful: Sign up for a free account at the site to view each pollen count in detail.

Example: If you are allergic to pollen from oak trees but not maple trees, you can find out which specific type of tree has a high count each day.

Martha V. White, MD, director of research, Institute for Asthma & Allergy, Wheaton, Maryland.

Four Best Natural Remedies for Allergies

Jamison Starbuck, ND, a naturopathic physician in family practice and a lecturer at the University of Montana, both in Missoula. She is past president of the American Association of Naturopathic Physicians and a contributing editor to *The Alternative Advisor: The Complete Guide to Natural Therapies and Alternative Treatments*. Time-Life.

This time of year, I treat a lot of people who are miserable because of seasonal allergies—they suffer from itchy eyes and throat, sneezing and a runny nose. Seasonal allergies typically result from exposure to allergens, such as pollen from grass, trees and ragweed. But there's another type of allergy that can affect people year-round. Dust, feathers and animal dander are the most common causes of these so-called "perennial" allergies.

Regardless of the trigger, an allergy is an immune disorder. When an airborne irritant, such as pollen or dust, is inhaled, the body recognizes it as a harmful substance. This activates the body's defensive response, which leads not only to sneezing and a runny nose but also to watery eyes, sinus congestion and/or ear pain. When the body is under assault from allergens, the immune system works hard. That's why for some people, the only sign of seasonal allergies is lethargy (extreme physical and mental sluggishness).

When allergies are treated with medication (such as antihistamines and corticosteroids), symptoms are *temporarily* relieved. Allergy shots can reduce allergic reactions in some people but, like medication, they do not cure the problem. To address the root cause of allergies, try my natural allergy-fighting regimen (products are available at most health food stores)...*

•**Get more flavonoids.** These powerful antioxidants strengthen the cells in your upper respiratory tract (particularly the membranes of your nose), which helps protect your body from the ill effects of inhaled irritants. Take 300 milligrams (mg) each of supplements containing the

*Check with your doctor before taking any of these supplements.

flavonoids *quercetin* and *hesperidin* four times daily during allergy season. Fruits—particularly citrus and berries—are rich in flavonoids. Eat them daily. Organic fresh fruits are best.

•**Reduce stress.** Researchers at the University of Texas Medical School in Houston have linked worsening allergy symptoms to anxiety, depression and psychological stress. That's because chronic stress triggers immune dysfunction, weakening the body's ability to defend against irritants. If you have allergies, review what causes stress in your life and take steps to remedy these situations, especially during allergy season.

•**Take herbs.** *Adaptogen* herbs help the body "adapt" to stress, generally by supporting adrenal gland health. I recommend astragalus and borage for allergy season. Mix one-eighth teaspoon each of a tincture of astragalus and a tincture of borage in two ounces of water and take 15 minutes before or after meals, twice daily throughout allergy season.

•**Drink tea.** To safely relieve allergy symptoms, try flavonoid-rich elderflower tea, which reduces nasal and sinus congestion, fights sneezing and relieves watery eyes. Pour one cup of boiling water over two teaspoons of dried elderflower blossoms (or an elderflower tea bag) and steep for 10 minutes. Strain and drink hot (add lemon and/or honey, if you like) three times daily until symptoms improve.

■ ■ ■ ■

Play the Harmonica For Healthier Lungs

Blowing into a harmonica lowers air pressure in the airways and expands the air sacs in the lungs, reducing the risk that they will narrow or collapse, as occurs in patients with asthma or emphysema. It also forces you to frequently change the pace and depth of your breath, which strengthens the diaphragm (a muscle separating the lungs from the abdomen).

If you have asthma, chronic bronchitis or emphysema: Consider learning to play the harmonica.

Dan Hamner, MD, a physiatrist and sports medicine physician, New York City.

3

Breast Cancer

Breakthroughs in Breast Cancer Screening

**O**ne in eight—that's how many American women discover that they have breast cancer. But this diagnosis is not a death sentence. More than two million women in the US today have survived breast cancer. Many can thank screening techniques that detect the disease early—which often allows for additional treatment options and a better outcome.

MAMMOGRAPHY: A PROVEN TOOL

Women who get mammograms (X-rays of the breast) every one to two years have a lower risk of dying from breast cancer—about 20% lower for women in their 40s and about 25% lower for women in their 50s and 60s. Among breast cancer screening techniques, only mammography has been proven to reduce death rates from the disease.

Controversy: The American Cancer Society recommends that women age 40 and over have yearly mammograms. Yet in April 2007, the American College of Physicians advised against automatic yearly mammograms for women in their 40s, citing the physical discomfort of screening procedures…radiation exposure…and risk for false-positive results.

My view: Get annual mammograms beginning at age 40. *Reasons…*

•**The death rate reduction due to mammography,** though greater in older women, is still substantial in women ages 40 to 49.

•**Cancers in women under age 50 often grow faster** and are deadlier than those in older women.

•**The needle biopsy used to confirm or exclude a mammogram's findings usually is minimally invasive,** takes less than 30 minutes and leaves only a freckle-sized scar.

Ellen Mendelson, MD, chief, section of breast imaging at Northwestern Memorial Hospital, and professor of radiology at Northwestern University Feinberg School of Medicine, both in Chicago. She is the author or coauthor of more than 60 scientific studies on imaging and breast cancer.

CAD MAMMOGRAPHY

With computer-aided detection (CAD) mammography, computer software analyzes a digital (rather than film) mammogram, marking suspicious areas. It now is offered by about 30% of mammography centers.

Controversy: A study in *The New England Journal of Medicine* found that CAD resulted in 31% more callbacks for additional tests and 20% more biopsies. Often, additional testing revealed no abnormalities.

My view: If a local facility offers it, it is preferable to use CAD (ask your doctor for a referral). *Reasons…*

• **CAD mammography increases detection of *ductal carcinoma in situ* (DCIS),** perhaps cancer's earliest stage.

• **CAD mammography can spot various breast abnormalities.** Some may be cancer, some may not. But all merit subsequent testing.

ULTRASOUND: THE NEXT STEP

This noninvasive test is routinely performed after a suspicious area is found. It uses sound waves to create a picture (sonogram) that shows if the area is a harmless fluid-filled cyst…a harmless variation of normal tissue…or a solid mass that should be biopsied. Ultrasound is safe, painless, widely available, relatively inexpensive and usually covered by insurance.

The American College of Radiology Imaging Network recently presented the results of a three-year study designed to show whether annual screening with mammography and ultrasound effectively detects cancer in women whose breasts are dense (have more glandular and connective tissue and less fatty tissue). If so, ultrasound may become a standard precancer screening technique for such women. Ultrasound may help distinguish between normal dense breast tissue and cancerous tissue, which also is dense.

MRI: THE NEW RECOMMENDATION

Magnetic resonance imaging (MRI) uses a magnetic field and radio waves to generate detailed pictures revealing cancers that mammograms may miss.

Note: Any woman recently diagnosed with breast cancer in one breast should have an MRI of the other breast.

The American Cancer Society recommends that women with the highest risk for breast cancer—20% or greater—receive a yearly mammogram and yearly MRI. Any one of the following criteria places a woman in this group…

• **Testing positive on genetic tests for the BRCA1 or BRCA2 gene**—linked to breast cancer.

• **Having a first-degree relative** (mother, sister or daughter) who tested positive for either gene.

• **Having two or more first-degree relatives** with breast cancer.

• **Having had chest radiation treatment for Hodgkin's disease** (a cancer of the lymphatic system).

MRI is very expensive, and insurance may not cover it. Women at "moderately increased" lifetime risk—a 15% to 20% risk—should talk to their doctors about the most appropriate screening method for them. This group includes…

• **Women with dense breasts.** Cancer is three to five times more likely to develop in dense breasts.

• **Women with fibrocystic or lumpy breasts,** since such breasts often are dense.

• **Women who have had a biopsy that showed *lobular carcinoma in situ* (LCIS),** an irregular growth of noncancerous cells. LCIS increases breast cancer risk.

PROMISING TECHNOLOGIES

Several other breast cancer screening techniques show promise.

• **Gamma camera.** A woman is injected with a short-lived radioactive substance that gravitates to a diseased area, where it emits gamma waves recorded by the camera. Several companies recently have created gamma cameras specifically for breast imaging, and early test results are promising. Already some breast centers use gamma cameras as a next step after a suspicious mammogram—because the test is far less expensive than MRI.

• **Positron emission tomography (PET).** This technique scans the whole body to see if diagnosed breast cancer has spread. When radioactive glucose is injected into the body, cancerous tissues accumulate more of it…and emit more positrons (positively charged molecular particles), which appear as bright areas on the PET images.

Caution: A technique called *thermography* cannot accurately screen for breast cancer. Thermography detects tissues with higher temperatures—including inflamed or diseased tissues, not just cancer. Do not risk your health by putting your faith in it.

■ **More from Ellen Mendelson, MD…**

Screening Guidelines

The American Cancer Society recommends the following…

•**Get a clinical breast exam** (manual exam by a doctor) every three years in your 20s and 30s and yearly thereafter.

•**Know how your breasts normally feel.** Report any change promptly to your doctor.

Watch for: A new lump…new asymmetry…dimpling of skin…inverted nipple…spontaneous nipple discharge…rash or color change…unusual soreness or swelling.

•**Have a yearly mammogram** starting at age 40.

•**If you're at high risk,** get a yearly mammogram and MRI.

Stereo Mammograms May Be Better at Finding Breast Cancer

David Getty, PhD, division scientist, BBN Technologies, Cambridge, Massachusetts.

David A. Bluemke, MD, PhD, professor, radiology and medicine, and clinical director of MRI, Johns Hopkins Medical Institutions, Baltimore.

Kristin C. Byrne, MD, chief, breast imaging, Lenox Hill Hospital, New York City.

Radiological Society of North America annual meeting, Chicago.

A 3-D view of breast tissue may give women a more accurate method of detecting breast cancers, according to a trial of a new technology called stereoscopic digital mammography.

False-positive results were almost cut in half with stereo mammography, said the technology's developer David Getty, PhD, a division scientist at BBN Technologies in Cambridge, Massachusetts.

"These are women who at the moment are getting a call back from a radiologist saying something suspicious has been found," he explained. However, after subsequent testing, "most of them are finding out there was nothing there," Dr. Getty added. "Being able to cut that number in half would have a dramatic impact" in reducing both patient anxieties and cost, he said.

A second benefit to the new technology lies in "finding lesions that are being missed on standard mammography. Most of them will turn out to be benign, but some additional cancers will be found," Dr. Getty said.

THE STUDY

The five-year trial, conducted at Emory University in Atlanta focused on nearly 1,100 women at elevated risk for breast cancer. According to Dr. Getty, the trial was a collaboration with Carl D'Orsi, MD, the director of Emory's breast imaging center.

STUDY FINDINGS

Results so far show that stereo mammography reduced false-positives by 49%. The stereoscopic equipment failed to detect 24 out of 109 cancerous lesions, compared to 40 out of 109 lesions not found through standard digital mammography, Dr. Getty said.

Another advantage of the stereoscopic digital mammography is that it "is much better at picking up cluster calcifications [that] can be associated with malignancy," Dr. Getty added.

HOW IT WORKS

This technology also allows radiologists to get a picture of the entire breast volume in a slice-by-slice view. "It certainly helps, because you're seeing all of the tissue in depth," Dr. Getty explained. The capacity of mammography to detect problems in dense breasts is not an issue with the stereoscopic digital equipment because it "doesn't look as dense, because tissue is being spread out in depth," he said.

A stereoscopic mammogram image works on principles similar to the old Viewmaster slide viewers used by children, Dr. Getty explained.

Each of two images inserted in the Viewmaster were channeled to a different eye, and the brain's "visual cortex—the magician in all this—then combines the two images, artificially recreating what your two eyes normally create when you walk around in a three-dimensional world," Dr. Getty said. Similarly, the viewing monitor for stereo mammography merges two distinct images to create a 3-D look at tissue.

EXPERT REACTION

"Stereo mammography is a step in the right direction, but it is not a breakthrough," said David Bluemke, MD, PhD, a professor of radiology and medicine at Johns Hopkins Medical Institutions in Baltimore. "True 3-D tomographic imaging of the breast is ultimately needed." By giving radiologists a view of slices through the breast, 3-D tomography would allow them to see lesions that are otherwise obscured by being superimposed on normal breast tissue, he explained.

Stereoscopic digital mammography "seems very promising," added Kristin C. Byrne, MD, the chief of breast imaging at Lenox Hill Hospital in New York City. "It would make mammography that much better."

With current technology, the problem of calling back a woman whose breasts show a suspicious area is that radiologists often can't find that same suspicious tissue in a second view, so the woman has to follow-up with further monitoring in another six months or have a biopsy, she noted.

info For more information on breast cancer, go the National Cancer Institute's Web site at *www.cancer.gov* and click on "Breast Cancer."

■ ■ ■ ■

Better Breast Cancer Detection

In a recent study, 969 women who had recently been diagnosed with cancer in one breast but had no abnormalities in the opposite breast (based on mammography and clinical examination) where given a magnetic resonance imaging (MRI) scan. In 30 women, the scans revealed opposite-breast malignancies missed by the standard testing methods.

Theory: MRI scans evaluate the subtle differences in blood flow of cancerous tissue versus normal tissue.

If you have breast cancer or are at high risk (due to family history): Ask your doctor about receiving an MRI scan in addition to your mammogram.

Connie Lehman, MD, PhD, director of radiology, Seattle Cancer Care Alliance.

Diagnostic Mammogram Readings Vary by Radiologist

Diana Miglioretti, PhD, associate investigator, Group Health Center for Health Studies, Seattle.
Jay Brooks, MD, chairman of hematology/oncology, Ochsner Health System, Baton Rouge, Louisiana.
Journal of the National Cancer Institute.

Radiologists are human, too, and vary widely in their interpretations of diagnostic mammograms, a new study found. The variations were linked to differences in the radiologists' experience and affiliation.

BACKGROUND

Previous studies have also shown variability in how radiologists interpret mammograms, but those studies primarily involved screening mammograms. Diagnostic mammograms are performed after an abnormality of some kind has already been detected either from a screening mammogram or a physical exam.

The accuracy of diagnostic mammograms is extremely important, given that the rate of breast cancer is 10 times higher with those images than in screening mammograms, the study authors said.

THE STUDY

The researchers looked at the records of 123 radiologists who had collectively interpreted 35,895 diagnostic mammograms at 72 different US facilities.

Close to 80% of breast cancers were diagnosed correctly. But sensitivity—or the ability to accurately detect cancer—ranged from 27% to

100% for different radiologists. False-positives (biopsies performed when there was no cancer) ranged from zero to 16%.

But 4.3% of women who had no cancer were tentatively told they had the disease, based on the mammogram (i.e., they received a false-positive reading).

The strongest factor linked to better accuracy was if the radiologist was affiliated with an academic medical center. Such radiologists were correct 88% of the time, compared to 76% for other radiologists. Radiologists at academic institutions were also less likely to report false-positive findings.

But the study results have to be taken with a grain of salt, the authors said, because only seven radiologists affiliated with academic institutions were represented in the study. This is more or less in keeping with the "real world," where academic radiologists interpret only 6.5% of mammograms across the nation, the authors said.

Radiologists who spent 20% or more of their time on breast imaging were more accurate than those who spent less time on breast imaging—80% versus 70%.

Interestingly, more experienced radiologists were less likely to recommend biopsies, but they missed more cancers than those with less experience, the study authors said.

"Radiologists who had been in practice longer had a lower threshold for recalling women for biopsies," said Diana Miglioretti, PhD, study lead author and an associate investigator at Group Health Center for Health Studies in Seattle. "They had fewer false-positives but lower sensitivity, meaning they missed more cancers."

WHAT TO DO

"This is a little bit of a warning that there is a wide variation," said Dr. Miglioretti. "If possible, go to a facility with a breast-imaging specialist, someone who also does biopsies and ultrasounds."

"You definitely want to have radiologists interpreting mammograms who do a substantial number of mammograms in a year—that's number one," added Jay Brooks, MD, chairman of hematology/oncology at Ochsner Health System in Baton Rouge, Louisiana. "Number two, you want to make sure that they read mammograms in a continuum so that they have previous mammograms to read it against. That's why I encourage patients to stay in one system where X-rays are looked at longitudinally. The third thing is that the radiologist is not reading this by him or herself, that there are other radiologists that can come into the room and look at the films."

info For more information on mammography, log on to the Internet site of the Radiological Society of North America at *www.radiologyinfo.org*. Under "Procedures A to Z," click "M" for "Mammography."

■ ■ ■ ■

Improved Mammogram Readings Drop Misdiagnosis by 44%

Comparing a new mammogram with previous ones improves accuracy of diagnosis.

Recent finding: When radiologists followed this protocol, the number of false-positive diagnoses declined by 44%.

Self-defense: Provide your radiologist with a copy of your prior mammogram results whenever possible.

Nico Karssemeijer, PhD, associate professor, department of radiology, Radboud University Nijmegen Medical Center, the Netherlands, and coauthor of a study published in *Radiology*.

Expert Tips for Easing Mammogram Discomfort

Baylor Health Care System, news release.

Mammograms can be uncomfortable, causing some women to skip the potentially lifesaving annual exam. But experts at Baylor Health Care System in Texas offer tips on how to ensure the test's accuracy and ease any possible discomfort during the procedure…

•**Don't drink coffee, tea or caffeinated soft drinks** during the week before having a mammogram. Caffeine can make breasts tender and lumpy, which may lead to discomfort during a mammogram. Chocolate and some over-the-counter pain relievers also contain caffeine. Check the label of OTC medications.

•Don't use deodorant, perfumes, talcum powder, or oils on the day of a mammogram. These products can leave a residue that can be picked up by the X-rays, obscuring the mammogram and possibly interfering with the results, leading to the need for a second mammogram.

•Don't have a mammogram the week before your period. "Most women's breasts are naturally more tender or slightly swollen during the week prior to their menstrual period," according to Dr. Alicia Starr, medical director of the Women's Imaging Center at Baylor Regional Medical Center at Plano, Texas. "Try to avoid scheduling your annual mammogram during this time."

•Wear a two-piece outfit with a blouse or sweater. It's easier and faster to take off a blouse or sweater than removing a one-piece dress.

Mammography is currently the most effective way of finding breast cancer in its earliest and most treatable stages, experts note.

info For more information on mammography, consult the Web site of the National Women's Health Information Center at *http://womenshealth.gov/faq/mammography.htm.*

Breast Cancer Surgery Breakthrough

Laura A. Klein, MD, director of breast surgical oncology at St. Barnabas Hospital and an instructor in clinical surgery at Columbia University College of Physicians and Surgeons, both in New York City. Dr. Klein is one of the few surgeons trained in oncoplastic surgery and is an innovator in its continued development.

Traditionally, women whose breast cancers have been treated with lumpectomies (surgical removal of the tumor, leaving the rest of the breast intact) often had to either live with a breast marred by the procedure…or plan for reconstructive breast surgery in the future.

Good news: An innovative new approach enables women undergoing lumpectomy to receive cosmetic repair at the same time. The result is a more attractive, natural-looking breast—right away.

Called *oncoplastic surgery*, this technique combines oncology surgery (treatment of cancer) and plastic surgery (reconstruction of the affected breast).

How it's done: Using a technique called the "advancement flap," the surgeon moves or rotates replacement tissue from the same breast. This is done without detaching it from the original blood supply.

While the result is a somewhat smaller breast, the doctor can immediately reshape the other to match. This means that there's no need for further surgery.

The patient usually ends up with a breast lift —a silver lining of sorts. This technique eliminates the need to use implants or relocate tissue from another part of the body.

Who it's for: Oncoplastic surgery is an alternative for many breast cancer patients, even small-breasted women who may otherwise have required mastectomy.

Also, this approach is particularly advantageous in treating a noninvasive cancer called *ductal carcinoma in situ* (DCIS). This refers to cancer that does not migrate outside the ducts and into the breast tissue, and comprises about 20% of diagnosed breast cancers today. DCIS radiates from the nipple and may be distributed throughout the ductal system, and can necessitate removal of a substantial amount of breast tissue.

Important: This is a new and emerging technique, and only a limited number of surgeons in this country have experience with it.

To learn more or find a physician who performs this innovative surgery, consult with a fellowship-trained breast surgeon or someone whose practice is 100% breast surgery, since he/she is apt to be most current in breast surgery advances.

Hypnosis Eases Pain of Breast Cancer Surgery

Guy Montgomery, PhD, associate professor of oncological sciences, Mount Sinai School of Medicine, New York City.

David Spiegel, MD, Willson Professor and associate chairman of psychiatry and behavioral sciences, Stanford University School of Medicine, Palo Alto, California.

Darlene Miltenburg, MD, assistant professor of surgery, Texas A&M Health Science Center College of Medicine, and chief, section of breast surgery, Scott & White Clinic, Temple.

Journal of the National Cancer Institute.

Hypnosis may ease the pain of surgery and speed recovery. According to a new study, women who received hypnosis before breast cancer surgery needed less anesthesia during the procedure, reported less pain afterward, needed less time in the operating room and had reduced costs.

"This helps women at a time when they could use help, and it has no side effects. It really only has side benefits," said Guy Montgomery, PhD, lead author of the report and an associate professor in the department of oncological sciences at Mount Sinai School of Medicine in New York City.

Dr. Montgomery hopes the study will promote greater use of hypnosis in medical treatments.

BACKGROUND

Side effects, such as pain, nausea and fatigue, both during and after breast cancer surgery, are commonplace. Previous research has suggested that hypnosis, a simple and inexpensive procedure, can help ease these problems.

NEW RESEARCH

For the new study, 200 women set for breast cancer surgery were randomly assigned to receive either 15 minutes of hypnosis with a psychologist, or assigned to a group that simply spoke with a psychologist.

During the hypnosis session, the patients received suggestions for relaxation and pleasant imagery as well as advice on how to reduce pain, nausea and fatigue. They also received instructions on how to use hypnosis on their own.

NEW FINDINGS

The researchers found that women in the hypnosis group required less anesthesia and sedatives than patients in the control group, and also reported less pain, nausea, fatigue, discomfort and emotional upset after the surgery.

Those who received hypnosis also spent almost 11 fewer minutes in surgery and had their surgical costs reduced by about $773, mainly as a result of the shorter time.

POSITIVE FEEDBACK

Although people think that hypnosis strips a person of control, it actually does just the opposite, said David Spiegel, MD, Willson Professor and associate chairman of psychiatry and behavioral sciences at Stanford University School of Medicine. "This is something that empowers patients," Dr. Spiegel explained. "If you're fighting, you think you're protecting yourself, but, actually, you're losing control, because you're getting into a struggle with your own body. You can teach people to float instead of fighting. You get the body comfortable and think more clearly. The weird thing is it actually works. If thoughts can make the body worse, it follows that thoughts could actually make the body feel better."

But will hypnosis catch on with health care providers?

"We have this in-built skepticism of what goes on in the brain and the mind, and the idea is that the only real intervention is a physical one. Yet what supposedly distinguishes us is this huge brain on top of our bodies," Dr. Spiegel said. "It seems more scientific and desirable to give drugs than it does to talk to people and have them reorganize the way they're managing their bodies."

There are other obstacles. Many doctors find it more expedient to write a prescription than learn to perform hypnosis. Also, there's no industry pushing the technique as there is with drugs, Dr. Spiegel said.

On the positive side, little investment is needed to get a hypnosis program going, Montgomery said. "A psychologist or nurse could get training in a short period of time," he said. "It's not that involved."

Darlene Miltenburg, MD assistant professor of surgery at Texas A&M Health Science Center

College of Medicine, hailed the new study, calling it "superb."

"Anybody who has an open mind would realize that this treatment works and is scientifically proven. It's not black magic," Dr. Miltenburg said. "It's real, and we do use it here. It's very time consuming, that's part of the problem, taking a pill is much easier. But just like many things in life, we want a quick fix rather than something that takes longer."

info To learn more about medical hypnosis, go to the Medical Hypnosis Web site at *www.medicalhypnosis.org.*

■ ■ ■ ■

Radiation During Surgery

New breast cancer treatment eliminates the need for later radiation. With *intraoperative radiation therapy*, during surgery to remove the cancerous tissue, a one-time dose of radiation is given. The procedure adds one hour to the surgery.

Best for: Women over age 55 with early-stage breast cancer that has not spread.

David McCready, MD, head of Princess Margaret Hospital Breast Cancer Program, Toronto.

Marijuana Compound May Stop Metastatic Breast Cancer

Sean D. McAllister, PhD, associate scientist, California Pacific Medical Center Research Institute, San Francisco.
Pierre-Yves Desprez, PhD, staff scientist, California Pacific Medical Center Research Institute, San Francisco.
Manuel Guzman, PhD, professor, biochemistry and molecular biology, Complutense University, Madrid, Spain.
Molecular Cancer Therapeutics.

A non-toxic, non-psychoactive compound in marijuana may block the progress of metastatic breast cancer, according to a new study by researchers in California.

"This is a new way to treat a patient that is not toxic like chemotherapy or radiotherapy. It is a new approach for metastatic cancer," said lead researcher Sean D. McAllister, PhD, an associate scientist at the California Pacific Medical Center Research Institute in San Francisco.

HOW IT WORKS

The compound found in cannabis, called cannabidiol (CBD), inhibits a gene, Id-1, that researchers believe is responsible for the metastatic process that spreads cells from the original tumor throughout the body.

Opting for a musical metaphor, senior researcher Pierre-Yves Desprez, PhD, likened Id-1 to "an (orchestra) conductor. In this case, you shoot the conductor, and the whole orchestra is going to stop. If you shoot the violinist, the orchestra just continues to play."

In humans, the Id-1 gene is found only in metastatic cancer cells, said Dr. Desprez, a staff scientist at the institute. Before birth, they are present and involved in the development of human embryos, but after birth, they go silent—and should stay that way, he said.

But in metastatic cancer "when (the genes) wake up, they are very bad," he said. "They push the cells to behave like embryonic cells and grow. They go crazy, they proliferate, they migrate." Dr. Desprez said, "We need to be able to turn them off."

NEW FINDINGS

According to the new study, CBD does exactly that.

"We are focusing on the latest stages of cancer," Dr. Desprez added. The cancer cell itself is not the problem, because a tumor can be "removed easily by surgery," he said. The problem is the development of metastatic cells, which is "conducted" by Id-1.

Drs. McAllister and Desprez said they are *not* suggesting that patients with hormone-independent metastatic breast cancer smoke marijuana. For one thing, a sufficient amount of CBD could never be obtained in that way, they said.

The research that has been done on marijuana and its compounds, however, is helpful, Dr. McAllister, said. CBD has been around for a long time, and researchers have found it is not psychoactive, and its "toxicity is very low," he added.

If Drs. McAllister and Desprez's work results in the development of a cancer treatment, someone with metastatic cancer might be placed on

CBD for several years. That means low toxicity is important, Dr. McAllister explained.

Dr. McAllister also suggested that Id-1 is "so important in providing the [metastatic] mechanism in these cells in so many types of cancers" that they "provide us an opportunity potentially to target other types of cancers."

TREATMENT WITH CBD

Further study is needed before CBD can be conclusively identified as a treatment option, Drs. McAllister and Desprez said. "We need to involve a team of physicians, because we are bench (basic) scientists," Dr. McAllister noted.

One expert called the findings intriguing but preliminary.

"This is the first evidence that a cannabinoid can target the expression of an important breast cancer metastasis gene," noted Manuel Guzman, PhD, a Spanish expert on cannabinoids and cancer. He described the California study as giving "preliminary insight into the question of whether CBD could be used clinically to treat metastatic breast cancer."

However, "all the experiments in the paper have been conducted in cultured cells and none of them in any animal model of breast cancer, which would be one of the steps for further research," added Dr. Guzman, who is a professor of biochemistry and molecular biology at Complutense University in Madrid.

info For more on breast cancer, go to the National Breast Cancer Foundation Web site at *www.nationalbreastcancer.org.*

New Drug Beats Tamoxifen at Keeping Women Cancer Free

Aman Buzdar, MD, professor, medicine and deputy chair, department of breast medical oncology, University of Texas M.D. Anderson Cancer Center, Houston.

Jay Brooks, MD, chairman, hematology/oncology, Ochsner Health System, Baton Rouge, Louisiana.

San Antonio Breast Cancer Symposium.

The aromatase inhibitor drug *anastrozole* (Arimidex) continues to outpace the old standard *tamoxifen* (Nolvadex) when it comes to preventing recurrences of hormone-receptor-positive breast cancers in postmenopausal women.

Even three years after treatment was stopped, women taking Arimidex still saw a benefit, researchers said.

"It has been very good news," said Aman Buzdar, MD, US principal investigator of the ATAC (Arimidex or Tamoxifen Alone or in Combination) trial. "A lot more women receiving Arimidex are free of cancer compared to tamoxifen, and the 100-month data show that these differences, if anything, with time actually continued to increase—meaning there were fewer and fewer recurrences on Arimidex compared with tamoxifen," Dr. Buzdar said.

"Arimidex is the standard of care for postmenopausal women with receptor-positive breast cancer," confirmed Jay Brooks, MD, chairman of hematology/oncology at Ochsner Health System in Baton Rouge, Louisiana. "One hundred months [over eight years] of follow-up is very profound."

BACKGROUND

Hormone-receptor-positive cancers respond to circulating hormones estrogen or progesterone. Experts estimate that from 50% to 70% of breast cancers are hormone receptor positive.

Arimidex is an aromatase inhibitor, a relatively new class of compounds that blocks estrogen production in the body. According to Dr. Buzdar, who is professor of medicine and deputy chair of the department of breast medical oncology at the University of Texas M.D. Anderson Cancer Center, Arimidex is now indicated for postmenopausal women who have a hormone-dependent cancer.

Tamoxifen, which has been the gold standard of care in breast cancer treatment for more than 20 years, hinders the tumor's ability to use estrogen. Because Arimidex does not interfere with ovarian function, premenopausal women with active ovaries should still use tamoxifen, Dr. Buzdar said.

The first major results from ATAC, reported in 2001, found that Arimidex was more effective than tamoxifen in preventing breast cancer recurrence and was better tolerated.

NEW STUDY

The current data represent five years of active treatment plus three additional years of follow-up. In all, more than 9,000 women in 21 countries were involved in the study.

All the women had early-stage disease and had undergone surgery with or without chemotherapy and/or radiation. The mean age of participants was 72 years and 84% had hormone-receptor-positive tumors.

The women were randomized to receive Arimidex alone or tamoxifen alone.

NEW FINDINGS

Arimidex improved disease-free survival by 15% compared with tamoxifen in women with hormone-receptor-positive breast cancer. The drug reduced the risk of all recurrences by 24%.

The improvement persisted even after treatment was stopped.

"The other question which was in all of our minds was what happens after you stop the pill," Dr. Buzdar said. "But the pill was stopped three years ago, and we're still seeing the effects. Even after stopping therapy, there are fewer recurrences in people who took Arimidex in the past."

The most common side effects were joint pain and estrogen deprivation leading to osteoporosis. Once the pill was stopped, however, a woman's risk of developing osteoporosis returned to normal. No additional side effects were observed.

"Not only are you keeping more patients alive free of disease, but the safety profile is much more predictable and much more favorable than tamoxifen," Dr. Buzdar said.

info For more information on aromatase inhibitors visit the National Cancer Institute's Web site at *www.cancer.gov/cancertopics/aromatase-inhibitors.*

■ ■ ■ ■

Breast Cancer Treatment Increases Survival Rate

Women with early-stage breast cancer who took *tamoxifen* for two to three years, then an aromatase inhibitor (AI), such as *anastrazole* (Arimidex) or *letrozole* (Femara), were less likely to have a recurrence than women who kept taking tamoxifen.

Caution: Women taking AIs should be monitored for high cholesterol, musculoskeletal disorders and heart disease.

R. Charles Coombes, MD, PhD, professor, medical oncology, Imperial College, London, and leader of a study of 4,724 women, published in *The Lancet.*

■ ■ ■ ■

Fight Forgetfulness Caused by Chemo

Forgetfulness may result from breast cancer treatment. Patients who had chemotherapy for breast cancer reported having reduced memory even 10 years after treatment. The condition, called "chemobrain," was previously thought to be short-term.

To keep memory sharp: Do crossword puzzles...exercise, eat well and be sure to get enough sleep.

If symptoms persist a year after treatment: Consult a neuropsychologist.

Ellen Coleman, MSSA, associate executive director, Cancer*Care*, New York City.

■ ■ ■ ■

Higher-Dose Chemo Lowers Cancer Recurrence by 22%

Older breast cancer patients benefit from higher-dose chemotherapy as much as younger patients do. Otherwise healthy patients age 65 and older have about the same lowered recurrence rate—approximately 22%—as younger patients.

Doctors tend to underuse chemotherapy in older patients because of its side effects, such as weakness and nausea.

Hyman B. Muss, MD, professor of medicine, Vermont Cancer Center, Burlington, and leader of a study of 6,487 chemotherapy cases from 1975 to 1999, published in *The Journal of the American Medical Association.*

Relieve Lymphedema With Weight Loss

Mark A. Stengler, ND, naturopathic physician in private practice, La Jolla, California...adjunct associate clinical professor at the National College of Natural Medicine, Portland, Oregon...author of many books, including *The Natural Physician's Healing Therapies* and coauthor of *Prescription for Natural Cures* (both from Bottom Line Books)...and author of the *Bottom Line/Natural Healing* newsletter.

Lymph nodes, lymph vessels and lymph fluid are all part of the immune system. Up to 42% of women who have surgery and/or radiation for breast cancer get arm *lymphedema* (abnormal swelling) caused by damage to the lymphatic system.

A recent study followed 64 women with breast cancer–related lymphedema. Most of them overweight, they followed a low-fat diet, a reduced-calorie diet or their usual diet for 24 weeks.

Result: Among the women who lost weight (about six to nine pounds), arm swelling decreased by 15%.

My view: Lymphedema can swell an arm to three times its normal size. Unless treated, this can become permanent as fat and fibrous tissue increase, skin thickens and lymph fluid becomes "fixed" in the arm. For overweight patients, losing weight can help to relieve lymphedema, perhaps by increasing the muscles' ability to pump out lymph and by reducing excess fat that presses on lymph vessels.

Hormone That Helps Stop the Spread of Cancer

University of North Carolina at Chapel Hill, news release.

A hormone called *adrenomedullin* may prove an effective drug target for treating lymphedema, a painful swelling of the limbs that can follow breast cancer or other cancer treatment, researchers say.

It may also help prevent the spread of cancer, according to a team from the University of North Carolina at Chapel Hill School of Medicine.

THE STUDY

Adrenomedullin, which is secreted by cells throughout the body, is known to play a role in cardiovascular disease and other cell functions. In a new study, the UNC group found that adrenomedullin also plays an important role in the formation of the lymphatic system in mice.

TREATING LYMPHEDEMA

Researchers said it might be possible to develop drugs that target this hormone in order to help the more than 100 million people worldwide who suffer from lymphedema. The condition occurs when the lymphatic system fails to work properly. In rare cases, it is genetic, but millions suffer lymphedema due to parasitic infections or as the aftermath of cancer therapies.

Currently, the only treatments for lymphedema include massage and the use of low-compression stockings and other garments. But these aren't much help, the UNC researchers said.

STOPPING CANCER SPREAD

"Our research also may lead to therapies to prevent cancer cells from traveling through these lymphatic vessels to infiltrate other parts of the body," said senior study author Kathleen M. Caron, PhD, assistant professor of cell and molecular physiology and genetics at UNC.

info The Society for Vascular Surgery has more information about lymphedema at *www.vascularweb.org* and type "lymphedema" into the search box.

∎ ∎ ∎ ∎

Beware! Grapefruit Raises Breast Cancer Risk by 30%

In a recent study of postmenopausal women, those who ate a quarter grapefruit daily increased their breast cancer risk by as much as 30%. Grapefruit is thought to boost levels of estrogen, a hormone associated with higher risk. This is the first study to link a commonly eaten food to increased breast cancer risk in older women.

Kristine R. Monroe, researcher, department of preventive medicine, Keck School of Medicine, University of Southern California, Los Angeles.

■ ■ ■ ■

Drinking Alcohol Increases Breast Cancer Risk

Drinking alcohol increases breast cancer risk, warns Heather Feigelson, PhD, MPH. The increased risk is 20% or less for women who have one drink daily. (One drink is defined as 12 ounces of beer, five ounces of wine or 1.5 ounces of 80-proof distilled spirits.) The more alcohol consumed, the greater the risk. Women who have two or three drinks daily have about 150% higher risk than women who do not drink.

Heather Feigelson, PhD, MPH, strategic director of genetic epidemiology, American Cancer Society, Atlanta. *www.cancer.org.*

■ ■ ■ ■

Grilled and Smoked Meat Raise Breast Cancer Risk

Grilled and smoked meat raise breast cancer risk, we hear from Susan Steck, PhD, RD, and MPH.

New finding: Based on an analysis of dietary information, postmenopausal women who ate the highest amounts of grilled or smoked meat were found to have a 47% greater lifetime risk, on average, for breast cancer than those who consumed the lowest amounts of such meat.

Theory: Cooking meat at high temperatures to the very well-done stage creates carcinogenic (cancer-causing) compounds.

To lower breast cancer risk: Limit intake of grilled or smoked meats…opt for roasted or baked meats instead.

Susan Steck, PhD, RD, MPH, research assistant professor, department of epidemiology and biostatistics, University of South Carolina, Columbia.

■ ■ ■ ■

Different Sized Breasts Mean Greater Cancer Risk

Women with different-sized breasts have a greater risk for breast cancer than women whose breasts are almost the same size.

Recent finding: Risk increases by 50% for every 100-milliliter difference in breast volume (about half a cup size).

Theory: Mutations that cause asymmetry may be linked to breast cancer.

Diane Scutt, PhD, director of research in health sciences, faculty of medicine, University of Liverpool, UK, and leader of a study of more than 500 women, published in *Breast Cancer Research.*

■ ■ ■ ■

Half of Genetic Breast Cancers Come from Dads!

Half of genetic breast cancers can be inherited from a woman's father. The breast cancer BRCA gene mutations may pass through generations unobserved if there are few women in the family tree. About 8,000 young women with breast cancer in the US per year are not offered genetic testing, because they have no apparent family history of the disease.

Problem: Genetic testing can determine if a BRCA mutation is present. If it is, a woman can consider certain measures to prevent the cancer from returning, such as taking an estrogen-suppressing medicine like *tamoxifen.*

Self-defense: Seek genetic counseling if you had breast cancer before age 50—even if you don't have a family history of the disease.

Jeffrey Weitzel, MD, director of clinical cancer genetics, City of Hope, Duarte, California, and leader of a study of the genetic test results of 306 women diagnosed with breast cancer before age 50, published in *The Journal of the American Medical Association.*

■ ■ ■ ■

Breast Cancer Increases Risk for Skin Cancer

Women diagnosed with a breast tumor are nearly twice as likely to develop malignant melanoma as healthy women.

Theory: Genetic susceptibility may play a role.

If you've been diagnosed with breast cancer: See a dermatologist for a skin exam as soon as possible and yearly thereafter.

Rony Weitzen, MD, senior oncologist, Oncology Institute, Sheba Medical Center, Tel Hashomer, Israel.

4

Cancer Breakthroughs

Seven Breakthrough Cancer Treatments

Chemotherapy has proven to be lifesaving for many cancer patients, but the treatment often inflicts massive "collateral" damage on surrounding healthy cells as the malignancy is being treated. The result can be serious side effects, such as nausea, vomiting and hair loss.

To treat cancer patients more effectively, doctors have recently begun prescribing newly developed "smart" drugs (taken as daily pills or intravenously) that precisely target the malignancy through sophisticated molecular processes. The new drug therapy typically results not only in improved outcomes, but also in far fewer serious side effects.

David G. Nathan, MD, a professor at Harvard Medical School and president emeritus of the Dana-Farber Cancer Institute in Boston, one of the world's leading centers for cancer research and treatment, recently shared his insights on the use of smart drugs.

Cancers that may be treated with smart drugs...

BREAST CANCER

About 25% of women with breast cancer have a receptor known as HER2 on the cancer cells. The receptor is activated by a protein called *epidermal growth factor* (EGF), which speeds up the division of cancer cells, leading to faster-growing, deadlier tumors.

In a landmark study, breast cancer patients with HER2 receptors were treated with either the smart drug *transtuzumab* (Herceptin) and chemotherapy after surgery, or chemotherapy alone. Those receiving Herceptin had a 52% lower rate for tumor recurrence and a 33% lower risk of dying over a three-year period than women given only standard chemotherapy.

David G. Nathan, MD, a professor of pediatrics and medicine at Harvard Medical School and president emeritus of the Dana-Farber Cancer Institute, both in Boston. Dr. Nathan is the author of *The Cancer Treatment Revolution*. Wiley.

How Herceptin works: It binds to the HER2 receptor and inhibits tumor cell growth. Herceptin may cause mild side effects, such as fever, muscle aches and nausea. (Nausea is milder and less common with smart drugs than with chemotherapy alone.)

LEUKEMIA

Chronic myelogenous leukemia (CML) is a form of leukemia (cancer of blood and bone marrow) that most commonly develops between ages 40 and 60.

In a five-year study of 454 CML patients who were given the smart drug *imatinib* (Gleevec), 46% survived in complete remission far longer, on average, than those given interferon, a standard therapy for certain cancers.

How Gleevec works: It blocks the signals of a protein (Bcr-Abl) that can cause bone marrow to make very high numbers of white blood cells and immature stem cells that crowd out the red blood cells and platelets.

Like many smart drugs, Gleevec usually causes fewer side effects than chemotherapy—because it blocks the action of a specific protein rather than eliminating millions of cancer cells *and* healthy cells. Gleevec may cause mild side effects, such as swelling around the eyes and muscle cramps.

Problem: Some CML patients become resistant to Gleevec, a problem that has traditionally necessitated a stem cell transplant, a sometimes fatal procedure that can involve high-dose chemotherapy and total body radiation.

Now: CML patients can try newly developed, second-generation smart drugs, such as *nilotinib* (Tasigna) and *dasatinib* (Sprycel).

LUNG CANCER

The two main types of lung cancer are non-small-cell and small cell, named according to how the cells look under a microscope. (Non-small-cell is the more common form.)

In a recent study, the smart drugs *erlotinib* (Tarceva) and *gefitnib* (Iressa) improved survival from 1.6 years to 3.1 years in the 10% of non-small cell cancer patients who have a particular mutation in a protein that stimulates lung cancer growth.

How Tarceva and Iressa work: Their mechanism of action is similar to that of the breast cancer drug Herceptin. Tarceva may cause mild side effects, such as dizziness and swelling in the hands or feet. Iressa's side effects may include diarrhea, rash and acne.

LYMPHOMA

Non-Hodgkin's lymphoma is a type of lymphoma (cancer of the lymph nodes) that develops in B or T lymphocytes (a type of white blood cell).

An analysis of five clinical studies on follicular lymphoma (a common type of non-Hodgkin's lymphoma) found that 90% of patients who received the smart drug *rituximab* (Rituxan), along with chemotherapy, survived for three to five years, compared with 80% of patients who had chemotherapy alone.

How Rituxan works: It targets a protein on the surface of the malignant cells that are generated during follicular lymphoma, thus triggering the immune system to attack the cells. Healthy cells are also targeted and attacked, but the body quickly replaces them after the therapy. Rituxan may cause mild side effects, such as headache, cough and skin flushing.

Smart drugs that show promise…

COLON CANCER

When cancer metastasizes, it spreads beyond the original site to other parts of the body.

In one study, doctors from the University of California at Los Angeles analyzed the results of three studies focusing on the treatment of metastatic colon cancer with the smart drug *bevacizumab* (Avastin) and chemotherapy, compared with chemotherapy alone. Patients who took the combined treatment survived 17.9 months, on average, compared with 14.6 months, on average, for those who had only chemotherapy.

How Avastin works: The drug blocks a protein that triggers *angiogenesis* (formation of new blood vessels—a process that can promote tumor growth). Avastin's potential side effects include tiredness, stomach pain and headache.

KIDNEY CANCER

Renal cell carcinoma is a malignant tumor of kidney cells that most often develops after age 50.

In a recent study of 903 patients with renal cell carcinoma that was resistant to standard cancer therapy with interferon, half the patients took the smart drug *sorafenib* (Nexavar) for about 19 months and half took a placebo. Sorafenib reduced the risk for death by 28%, with the sorafenib group living an average of 19.3 months, compared with 15.9 months for the placebo group.

How Nexavar works: One of a new class of smart drugs, Nexavar works by inhibiting the proteins inside cancer cells that control cell division…like Avastin, Nexavar also inhibits angiogenesis. Nexavar may cause mild side effects, including skin rash, fatigue and nausea.

HOW TO FIND OUT MORE

To find out whether smart drugs are right for you or a family member with cancer—and to learn more about current or future clinical trials with the drugs—talk to an oncologist. Or visit the Web sites of the National Cancer Institute (*www.cancer.gov*) or the American Cancer Society (*www.cancer.org*).

Amazing! These Natural Cancer Treatments Really Work

Keith I. Block, MD, medical director of Block Center for Integrative Care in Evanston, Illinois…director of Integrative Medical Education at University of Illinois College of Medicine, Chicago…and scientific director of the Institute for Integrative Cancer Research and Education, Evanston. He is editor of *Journal for Integrative Cancer Therapies*. His new book, *Life Over Cancer* (Bantam), is scheduled for publication in 2009.

Many cancer patients augment conventional medical treatment with complementary medicine, such as nutritional or herbal supplements. The newest research and decades of successful clinical use show that some of these natural treatments work very effectively to fight cancer and reduce side effects.

Here are the best science-based complementary treatments for cancer. It's usually fine to take several of these supplements simultaneously, but be sure to talk to your doctor first. To learn how to find an integrative practitioner, go to *http://nccam.nih.gov/health/practitioner*.

ANTIOXIDANTS

Cancer specialists often advise patients not to take antioxidant supplements, such as vitamin A or vitamin E, during chemotherapy and radiation treatments. Reason: One way chemotherapy and radiation destroy cancer cells is by causing oxidative stress. According to one theory, antioxidants may be counterproductive because they might have the ability to protect against this oxidative damage.

But new scientific research shows that the opposite is true—antioxidant supplements aren't powerful enough to counter chemotherapeutic medicines or radiation, but they can reduce the side effects of those treatments and also may battle tumors and extend life.

Recent study: Researchers from the University of Illinois at Chicago and the Institute for Integrative Cancer Research and Education analyzed 19 studies involving 1,554 cancer patients who took antioxidants during chemotherapy. They concluded that most cancer patients are better off using antioxidants in conjunction with chemotherapy and radiation than not using them.

Typical doses…

•**Vitamin A:** 7,500 daily international units (IU), which should only be taken under a doctor's supervision—patients should have their liver enzymes monitored on an ongoing basis.

•**Vitamin E:** 400 IU daily, taken under a doctor's supervision (patients should have their platelet counts monitored). It's best to divide the dose, taking half in the morning and half in the evening. Ideally, take it on an empty stomach.

ASTRAGALUS

The herb astragalus has been used in traditional Chinese medicine for thousands of years. Scientific studies show that it strengthens the immune system, increasing the activity of cancer-fighting cells and inhibiting the activity of immune cells that increase inflammation and thereby worsen cancer. Research shows that the herb also can boost the power of some types of chemotherapy.

Recent study: Researchers from the School of Public Health at the University of California, Berkeley, analyzed 34 studies involving 2,815 patients with non-small-cell lung cancer who were treated with chemotherapy alone or who were treated with chemotherapy and astragalus. Patients taking astragalus had a 33% lower risk for death after 12 months and a 24%-to-46% better tumor response than those not taking the herb.

Typical dose: 750 milligrams (mg) to 2,500 mg a day of astragalus extract.

GINSENG

Extracts from the root of this herb often are used as a natural stimulant—to boost mental and physical energy, improve athletic performance and relieve fatigue. Ginseng also may boost energy in cancer patients.

Recent study: Doctors from the North Central Cancer Treatment Group at the Mayo Clinic gave either a placebo or ginseng—at daily doses of 750 mg...1,000 mg...or 2,000 mg—to 282 cancer patients. Those taking 1,000 mg or 2,000 mg of ginseng had more energy and vitality and less fatigue. Those taking 750 mg or a placebo had no such improvement. The patients taking the higher doses of ginseng also reported greater physical, mental, emotional and spiritual well-being.

Typical dose: 500 mg to 1,000 mg twice daily of American ginseng (not Asian red ginseng). Medical supervision is needed for the higher dosage, particularly if you are taking blood-thinning medication.

GLUTAMINE

Chemotherapy can damage the mucous lining of the digestive tract, which stretches from the inside of the mouth to the rectum. One common result is *oral mucositis* (OM), a condition in which the mucous lining of the mouth and throat becomes inflamed, painful, ulcerated and prone to infection. The amino acid *glutamine* fuels the daily maintenance of the mucous lining of the digestive tract—and supplemental glutamine helps limit or stop its destruction by chemotherapy.

Recent study: Researchers at the University of Connecticut Health Center gave either glutamine powder or a placebo to 326 cancer patients undergoing chemotherapy who were developing OM. Those taking glutamine experienced a significant reduction in the severity of the condition compared with those taking the placebo. In fact, many of those taking glutamine

didn't develop OM at all during their second cycle of chemotherapy.

Typical dose: 5 to 10 grams (g), twice daily.

OMEGA-3 FATTY ACIDS

Chronic inflammation is known to fuel the growth of tumors. Omega-3 fatty acids, nutrients abundant in fish oil and flaxseed, are potent anti-inflammatories that slow tumor growth and shrink tumors in animal studies. Recent research shows that omega-3 fatty acids may do the same for men with prostate cancer.

Recent study: Researchers at Duke University Medical Center, the University of Michigan and the University of North Carolina studied 140 men with prostate cancer who were scheduled to undergo prostate surgery in 30 days. They divided the men into four presurgical groups—some took 30 g (about one ounce) of ground flaxseed daily...some ate a low-fat diet and took the flaxseed...some just ate a low-fat diet...and a control group used none of the regimens. After the surgery, researchers found that the tumors of the men who took flaxseed had grown more slowly—at a 30%-to-40% slower rate than those of the other men. The men mixed the ground flaxseed in drinks or sprinkled it on yogurt and other foods. The study was reported at the 2007 annual meeting of the American Society of Clinical Oncology.

Typical dose: One ounce of ground flaxseed...or 3 g of fish oil.

ACUPUNCTURE

Acupuncture is a healing technique from traditional Chinese medicine. An acupuncturist inserts tiny needles into the skin along *meridians* (energy channels in the body) in order to restore and enhance *chi*, the fundamental force of health and well-being.

Recent study: Doctors at the Osher Center for Integrative Medicine at the University of California, San Francisco, studied 138 cancer patients undergoing surgery, dividing them into two groups. One group received acupuncture and massage after surgery, along with standard care, such as pain-relieving medications. The other group received standard care only. The acupuncture and massage group had 58% less postsurgical pain and less depression, reported the doctors in the *Journal of Pain and Symptom*

Management. It's hard to tell specifically what role acupuncture played and what role massage played, but other studies that look at acupuncture and massage alone show that each has benefits, including reducing surgical pain.

Other studies show acupuncture may help prevent or relieve chemotherapy-induced nausea and fatigue…chemotherapy-induced decrease in white blood cell count…radiation-induced dry mouth…shortness of breath…and insomnia and anxiety.

■ ■ ■ ■

Aspirin Fights Cancer

Aspirin fights cancer, according to Aditya Bardia, MD, MPH, of the Mayo Clinic. In a recent study, people who took aspirin daily were 16% less likely to get any type of cancer than people who didn't take it. But aspirin has known disadvantages, such as increased risk of bleeding and gastrointestinal side effects.

Best: Talk to your doctor about the benefits and risks of aspirin.

Aditya Bardia, MD, MPH, researcher at Mayo Clinic, Rochester, Minnesota, and leader of an analysis of data on 22,500 postmenopausal women, published in *Journal of the National Cancer Institute.*

How to Conquer Chemotherapy Side Effects

Sarah Hope Kagan, PhD, RN, professor of gerontological nursing at the University of Pennsylvania School of Nursing in Philadelphia, specializing in older adults with cancer. She received the 2006 Excellence in Care of the Older Adult with Cancer Award from the Oncology Nursing Society.

For someone recently diagnosed with cancer, facing the prospect of chemotherapy and the possibility of side effects can feel like a double whammy.

Good news: Advances in treatments designed to manage chemotherapy side effects have drastically reduced the discomfort associated with the use of this common cancer therapy.

THE DOWNSIDE OF CHEMO

Chemotherapy drugs (which come in oral, intravenous and topical forms, depending on the drug and its use) are prescribed alone or with radiation and/or surgery in an effort to cure or control many types of cancer, including malignancies of the breast, lung and colon.

Unfortunately, most of these drugs kill not only cancer cells but also some healthy cells found in many parts of the body, including the hair follicles, leading to such side effects as hair loss. The type of chemotherapy drug used largely determines which—if any—side effects will occur. Following chemotherapy, noncancerous cells that were affected by the drugs recover, allowing hair, for example, to grow back. *After 21 years of working with cancer patients, here's what I recommend to curb side effects…*

APPETITE LOSS

Chemotherapy can affect the taste buds and mucous membranes of the mouth, causing strong-tasting foods to taste offensive or less than palatable. This can result in a diminished appetite and other nutritional problems. *What to do…*

•**Talk to an oncology dietitian.*** People receiving chemotherapy often need more protein and calories in a relatively smaller amount of food (known as nutrient-dense food) because they feel too tired to eat or have experienced taste and/or smell changes. An oncology dietitian can suggest nutrient-dense foods, such as chicken and other lean meats, fish or eggs. Be sure these foods are fully cooked and eaten immediately or chilled to prevent the growth of bacteria.

Also helpful: If your dietitian, nurse or doctor recommends extra protein, try adding non-fat, dry-milk powder to cereal, spaghetti sauce or other foods (as long as you're not lactose-intolerant). Also, eating five or six mini-meals each day can reduce the "work" of eating and make it easier to get the nutrition you need.

FATIGUE

Fatigue is a common side effect of chemotherapy, especially for older adults who may have other chronic health conditions that also

*Ask your oncologist or oncology nurse to refer you to a dietitian who works with cancer patients.

cause fatigue, such as arthritis or heart failure. *What to do...*

•**Set priorities.** It may seem obvious, but far too many cancer patients put pressure on themselves to maintain their normal schedules—even if they don't feel up to it. For example, if you're the family cook and typically prepare big breakfasts, ask yourself, "Do I value cooking more than showering in the morning?" If so, shower at night and just wash your face and brush your teeth in the morning, so you can cook. Or delegate the task of cooking to someone else.

•**Ask for help.** It's likely that many people know about your cancer and want to help but don't know how. If you're overwhelmed by multiple offers, appoint a friend or relative to coordinate help with meals, transportation, etc. If you don't have offers of help, contact people you may have met through volunteering, work and community activities.

HAIR LOSS

If hair loss occurs from chemotherapy, it is generally temporary. Still, it makes sense to plan ahead. *What to do...*

•**Get a haircut.** As surprising as this might sound, you can ease the psychological pain of losing your hair by getting a short haircut or your head shaved *before* long strands start falling out. (Men and women can follow this advice.) This allows you—rather than the chemotherapy—to be in charge.

•**Choose appropriate head coverings.** If you are comfortable with baldness, there's no reason to worry about head coverings. Just be sure to use sunblock on your head—as well as the rest of your body. Otherwise, go for a hat or a wig, depending on your own personal style. Head covers, including scarves and turbans, also are an option.

The American Cancer Society's Look Good... Feel Better program offers guidance on the use of head coverings. For more information, call 800-395-5665 or visit the Web site *www.cancer. org.* Or ask a hospital about boutiques that cater to cancer patients.

NAUSEA

Nausea is among the most dreaded potential side effects of chemotherapy. *What to do...*

•**Ask your doctor about anti-nausea medication.** A number of medications are available to prevent and treat nausea, including *ganisetron* (Kytril) and *ondansetron* (Zofran).

Also helpful: Lemon or ginger-flavored foods, such as lemon gelatin, ginger ale and candied ginger, may reduce nausea.

•**Get some exercise.** Mild aerobic exercise, such as walking, fights nausea by helping move food through the digestive tract. Ask your doctor or nurse about an exercise program that is suitable for you.

SKIN PROBLEMS

Some chemo drugs affect skin cells, leading to cracking, itching or sensitive skin. *What to do...*

•**Use care when bathing.** Take a brief daily shower, using a non-irritating, soothing soap, such as Tone, Camay or Dove, only where you need it, such as your groin area and armpits. For dry skin, apply a fragrance-free lotion or cream, such as Cetaphil or Eucerin.

For a line of skin-care products specifically formulated for people undergoing chemotherapy or radiation, contact Lindi Skin, 800-380-4704, *www.lindiskin.com.*

WEAKENED IMMUNITY

•**Wash your hands often.** Because chemotherapy can weaken immunity, scrupulous handwashing—in addition to avoiding large crowds and sick people—is an important defense against contracting a viral or bacterial infection. Wash up before preparing food and eating, after using the toilet and whenever you come in contact with something that may have been touched by someone else, such as an elevator button, a doorknob or a pen at the bank or drugstore. For convenience, carry your own pen and an alcohol-based hand sanitizer.

■ ■ ■ ■

Effective Cancer Treatment Many Hospitals Don't Offer

Treatment for blood cancers is underused, says Mitchell R. Smith, MD, PhD. Many patients with leukemia or non-Hodgkin's B-cell lymphoma go into remission after receiving *radioimmunotherapy*—a radioactive drug combined with antibodies that seek out malignant cells. The treatment requires only a few out-patient visits over one week to three weeks.

Why it may be underused: Few hospitals offer radioimmunotherapy because it requires a multispecialist team, including a physician licensed in the delivery of radioactive drugs. Cancer centers and teaching hospitals are most likely to provide it.

Mitchell R. Smith, MD, PhD, is director of lymphoma service, Fox Chase Cancer Center, Philadelphia.

New Study Shows Virtual Colonoscopies Work!

David Kim, MD, assistant professor, radiology, University of Wisconsin, Madison.

David Weinberg, MD, director, gastroenterology, Fox Chase Cancer Center, Philadelphia.

The New England Journal of Medicine.

A new study supports the effectiveness of an innovative form of colonoscopy that relies on a CT scanner to image a patient's colon.

When it comes to detecting polyps that might become malignant, this so-called "virtual colonoscopy" is just as effective as the traditional approach of using a fiber-optic device, explained study lead David Kim, MD, assistant professor of radiology at the University of Wisconsin.

The real advantage to the technology is that "it can do it in a less invasive manner for less cost and at less risk," he said.

BACKGROUND

According to the American Cancer Society, colorectal cancer is the third most common cancer in the United States among both men and women. It's especially common among people over the age of 50. An estimated 112,000 people in the United States will be diagnosed with the disease this year, and 52,000 will die.

Colonoscopies are considered essential to preventing the disease, but many people don't get them because of the cost or because of their reputation as being uncomfortable.

Virtual colonoscopies, by contrast, offer patients less discomfort, and Dr. Kim said could cost only one-third of the price.

COMPARING METHODS

Just as happens with the conventional test, patients using the virtual screen must still cleanse their bowels by using laxatives beforehand and have a catheter inserted into the rectum to expand their colon with carbon dioxide, Dr. Kim said.

However, unlike the traditional procedure, the patients aren't sedated, although Dr. Kim said they might feel "crampy" until the procedure is over.

CT scanners image the colons to look for signs of trouble. Doctors look at three-dimensional images on computers that "put you inside of the colon so you can navigate your way to look for polyps," Dr. Kim explained.

THE STUDY

In the new study, Dr. Kim's team compared the effectiveness of traditional colonoscopies in 3,163 consecutive patients to virtual colonoscopies in 3,120 consecutive patients.

Researchers found that the two approaches were about equal in terms of detecting potentially dangerous polyps—virtual colonoscopy detected 123 and the traditional approach detected 121. About 8% of the patients who underwent the new approach had to return for traditional colonoscopies.

IMPLICATION

In the near future, doctors will need to screen patients using both approaches, he said. "The bottom line is that there's a huge number of people who should be screened but aren't—40 million people over the age of 50 aren't screened. We're going to need both modalities to make an impact on this number."

EXPERT COMMENTARY

David Weinberg, MD, director of gastroenterology at Fox Chase Cancer Center said the study didn't look at overall colon cancer risk, "and it's premature to declare that virtual colonoscopy should be a routine first-line screening test."

It's also unclear whether the new test is cost-effective or will be covered by insurance. Still, said Dr. Weinberg, "it has potential to be useful because patients, when they know nothing about either, think they will prefer virtual colonoscopy." That could lead to more of potentially lifesaving screenings.

But once they know the details—particularly about how laxatives must still be used—fewer people may think there's a huge difference between the two approaches, he said.

info For more about colorectal cancer screening options, visit the American Cancer Society Web site at *www.cancer.org*. Search "how is colorectal cancer found?"

New Drug Fights Colon Cancer When Chemo Can't

Derek Jonker, MD, assistant professor, oncology, University of Ottawa, and medical oncologist, Ottawa Hospital, Ottawa, Ontario, Canada.

Axel Grothey, professor, oncology, and chair, colorectal cancer group, Mayo Clinic, Rochester, Minnesota.

The New England Journal of Medicine.

A highly targeted drug called *cetuximab* (Erbitux) is the first to extend the survival of patients with advanced colon cancer who have otherwise proved resistant to conventional chemotherapy, Canadian researchers confirmed.

Cetuximab is one of a special class of medications called biologically targeted therapies, which destroy some types of cancer cells while causing little harm to healthy cells. The drug, which costs about $10,000 a month in the United States, appears to be effective in only about one-third of colon tumors, based on their specific gene profile, experts added.

"That's a significant number, but it still leaves a large proportion [of patients] who aren't benefiting," noted lead researcher Derek Jonker, MD, assistant professor, division of medical oncology, at the University of Ottawa and a medical oncologist at the Ottawa Hospital.

Nevertheless, the success of any new drug is welcome, he added.

"Until now, no anticancer therapy had demonstrated an improvement in survival in patients for whom chemotherapy was no longer effective,

and for whom supportive care was the only available treatment," Dr. Jonker said. "So, cetuximab provides new hope for these patients."

The National Cancer Institute of Canada funded the study, along with ImClone Systems and Bristol-Myers Squibb, the two companies that developed the drug.

BACKGROUND

Colorectal cancer is the third most common kind of cancer and the third leading cause of cancer death in the United States. As Dr. Jonker explained, most patients are treated with either surgery or conventional chemotherapy, which typically targets cellular DNA.

Unfortunately, almost all patients with advanced or metastasized colon cancer will develop resistance to standard chemotherapy drugs, he said.

BIOLOGICALLY TARGETED THERAPIES

"However, now we have a new class of drugs known as the biologically targeted therapies, such as cetuximab, and these drugs are targeted to different aspects of the tumor biology," Dr. Jonker explained. "Many of them are targeted at receptors or signals that trigger a cancer cell to grow."

In the case of cetuximab, the drug's target is the epidermal growth factor receptor (EGFR), which is found in especially high concentrations on colon cancer cells. Because biologic drugs are finely targeted to affect cancer cells and not healthy cells, they typically have fewer side effects than standard chemotherapy.

In 2004, the US Food and Drug Administration granted cetuximab conditional approval for use in patients with late-stage, chemotherapy-resistant colon cancer. At the time, the agency stated that full approval hinged on the outcome of the Canadian trial.

Based on the new findings, the agency followed through and gave the drug its full approval for this new indication.

THE STUDY

In the trial, Dr. Jonker's team administered individualized doses of cetuximab to 287 colon cancer patients treated between late 2003 and August 2005. All of the patients had proven resistant to standard chemotherapy. Another 285 patients received supportive/palliative care only—the usual option for patients in this situation.

Compared to those who didn't receive the drug, overall survival for patients receiving cetuximab improved by 23%, while survival without any sign of disease progression rose by 32%, the research team reported.

The incidence of side effects—including skin rash—was 78.5% in the cetuximab group versus about 59% for the control group.

GENE TESTING

One key point, however, was that increases in survival were found only among the 31.4% of patients who actually responded to cetuximab, meaning that their cancer stopped growing.

That's probably due to the fact that cetuximab (as well as a related drug, *panitumumab*) only works against a specific subtype of colon cancer cell—those carrying an unmutated version of a particular gene called KRAS.

"Mutated KRAS almost guarantees no benefit" from cetuximab, said one expert, Axel Grothey, MD, a professor of oncology and chairman of the colorectal cancer group at the Mayo Clinic, in Rochester, Minnesota.

For that reason, he said, pre-treatment gene testing may prove crucial to decisions as to whether a particular patient receives cetuximab or not.

Because it is so expensive—the costliest drug used today against colon cancer—and because it can induce side effects, "I would like cetuximab to be used in a more individualized way," Dr. Grothey said.

He said that most cancer centers, including the Mayo Clinic, do not yet have technologies in place to test tumors for KRAS, but many are looking into it.

Dr. Jonker agreed that, ideally, KRAS testing and the use of cetuximab would go hand-in-hand. That way, he said, "We wouldn't have to put [patients] through treatment, and we wouldn't have to suffer the cost of treatment for people who may not even respond to the drug."

IMPLICATIONS

Studies are already under way to see if adding cetuximab to other therapies will boost survival even further, Dr. Jonker said. "The future of cetuximab is likely to be in combination with chemotherapy or other biologically targeted therapies, where the benefits of cetuximab might be further enhanced," he said.

The drug might also work better if given earlier in the disease process, before patients have developed resistance to chemotherapy.

In any case, the Canadian trial does give colon cancer patients some new reason for hope, Dr. Grothey said. "We need this drug," he said, "and we probably need it even earlier."

info For more about cancer updates and research, visit *www.curetoday.com*.

■ ■ ■ ■

Being Overweight Raises Risk for Colon Cancer

A recent study found that men who carry the most excess weight had more than twice the risk of thin men. Excess weight raises blood levels of *insulin*, which is believed to influence colon cancer risk. The risk also increased in women up to age 66. In older women, the relationship between colon cancer and body mass was not significant.

Kenneth F. Adams, PhD, a postdoctoral fellow in nutritional epidemiology, National Cancer Institute, Rockville, Maryland, and lead author of a study of more than 517,000 people, published in *American Journal of Epidemiology*.

■ ■ ■ ■

Treatment Restores Healthy Tissue in 50% of Cancer Patients

In a recent study of patients with Barrett's esophagus (damage to the lining of the esophagus that can lead to esophageal cancer) 12 individuals received *radiofrequency ablation*, which uses concentrated radio waves to burn away the layer of abnormal cells in the esophageal lining.

Result: Three months later, 50% of the patients had healthier esophageal tissues. To find more information about clinical trials of the procedure, go to *www.clinicaltrials.gov* and click on "Search for Clinical Trials."

Darren Pavey, MD, gastroenterologist, Duke University Medical Center, Durham, North Carolina.

■ ■ ■ ■

Kidney Cancer Treatment Alternative

In a recent study of 104 patients with a type of kidney cancer known as renal cell carcinoma (RCC), participants were treated with *radiofrequency ablation* (RFA), in which a needle-like probe heats and destroys cancerous tissue. A single treatment destroyed all tumors smaller than 3.7 centimeters (about 1.5 inches).

Self-defense: If you have been diagnosed with RCC and are not a good candidate for surgery because of high risk for surgical complications, ask your doctor about RFA.

Ronald J. Zagoria, MD, professor of radiology, Wake Forest University Health Sciences, Winston-Salem, North Carolina.

Three Chemo Drugs Better Than Two for Advanced Head/Neck Cancers

Marshall R. Posner, MD, associate professor, medicine, and medical director, head and neck oncology program, Dana-Farber Cancer Institute, Boston.

David Pfister, MD, chief, head and neck medical oncology service, Memorial Sloan-Kettering Cancer Center, New York City.

New England Journal of Medicine.

The addition of the chemotherapy drug, *docetaxel* (Taxotere), to the standard two-drug regimen used for head and neck cancers improved the efficacy of the treatment while reducing the toxicity, two different studies report.

The triple drug chemotherapy regimen was so effective that it increased survival in both studies and more than doubled the average overall survival in one of the studies.

"This is a study that demonstrates that a three-drug regimen is better by a substantial amount in terms of survival for head and neck cancer. There was a 30% reduction in mortality with less toxicity," said Marshall R. Posner, MD, lead author of the first study and medical director of the head and neck oncology program at the Dana-Farber Cancer Institute in Boston. "This is a wonderful step forward for patients."

Both studies were funded, at least partially, by Sanofi-Aventis, the manufacturer of docetaxel.

BACKGROUND

About 3% to 5% of all cancers in the United States are head and neck cancers, according to the National Cancer Institute. That means almost 40,000 Americans are diagnosed with these cancers each year. They most commonly occur in people over age 50. The biggest risk factor for head and neck cancers is tobacco use.

Treatment for these cancers can be difficult, because surgical removal of tumors can affect the way a person chews, talks and swallows. It is impossible to surgically remove some of these cancers, because the risk of harm outweighs the potential benefit. The cancer is then referred to as unresectable.

STUDY #1

The first study, conducted by Dr. Posner and his colleagues, included 501 people with advanced—stage III or IV—head and neck cancers. None of the volunteers had any signs of cancer in areas far from the original tumor site. The study included participants with both unresectable and resectable tumors.

The study participants were randomly assigned to receive the standard two-drug regimen—*cisplatin* (Platinol AQ) and *fluorouracil* (Adrucil)—or the new three-drug treatment, which included cisplatin, fluorouracil and docetaxel. People in both groups then received seven weeks of weekly chemoradiotherapy (chemotherapy and radiation combined) with the drug *carboplatin* (Paraplatin), and radiotherapy (radiation treatment) for five days a week. Those who became eligible for surgery were able to have surgery six to 12 weeks after completing chemoradiotherapy.

Overall survival after three years was estimated to be 62% for the three-drug group compared to 48% for the two-drug group. Median overall survival was 71 months for the newer treatment versus just 30 months for the older regimen, according to the study.

STUDY #2

The second study, conducted by European researchers, randomly assigned 358 people with unresectable stage III or IV head and neck cancer to receive either the two-drug regimen or the newer three-drug treatment. If there was no progression of disease after the study participants completed chemotherapy, they were given radiotherapy.

Overall survival increased from 14.5 months for the two-drug group to 18.8 months for the three-drug group in this study.

PROMISING RESULTS

In both studies, the three-drug regimen had a similar, though slightly reduced, side-effect profile than the two-drug therapy. Dr. Posner said that's because they were able to use less fluorouracil in the three-drug regimen.

"We maximized efficacy and reduced toxicity. With the inclusion of the [three-drug induction chemotherapy] followed by chemoradiotherapy, we saw unprecedented survival," said Dr. Posner.

EXPERT REACTION

Of the new research, David Pfister, MD, chief of the head and neck medical oncology service at Memorial Sloan-Kettering Cancer Center in New York City, said that the "triple-drug regimen is more effective than the standard regimen alone when given prior to radiation-based treatment and not at a cost of side effects. There was no increase in overall toxicity."

He said oncologists want to know whether induction chemotherapy (as was done in these studies) plus chemoradiotherapy is more effective than chemoradiotherapy alone. The addition of induction therapy, said Dr. Pfister, adds about three months to the treatment process.

info To learn more about head and neck cancers, visit the Web site of the National Library of Medicine at *http://www.nlm.nih. gov/medlineplus* and search "head and neck cancer."

Knee Pain a Sign Of Lung Cancer?

The Annals of Rheumatic Diseases, news release.

Heavy smokers with knee arthritis may be experiencing an early sign of a difficult-to-treat lung cancer, research shows.

THE STUDY

Researchers at Prato Hospital in Italy reviewed the case files of 296 patients with inflammation in one knee between 2000 and 2005.

In just under 2% of these patients, the mild knee arthritis was accompanied by non-small cell lung cancer. All patients were middle-aged men who had been heavy smokers for most of their lives. Once the cancer tissue was surgically removed, the knee pain cleared up as well.

DIAGNOSIS AND TREATMENT

According to the American Cancer Society, about 85% of all lung cancers are non-small cell lung cancer. Unless it is caught early, this type of lung cancer is difficult to treat. It spreads to the bones in one in five cases and is well advanced by the time it is diagnosed in half of all cases.

The researchers noted that early warning signs such as knee pain could lead to earlier diagnosis and more successful treatments.

info For more information about non-small cell lung cancer, visit the Web site of the American Cancer Society at *www.cancer.org*. Under "Learn About Cancer" click "Choose a Cancer Topic" then "Lung Cancer—Non-Small Cell."

■ ■ ■ ■

Nonsmokers Still at Risk For Lung Cancer

About 20% of lung cancer cases in women occur in nonsmokers. Only 8% of cases in men are nonsmokers.

Possible reason: Secondhand smoke exposure is the biggest risk factor among people who have never smoked. It is likely that more women nonsmokers live with men who smoke than men nonsmokers live with women who smoke.

Heather Wakelee, MD, assistant professor of medicine, division of oncology, Stanford University School of Medicine, Stanford, California, and leader of a study of one million people, published in *Journal of Clinical Oncology*.

■ ■ ■ ■

Better Lung Cancer Treatment

A recent study followed 286 patients (ages 18 to 75) who received chemotherapy for small-cell lung cancer (an aggressive form that often spreads to the brain). Those who received radiation to the brain were 15% less likely to develop cancerous tumors in the brain one year later than those who received chemotherapy alone.

Self-defense: If you have small-cell lung cancer that has responded to initial treatment with chemotherapy, ask your doctor if radiation to the brain should be part of your overall treatment plan.

Ben Slotman, MD, PhD, Vrije University Medical Center, Amsterdam, The Netherlands.

Three Early Warning Signs of Oral Cancer

Sol Silverman, Jr., DDS, professor of oral medicine at the University of California, San Francisco. He is the editor of the 5th edition of the textbook *Oral Cancer* (B.C. Decker) and the principal investigator of a five-year project funded by the National Cancer Institute to create a comprehensive oral cancer prevention program.

C ancers of the mouth are among the most curable malignancies—but only when they're detected early. However, the signs and symptoms are subtle, so most people overlook them.

Each year, approximately 34,000 Americans are diagnosed with oral or pharyngeal (throat) cancers, and about 8,000 die from those cancers—primarily because of delayed diagnosis.

What you may not know: The number of oral and pharyngeal cancer cases is on the rise—increasing by about 9% between 2006 and 2007—and studies are under way to find out why in hopes of curbing this increase. *How to protect yourself...*

EARLY WARNING SIGNS

The tongue, the lips and the floor of the mouth are the most common sites for oral cancers. Malignancies also can develop on the gums, the roof of the mouth and the inside of the cheeks.

Initially, most early oral cancers are painless or cause minor irritation. However, early signs often can be spotted by looking inside the mouth. *Warning signs include...*

•**White patches,** known as *leukoplakia*, which can occur on any mouth surface, including the tongue or the inside of the cheeks, and are usually flat.

•**Red raised patches,** known as *erythroplakia*, can occur in any area of the mouth, but most commonly on the tongue. Erythroplakia is sometimes tender and may bleed when you brush the area or eat hard foods.

•**Sores in the mouth** that don't heal within three weeks. They typically appear as an ulcer, lump, red patch, white patch or a combination of red and white patches.

Symptoms associated with early-stage oral cancer can easily be mistaken for a minor ailment such as an injury, toothache or infection. That's why it's so important to pay attention to subtle changes that you may feel inside your mouth. Primary symptoms of oral cancer include pain or numbness anywhere in the mouth...difficulty swallowing...a sore throat...and recently developed bad breath.

Important: If any of these signs or symptoms persists for more than three weeks, see your dentist or physician for an evaluation. Any suspicious area in the mouth usually requires a biopsy to confirm (or rule out) the presence of cancer.

ARE YOU AT RISK?

Like most cancers, oral malignancies occur most often (although not solely) in older adults. In addition to age, there may be a genetic risk factor for oral cancer, but this is not well understood at this time.

Other factors...

•**Tobacco use.** Cigarettes and cigars are considered equally harmful as risk factors for oral cancer. Chewing tobacco and smokeless tobacco (snuff) are even worse—they increase the risk for cancers of the cheek, the inside of the lips and the gums, with the risk rising with the years of usage. Pipe smoking is the least dangerous but also increases risk for oral cancer.

What to do: If you use any form of tobacco, talk to your dentist or physician about ways to quit, including stop-smoking medications—such as nicotine-replacement patches or *varenicline* (Chantix), a prescription drug that diminishes the desire to smoke—and smoking-cessation programs.

•**Excessive alcohol consumption.** People who have three to five hard-alcoholic beverages daily are far more likely to develop oral cancer than those who drink less.

Warning: The risk is greater for those who smoke and drink.

What to do: Abstain from alcohol or limit consumption. Beer and wine present less of a risk than hard liquor. Alcohol-containing mouthwash is not known to increase oral cancer risk.

•**Sunlight exposure.** Ultraviolet light increases the risk not only for skin cancers, in general, but for lip cancer, in particular.

What to do: If you spend a lot of time outdoors—regardless of the season—use a lip balm that protects against ultraviolet-A and ultraviolet-B rays. Especially in the summer, wear a broad-brimmed hat to keep the sun off your face.

•**Human papilloma virus (HPV).** This sexually transmitted virus is strongly associated with cervical cancer—and there's some evidence that the virus, which can be contracted through oral sex, might be linked to some oral cancers.

What to do: If you have HPV, be vigilant about getting oral cancer exams from your dentist.

BEST TREATMENT OPTIONS

Without treatment, oral cancers will invade deeper layers of tissue and spread to the neck and, in some cases, to other parts of the body. Research has shown that the cancer can spread to the neck as soon as four to eight weeks after diagnosis.

Oral cancers that are detected early usually can be cured with surgery and/or radiation therapy. The lesions may be so small that they can be removed by a head and neck surgeon with very little hospital time, no complications and excellent recovery. Surgery may be combined with radiation to kill cancer cells that may have been left behind. Chemotherapy is required only for larger and/or more invasive tumors.

FOODS THAT REDUCE RISK

Scientific studies show that people who eat a produce-rich diet (about five servings daily of fruits and vegetables) are less likely to get oral cancers than those who eat less produce.

New finding: In a laboratory study, increasing concentrations of berry extracts (taken from blackberries, black raspberries, blueberries, cranberries, red raspberries and strawberries) were linked with inhibition of cancer cells—including cells involved in oral cancers. Berries contain potent phytochemicals, including some with antioxidant and anticancer properties.

30-SECOND MOUTH EXAM

Your dentist should examine your mouth for possible signs of oral cancer once or twice a year, but you can help by doing a self-exam to check for suspicious changes.

What to do: While standing in front of a mirror in a well-lit room, pull the sides of your cheeks away from your teeth so that you can see inside your mouth. Check all areas of your mouth, including under the tongue, as well as your lips. If you notice any bumps, tender areas or changes in color, see your dentist promptly.

■ ■ ■ ■

Gum Disease Linked to Cancer

In a recent study, researchers compared dental X-rays of 51 men diagnosed with tongue cancer and 54 men without cancer.

Result: Each millimeter of bone loss associated with gum disease equaled a 5.2 times greater likelihood that the study subject had tongue cancer.

Theory: Gum disease is caused in part by chronic inflammation, which has been linked to cancer.

Miné Tezal, DDS, PhD, assistant professor, School of Dental Medicine, University of New York at Buffalo.

Ultrasound Best For Gauging Ovarian Cancers

Dirk Timmerman, MD, PhD, researcher, Katholieke Universiteit Leuven, Belgium.

Robert Morgan, MD, co-director, gynecologic oncology/peritoneal malignancy program, City of Hope Cancer Center, Duarte, California.

Sherry Salway Black, executive director, Ovarian Cancer National Alliance, Washington, D.C.

Journal of the National Cancer Institute, online.

Ultrasound exams are better than blood tests at identifying whether ovarian tumors are benign or malignant, a team of international researchers reports.

Ultrasound correctly identified 93% of tumors as benign or cancerous, while the blood test was correct 83% of the time.

"To my knowledge, the IOTA (International Ovarian Tumor Analysis) study is the first study that clearly demonstrated that in experienced hands, ultrasound is significantly better than blood tests," said study leader Dirk Timmerman, MD, PhD, a researcher at Katholieke Universiteit Leuven in Belgium.

BACKGROUND

An estimated 22,430 new cases of ovarian cancer will be diagnosed in the United States, according to the latest yearly numbers American Cancer Society (ACS), with about 15,280 deaths. The disease typically strikes women over age 55. Symptoms include bloating, pelvic or abdominal pain, difficulty eating or feeling full quickly, or urinary symptoms such as a frequent need to urinate.

Because the symptoms are often similar to less serious conditions, only about 20% of ovarian cancers are found at an early stage, the ACS estimates. This makes the quest for the best techniques to detect the cancer early even more important.

THE STUDY

For the IOTA study, Dr. Timmerman and his colleagues compared ultrasound with blood tests to decide if the ovarian masses discovered in 1,066 women were benign or malignant.

Experts examined patterns in ultrasound images, and then compared those results with blood tests that detect an elevated level of the protein CA-125, considered an indicator of whether an ovarian tumor is cancerous or benign.

The ultrasound exams, including transvaginal gray-scale and color Doppler ultrasound exams, were given within 120 days of surgery to remove the tumors. Before surgery, 809 of the women gave blood, and the samples were analyzed later for CA-125 levels.

RESULTS

When the results from both methods were compared with the findings at surgery, the researchers found that ultrasound correctly classified 93% of tumors as cancerous or not, while the blood test was correct in only 83% of cases.

"The IOTA study not only demonstrated that ultrasound is better than blood tests but also that the blood tests do not give additional benefit in mathematical models developed to distinguish between benign and malignant masses," Dr. Timmerman said.

EXPERT COMMENTARY

Dr. Timmerman emphasized that the study only looked at the best method to decide if a tumor was cancerous after the mass had already been discovered. "Of course, this is different from screening," he said. "In screening studies, a healthy population is screened for a specific disease, for example, ovarian cancer. In that setting, a blood test might prove to be useful in the future." He noted that two large studies exploring that issue are expected to conclude in about five years.

According to Robert Morgan, MD, co-director of the gynecologic oncology/peritoneal malignancy program at the City of Hope Cancer Center in Duarte, California, "CA-125 is only elevated in about 50% of early stage ovarian cancer, and the data in this paper confirms that."

Most of these cancers are being picked up with ultrasound, not the blood test, Morgan said. "And, most of the time, when [the ultrasound] says it's not malignant, it's not," he said.

"CA-125 tests are not cheap and, particularly when you do them in a huge number of patients, the costs add up. And, apparently, they don't seem to be adding anything to the diagnostic accuracy," he added.

Sherry Salway Black, executive director of the Ovarian Cancer National Alliance, called the study results exciting. "It gives more information, more evidence that a transvaginal ultrasound can be effective under these circumstances."

Still, she said, the blood test might prove to have some benefit. "It may not be the best stand-alone diagnostic tool. This [study] appears to say transvaginal ultrasound is definitely better." But the study authors did find that CA-125 levels in women found to have cancer were higher for postmenopausal women than premenopausal women, for instance. And such details, Black said, might prove valuable.

info To learn more about ovarian cancer symptoms, visit the Web site of the Ovarian Cancer National Alliance at *www.ovariancancer.org*. Click "Symptoms" on the left side of the page.

Reduce Risk of Ovarian Cancer by 40%

Ross Prentice, PhD, professor, biostatistics, University of Washington School of Public Health and Fred Hutchinson Cancer Research Center, Seattle, and principal investigator, Women's Health Initiative Clinical Coordinating Center.
Robert Morgan, Jr., MD, section head, medical gynecologic oncology, City of Hope Cancer Center, Duarte, California.
Journal of the National Cancer Institute.

Older women who stick to a low-fat, high-fiber diet could cut their odds for deadly ovarian cancer, new research shows. In fact, postmenopausal women who stayed on the regimen for more than eight years reduced their risk for the disease by 40%, a US team said. Those who saw the greatest benefit from switching to a low-fat diet were women who had originally eaten a relatively high-fat diet, the researchers added.

On average, the women had managed to add one serving of fruits or vegetables to their daily diet by the end of the six-year follow-up. They had also reduced their daily fat consumption by about 8%.

BACKGROUND

Ovarian cancer is the fifth leading cancer killer of women. Some 20,000 women in the United States are diagnosed with the disease every year, and about 15,000 women will die from it during the same time frame.

As with most cancers, a woman's chances of survival are better if the disease is found early, but ovarian tumors are a "stealth killer," because they are notoriously difficult to detect in their early stages.

Ross Prentice, PhD, of the Fred Hutchinson Cancer Research Center in Seattle led the new multi-center study. Prior to the publication of this analysis, the impact of particular diets on ovarian cancer was unknown.

THE STUDY

Dr. Prentice's team recruited nearly 50,000 postmenopausal women between the ages of 50 and 79. Nearly 20,000 of those women were randomly assigned to eat a low-fat diet in which fat intake totaled less than 20% of daily calories. They also ate at least five servings of fruits and vegetables a day and at least six servings of whole grains.

The women received 18 diet-support group sessions in the first year to help keep them on track and then quarterly maintenance meetings during the following years.

The researchers then monitored the women's rates of ovarian and/or endometrial malignancies over the next eight years.

RESULTS

Rates of ovarian cancer were roughly similar for women during the first four years of the study, whether they were enrolled in the low-fat diet or not. But after more than eight years of follow-up, a clear trend emerged, with women on the healthier diet having a 40% reduction in ovarian cancer incidence.

There was no such effect on the risk of endometrial cancer, however, the researchers added. That was surprising, said Robert Morgan, MD, section head of medical gynecologic oncology at City of Hope Cancer Center in Duarte, California, because some experts theorize that fat increases estrogen levels in the body, which, in turn, may boost risk for both ovarian and endometrial cancer. Previous reports have indicated that low-fat diets lower circulating estrogen, said Morgan, who was not involved in the study, so he expected to see a similar effect for both tumor types.

THEORY

The potential link between dietary fat and cancer is not fully understood, he added. During the study, Prentice said the researchers did note lower levels of estradiol—an estrogen hormone produced by the ovaries—in the blood of dieting women. Estradiol is an important risk factor for cancer among women, he said.

"This or other circulating hormones could have a stimulatory effect on epithelial (blood vessel) tissue in the ovary or breast, possibly including effects on cells in yet undiagnosed cancers," Prentice explained.

DIETARY GUIDELINES

Women looking to duplicate the diet in their own lives should follow the Food Pyramid guidelines set out by the US Department of Agriculture, Morgan said. But he added that one of the components that made this study so unique was the intense dietary counseling and support the women received over time. The findings support "the idea that lifestyle changes can be made with intensive help," Morgan said.

"Restricting calorie consumption was not a goal, according to Prentice, "though participating intervention group women did lose some weight," he added. "Nor was there an attempt to reduce carbohydrates," said Prentice. "On the contrary, most of the reduced dietary fat was replaced by complex carbohydrates."

info For more information about the US Department of Agriculture's Food Pyramid and dietary guidelines, visit their Web site at *www.mypyramid.gov/guidelines.*

Broccoli and Tea Fight Ovarian Cancer

Brigham and Women's Hospital, Boston, news release.

A study from Boston's Brigham and Women's Hospital has found that regular consumption of foods containing the flavonoid *kaempferol*, including nonherbal tea

and broccoli, was associated with a reduced risk for ovarian cancer.

The study, funded by the National Cancer Institute, also found a decreased risk in women who consumed large amounts of the flavonoid *luteolin*, found in carrots, peppers and cabbage.

"This is good news, because there are few lifestyle factors known to reduce a woman's risk of ovarian cancer," said first author Margaret Gates, a research fellow at the hospital.

"Although additional research is required, these findings suggest that consuming a diet rich in flavonoids may be protective."

"Other flavonoid-rich foods, such as onions, beans and kale, may also decrease ovarian cancer risk, but the number of women who frequently consumed these foods was not large enough to clearly evaluate these associations. More research is needed," concluded Gates, who is also a research fellow at the Harvard School of Public Health.

info For more about the healthful compounds in foods, visit the Web site of the USDA Agricultural Research Service at *www.ars.usda.gov.* Then search "food and health."

■ ■ ■ ■

Pancreatic Surgery Increases Survival Rates

A surgical procedure for pancreatic cancer is not regularly considered, according to cancer surgeon Mark Talamonti, MD. Nearly 40% of patients with early stage pancreatic cancer are not offered surgery, even though the five-year survival rate is 25% higher for patients who have the operation. Called the *Whipple procedure*, the surgery takes about eight hours and removes most or all of the pancreas, part of the intestine, the gallbladder and part of a bile duct. Postsurgery treatment includes chemotherapy and radiation therapy. Risk of death from surgery has fallen from 25% to 3% in major cancer centers that perform this surgery frequently.

Mark Talamonti, MD, a cancer surgeon at Northwestern Memorial Hospital and chief of surgical oncology at Northwestern University Medical School, both in Chicago. He was leader of a study of 9,559 pancreatic cancer patients, published in *Annals of Surgery.*

New Ways to Beat Prostate Cancer

Patrick C. Walsh, MD, distinguished service professor of urology at the Brady Urological Institute of the Johns Hopkins Medical Institutions in Baltimore. The creator of the "nerve-sparing" procedures now used in most prostate cancer patients, Dr. Walsh has performed more than 4,000 prostate surgeries. He is the author of *Dr. Patrick Walsh's Guide to Surviving Prostate Cancer* (Warner Wellness) and is the recipient of the Castle-Connolly 2007 National Physician of the Year Award.

A diagnosis of prostate cancer once invariably carried with it a very real threat. It could mean urinary incontinence, impotence—and even death.

Now: The complication rate from prostate surgery is declining, and the number of men who die from this type of malignancy has fallen by one-third in the last 10 years—a greater drop than has occurred with any other cancer.

These improvements are largely the result of painstaking research that has helped doctors develop an aggressive approach to fighting prostate malignancies. *Among the most important recent findings...*

PSA VELOCITY

By the time prostate cancer causes symptoms, such as difficulty urinating and a frequent and/or urgent need to urinate, the malignancy has usually grown beyond the prostate and is rarely curable. Early detection—via a digital rectal exam (DRE) and blood test for prostate-specific antigen (PSA), an enzyme produced by the prostate gland—is the key to survival.

However, interpretation of PSA levels is tricky. A man can have a high PSA (above 4 nanograms per milliliter, or ng/ml) without having prostate cancer. Conversely, 15% of men with a PSA below 4 ng/ml have prostate cancer.

Latest scientific evidence: Increases in PSA are more significant than the initial reading. A gradual rise in *PSA velocity (*the rate of change from year to year) indicates that a man might have cancer—even if the overall levels are low (below 4 ng/ml). A PSA velocity that is greater than 0.2 ng/ml to 0.4 ng/ml per year is cause for concern.

My advice...

•**Get a baseline PSA (and DRE) at age 40.** The American Cancer Society recommends annual PSA screening beginning at age 50 for most men. But I recommend beginning PSA testing at age 40, because at that age men usually do not have the two most common conditions that also can raise PSA levels—prostate infection and benign prostate hyperplasia (BPH), enlargement of the prostate. The PSA test should be repeated at age 45 if the PSA level is lower than 0.6 ng/ml...or every two years if the reading is higher.

•**Get a biopsy if...**
You did not begin baseline PSA testing at age 40 and your PSA level is greater than 2.5 ng/ml and you're age 41 to 49...your PSA level is above 3 ng/ml and you're age 50 to 59...or your PSA level is greater than 4 ng/ml and you're age 60 or older. I also recommend a biopsy for men whose PSA level is below 4 ng/ml, and subsequent tests show an annual increase of 0.2 ng/ml to 0.4 ng/ml over the last two years...or if the PSA level is above 4 ng/ml, and subsequent tests show an annual increase of more than 0.75 ng/ml. An abnormal rectal exam (due to a suspicious lump or hard spot) warrants a biopsy—*regardless of your PSA level.*

FREE VS. BOUND PSA

Because many conditions besides cancer can elevate the PSA reading—a prostate infection or enlargement, for example, or ejaculation within 48 hours of the PSA test—men with a high PSA are often subjected to numerous—and sometimes *unnecessary*—biopsies. That's because the traditional PSA test cannot determine whether an elevated level results from cancer or some other cause.

Latest scientific evidence: The total PSA test measures both bound PSA (a form that's bound to proteins) and *free* PSA (a form that circulates freely in the blood). A man with a high percentage of free PSA (25% or above) is less likely to have cancer than a man with a lower percentage of free PSA.

My advice: Men who have had multiple negative biopsies should get the free PSA test. A man with a high percentage of free PSA can probably relax—but if it's low (below 20%), he should continue getting biopsies as often as his doctor recommends.

OBESITY

It's not yet known if obesity increases the risk for prostate cancer—but men who are obese are more likely to get an *advanced* form of the disease.

Latest scientific evidence: A study by the American Cancer Society found that men with a body mass index (BMI)—a measurement of weight relative to height—that is greater than 30 (an indication of obesity) were 20% to 25% more likely to die from advanced prostate cancer than thinner men.

My advice: Men with a BMI of 30 or more—as well as overweight men (BMI of 25 to 29)—need to lose weight.

To calculate your BMI: Go to the National Heart, Lung and Blood Institute Web site, *www. nhlbi.nih.gov/health/index.htm.*

OMEGA-3 FATTY ACIDS

Omega-3 fatty acids, a healthful form of fat found in cold-water fish, such as salmon, sardines and herring, have been linked to reduced rates of heart disease.

Latest scientific evidence: Research published in *The Lancet* found that men who ate no fish were two to three times more likely to get prostate cancer than men who ate two to three servings weekly. The anti-inflammatory effects of omega-3 fatty acids in fish are believed to inhibit prostate cancer development.

My advice: Eat cold-water fish two to three times weekly.

LYCOPENE

Lycopene, an antioxidant found in tomatoes, pink grapefruit and watermelon, was once believed to protect against prostate cancer.

Latest scientific evidence: Newer research shows that tomatoes (especially cooked tomatoes) most likely confer the protective effect. Also, men who eat five or more servings a week of cruciferous vegetables, such as broccoli and cauliflower, can lower prostate cancer risk by 10% to 20%.

My advice: Eat a plant-based diet rich in antioxidants. Supplemental selenium and vitamin E may help prevent prostate cancer, but do not exceed the amounts found in many men's multivitamins—60 international units daily of vitamin E or 55 micrograms daily of selenium. (Higher levels of these nutrients are not necessarily better

and may increase risk for other problems, such as heart disease.) If you take a calcium supplement for bone health, do not exceed 1,500 milligrams (mg) of calcium daily—higher levels have been shown to increase prostate cancer risk.

Prostate Cancer Survival Varies by Season

Oregon Health & Science University, news release.

Men diagnosed with prostate cancer in the summer and fall have a better chance of survival than those diagnosed in the spring and winter, a recent study of Norwegian men suggests.

"Summer and autumn months correspond to times when vitamin D is highest (in Norway). Although the study does not prove vitamin D is the determining factor, it does suggest that this possibility should be studied further," said study co-author Dr. Tomasz Beer, director of the prostate cancer program at the Oregon Health & Science University Cancer Institute.

THE STUDY

A team of American and Norwegian researchers analyzed data for more than 46,000 Norwegian men diagnosed with prostate cancer from 1964 to 1992.

Result: Compared with men diagnosed in the summer and fall, those diagnosed in the winter and spring were 20% more likely to die within three years after diagnosis. The study was published in the journal *The Prostate.*

The researchers also examined whether survival was affected by factors such as eating foods high in vitamin D (such as fatty fish), taking vacations in sunny southern locations, and where the men lived in Norway.

Result: Only age seemed to have an influence—younger men had a slightly better rate of survival. The researchers noted that the capacity of skin to produce vitamin D when exposed to sunshine is about 40% lower in men age 75 and older than in men age 60 and younger.

THEORY

Vitamin D, which has been shown to inhibit cancer growth, may also help maintain immune system health and help regulate cell growth and differentiation, Beer said.

info For more information about prostate cancer, go to the Prostate Cancer Foundation Web site at *www.prostatecancerfoundation.org*.

Alternative Treatments Lower Prostate Cancer By Nearly 80%

Mark A. Stengler, ND, naturopathic physician in private practice, La Jolla, California...adjunct associate clinical professor at the National College of Natural Medicine, Portland, Oregon...author of many books, including *The Natural Physician's Healing Therapies* and coauthor of *Prescription for Natural Cures* (both from Bottom Line Books)...and author of the *Bottom Line/Natural Healing* newsletter.

Over the course of a lifetime, one man in six eventually will be diagnosed with prostate cancer...one in 35 will die from it. The treatment path for prostate cancer is seldom clear. Even conventional doctors who specialize in prostate cancer frequently disagree about the best course of action.

Surgery to remove the prostate gland is often recommended, yet it can have onerous side effects—including incontinence and lifelong erectile dysfunction. What's more, statistics show that surgery does not necessarily increase a man's life span.

For these reasons, many doctors now recommend a "watch and wait" approach in certain cases rather than surgery. Prostate cancer usually is slow-growing. The older a man is, the more likely he is to die of some other condition before his prostate cancer becomes a real threat.

The holistic view: For prostate cancer patients age 65 and older, as well as for some younger men whose cancer does not appear to be fast-growing, I support the decision to watch and wait. But, instead of waiting passively while doing nothing, I recommend a proactive approach using natural therapies that may slow or halt cancer growth or even cause the cancer to diminish.

Unless noted otherwise, all supplements described below are available at health food stores, generally are safe to take indefinitely and cause no side effects.

Important: It is vital that men who have prostate cancer be monitored by an oncologist. Show your doctor this article, and discuss your desire to incorporate these natural therapies.

CUTTING-EDGE PROSTATE CARE

Aaron E. Katz, MD, associate professor of clinical urology and director of the Center of Holistic Urology at Columbia University Medical Center in New York City, is heading the research on two new supplements that are showing promise in the fight against prostate cancer. Studies are still in progress. *Here is what we know so far...*

•**Zyflamend.** This unique formula from New Chapter (800-543-7279, *www.newchapter. com*) combines *phytochemicals* (beneficial plant chemicals) with herbal extracts from turmeric, ginger, green tea, rosemary, *hu zhang* (Japanese knotweed), Chinese goldthread, barberry, oregano, baikal skullcap and holy basil.

Dr. Katz's laboratory study found that Zyflamend reduced prostate cancer cell proliferation by up to 78% and may even have killed some existing prostate cancer cells.

Dr. Katz's team is now analyzing results of a clinical trial of Zyflamend among men at high risk for prostate cancer. The trial included 23 men, ages 46 to 75, who were diagnosed via biopsy with a type of precancerous cell proliferation called high-grade *prostatic intraepithelial neoplasia* (PIN)—a marker suggesting an 80% chance that cancer will develop within 10 years. The men also had elevated levels of *prostate specific antigen* (PSA)—a substance produced by prostate gland cells and often elevated when cancer exists. *After 18 months on Zyflamend, blood tests and biopsies then showed...*

•The PIN disappeared in 62% of patients.

•Half of the men had decreases in PSA levels—some by more than 50%—indicating a return to more normal prostate cell activity.

• For all of the nine patients who did develop cancer, the disease was the slow-growing type and confined to a small area.

If you are at risk: Based on the evidence that Zyflamend can reverse PIN and reduce PSA, I recommend taking three Zyflamend capsules daily (with meals to avoid gastric upset), continuing indefinitely, if you have any of the following…

• An enlarged prostate (identified by a doctor)

• Any abnormal prostate PIN

• PSA that is elevated for your age. PSA is considered elevated if it is at or above 2.5 nanograms per milliliter (ng/ml) in your 40s…3.5 ng/ml in your 50s…4.5 ng/ml in your 60s…or 6.5 ng/ml in your 70s.

• An ultrasound or other imaging test showing prostate lesions

• One or more immediate family members with a history of prostate cancer, if you are over age 50.

If you have high-grade PIN or prostate cancer: In addition to taking Zyflamend, consider taking a second new supplement, Prostabel, described below…

• **Prostabel.** Available on-line from Natural Source International (888-308-7066, *www.natural-source.com.*)

Dr. Katz's team at Columbia is now conducting a clinical trial on Prostabel. The study currently has 25 men, ages 40 to 75, with negative biopsy reports but elevated PSA levels. Participants were assigned to take from two to eight capsules of Prostabel daily for 12 months.

Findings are preliminary—eight men have completed the 12-month course of treatment to date. Prostabel significantly lowered PSA in five of the eight men. While four of the men have developed cancer, their cancers are small and slow-growing. Researchers are waiting to see if Prostabel suppresses cancer cell growth in the remaining 17 participants. Just one patient, who was on the highest dosage, developed liver enzyme problems as a side effect.

Surprising: Patients experienced significant improvements in urination problems common among older men, such as frequent need to urinate and slowed stream.

Recommended dosage: Three Prostabel capsules daily. Take on an empty stomach to maximize absorption. If it causes digestive upset, take with meals instead.

MORE CANCER FIGHTERS

In addition to taking Zyflamend and/or Prostabel, I recommend that men who have had a diagnosis of prostate cancer take all of the following, continuing indefinitely…

• **Zinc.** 50 mg daily.

Caution: Check with your doctor before taking zinc if you are undergoing chemotherapy—zinc may not be compatible with some chemotherapy drugs.

• **Copper.** Long-term zinc supplementation can lead to a copper deficiency, so also take 2 mg of copper daily.

• **Selenium.** 200 micrograms (mcg) daily.

Note: Although evidence is not conclusive, selenium has been linked to increased risk for diabetes—so have your blood sugar monitored regularly.

• **Vitamin E.** 200 international units (IU) daily of "mixed" vitamin E (as indicated on label).

• **Calcium limit.** Take no more than 500 mg daily. Some evidence links high doses to increased prostate cancer risk.

Men who have been diagnosed with prostate cancer and who want a more aggressive approach can add the following and continue taking them indefinitely…

• **Indole 3-carbinol.** 400 mg daily.

• **Maitake mushroom extract.** Use capsules or tincture labeled "standardized MD-fraction."

Take 1 mg per day for every 2.2 pounds of body weight (for instance, a 165-pound man would take 75 mg daily…a 200-pound man would take 90 mg daily). Take in two divided doses on an empty stomach.

• **Beta glucan.** 500 mg twice daily.

■ ■ ■ ■

Beware! Aspirin Blocks Prostate Cancer Treatment

Men who are taking daily low-dose aspirin to head off a heart attack should stop taking it before starting hormone therapy for prostate cancer and then resume taking it after the therapy ends. For men who already have had a cardiovascular event and who are taking aspirin to prevent another one, it may be necessary to continue taking aspirin and forgo part of the hormone therapy.

Anthony V. D'Amico, MD, PhD, professor of radiation oncology, Harvard Medical School, and chair of gastrourinary radiation oncology, Dana-Farber Cancer Institute, both in Boston.

■ ■ ■ ■

Obesity May Hide Prostate Cancer

Prostate cancer in obese men can be harder to detect because measurements of prostate-specific antigen (PSA) may seem normal when they aren't.

Reason: Obese men have more blood in their bodies than normal-weight men—so PSA may be diluted, and a test may show PSA within normal limits. Doctors need to adjust their interpretation of PSA scores for men with high body-mass indexes.

Stephen Freedland, MD, assistant professor, and Lionel Bañez, MD, research fellow, department of surgery and division of urology, Duke University, Durham, North Carolina, and coauthors of a study of the medical records of almost 14,000 prostate cancer patients, published in *Journal of the American Medical Association*.

New Sunscreen Gives Ray of Hope For Skin Cancer

Mohammad Athar, PhD, professor, dermatology, University of Alabama, Birmingham.

Robin Ashinoff, MD, medical director, dermatologic, Mohs and laser surgery, Hackensack University Medical Center, Hackensack, New Jersey.

The Journal of Clinical Investigation.

Research is shedding new light on sunscreens that might someday prevent or treat skin cancer by reversing dangerous genetic mutations caused by overexposure to the sun.

THE STUDY

Working with hairless mice, the researchers found that a synthetic compound called CP-31398 helped stabilize damage in the tumor-suppressing p53 gene. This type of damage occurs in humans and mice alike after sustained exposure to the sun's ultraviolet B (UVB) rays.

Once treated and repaired, the UVB-exposed p53 mouse gene resumed its normal cancer-preventing activity, inhibiting the spread and proliferation of tumor cells.

"Once the skin is exposed to UVB it leads to mutations in the p53 gene, and it becomes non-functional, and then you see induction of skin cancer," explained study lead author Mohammad Athar, PhD, a professor of dermatology at the University of Alabama, Birmingham.

"But this compound we used interacts with the p53 mutant genes and converts them back into functional genes," he said. "And that led to less incidence of skin cancer tumors, fewer numbers of tumors, and slower tumor growth in the UVB-exposed mice populations we tested."

PREVENTING MORE CANCERS

Dr. Athar pointed out that p53 mutations linked to skin cancer are also present in more than half of all tumor types, so the current work could theoretically lead to cancer prevention applications for a range of diseases beyond melanoma.

"We are also planning to conduct more studies in mice to see if the compound we used has any toxicity, although we did not find that to be the case so far," he said. "So, we are planning long-term studies with mice. Once that is complete, we will certainly go for clinical trials with humans."

EXPERT COMMENTARY

Robin Ashinoff, MD, the medical director of dermatologic, Mohs and laser surgery at Hackensack University Medical Center in Hackensack, New Jersey, said that the current findings should be viewed with a mix of interest and caution.

"This still needs to be studied in human trials in a placebo-controlled fashion," she noted. "And bringing this kind of technology to market is always a long road."

"But if we can work at the genetic level to try and prevent skin cancer where it starts and correct and suppress the abnormal clones that arise from UVB exposure, that would certainly be quite advantageous," she added. "And it would be wonderful to be able to put this approach into a cream or a sunblock. That—when it happens—will certainly become the new gold standard."

info For more on melanoma risk factors, visit the Web site of the Skin Cancer Foundation at *www.skincancer.org.* and click "Melanoma" on the left side of the page.

■ ■ ■ ■

Can Exercise and Coffee Fight Skin Cancer?

Skin cancer develops in cells whose DNA has been damaged by UV radiation—but damaged cells often die before becoming malignant. The death rate of precancerous skin cells in mice that received exercise and oral caffeine was nearly 400% greater than in mice that had neither exercise nor caffeine.

Allan Conney, PhD, director of the Susan Lehman Cullman Laboratory for Cancer Research, Rutgers State University of New Jersey, Piscataway, and coauthor of a study published in *Proceedings of the National Academy of Sciences.*

■ ■ ■ ■

A Different Kind of Skin Cancer

The sexually transmitted *human papillomavirus* (HPV), linked to cervical cancer, can cause genital skin cancer. This cancer—squamous cell carcinoma—is more common in the genitalia of women than men. If treated early, there is a high cure rate. Women are three times more likely to die from this type of skin cancer than men.

Self-defense: Examine genitals monthly using a mirror, and contact your gynecologist if you find anything unusual.

Martin A. Weinstock, MD, professor of dermatology and community health, Brown University, Providence, and senior author of a study of 75,000 skin cancer deaths, published in *Journal of Investigative Dermatology.*

■ ■ ■ ■

Melanoma Warning: Check Your Feet!

Melanomas on the feet or ankles have a higher mortality rate than other melanomas. That's because the cancer tends to be diagnosed at a later stage.

Self-defense: Check the entire foot monthly—ankles, tops of feet, soles (use a mirror), between the toes and around the toenails. Look for small areas of pigmented skin, moles that have changed in size or appearance and any unexplained discoloration under a toenail. If you see any of these signs, consult a doctor.

Neil A. Campbell, DPM, podiatrist, Yoakum, Texas, and spokesperson for the American College of Foot and Ankle Surgeons.

Hidden Signs of Stomach Cancer

Jonathan D. Cheng, MD, medical oncologist specializing in gastrointestinal diseases, and associate member of Fox Chase Cancer Center in Philadelphia, a nonprofit institution formed in 1974 by the union of the American Oncologic Hospital (the nation's first cancer hospital, established in 1904) and the Institute for Cancer Research (founded in 1927). He has coauthored dozens of scientific papers and book chapters on stomach and esophageal cancers.

Stomach cancer is one of the few types of cancer for which scientists have strong evidence that diet is a primary cause, yet an estimated 22,000 Americans develop the illness each year and half of them die from it. Why does this occur?

A diet rich in salted, smoked or pickled foods and/or processed meats, such as salami and corned beef, has been identified as a risk factor for stomach cancer. Infection with *Helicobacter pylori* (H. pylori)—the bacterium that causes most ulcers—also increases risk for the disease. It's estimated that half of Americans age 60 and older are infected with H. pylori, but most of them don't know it.

In addition, smokers are twice as likely as nonsmokers to develop stomach cancer. In former smokers, risk for the disease is 50% higher than in someone who never smoked. *How to protect yourself...*

HIDDEN SYMPTOMS

Most patients with stomach cancer have few or no symptoms in the early stages. Even when symptoms—such as abdominal pain, nausea and/or heartburn—are present, they're often mistaken for other, less serious problems.

Result: The cancer usually isn't detected until it reaches an advanced stage, in which it has spread to other organs and/or distant lymph nodes.

Symptoms to watch for...

•**Dull, achy pain in the upper abdomen** that isn't relieved with antacids, such as *famotidine* (Pepcid) or *ranitidine* (Zantac).

•**Abdominal pain and/or cramping that's worse after eating.**

•**An unusual feeling of fullness after eating,** even when you're eating less than usual.

•**Vomiting after meals.**

•**Sudden weight loss.**

Important: If you have any of these symptoms, talk to your doctor.

STEPS TO PROTECT YOURSELF

With the exception of not smoking, there is no definitive evidence that preventive strategies can reduce stomach cancer risk. *However, cancer experts agree on the following approaches as prudent and reasonable precautions...*

•**Treat ulcers promptly.** Ulcers were once believed to be caused mainly by lifestyle factors, such as chronic stress and eating spicy foods. It's now known that the vast majority of duodenal ulcers (which develop in the part of the small intestine that connects to the stomach) are caused by H. pylori, an organism that burrows into the protective layer (mucosal lining) of the stomach. Ulcers don't necessarily increase the risk for stomach cancer, but H. pylori does—by 200% to 600%.

Reason: Infection with H. pylori causes chronic inflammation in the stomach lining and increases the risk for cell changes that can lead to cancer. In patients with duodenal ulcers, antibiotic therapy is the standard approach to eradicate the bacteria.

Self-defense: If you have ulcers or gastritis (inflammation of the stomach lining), ask your doctor for an H. pylori blood test, and consider antibiotic therapy (usually for two weeks) if an infection is present.

•**Avoid foods with certain preservatives.** Certain types of preserved foods, such as smoked or salted meat or fish...pickled vegetables...and processed or cured meats, including bologna, salami, hot dogs, bacon or ham, usually contain high levels of nitrates and nitrites, chemicals that combine with other compounds in the stomach to form carcinogens. People who eat these foods regularly have at least double the risk for stomach cancer as those who don't—and the risk rises with increased consumption.

Recent finding: A diet rich in red meat—particularly meat that's well-done and/or barbecued—also may increase risk for stomach cancer.

Self-defense: Do not exceed one or two weekly servings of foods that contain nitrates and/or nitrites. (Check the ingredients list on the label.) The evidence isn't strong enough to recommend giving up these foods altogether.

•**Eat more fresh produce.** Studies suggest that people who eat many fruits and vegetables—particularly brightly colored produce, such as spinach, cantaloupe, broccoli and winter squash—have lower rates of stomach cancer.

Self-defense: Eat five to nine one-half cup servings of nonpickled fruits and vegetables daily.

BEST DETECTION TECHNIQUES

Most cases of stomach cancer can be diagnosed with endoscopy, in which a lighted tube is inserted through the mouth into the stomach. If an area looks abnormal (for example, discoloration or masses are present), a biopsy will be taken and analyzed in a laboratory. Although stomach cancer is relatively easy to diagnose with endoscopy, most people with the disease don't receive this test until the malignancy is advanced.

For earlier detection: A fecal occult blood test (FOBT) detects trace amounts of blood in stool samples. This test is mainly used as part of colon-cancer screening, but it also can detect bleeding that may be present with early-stage stomach cancer.

Self-defense: Ask your doctor if you should have an FOBT annually. The FOBT doesn't identify the source of bleeding—a positive test needs to be followed by other screenings, such as colonoscopy (for colon cancer) or endoscopy (for stomach cancer).

TREATMENT OPTIONS

Surgery is the main treatment for stomach cancer. If the cancer involves a small area, a subtotal gastrectomy (only part of the stomach is removed) is usually performed. More advanced cancers may require a total gastrectomy (removal of the entire stomach). After a total gastrectomy, food is digested in the small intestine.

Most patients with locally advanced stomach cancer (which occurs when the tumor affects only the stomach and nearby tissues) are also treated with chemotherapy and radiation. The combination of surgery, chemotherapy and radiation is more effective for this stage of stomach cancer than surgery alone.

With very early-stage, localized cancers, about two-thirds of patients recover completely. Once the cancer has spread through the stomach wall to nearby lymph nodes and/or organs, treatment is less successful and the survival rate ranges from less than 10% to 40%.

CT Scans Raise Your Cancer Risk

David J. Brenner, PhD, DSc, director, Columbia University Radiological Research Accelerator Facility at the Columbia University Center for Radiological Research, and professor, radiation oncology, Columbia University College of Physicians and Surgeons, New York City.

Eric J. Hall, PhD, DSc, director, Center for Radiological Research, Columbia University College of Physicians and Surgeons, New York City.

G. Donald Frey, PhD, professor, radiology, Medical University of South Carolina, Charleston.

New England Journal of Medicine.

The number of CT scans performed in the United States has increased dramatically since the 1980s, and that means an increased risk of cancer for patients caused by exposure to high doses of radiation, according to a new report.

A CT scan—an imaging method that uses X-rays to create cross-sectional pictures of the body—can have radiation doses 50 to 250 times greater than the dose of a conventional X-ray, the report's authors note. Today, more than 62 million CT scans a year are done in the United States, compared with 3 million in 1980.

"The radiation doses from CT scans have been clearly demonstrated to increase cancer risk," said David J. Brenner, PhD, director of the Columbia University Radiological Research Accelerator Facility. "On an individual basis, not a big individual risk, but a small risk applied to an increasingly large population spells trouble down the road," he added.

RADIATION'S LINK TO CANCER

Cancers from radiation, except leukemia, take years to develop, Dr. Brenner said. "However, in a few decades, 1.5% to 2% of all cancers in the United States may be due to the radiation from CT scans being done now," he said.

It takes 20 to 50 years after exposure to radiation before the full legacy of that exposure becomes evident, said Eric J. Hall, PhD, DSc, director of the Center for Radiological Research at Columbia University College of Physicians and Surgeons. "It takes a long time before the solid cancers emerge," he said. "The leukemias may come up in the first decade, but the solid cancers take a long time."

CT SCANS AND CHILDREN

Some 4 million to 5 million CT scans are done on children each year, and children are more sensitive to radiation than adults, Dr. Hall added. "A CT scan of the abdomen in a child gives a risk of about one in a 1,000 of an induced cancer," he said.

UNNECESSARY CT SCANS

One-third of all CT scans, about 20 million a year, are medically unnecessary, Dr. Brenner said. "Anyone presenting to an emergency room with a belly ache or chronic headache will automatically get a CT scan," he said. "Is this justified? Well, maybe not."

Dr. Brenner said many CT scans could be replaced by other tests that don't involve X-rays, with ultrasound being one example.

"We were astonished to find how many doctors, particularly emergency room physicians, really have no idea of the magnitude of the doses or the potential risks that are involved in CT scans," Dr. Hall said.

Dr. Brenner said the use of CT scans is growing. New uses include diagnosing lung cancer, virtual colonoscopy and whole-body scans. "Most of these have not been proven to have a benefit over the risk," Dr. Hall said.

DIMINISHING RISK FROM CT SCANS

Drs. Brenner and Hall said they aren't saying that people should avoid CT scans when they are appropriate. "Clearly, in a patient that's symptomatic, a CT is a wonderful diagnostic tool," Hall said. "What we are pushing for is to limit the use of CT to situations where it really is needed."

Drs. Brenner and Hall suggested three ways to diminish the risk from CT scans. First, the radiation dose should be reduced and tailored to individual patients. Second, CT scans should not be used when other options that have no radiation risk, such as ultrasound or magnetic resonance imaging (MRI), are appropriate. And the third suggestion—reducing the number of CT scans prescribed.

Adopting these strategies could keep some 20 million adults and more than one million children from unnecessary radiation exposure each year, the researchers said.

EXPERT COMMENTARY

G. Donald Frey, PhD a professor of radiology at the Medical University of South Carolina, said he agreed that too many unnecessary CT scans are probably being performed. But, for those who need such a scan, the benefit outweighs the risk, he said.

"We are concerned that many CTs are done inappropriately," Dr. Frey said. "The whole community should work together to reduce inappropriate scans, but it would be absolutely tragic if a patient who needed a CT failed to get one because of concerns of the radiation dose."

Also, newer CT scanners have the ability to adjust the dose of radiation, Dr. Frey said.

"When CT scans are done on modern equipment where the dose can be adjusted to individual patient size, and when they are done in facilities that are accredited, the actual doses are being reduced," he said.

info For more information on CT scans, visit the Web site of the National Library of Medicine at *http://medlineplus.gov*. Click on "Medical Encyclopedia" then "Cp–Cz" and then "CT scan."

Delicious Foods That Fight Cancer

Timothy C. Birdsall, ND, vice president of integrative medicine for Cancer Treatment Centers of America, a national network of cancer care facilities. Based in Zion, Illinois, he is the coauthor of How to Prevent and Treat Cancer with Natural Medicine. *Riverhead. www.cancercenter.com.*

Take healthy cells and expose them to a damaging substance—a toxic chemical, tobacco, radiation, a virus or a bacterium—and the result may be a *mutation*, a permanent change in cell DNA. Expose the cells again, and you get more mutations. Eventually, the healthy cells can turn into cancer cells.

Mutations also can be triggered by breathing, digesting, moving—in other words, living. As part of metabolism, our bodies create harmful molecules called *free radicals*, which can damage cell DNA, cause mutations and induce cancer.

First line of defense: An anticancer diet.

FREE RADICAL WEAKENERS

To combat free radicals, we need beneficial nutrients known as antioxidants. *How they work…*

A free radical is an unstable molecule that's missing an electron. To stabilize it, an antioxidant donates one of its own electrons, neutralizing the free radical. Problem solved…except now the antioxidant is missing an electron, so it becomes a free radical. This new free radical is less dangerous than the original one, but it still can damage cells. So you need another antioxidant to give up its electron—and so on. *To get enough antioxidants, eat…*

•**A rainbow of produce.** Varied colors of fruits and vegetables come from antioxidant pigments called phytochemicals. Each plant food contains hundreds of phytochemicals in different combinations.

Remember "Roy G. Biv": The old mnemonic for the colors of the rainbow helps you shop for variety. Go for *red* raspberries, cranberries, tomatoes…*orange* pumpkin, papayas, yams…*yellow* peppers, pineapple, corn…*green* grapes, asparagus, kale…*blue, indigo* and *violet* blueberries, plums and eggplant.

•**Green tea.** These leaves contain antioxidants called *flavonoids*. Consuming green tea daily may reduce risk for various cancers, including bladder and pancreatic cancers.

Recommended: Decaffeination removes flavonoids, so opt for regular green tea rather than decaf. Aim for at least three cups daily, or take green tea extract capsules.

ESTROGEN CONNECTION

The hormone estrogen affects many body functions, including menstruation and cognition. It also may promote some types of breast, ovarian and uterine cancers, although the exact mechanisms are not known. *Protective foods include…*

•**Cruciferous vegetables.** After being used by the body, estrogen is broken down and excreted. The breakdown produces two *metabolites*, or chemical compounds—one that promotes breast cancer and one that does not. Cruciferous vegetables contain the phytochemical *indole-3-carbinol* (I3C), which promotes formation of estrogen's harmless metabolite instead of its carcinogenic one.

I3C foods: Cabbage, broccoli, cauliflower, kale, brussels sprouts. Have four or five half-cup servings weekly.

•**Soy foods.** Soy contains *phytoestrogens* (compounds that mimic natural estrogen in the body), including isoflavones.

Paradox: Some test-tube studies indicate that concentrated phytoestrogens promote breast cancer cell growth—but in real life, soy seems to protect against breast cancer. In Japan and China, where the typical diet is rich in soy

isoflavones, breast cancer incidence is about one-third of the US rate.

Theory: Lifelong intake of isoflavones may reduce levels of natural estrogen in breast tissue.

Isoflavone sources: Soy milk, tofu, miso (soybean paste), tempeh (soybean cake), edamame (green soybeans) and soy nuts (roasted soybeans).

Goal: One cup of soy milk or one-half cup of another soy food daily.

Caution: Limit soy foods to three servings weekly if you have a history of breast cancer, or are pregnant or nursing. Women with thyroid problems should consult their doctors before eating soy.

•**Fiber.** Estrogen metabolites and toxins pass through the colon on their way out of the body. If they linger there, they can be reabsorbed by the body and cause damage. Fiber may bind to estrogen metabolites and toxins, so they are excreted before they can be reabsorbed.

Goal: Five or more servings per day. Good sources: Whole-grain bread (one slice) or cereal (typically three-quarters of a cup)…fruit (one piece or one-half cup)…vegetables and legumes (one-half cup)…nuts and seeds (one-quarter cup).

INFLAMMATION FIGHTERS

Inflammation is part of the normal healing process. However, when this mechanism does not turn itself off properly, inflammation becomes chronic.

Result: More free radicals and cell damage that can lead to cancer. *To reduce inflammation, eat…*

•**Fish.** Many fish are rich in beneficial omega-3 fatty acids. Omega-3s contain an inflammation-fighting component called *eicosapentaenoic acid* (EPA).

Best: Three four-ounce servings weekly of cold-water fatty fish, such as salmon, mackerel, herring and sardines.

Alternative: Take fish oil supplements that provide 1,500 milligrams (mg) daily of combined EPA and *docosahexaenoic acid* (DHA).

•**Flaxseeds.** Ground flaxseeds also provide anti-inflammatory omega-3s.

Bonus: Flaxseeds contain compounds called *lignans* that may kill some types of cancer cells.

Smart: Add one tablespoon of ground flax-seeds to your daily diet. Sprinkle on cereal or salad, or add to a fruit smoothie.

•**Turmeric.** This yellow spice, commonly used in curry, contains *curcumin*, a compound that neutralizes free radicals and shuts down proteins that promote an abnormal inflammatory response.

Use liberally: Sprinkle turmeric on pasta and rice...add it to fish...stir into soups and salad dressings.

■ **More from Timothy C. Birdsall, ND...**

Why Meat and Poultry Raise Your Cancer Risk

A diet high in meat and poultry increases cancer risk. *Here's why...*

•**Sedentary farm animals tend to have more body fat than wild or free-range animals.** High-fat meat and poultry contain more *arachidonic acid*, a fatty acid that promotes cell-damaging inflammation.

•**Cattle often are given hormones to make them bigger.** When we eat their meat, we ingest residual hormones that may stimulate cancer growth.

•**Preserved, cured and smoked meats—** such as hot dogs, ham, bacon, salami and smoked turkey—contain preservatives called *nitrites*, which the body can convert into carcinogenic nitrosamines.

•**Grilling meat or poultry allows fat to drip onto coals,** forming carcinogenic *polycyclic aromatic hydrocarbons* (PAHs)—which smoke then deposits onto the food.

To decrease your risk...

•**Choose meats and poultry labeled "free-range,"** which generally contain less fat.

•**To avoid hormones,** opt for poultry or pork (the USDA prohibits hormone use in these animals)...or buy beef labeled "hormone-free."

•**Select nitrite-free brands of deli meats,** hot dogs and bacon.

•**When grilling, stick to vegetables,** which do not form PAHs. If you do grill meat, cut off charred bits.

•**Limit serving sizes of meat and poultry to three or four ounces—**about the size of a woman's palm.

Eat Black Raspberries and Broccoli to Battle Cancer

Laura Kresty, PhD, assistant professor, Ohio State University, Columbus, Ohio.

Wendy Demark-Wahnefried PhD, RD, professor, behavioral science, M.D. Anderson Cancer Center, University of Texas, Houston.

Yuesheng Zhang, MD, PhD, professor, oncology, Roswell Park Cancer Institute, Buffalo, New York.

Colleen Doyle, MS, RD, director, nutrition and physical activity, American Cancer Society.

American Association for Cancer Research's Sixth Annual International Conference on Frontiers in Cancer Prevention, Philadelphia.

Your local farmer's market might hold the key to cancer prevention, since new research shows that black raspberries, broccoli sprouts and some raw vegetables reduce the risk of esophageal and bladder cancers.

BLACK RASPBERRIES VS. ESOPHAGEAL CANCER

Ohio State University researchers found black raspberries may protect against esophageal cancer by reducing the oxidative stress associated with Barrett's esophagus, a precancerous condition usually caused by gastroesophageal reflux disease. The esophagus is a long tube that connects the throat to the stomach. Reflux disease causes stomach acid to continually splash back up into the esophagus.

"Specifically in the case of Barrett's patients, reflux of the stomach and bile acid contribute to ongoing oxidative damage. Thus, our hypothesis is that feeding a food that is high in potential protective constituents, such as antioxidants, vitamins, minerals and other phytochemicals, may help restore the oxidative balance," said lead researcher Laura Kresty, PhD.

People who have Barrett's esophagus typically are 30 to 40 times more likely to develop esophageal cancer, which has a poor five-year survival rate of 15%.

Black raspberries previously have been shown to reduce the risk of oral, esophageal and colon cancer in animal models, according to the researchers, who called for further study in humans.

The team gave 32 grams to 45 grams of black raspberries daily for six months to 20 patients with Barrett's esophagus. They analyzed changes in blood, urine and tissue before, during and after the treatment, and found reduced levels of some of the chemical markers of oxidative stress in both urine and tissue samples.

Recommendation: Dietitian Wendy Demark-Wahnefried, PhD, a professor of behavioral science at M.D. Anderson Cancer Center at the University of Texas in Houston, said she would feel comfortable advising people with Barrett's to eat black raspberries. "It couldn't hurt," she said, but added that further studies need to find out if the berries really do prevent cancer.

BROCCOLI SPROUTS VS. BLADDER CANCER

A team lead by Yuesheng Zhang, MD, PhD, a professor of oncology at Roswell Park Cancer Institute in Buffalo, New York, demonstrated that a broccoli sprout extract reduced bladder cancer in rats by 70%.

"Our present study shows that broccoli sprout extracts fed to rats in the diet inhibits bladder cancer development induced by a carcinogen. We don't yet know if the extracts inhibit the growth of a existing bladder cancer," said Dr. Zhang, who explained that broccoli sprouts are a rich source of a well-known cancer preventive agent known as sulforaphane.

"We next plan to find out if broccoli sprout extracts can fight bladder cancer in humans," Dr. Zhang noted.

CRUCIFEROUS VEGETABLES VS. BLADDER CANCER

A second team at the Roswell Park Cancer Institute found that people who ate three or more servings of raw, cruciferous vegetables per month reduced their risk for bladder cancer by 40%. Cruciferous vegetables include broccoli, cabbage and cauliflower.

The team analyzed the dietary habits of 275 people with early bladder cancer and 825 people who were cancer-free. The researchers specifically asked how many servings of raw or cooked cruciferous vegetables they ate before their diagnosis and whether they smoked.

Analysis of the data showed that the more raw, cruciferous vegetables people ate, the lower their risk for bladder cancer. In comparison to people who smoked and ate fewer than three servings of raw vegetables a day, nonsmokers eating at least three servings of cruciferous vegetables daily were 73% less likely to develop bladder cancer.

The intake of raw cruciferous vegetables showed risk reduction of bladder cancer in smokers, and even the heavier smokers, according to researchers.

The researchers stressed that the benefits are derived from raw cruciferous vegetables, giving coleslaw the edge over cabbage soup when it comes to cancer prevention.

AMERICAN CANCER SOCIETY RECOMMENDATIONS

"This confirms that there are a variety of compounds within fruits and vegetables that contribute to reducing the risk of cancer. Research like these studies contribute to our knowledge about what the impact of specific nutrients may be on specific types of cancer," said Colleen Doyle, MS, RD, director of nutrition and physical activity for the American Cancer Society.

"Cooking leaches out some nutrients but makes others more absorbable. Until we know more in this regard, the bottom-line message for consumers is eat at least five servings of fruits and vegetables each day, raw and/or lightly cooked," Doyle advised. "Focus on those with the most color, since, in general, fruit and vegetables with the most color have the most cancer-fighting antioxidants and phytochemicals."

"Surveys we've done indicate many people don't think they have control over their cancer risk, but studies clearly indicate they do. For the majority of people who don't smoke, watching their weight, being more active and eating a healthy diet are the most important ways to reduce cancer risk," Doyle said.

info To learn more on how diet and physical activity can help prevent cancer, visit the Web site of the National Cancer Institute at *www.cancer.gov* and search "food and fitness."

High Meat Consumption Linked to Heightened Cancer Risk

Amanda J. Cross, PhD, Nutritional Epidemiology Branch, Division of Cancer Epidemiology and Genetics, National Cancer Institute.

Colleen Doyle, MS, RD, director, nutrition and physical activity, American Cancer Society.

Mary K. Young, MS, RD, vice president of nutrition, National Cattlemen's Beef Association.

PLoS Medicine.

A quarter-pound hamburger or a small pork chop eaten daily could put you at increased risk for a variety of cancers, US government health researchers report.

The more red meat and processed meat you eat, the greater your risk, the researchers from the National Cancer Institute (NCI) concluded.

"Red and processed meats have been associated with an elevated risk of colorectal cancer. We investigated whether this association was also evident for cancers at other anatomic sites," explained lead author Amanda Cross, an epidemiologist at the NCI. "This is the largest study to look at the effect of red and processed meat on multiple cancer sites, including rarer cancers, such as laryngeal and liver cancer."

THE STUDY

For the study, red meats included beef, pork and lamb. Processed meats included bacon, red-meat sausage, poultry sausage, luncheon meats, cold cuts, ham, regular hot dogs and low-fat hot dogs.

Cross and her team from the National Institutes of Health and the AARP analyzed health data from 500,000 people ages 50 to 71. They followed participants for about eight years, during which time they recorded 53,396 cases of cancer. In addition to meat consumption habits, the participants detailed other lifestyle choices such as smoking and exercise.

The team then grouped the people into categories, according to their level of meat consumption.

"In the top category of red meat eaters were those consuming the equivalent of a quarter pound hamburger or a small steak or a pork chop per day," said Cross, who added that in the lowest category, participants ate approximately three thin slices of ham or less per day.

For processed meat, those in the lowest category ate no more than one slice of bacon a day, while those in the top consumption category ate four slices a day.

The median consumption of red meat was 31.4 grams per 1,000 calories. This works out to about two and a half ounces of red meat a day for a person consuming the average 2,000-calorie diet.

STUDY FINDINGS

Overall, the researchers found elevated risks for colorectal and lung cancer with high consumption of both meat types along with borderline higher risks for advanced prostate cancer. High red meat intake was also associated with increased risk for esophageal cancer and liver cancer and a borderline increased risk for laryngeal cancer. And high processed meat consumption also was associated with borderline increased risk for bladder cancer and myeloma, a kind of bone cancer.

In addition, both red meat and processed meat consumption were associated with increased pancreatic cancer risk in men, but not women.

And the research team noted an unexpected effect of red meat on endometrial cancer: The more red meat women consumed, the less likely they were to suffer from endometrial cancer.

THEORIES

There are several possible routes by which red and processed meats may contribute to cancer, the NCI researchers said. Meats are a source of saturated fat and iron, both of which have been linked to cancer, and also the source of several compounds that are known to affect cell development, they added.

Cooking at high temperatures might also contribute to cancer risk, Cross added.

"Compounds such as heterocyclic amines and polycyclic aromatic hydrocarbons are formed when meats are cooked well-done by high temperature cooking methods, such as barbecuing," she said. Studies have linked these compounds to increased risk for cancer.

EXPERT COMMENTARY

"This adds to the body of knowledge that supports recommendations that to reduce the risk of colon cancer, you should reduce your consumption of red and processed meats," said Colleen Doyle, director of nutrition and physical activity for the American Cancer Society. "It also adds to the smaller amount of research tying red and processed meats to other types of cancer risk. The American Cancer Society recommends reducing red and processed meat consumption to reduce the risk of prostate cancer."

"We really see this study that it further illustrates the complexity and challenges of understanding research related to diet and cancer. They also could have said red meat is protective against endometrial cancer. The challenges of looking at diet and cancer are just vast," said Mary K. Young, vice president for nutrition with the National Cattlemen's Beef Association. She noted that the researchers did not ask how food was prepared, which she said could have affected the health outcomes.

Doyle and Young, both dietitians, agreed that diet plays a critical role in health.

"One of the most important things people can do to lower their risk of chronic disease, including cancer, is maintain a healthy weight," added Young, who recommended that people follow national dietary guidelines, watch their serving sizes and stay physically active.

People worrying about cancer and diet should take a balanced approach, said Doyle. "No one food is going to put our cancer risk over the top. If you are someone who eats steak or pork or lamb or salami or hot dogs, etc., on a regular basis and/or in large portion sizes, I would probably suggest you look for healthier protein sources to include in your diet," she added. The American Cancer Society recommends that people eat lots of fruits, vegetables and whole grains with some lean proteins to prevent cancer.

info To learn more about how diet and physical activity choices can help prevent a number of health conditions, visit the Web site of the Centers for Disease Control and Prevention at *www.cdc.gov* and click on "Healthy Living."

5

Diabetes Update

Lack of Deep Sleep Raises Diabetes Risk

Failing to sleep deeply for just three nights running has the same negative effect on the body's ability to manage insulin as gaining 20 to 30 pounds, diabetes researchers report.

In fact, young adults who do not get enough deep sleep may be increasing their risk for type 2 diabetes, according to the study.

Researchers reported that three nights of interrupted sleep effectively gave people in their 20s the glucose (blood sugar) and insulin (the hormone that controls glucose uptake) responses of people three times their age.

Previous studies have demonstrated that not getting enough hours of sleep affects the body's ability to manage blood sugar levels and appetite, increasing the risk of obesity and diabetes. This current study provides the first evidence linking poor sleep quality—specifically the loss of deep or slow-wave sleep—to increased diabetes risk, said the University of Chicago Medical Center research team.

THE STUDY

The researchers recruited five men and four women, all lean and healthy, who were between the ages of 20 and 31. They first observed the participants for two nights of uninterrupted sleep, during which they slept for 8.5 hours, to establish their normal sleep patterns.

Then they observed the same participants over a three-night study period, during which the researchers deliberately disturbed their sleep when their brain waves indicated the beginning of slow-wave sleep.

The sounds used to interrupt the sleep patterns were loud enough to move the participants to a different level of sleep but not loud enough to fully wake them. According to the researchers, the participants could recall hearing between three and 15 noises at night, although they were interrupted on average 250 to 300 times. The

University of Chicago Medical Center, news release.

85

interruptions increased in number each night, as the participants' need for deep sleep increased.

"This decrease in slow-wave sleep resembles the changes in sleep patterns caused by 40 years of aging," said lead author Esra Tasali, MD, assistant professor of medicine at the University of Chicago Medical Center. Young adults spend 80 minutes to 100 minutes per night in slow-wave sleep, while people over age 60 generally have less than 20 minutes. "In this experiment," she said, "we gave people in their 20s the sleep of those in their 60s."

At the end of each study, the researchers gave intravenous glucose (a sugar solution) to each subject, and then took periodic blood samples to measure the levels of glucose and insulin.

RESULTS

Participants were nearly 25% less sensitive to insulin after nights of interrupted sleep. As their insulin sensitivity declined, they needed to make more insulin to process the same amount of glucose, or blood sugar. However, in all but one subject, their bodies did not make more insulin. As a result, they had 23% more blood glucose, the equivalent of glucose levels in an adult over 60 with impaired glucose tolerance.

The researchers also found that the participants who typically had the least amount of slow-wave sleep during the nights they were not interrupted experienced the greatest decline in insulin sensitivity during the study.

"These findings demonstrate a clear role for slow-wave sleep in maintaining normal glucose control," according to Dr. Tasali. "A profound decrease in slow-wave sleep had an immediate and significant adverse effect on insulin sensitivity and glucose tolerance."

The researchers suggested that improving the quality of sleep, especially for people as they age or if they are obese, could be an important step in preventing the onset of type 2 diabetes.

info To learn more about sleep, its health benefits and how to improve sleep quality, visit the Web site of the American Academy of Sleep Medicine at *www.aasmnet.org* and click on "Patients & Public."

Childhood Diabetes Boosts Risk for Kidney Problems

Robert G. Nelson, MD, PhD, staff clinician, Diabetes and Arthritis Epidemiology Section, Phoenix Epidemiology and Clinical Research Branch, National Institute of Diabetes and Digestive and Kidney Diseases, National Institutes of Health, Phoenix.
Pascale H. Lane, MD, Helen Freytag Distinguished Professor and Associate Chair for Research, Department of Pediatrics, University of Nebraska Medical Center, Omaha.
Centers for Disease Control and Prevention, Atlanta.
National Institute of Diabetes and Digestive and Kidney Diseases, Bethesda, Maryland.

As more and more American children are diagnosed with type 2 diabetes, another serious problem is threatening their health. Children and teens diagnosed with type 2 diabetes are five times more likely to develop kidney disease later in life than those who develop diabetes as adults, a recent study found.

The findings underscore the importance of preventing—or at least delaying—the onset of type 2 diabetes, doctors say.

"Since the development of diabetic kidney disease is strongly dependent on the duration of diabetes, developing diabetes in youth leads to a high risk of kidney disease in early- to mid-adulthood," said study author Robert G. Nelson, MD, PhD, a staff clinician with the National Institute of Diabetes and Digestive and Kidney Diseases (NIDDK).

"For example," he said, "a 15-year-old person with 10 years of type 2 diabetes has the same risk of kidney disease as a 55-year-old with 10 years of type 2 diabetes."

BACKGROUND

Diabetes is becoming increasingly prevalent among children and teens, largely due to the obesity epidemic. The Centers for Disease Control and Prevention (CDC) estimates that among new cases of childhood diabetes, up to 43% are type 2 disease.

While type 2 diabetes can affect children of any race or ethnic group, it's more common among non-white individuals, the CDC reports. The Pima Indians of Arizona currently have the highest recorded rates of diabetes in the world, at 50.9 per 1,000 individuals ages 15 to 19, according to the CDC.

Diabetes is the most common cause of kidney failure. Initially, small amounts of albumin, a blood protein, begin to leak into the urine. The filtering function of the kidneys begins to decline as the amount of albumin in the urine increases. It may take 15 to 25 years for kidney failure to occur. Native Americans, blacks and Hispanics have higher rates of kidney failure from diabetes, the NIDDK said.

THE STUDY

Dr. Nelson and his colleagues examined the relationship between a person's age at the onset of diabetes and the likelihood that they would have "end-stage renal disease," or kidney failure. The study, published recently in the *Journal of the American Medical Association*, was based on data collected over four decades from more than 1,800 members of the Pima and closely related Papago Indian tribes. The researchers compared people who were diagnosed with type 2 diabetes before the age of 20 with those who developed the disease between ages 25 and 55.

RESULTS

Breaking down the numbers by age range, people who developed type 2 diabetes before age 20 were eight times more likely to experience kidney failure between ages 25 and 34 than those diagnosed after 20. And the younger diabetics were four times more likely to experience kidney failure between the ages of 45 and 54 than those diagnosed at an older age.

EXPERT RECOMMENDATIONS

Pascale H. Lane, MD, is a diabetic neuropathy specialist and associate chairwoman for research at the University of Nebraska Medical Center's Department of Pediatrics. She believes that patients and parents of children with diabetes need to be aware of the potential complications of type 2 diabetes and ways to minimize the risk.

"Nephropathy [kidney failure] may be prevented by strict control of blood sugar levels and by not smoking," Dr. Lane said. "Diagnosing and treating high blood pressure early and aggressively may also prevent or slow the development of this kidney disease."

Efforts also need to focus on preventing type 2 diabetes in children through lifestyle changes that emphasize weight loss and increased exercise, Dr. Nelson added.

"The explosion of obesity in children and adolescents is a cause for great concern and must be reversed," he said. "Calorie-dense fast foods must be replaced by healthy alternatives provided in reasonable portions, and hours of TV watching must be replaced by activities that require exercise."

info For more information on diabetes and kidney disease, visit the National Kidney Foundation's Web site, *www.kidney.org*, and search "diabetes and kidney disease."

■ ■ ■ ■

Diabetes Increases Stroke Risk

Type 1 (insulin-dependent) diabetes and type 2 (non-insulin-dependent) diabetes increase risk of ischemic stroke, triggered by a blood clot that blocks a blood vessel in the brain. Type 1 also is linked to hemorrhagic stroke, triggered by a vessel bleeding into the brain.

Self-defense: If you have either type, ask your doctor about controlling stroke risk factors.

Mohsen Janghorbani, PhD, professor of epidemiology, department of epidemiology and biostatistics, School of Public Health, Isfahan University of Medical Sciences, Iran, and lead author of study of 116,316 women, published in *Diabetes Care*.

Living Well with Diabetes

Anne L. Peters, MD, professor of medicine and director of the University of Southern California Clinical Diabetes Programs and former chairperson of the American Diabetes Association Council on Health Care Delivery and Public Health. She is the author of *Conquering Diabetes: A Complete Program for Prevention and Treatment.* Plume.

Even though people who are newly diagnosed with type 2 diabetes *intend* to control the disease with lifestyle changes, such as diet and exercise, only 3% are successful—often because these steps can be difficult to follow on a long-term basis.

Solution: Recent research has identified simple, more effective ways to control diabetes, with little or no use of medication. Sometimes, they can even reverse the signs of the disease

Bonus: These strategies also can help prevent full-blown diabetes in the 40% of Americans ages 40 to 74 who have a precursor to the disease known as prediabetes.

What you should know now…

DANGERS OF DIABETES

Diabetes causes elevations in blood sugar (glucose), the primary fuel that powers our bodies' cells. A normal fasting blood sugar level (measured after eight hours without eating) is below 100 milligrams per deciliter (mg/dL).

Nearly 20 million Americans—more than half of them over age 60—have type 2 diabetes. The pancreas no longer manufactures sufficient amounts of the blood sugar–regulating hormone *insulin* or the body becomes insensitive to insulin effects, and blood sugar levels rise above 125 milligrams per deciliter (mg/dL). Another 54 million Americans have prediabetes, where fasting blood sugar levels increase to 100 mg/dL to 125 mg/dL.

It's a common misconception that being overweight and having a sedentary lifestyle are enough to cause the glucose-regulating hormone insulin to lose its effectiveness. In fact, most people who develop diabetes are genetically predisposed to the disease. Excess body weight and inactivity simply *activate* the genes that trigger diabetes.

Type 2 diabetes is often downplayed as a "little blood sugar problem," but the disease can have devastating consequences. Prediabetes and diabetes damage arteries, increasing the risk for heart disease and stroke two- to fourfold. In addition, diabetes is the leading cause of blindness (from damaged blood vessels in the eyes)…and nontraumatic amputation of lower limbs (due to chronic foot ulcers that are caused and complicated by poor circulation and abnormal nerve conduction resulting from diabetes).

In a 40-year-old man, diabetes shortens his normal life expectancy by 12 years…in a 40-year-old woman, it cuts her life expectancy by 14 years, according to estimates by the Centers for Disease Control and Prevention (CDC).

THE BASICS MADE EASIER

Eating right, getting regular exercise and reducing stress may sound like all-too-familiar advice for preventing and controlling diabetes, but new research has uncovered ways to make these practices simpler than ever before…

•**To lose weight**. Risk for diabetes is reduced by 16% with every kilogram (2.2 pounds) of weight loss.

Best weight-loss diet: For long-term health, weight-loss *and* diabetes control, research supports the use of a low-fat vegan (pronounced "vee-gun") diet, which does not include any meat, poultry, fish, dairy or eggs, and includes only vegetables, fruits, whole grains and legumes, such as lentils and black beans.

Recent research: Ninety-nine people with type 2 diabetes were asked to go on either a low-fat, low-sugar vegan diet or a diet following American Diabetes Association (ADA) guidelines, focusing on calorie counting and portion control. After 22 weeks, those on the vegan diet had lost an average of 14 pounds, while those on the ADA diet lost 6.8 pounds. The vegan group also had a greater decrease in blood sugar levels, LDL "bad" cholesterol and the need for oral diabetes medications.

Also helpful: Using "meal-replacement" products, such as Slim-Fast or Medifast, for one or two meals a day is an excellent calorie-reducing practice that results in weight loss.

Recent study: 104 people with diabetes were asked to follow a weight-loss diet using meal replacements or ADA guidelines. After 34 weeks, those using meal replacements had lost twice as much weight and had significantly lower blood sugar levels.

Bottom line: A low-fat vegan diet and meal replacements are two among *many* healthful approaches to weight loss for people with diabetes. *Whatever approach you choose to lose and maintain weight, follow these principles of healthful eating…*

•**Minimize refined carbohydrates,** such as white flour and sugar, and starches, such as potatoes and white rice.

•**Focus on vegetables, fruits, whole grains and legumes**.

Helpful: Work with a dietitian for a personalized meal plan.

•**Eat balanced meals**—half of your calories from vegetables and salad…one-quarter from grains and other unrefined carbohydrates, such as cereals and whole-wheat bread…and one-quarter from protein and fat.

The strictness of a vegan diet won't be practical for everyone—and, fortunately, there are ways to incorporate lean meat and fish into your diet and still prevent diabetes or keep it under control.

Sample lunch: A large green salad, one-half cup of brown rice and two ounces of fish.

•**To exercise the right way.** Research shows that people with diabetes who exercise regularly have lower blood sugar levels than those who do not exercise.

Best exercise routine: Four to five days a week, perform 45 minutes of aerobic exercise, such as brisk walking, to condition the heart… and at least one to two nonconsecutive days a week, do 15 minutes of resistance-training with weights to increase muscle mass (this helps the body use insulin more efficiently).

New finding: In a study published in the September 18, 2007, issue of *Annals of Internal Medicine*, 251 people with type 2 diabetes were asked to participate in aerobics, resistance training or both. Improvements in blood sugar control were greatest in the *combined* group.

Trap: Many people begin an exercise program and immediately overdo it, causing an injury.

Best: Increase exercise *gradually.*

Example: The first week, walk five minutes away from your house and five minutes back on four or five days. Each week for the next three weeks, increase the time by five minutes each way. By week four, you'll be walking 40 minutes, four to five days a week.

•**To reduce stress.** *Cortisol*, a hormone produced during stress, boosts blood sugar levels.

Best stress-reducing strategies: Staying centered and calm, through the use of yoga, meditation, mindfulness (focusing attention on the here and now rather than the past or future) or other stress-relieving techniques, helps normalize blood sugar.

New study: Researchers divided 81 people with diabetes into two groups. Both were taught how to manage the disease, but only one group received training in stress-reducing psychological skills, such as mindfulness. Three months later, the people who had learned psychological techniques were more likely to have lower blood sugar than they'd had before.

SMART USE OF MEDICATION

In 2007, the ADA recommended that people newly diagnosed with diabetes use lifestyle modification and an oral diabetes medication, such as *glucophage* (Metformin), to control high blood sugar.

However, research published earlier this year showing that the diabetes drug *rosiglitazone* (Avandia) increased the risk for heart attack by 42% and doubled the risk for heart failure has made some people with the disease wary of diabetes medications.

When used appropriately—and in conjunction with a healthful lifestyle—most diabetes drugs don't cause significant side effects. But it's important to know the risks and benefits of every drug you take, and how to minimize the risks.

Example: If you take rosiglitazone and notice that your ankles are swollen or that you are short of breath—signs of a possible drug-related heart problem—inform your doctor immediately. He/she may change your drug or decrease the dose and add another diabetes drug, such as glucophage or *glimepiride* (Amaryl), to your regimen.

Urgent: How to Tell If You Have Prediabetes

Mark A. Stengler, ND, naturopathic physician in private practice, La Jolla, California…adjunct associate clinical professor at the National College of Natural Medicine, Portland, Oregon…author of many books, including *The Natural Physician's Healing Therapies* and coauthor of *Prescription for Natural Cures* (both from Bottom Line Books)…and author of the *Bottom Line/Natural Healing* newsletter.

As Americans continue to pack on the pounds, doctors are seeing a surge in weight-related health problems. One such common condition that now affects about 40% of American adults is *prediabetes*, characterized by blood glucose (sugar) levels that are higher than normal but not yet at diabetic levels. People with prediabetes are five to 15 times more likely to develop full-blown diabetes than people without this condition.

These are alarming statistics. Diabetes has serious potential consequences, including blindness, kidney failure, nerve damage, erectile dysfunction, heart failure, stroke and circulation problems that can necessitate amputation.

Good news: Diabetes and its devastating consequences often can be prevented—by reversing prediabetes.

HOW THE DISEASE PROGRESSES

The development of type 2 diabetes—which accounts for about 90% of all diabetes cases—is greatly influenced by prediabetes and excess weight. An obese person is *80 times* more likely to develop type 2 diabetes than a person of normal weight. With type 2 diabetes, the pancreas usually does produce insulin, but the body's cells cannot use it properly. A person often passes through many stages on the way to developing type 2 diabetes. *What happens…*

When we eat, the amount of glucose in our blood rises, alerting the pancreas that it needs to release insulin. Excess fat, nutritional deficiencies and the stress hormone *cortisol* interfere with cells' ability to accept and use insulin, leaving excess glucose in the blood. When this happens, a person is said to have *insulin resistance.*

Sensing that the insulin is not doing its job, the pancreas churns out even more. But since the cells cannot accept the excess insulin, it remains in the blood, along with the excess glucose. When blood glucose levels reach a certain point (as measured with blood tests), the condition qualifies as prediabetes…and if levels climb higher still, it qualifies as diabetes.

High blood glucose levels cause many of the complications of diabetes, including damage to the kidneys, nerves and eyes. However, while prediabetes and diabetes are developing, a bigger problem is high blood insulin.

Reason: Insulin helps produce muscle—but when insulin levels get too high, the hormone instead promotes formation of belly fat, which in turn makes insulin resistance even worse. Insulin elevations also increase production of triglycerides and cholesterol, which clog arteries

…of *C-reactive protein*, which promotes damaging inflammation…and of cortisol, which contributes to various diseases.

WHAT THE TESTS SHOULD TELL US

Too many doctors use antiquated guidelines for interpreting test results, then tell patients all is well when, in fact, the patients are at risk. I urge you to ask your doctor for the specific results of your tests and compare them with my guidelines below, which I have based on the most recent evidence. You may spot a warning sign that your doctor missed.

•**Fasting glucose test.** This test involves fasting for at least eight hours (optimally 12 hours), usually overnight, then having blood drawn to measure glucose levels.

Problem: The range generally accepted as "normal"—from 65 milligrams per deciliter (mg/dL) to 99 mg/dL—is much too broad.

Evidence: A study published in *The New England Journal of Medicine* found that men with a fasting blood glucose level of 87 mg/dL had almost twice the risk of developing diabetes as did men whose level was 81 mg/dL or less. *My guidelines…*

- •Optimal—76 mg/dL to 81 mg/dL
- •Normal—82 mg/dL to 85 mg/dL
- •At risk—86 mg/dL to 99 mg/dL
- •Prediabetic—100 mg/dL to 125 mg/dL
- •Diabetic—126 mg/dL and above

Though most doctors don't order it routinely, you can ask your doctor to have your insulin levels checked as part of your fasting glucose test. These results are not used to officially diagnose diabetes, but they do provide additional information about your risk. Although the generally accepted guidelines put the normal range for blood insulin levels at six micro-international units per milliliter (mcU/ml) to 35 mcU/ml, I think this range is far too wide to be meaningful. *My guidelines…*

- •Optimal—7 mcU/ml or less
- •At risk—8 mcU/ml to 10 mcU/ml
- •Prediabetic—11 mcU/ml to 25 mcU/ml
- •Dangerous—above 25 mcU/ml

•**Oral glucose tolerance test with glucose and insulin levels.** A more accurate way to measure blood insulin levels, this test requires fasting for 12 hours and having blood drawn… then drinking a glucose solution and having blood drawn again after one, two and up to three hours. I often order this test for patients who are overweight, have a strong family history of diabetes or have a history of elevated fasting glucose levels—even if their most recent fasting glucose test results appeared normal. In this way, I have diagnosed type 2 diabetes in several patients whose fasting glucose results did not suggest any problems. *My guidelines for blood drawn at the two-hour point…*

•Normal—blood glucose below 140 mg/dL …or insulin levels at or below 55 mcU/ml.

•Prediabetic—blood glucose of 140 mg/dL to 159 mg/dL, or an increase in glucose of 50 mg/dL or more within one hour…or insulin levels at 56 mcU/ml to 90 mcU/ml.

•Dangerous—blood glucose of 160 mg/dL or higher…or insulin levels above 90 mcU/ml.

•**Hemoglobin A1C (HbA1c).** A British study involving 10,232 adults indicated that HbA1c results accurately predict health problems, including heart attacks (for which prediabetes and diabetes are risk factors). For each 1% rise in HbA1c, study participants' heart attack risk increased by 20%. *My guidelines…*

•Normal—4.5% to 4.9%

•At risk—5.0% to 5.6%

•Prediabetic—5.7% to 6.9%

•Diabetic—7.0% or higher

STEPS TO TAKE TO PREEMPT PREDIABETES

Fortunately, there is a lot you can do to prevent prediabetes—or even to reverse it if you have it.

1. Lose excess weight. This is without question the most important step. To determine if you are at a healthful weight, calculate your *body mass index* (BMI), a ratio of your weight to the square of your height (for a free on-line BMI calculator, go to *www.nhlbisupport.com/bmi*). BMI of 30 or higher indicates obesity and a strong likelihood of developing prediabetes or

diabetes…BMI between 25 and 29.9 puts you at risk for prediabetes.

2. Reduce body fat percentage. Apart from its effect on weight, excess body fat increases prediabetes risk. I measure a patient's body fat percentage with *bioelectrical impedance*, a painless test that involves placing electrodes on your hand and foot. For women, an ideal range is 21% to 24%…anything above 31% is risky. For men, ideal is 14% to 17%…above 25% is risky.

Self-defense: Build muscle and banish excess fat by doing 30 minutes of aerobic exercise, such as brisk walking, five days a week…plus 30 minutes of strength training twice weekly.

3. Eat right. Good dietary habits help to control weight…prevent spikes and drops in blood glucose levels…slow nutrient absorption, giving the pancreas time to produce insulin…boost energy, making it easier to exercise…and provide nutrients that optimize health.

•**Eat three meals a day at regular times.** Keep portions moderate. Never skip breakfast.

•**Keep snacks small.**

Options: Nuts, seeds, low-sugar protein drinks, vegetables or fruit.

•**Include a small portion of protein at every meal.**

Good choices: One or two eggs…1.5 ounces of nuts…or three ounces of fish, chicken, turkey or lean meat.

•**Eat at least one or two servings of whole grains daily.** For variety, try quinoa, couscous, and bread made with spelt or kamut flour.

•**Avoid sugary foods, processed foods, trans fats** (found in some margarines, baked goods and crackers) and saturated fats (in meats, dairy foods and many vegetable oils).

•**Have at least two servings of fruits and three or more servings of vegetables daily.**

4. Take appropriate supplements. Many manufacturers offer a "blood sugar control formula" that provides a combination of nutrients to help stabilize blood glucose and promote proper insulin function. Alternatively, you can follow the guidelines below.

If you are at risk for prediabetes, take...

•**Chromium,** a mineral, at 500 micrograms (mcg) daily.

•**Pycnogenol** (maritime pine extract) at 200 mg daily.

If you have been diagnosed with prediabetes, also take...

•**Biotin** (vitamin B-7) at 500 mcg daily.

•**Alpha lipoic acid,** an antioxidant, at 300 mg daily.

•**Magnesium** at 400 mg daily.

•**Vitamin D** at 1,000 international units (IU) daily.

If you use diabetes medication, check with your doctor before taking these supplements—your medication dosage may need to be adjusted. These supplements are sold in health food stores, generally are safe, rarely cause side effects and can be taken indefinitely. Ideally, however, your improved diet and more healthful lifestyle will decrease your risk for prediabetes or reverse the condition, so the supplements eventually will no longer be necessary.

■ ■ ■ ■

Important News for Women with Diabetes

The death rate for women with diabetes has not declined, even though the rate for men with diabetes has declined by 43% over the last three decades, says Ronald B. Goldberg, MD.

Likely reason: The primary cause of death in people with diabetes is cardiovascular disease—which appears to be diagnosed and managed less efficiently in women.

Self-defense: Women with diabetes should be in the regular care of a physician and alert to symptoms such as chest and abdominal discomfort, shortness of breath, profound weakness and unexplained ankle swelling.

Ronald B. Goldberg, MD, professor of medicine, biochemistry and molecular biology, University of Miami School of Medicine, and principal investigator for the university's Diabetes Prevention Program. He also is associate director of the Diabetes Research Institute, also in Miami.

Ladies: Know These Hidden Signs Of Diabetes

Robert A. Rizza, MD, professor of medicine at Mayo Clinic in Rochester, Minnesota. He is a past president of the American Diabetes Association.

For many women, a diagnosis of diabetes seems to come like a bolt out of the blue, with little or no warning. This is worrisome, because once the disease has developed, it can bring on a multitude of health problems. Yet if women at risk are identified when still in the prediabetic stages, the condition is much easier to control and its consequences are far less severe.

Most know that being overweight increases the likelihood of developing type 2 diabetes—but few people recognize the various hidden risk factors that can contribute to the disease.

UNRECOGNIZED RISK FACTORS

Insulin resistance is a prediabetic condition in which the body's cells do not efficiently use the hormone insulin to regulate blood sugar levels. Often this progresses to type 2 diabetes, in which the body no longer produces enough insulin or the cells become insensitive to the insulin.

Here are seven risk factors for insulin resistance and/or diabetes. If any apply to you, talk to your doctor now—before diabetes creeps up on you.

•**You are of African-American, Hispanic, Asian or Native American descent.** For unknown reasons, people within these ethnic groups are at increased risk for diabetes.

•**Your mother or father has or had type 2 diabetes.** If a parent developed the disease by age 50, your risk is about one in seven—or one in 13 if the parent was diagnosed after age 50. Having a sibling with diabetes also increases your risk.

•**You had high blood sugar when pregnant.** During pregnancy, a woman's insulin resistance rises, so the pancreas needs to produce more insulin. If the pancreas can't meet this demand, you develop high blood sugar.

If the insulin shortage is severe, you may develop gestational diabetes (diabetes caused by pregnancy). This usually goes away after the baby is born, but it's a clue that your pancreas doesn't produce plentiful levels of insulin. The amount it does make will be enough to do the job if you maintain a normal weight, but if you gain weight, you may not be able to produce enough insulin to supply your larger body.

•**Your mother had gestational diabetes** when she was pregnant with you.

Theory: Animal studies suggest that excess blood glucose in the fetus's system may be harmful, "programming" the baby to be prone to diabetes in the future.

•**You weighed nine pounds or more at birth**—which suggests that your mother may have had undiagnosed gestational diabetes. Babies born to mothers with gestational diabetes often are large. As the mother's extra blood glucose goes through the placenta, the baby receives more energy than he/she needs to grow —and this excess energy is stored as fat.

•**You're 45 or older.** A woman's risk for diabetes rises in midlife, especially after menopause. The reasons are unclear but may be related to the weight gain that often accompanies menopause.

•**You have polycystic ovary syndrome (PCOS),** a disorder characterized by irregular menstrual periods, excessive hair growth, acne, obesity and/or insulin resistance. PCOS affects up to 10% of women of reproductive age. We don't know the exact cause, but researchers believe PCOS is linked to excess insulin, which may stimulate ovaries to produce excess *androgens* (male hormones, such as testosterone). Women with PCOS usually have high blood sugar and are at greater risk for developing diabetes.

LESSER-KNOWN DANGERS

Why is it so important to protect yourself from diabetes? In part because the disease itself can have grave consequences—including seizures, blindness, kidney failure, coma and nerve and/or circulatory problems that can lead to loss of limbs and even death.

Diabetes also increases your risk for other serious diseases.

Reason: Because people with diabetes cannot use their blood sugar efficiently, excess amounts stay in the bloodstream. *If left untreated, this can lead to...*

•**Heart disease.** Before menopause, women usually have less risk for heart disease than men of the same age—but diabetes erases this female advantage. Women of any age with diabetes are more prone to cardiovascular problems than are women without diabetes. Over time, high blood glucose levels lead to increased buildup of fatty plaque on the insides of the blood vessel walls. These plaque deposits impede the flow of blood and cause the arteries to harden, raising your risk for heart attack and stroke.

•**Breast cancer.** Being obese increases a woman's risk for breast cancer after menopause. Many researchers believe that type 2 diabetes, independent of obesity, also increases risk— perhaps due to insulin's effects on estrogen, a hormone that is linked to breast cancer.

•**Other cancers.** Every cancer studied shows a small but consistent increase in incidence among overweight people with diabetes.

SELF-PROTECTION

You can decrease your risk for developing diabetes—or for suffering severe consequences if you do have the disease. *To optimize your health...*

•**Maintain a normal weight.** If you are overweight, losing even a small amount can improve insulin resistance and lower blood sugar levels.

•**Exercise more,** even if all you do is add some walking to your daily routine. Try to work up to a brisk 30-minute walk most days. Exercise reduces insulin resistance.

•**Eat sensibly.** Focus on fruits, vegetables and whole grains. Ask your doctor for a referral to a diabetes educator for help working out the best diet for you.

•**Take appropriate medications,** if necessary, to help keep your blood sugar at normal levels. Also be conscientious about taking any other medications—for high blood pressure, for example—as prescribed by your doctor.

Best Exercise to Fight Diabetes

Ronald J. Sigal, MD, associate professor, medicine and cardiac sciences, University of Calgary, Alberta, Canada.

Cathy Nonas, RD, MS, director, physical activity and nutrition, New York City Department of Health and Mental Hygiene, and certified diabetes educator.

Annals of Internal Medicine.

Most people know that exercise can help beat type 2 diabetes, but one type of fitness regimen might work best, a new study shows.

Specifically, workouts that combine aerobic and resistance training exercises appear better at controlling blood sugar than either type of activity alone, researchers say.

The finding is new, because "most other studies have looked at just one kind of exercise, either aerobic or resistance," noted lead researcher Ronald J. Sigal, MD, an associate professor of medicine and cardiac sciences at the University of Calgary, in Alberta, Canada.

THE STUDY

Dr. Sigal's team evaluated 251 adults, ages 39 to 70, with type 2 diabetes who did not exercise regularly. The participants were assigned to one of four groups: those who did 45 minutes of aerobic training three times a week, those who did 45 minutes of resistance training three times a week, those who did 45 minutes each of both forms of exercise three times a week, and those who did no exercise at all.

The aerobic group worked out on a treadmill or a bike at the gym. The resistance group also worked out at the gym doing seven different exercises on weight machines.

Dr. Sigal's team evaluated changes in A1c values—a measurement reflecting blood sugar concentrations over the previous two to three months. A1c is expressed as a percentage.

RESULTS

As expected, blood sugar control improved in all the exercise groups. In those who did either aerobic or resistance exercise, the A1c value declined by about 0.5% compared to the non-exercisers. Those who did both kinds of exercise had double that level of success, with their A1c value dropping by 0.97% compared to the non-exercising group. Non-exercisers experienced no change in their A1c values over the 26-week study.

The bottom line: "There is additional value to doing both resistance and aerobic exercise," according to Dr. Sigal.

He said the decrease of nearly 1% of A1c seen in the study "translates to a 15% to 20% reduction in risk of heart attack or stroke and a 25% to 40% reduced risk of other complications, such as retinopathy," an eye problem related to diabetes.

EXPLANATION

How does physical activity fight type 2 diabetes? According to Dr. Sigal, "exercise decreases insulin resistance. It makes the transport of glucose [blood sugar] more efficient."

EXPERT REACTION

Another expert said the study gives new information for people hoping to beat back diabetes. "Basically, aerobic and resistance training both do very well, and the combination does even better," said Cathy Nonas, RD, director of physical activity and nutrition for the New York City Department of Health and Mental Hygiene and a registered dietitian and certified diabetes educator.

But, she said, couch potatoes often need to ease into exercise to maintain a fitness regimen over time.

The study participants built up to their 45-minute fitness sessions, Dr. Nonas noted, and the combination group ended up doing about 4.5 hours of exercise a week—an amount some might find daunting.

"I would never talk about 4.5 hours a week to someone who doesn't exercise at all," Dr. Nonas said. Rather, she encourages physical activity in any amount to start. "Anything you do is good," she said. Then she encourages people to slowly build up their time.

"I think this is a very uplifting study," she added. "It says whatever you do will have an effect, and the more you do, the better the effect."

info To learn more about the benefits of exercise for diabetes, visit the Web site of the American Diabetes Association, *www.diabetes.org*, and search "types of exercise."

Cheer Up! Treating Depression Lowers Diabetes Death Risk 50%

University of Pennsylvania School of Medicine, news release.

Treating depression can help extend the lives of people with diabetes, concludes a University of Pennsylvania School of Medicine study published in the journal *Diabetes Care*.

It found that providing depression care management to older adults with diabetes and depression reduced the risk of death over five years by about 50%.

"Depression is common among people with diabetes and contributes to issues with medication and diet adherence and also leads to an overall reduced quality of life," said study lead author Hillary R. Bogner, MD, an assistant professor in the department of family practice and community medicine.

THE STUDY

The study included 584 people, ages 60 to 94, with depression. Of these patients, 123 had a history of diabetes. The participants were randomly assigned to receive either usual care or depression care management, which involved a depression care manager who worked with the patient's primary care provider to recommend treatment for depression and help patients adhere to their treatment program.

Patients with diabetes who received depression care management were less likely to have died at the end of five years of follow-up than patients with diabetes who received usual care.

IMPLICATION

The findings support the integration of depression evaluation and treatment with diabetes management in primary care, the study authors concluded.

info For more information about diabetes and depression, visit the American Diabetes Association Web site at *www.diabetes.org*. Under "All About Diabetes," click on "Type 2 Diabetes" and then "Complications."

■ ■ ■ ■

The Depression–Diabetes Link

In a new study, researchers followed 4,681 people (average age 73) for 10 years, screening them annually for signs of depression. People with a high number of depression symptoms were 50% to 60% more likely to develop type 2 diabetes than those who were not depressed.

Theory: Depressed people may be more vulnerable to diabetes because they typically have high levels of the stress hormone *cortisol*, which can reduce insulin sensitivity (the body's ability to respond to insulin).

If you have been diagnosed with depression: Discuss a possible screening for diabetes with your doctor.

Mercedes R. Carnethon, PhD, assistant professor of preventive medicine, Feinberg School of Medicine, Northwestern University, Chicago.

Why You Must Ask Your Doctor About Statin Therapy Now!

The Lancet, news release.

Most people with diabetes should be considered for treatment with a statin drug, a class of cholesterol-lowering medications.

The British and Australian researchers found that statins reduced the risk of major vascular events in a wide range of people with diabetes, regardless of age, sex and other clinical characteristics, and irrespective of whether they already had cardiovascular disease.

Diabetes is associated with an increased risk of cardiovascular disease.

THE STUDY

Researchers conducted a meta-analysis of 18,686 people with diabetes and 71,370 without diabetes who took part in 14 randomized trials that examined the use of statins to reduce levels of low-density lipoprotein (LDL), or "bad" cholesterol.

During a mean follow-up of 4.3 years, 3,247 of the people with diabetes experienced heart attacks, strokes or other vascular events.

Among people with diabetes, all-cause mortality decreased by 9% for every 1 millimole/liter (mmol/L) reduction in LDL cholesterol, which was similar to the 13% reduction noted in people without diabetes.

The study authors said they found a significant 20% reduction in major vascular events with each mmol/L reduction in LDL cholesterol in people with diabetes, a decline similar to that seen in people without diabetes.

IMPLICATION

According to the researchers, "This meta-analysis shows convincingly that the proportional benefits of statin therapy on major vascular events were similar in a wide range of individuals with diabetes, including those with no previous history of vascular disease, and benefits were similar to those observed in people without diabetes."

RECOMMENDATIONS

"Most people with diabetes should now be considered for statin therapy, unless their risk is low (for example, children) or statin therapy has been shown to be unsuitable for them (for example, when pregnant)," they concluded.

Statin drugs are among the most notable achievements of modern medicine.

However, cautioned Bernard Cheung, a professor of clinical pharmacology at the University of Birmingham in England, "one must not forget the importance of lifestyle changes, such as cessation of smoking, maintaining a healthy diet and implementing a regular exercise regimen."

info For more information regarding statins, visit the American Heart Association's Web site, *www.americanheart.org*, and search "cholesterol-lowering drugs." To read more information on the connection between diabetes and cholesterol-lowering drugs, go to the Medicinenet.com Web site, *www.medicinenet.com*. Then search "statins and diabetes."

Look! This Drug Protects Diabetics' Eyes

The Lancet, news release.

In people with type 2 diabetes, the cholesterol-lowering drug fenofibrate reduces the need for laser treatment for diabetic retinopathy, which is a leading cause of blindness in American adults.

THE STUDY

A team of researchers from the University of Sydney studied nearly 9,800 type 2 diabetes patients, ages 50 to 75, who received either 200 milligrams (mg) per day of fenofibrate or a placebo.

After an average follow-up of five years, fenofibrate reduced the frequency of first laser treatment for macular edema (swelling of the macula, the part of the eye responsible for highly-focused central vision) by 31% and for proliferative diabetic retinopathy (growth of new, abnormal blood vessels on the retina surface) by 30%.

The researchers noted that although fenofibrate is a drug that lowers levels of blood fats (lipids), it didn't lead to clinically important differences in "good" high-density lipoprotein (HDL) cholesterol in the type 2 diabetes patients who took it.

IMPLICATION

"These findings suggest that the mechanisms of benefit of fenofibrate in diabetic retinopathy must go beyond the effects of this drug on lipid concentrations or to lower blood pressure and might be conferred mainly by other means," said the study authors.

RECOMMENDATION

They concluded that, "The substantial benefits of fenofibrate on need for laser treatment for diabetic retinopathy are likely to be additive to those benefits arising from tight control of blood glucose and blood pressure in the management of type 2 diabetes mellitus and emerge rapidly after treatment is commenced."

The findings support the use of fenofibrate in the management of diabetic eye disease, said the researchers.

info For more information on diabetic retinopathy, go to the Web site of the US National Eye Institute at *www.nei.nih.gov* and click on "Diabetic Retinopathy."

Warning: Avandia Could Weaken Bones

Ron Evans, PhD, professor and March of Dimes Chairman in Molecular and Developmental Biology, Salk Institute for Biological Studies, La Jolla, California and investigator, Howard Hughes Medical Institute, Chevy Chase, Maryland.

Paul Brandt, PhD, associate professor, neuroscience and experimental therapeutics, Texas A&M Health Science Center College of Medicine, College Station.

Nature Medicine online.

A vandia, a drug used by millions of diabetes patients, may contribute to bone loss, according to a new study conducted in mice.

Experts fear that, over the long term, *rosiglitazone* (Avandia) may speed osteoporosis, the thinning of the bones that can lead to dangerous and even fatal fractures.

BACKGROUND

Avandia and four other diabetes drugs from the same class were given a "black box" warning by the US Food and Drug Administration (FDA). That warning advises users of an increased risk of heart failure while on the drug. The black box message is the FDA's strongest label warning.

With an estimated 3.5 million or more US patients taking Avandia, the public health impact from the point of view of both heart failure and bone degradation could be substantial, experts say.

THE STUDY

Avandia affects a key cellular protein called the *peroxisome proliferator-activated receptor* (PPAR-gamma). In their study, the California team discovered that, in mice, activating this receptor also stimulates the production of osteoclasts, cells whose key function is to degrade bone.

Proper bone health is maintained by a balance between osteoclasts and osteoblasts, the cells that build bone up. If either side is out

of whack, so to speak, bones become thinner, more fragile and prone to fracture.

The current results are particularly disturbing in light of prior studies, the experts said.

"It was previously known that Avandia mediates bone loss by inhibiting bone formation," explained study senior author Ron Evans, PhD, a professor at the Salk Institute for Biological Studies in La Jolla, California. "Our work identified an additional mechanism, in which Avandia promotes bone resorption. These are the two parts of the checks-and-balance system that maintains bone in good shape. The drug weakens both sides of the balance mechanism, leading to an increased risk for osteoporosis."

"Previous research showed that Avandia reduced osteoblasts," added Paul Brandt, PhD, an associate professor of neuroscience and experimental therapeutics at Texas A&M Health Science Center College of Medicine, in College Station. "Combine the two, and you're going to get thinning of the bone."

RECOMMENDATIONS

"Our study suggests that long-term rosiglitazone usage in the treatment of type 2 diabetes may cause osteoporosis due to both increased bone resorption and decreased bone formation," said Evans. "Because Avandia is effective in controlling glucose and restoring the body's sensitivity to insulin, we do not recommend that people stop their treatment. You must balance the benefits against the complications."

"Anyone who is already at risk for osteoporotic fractures should consider an alternative anti-diabetic drug," added Dr. Brandt. "There are many alternatives," he said. "It may [also] be possible to blunt some of Avandia's effects with anti-osteoporosis drugs such as bisphosphonates, raloxifene, vitamin D and calcium."

info For more on diabetes drugs, visit the Web site of the US Food and Drug Administration at *www.fda.gov/diabetes/pills.html*.

■ ■ ■ ■

Better Insulin Therapy

In a recent five-year study, researchers followed 1,300 diabetes patients who received insulin therapy using either syringes to inject insulin extracted from a vial…or insulin pens, which contain a needle and a premeasured dose of the drug. The insulin pen group had average annual health care costs nearly $17,000 lower than those who used syringes (due to lower total hospital costs, for example, and fewer trips to emergency rooms).

Theory: When using an insulin pen, there is less risk of getting an incorrect dose. If you use a syringe for insulin therapy: Ask your doctor if switching to an insulin pen would be appropriate for you.

Rajesh Balkrishnan, PhD, professor of pharmacy, Ohio State University, Columbus.

■ ■ ■ ■

Diabetes and Hip Fracture

In a recent analysis of 16 studies involving 836,941 people, researchers found that people with diabetes were 70% more likely to fracture a hip than nondiabetics. The reason has not yet been determined.

If you have diabetes: Ask your doctor if you should have an annual bone density test.

Mohsen Janghorbani, PhD, professor of epidemiology, School of Public Health, Isfahan University of Medical Sciences, Isfahan, Iran.

■ ■ ■ ■

Diabetics, Examine Your Feet!

People with diabetes are prone to foot problems that can be serious enough to require amputation. Good hygiene and regular inspection of the feet can help catch potential problems early.

Here are suggestions on how to care for feet and prevent injury, courtesy of the US National Diabetes Information Clearinghouse…

•**Wash feet thoroughly each day** in warm—not hot—water.

•**Make sure to dry them completely** after washing.

•**Gently file down corns and calluses** with a pumice stone after washing feet.

•**Inspect feet every day,** looking for blisters, calluses, cuts, sores or any signs of redness.

•**Apply lotion to dry skin**—but never between the toes.

•**Cut toenails regularly,** and file the edges with an emery board.

•**Avoid walking barefoot,** make sure shoes fit well, and always wear socks or stockings with shoes.

US National Diabetes Information Clearinghouse.

■ ■ ■ ■

Amazing New Device Prevents Foot Ulcers

In an 18-month study, 225 people with diabetes inspected their feet daily for signs of diabetes-related ulcers. One group also used a TempTouch thermometer (a probe is placed against the bottom of the foot).

Result: Patients who used the thermometer were three times less likely to develop ulcers than those who only visually examined their feet.

Theory: A wound heats up before the surrounding skin breaks down, providing an early warning of infection.

If you have diabetes: Ask your doctor if you should use a TempTouch, available with a prescription for about $150.

David G. Armstrong, DPM, PhD, professor of surgery, Rosalind Franklin University of Medicine and Science, North Chicago, Illinois.

■ ■ ■ ■

Warning: Selenium Can Raise Diabetes Risk

In a recent study about the effects of supplemental selenium, almost 5% of people taking 200 micrograms (mcg) of selenium daily developed type 2 diabetes, compared with 3% who develop the disease after using a placebo. Selenium has been promoted for improving glucose metabolism, but the new study suggests that it could be dangerous, not helpful. Most people get enough selenium from their diets to meet the Recommended Dietary Allowance of 55 mcg/day. It's best to avoid selenium supplements, even in multivitamins.

Saverio Stranges, MD, PhD, Clinical Sciences Research Institute, Warwick Medical School, University Hospitals Coventry and Warwickshire, Coventry, England.

Poor Hearing for Older Diabetics

Older people who have diabetes have poorer hearing than people the same age who don't have diabetes. In people age 60 and older with type 2 diabetes, high blood sugar may cause tiny blood vessels in the inner ear to break, disrupting sound reception.

Self-defense: If you have type 2 diabetes, have your hearing tested regularly and wear hearing protection (earplugs, earmuffs, etc.) in all noisy situations—mowing the lawn, using power tools, attending concerts.

Nancy E. Vaughan, PhD, investigator, Department of Veterans Affairs' National Center for Rehabilitative Auditory Research, Portland, Oregon.

How Environmental Toxins May Cause Diabetes

Mark A. Stengler, ND, naturopathic physician in private practice, La Jolla, California...adjunct associate clinical professor at the National College of Natural Medicine, Portland, Oregon...author of many books, including *The Natural Physician's Healing Therapies* and coauthor of *Prescription for Natural Cures* (both from Bottom Line Books)...and author of the *Bottom Line/Natural Healing* newsletter.

Few people would dispute that the root cause of diabetes often is a high-calorie diet that's loaded with simple sugars but deficient in fiber, combined with a lack of exercise. Yet it is increasingly clear that in a world full of man-made chemicals, environmental toxins are contributing to the growing epidemic of diabetes.

How so? *Certain toxic chemicals can...*

•**Destroy the *beta cells* of the pancreas** that are responsible for producing *insulin*, the hormone that regulates blood glucose (sugar) levels.

•**Interfere with the activity of cell receptors** that bring glucose to muscle and fat cells.

•**Exert an estrogenlike effect** that further impairs the cell receptors' ability to use insulin.

NEED-TO-KNOW FACTS ABOUT DIABETES

Insulin is required to transport glucose into our cells for energy production. A deficiency of insulin is the main cause of type 1 diabetes. Of the 20.8 million Americans with diabetes, 5% to 10% have type 1.

Far more common in the US is type 2 diabetes, in which the body's cells ignore insulin, allowing excess amounts of this hormone to build up in the blood. As cells become less effective at accepting and using insulin, blood glucose levels rise. Often, this causes the pancreas to pump out even more insulin.

The dangers: Excess glucose can damage kidneys, nerves and eyes...and excess insulin promotes harmful widespread inflammation and boosts cholesterol production, raising cardiovascular disease risk.

An additional 54 million Americans have the prediabetic condition *insulin resistance* (in which cells do not properly use the hormone insulin to regulate blood sugar). Insulin resistance is the root of a common health problem called *syndrome X* or *metabolic syndrome*, which is characterized by elevated insulin and glucose levels...elevated blood fats (particularly cholesterol and triglycerides)...high blood pressure...overall weight gain...and body fat accumulation around the waist. Insulin resistance frequently leads to type 2 diabetes.

THE CASE AGAINST TOXINS

How many types of toxins are found in the modern-day human body? No one knows. There may be as many as 75,000 man-made chemicals in the environment, so it's reasonable to estimate that several hundred and possibly many more are lodged within us. Since toxins are stored primarily in fatty tissue, being overweight may increase one's toxicity risk.

The federal Centers for Disease Control and Prevention (CDC) researches chemical accumulation in Americans (as measured in blood and urine samples) and publishes its findings biannually in its *National Report on Human Exposure to Environmental Chemicals*. The most recent report includes data on 148 chemicals—from toxic metals (such as mercury, lead, barium and uranium) to pesticides to cigarette smoke—found in air, water, food, soil, dust and consumer products.

The CDC says that *cadmium* (a by-product of cigarette smoke) was detected at alarming levels in 5% of adult Americans—probably due in part to secondhand smoke. Cadmium can cause kidney damage (to which people with diabetes are vulnerable) and weaken bones. Most of the subjects also had many pesticides in their bodies. Pesticides disrupt the cells' ability to accept glucose.

Other studies show that military veterans who were exposed to *dioxin*—a toxic chemical produced during manufacturing processes—have an increased incidence of diabetes. The US Department of Veterans Affairs has added type 2 diabetes to its list of diseases associated with exposure to the dioxin-containing herbicide Agent Orange, used in the Vietnam War.

A 2006 study in the journal *Epidemiology* showed that women with high blood levels of *polychlorinated biphenyls* (PCBs) had a greater risk of diabetes. PCBs are man-made chemicals used as coolants and lubricants. Production in the US halted in 1977, but PCBs break down slowly.

Another recent study involving more than 2,000 Americans published in *Diabetes Care* found a striking association between diabetes and blood levels of six *persistent organic pollutants* (POPs), including PCBs and various pesticides. These pollutants were found in about 80% of the people tested.

If you are concerned about known or unknown exposure to pesticides, dioxin or other toxic chemicals, talk to your doctor about getting blood and/or urine tests to measure the levels of toxins in your body.

POLLUTANT SELF-PROTECTION

Take steps to minimize buildup of the harmful toxins that can lead to diabetes and other health problems. (Supplements below are sold at health food stores, generally are safe and can be taken indefinitely.) *General recommendations for adults...*

•**Eat organic plant foods,** which are grown without harmful pesticides.

•**Select organic poultry and eggs labeled "free range"** (meaning that the animals were not constantly caged and were not fed antibiotics or hormones).

•**Get more fiber from fruits,** vegetables, grains, nuts and seeds. Fiber promotes proper digestive function, so toxins can be eliminated via urine and stool. Fiber also binds with toxins, preventing them from circulating through the body.

•**Drink fresh vegetable juice daily.** Beets, celery, parsley, carrots and burdock root all can be juiced and supply nutrients that help the body to detoxify.

•**Supplement daily with a green-food formula that includes chlorella, spirulina and wheatgrass.** This supports liver and kidney detoxification by binding to toxic metals, which then can be excreted.

Try: Greens+ from Orange Peel Enterprises (800-643-1210, *www.greensplus.com*).

•**Take a daily multivitamin and mineral supplement** to support liver function.

•**Take milk thistle extract daily** to aid liver and kidney detoxification.

A good brand: Nature's Way Thisilyn (800-962-8873, *www.naturesway.com*).

•**Also, take a daily probiotic supplement containing beneficial bacteria,** such as Lactobacillus acidophilus and bifidobacterium, to detoxify the digestive tract.

•**Exercise.** Sweating releases toxins stored in fat.

•**Consider a series of four weekly colonics each year** (a holistic doctor can provide a referral). This infusion of water into the rectum flushes out waste from the lower end of the colon for more complete elimination than bowel movements provide.

•**Take a sauna weekly** to clear toxins from cells.

•**Purify water at home** by installing a reverse osmosis filtering system on each tap...a chlorine-removal filter on your showerhead... and a charcoal filter on your main waterline.

6

Drug News

Breakthrough Antidepressants Bring Faster Relief

 A new class of antidepressants was found to cut the time needed to take effect dramatically when they were tested on rats, according to a recent study.

The study authors, from McGill University in Montreal, Canada, said they hope the finding will spur research into the family of drugs, raising the prospect of faster-acting antidepressants.

BACKGROUND

Antidepressant drugs known as selective serotonin reuptake inhibitors (SSRIs), which include *fluoxetine* (Prozac) and *citalopram* (Celexa), are widely prescribed but can take up to six weeks to take effect, and they don't work for everyone. Many patients have to try several different drugs before achieving success, and only about 65% of people end up responding to a drug, according to researchers.

That time lag can be critical for someone suffering from depression. "During that time, there is a risk of suicide," said Gerald Frye, PhD, Joseph H. Shelton professor of neuropharmacology and neurotoxicology at the Texas A&M Health Science Center College of Medicine's department of neuroscience and experimental therapeutics. "Anything you can do to get a faster response" is desirable, he added.

SSRIs work by enhancing the action of the neurotransmitter serotonin in the brain. The new study looked at a new class of drugs known as serotonin4 (5-HT4) receptor agonists, which have a more specific effect.

"SSRIs interfere with the serotonin system and increase naturally transmitted serotonin to help the system readjust itself," Dr. Frye, who

Gerald Frye, PhD, Joseph H. Shelton Professor of Neuropharmacology and Neurotoxicology, Department of Neuroscience and Experimental Therapeutics, Texas A&M Health Science Center College of Medicine, College Station.
Neuron.

was not involved in the study, explained. "The new drugs act only on one receptor. They're more selective."

THE STUDY

For the animal study, the researchers tested two serotonin receptor agonist compounds, called *RS 67333* and *prucalopride*, against the action of Celexa. Using different measures of depression, the researchers found that the two new drugs acted four to seven times faster and also seemed more powerful.

In one test, the researchers found that one of the serotonin receptor agonists took effect after only three days and completely erased the depressive symptoms after one week.

MORE STUDY NEEDED

The new drugs, however, may have side effects. "There are potential side effects, and that's where the rub could be with clinical trials. The only way we'll know is when a clinical trial [involving humans] is done," said Dr. Frye. "It looks promising from an animal standpoint, and the animal systems they're using are pretty good, but this can only predict. There's no guarantee."

info For more information on depression, visit the Web site of the National Institute of Mental Health at *www.nimh.nih.gov/health/topics/depression*.

Genes Might Make Antidepressant Users Have Suicidal Thoughts

Gonzalo Laje, MD, associate clinical investigator, National Institute of Mental Health, Rockville, Maryland.

Michael Slifer, MD, assistant professor of medicine, University of Miami Institute for Human Genomics.

Duke University Medical Center news release.
American Journal of Psychiatry.

Variations in two genes may help spur suicidal thinking in individuals taking a commonly prescribed antidepressant, research suggests.

Although preliminary, the findings could pave the way for genetic testing to determine which patients with depression are likely to have this unusual but dangerous side effect.

BACKGROUND

There is some evidence that people starting antidepressant medication can develop suicidal ideation, or suicidal thoughts and ideas, although this notion remains controversial.

In 2004, the US Food and Drug Administration (FDA) recommended that the class of drugs known as selective serotonin reuptake inhibitors (SSRIs) carry a strong "black box" warning on the label outlining the possibility of an increase in suicidal ideation.

SSRIs include drugs such as *citalopram* (Celexa), *paroxetine* (Paxil), *fluoxetine* (Prozac) and *sertraline* (Zoloft).

The black box warning was based on studies that found that 4% of those taking SSRIs had suicidal ideation, compared with 2% of the study group taking a placebo.

"It is a severe side effect, but it is unusual," Gonzalo Laje, MD, lead author of the study and associate clinical investigator at the US National Institute of Mental Health stated.

"Given the warnings by regulatory agencies, we thought this would be a very important side effect to look at," said Dr. Laje.

NEW STUDY

The current study was part of the Sequenced Treatment Alternatives to Relieve Depression (STAR*D) trial, the largest trial to date to look at depression in real-world settings. Participants in STAR*D were treated with the SSRI Celexa for up to 14 weeks.

For this study, Dr. Laje and colleagues analyzed DNA samples from 1,915 participants, looking for associations between reports of suicidal ideation and 68 genes.

RESULTS

Versions of two genes were more prevalent in participants reporting suicidal thinking.

While overall about 6% of the patients reported suicidal thoughts when taking Celexa, 36% of patients who carried both of the gene variations reported suicidal ideation. Overall, 59%

of those who reported suicidal ideation had at least one of the suspect gene types.

One percent of the participants had a version of the *kainate receptor gene* (GRIK2) that was associated with eight times the risk for suicidal thinking.

Forty-one percent had a version of the AMPA receptor gene (GRIA3) that was associated with almost double the odds.

Eleven participants, or one-half of one percent, had both versions, which was associated with a 15-fold increase in risk.

Since the researchers only looked at Celexa, it's unknown if the findings extend to other antidepressants, even those in the same class of SSRIs.

This study, published in the *American Journal of Psychiatry*, is the first to find a significant association between a genetic marker and suicidal ideation.

IMPLICATIONS

"These findings, if replicated, would provide a way to have a genetic test that would tell us who is at a higher risk of developing suicidal ideation when taking antidepressants," said Dr. Laje.

"Our long-term goal is to make sure that people with depression can take antidepressants, because treating depression is the best way to avoid suicide," he said.

EXPERT REACTION

Other experts stressed the need for more studies before getting too excited about the finding.

"It's a very important topic," said Michael Slifer, MD, an assistant professor of medicine at the University of Miami Institute for Human Genomics.

Dr. Slifer, who was not involved in the study, added, "Nobody has really looked into what might be different about the background of these folks that have such a difficult time in treatment and get suicidal thoughts. This is a first step, but it's only a first step."

info For more information on depression and its aftereffects, visit the Web site of the Depression and Bipolar Support Alliance at *www.dbsalliance.org*.

Antidepressants Boost GI Bleeding Risk

Wake Forest University Baptist Medical Center, news release.

Antidepressant drugs called selective serotonin reuptake inhibitors (SSRIs), which include *citalopram* (Celexa), *paroxetine* (Paxil), *fluoxetine* (Prozac) and *sertraline* (Zoloft), can double the risk for gastrointestinal bleeding, and the threat is more than six times higher if patients take aspirin and similar pain medications at the same time as SSRIs, a new study finds.

"Clinicians who prescribe these medications should be aware of the potential risk and may need to consider alternatives," said senior researcher Sonal Singh, MD, assistant professor of internal medicine at Wake Forest University School of Medicine, in Winston-Salem, North Carolina.

His team published the findings in the journal *Alimentary Pharmacology & Therapeutics*.

In addition to depression, SSRIs are also used to treat panic disorder and obsessive-compulsive disorder.

THE STUDY

Dr. Singh and colleagues analyzed data from four studies involving 153,000 patients. They found that those taking SSRIs were nearly twice as likely to develop upper GI bleeding as people who weren't taking the drugs.

When patients taking SSRIs also took such nonsteroidal anti-inflammatory drugs (NSAIDs) as aspirin, *ibuprofen* (Advil), *naproxen* (Aleve) and *celecoxib* (Celebrex) they were six times likelier to develop upper GI bleeding than those not taking either type of drug.

IMPLICATION

Dr. Singh and his colleagues estimated that one of every 411 patients over age 50 taking an SSRI, and one out of 82 taking both an SSRI and an NSAID, is likely to develop upper GI bleeding requiring hospitalization.

The combined use of SSRIs and NSAIDs may have a "synergistic effect" that greatly increases the risk for upper GI bleeding beyond the risk posed by each kind of drug alone, the study authors suggested.

info To find out more about GI bleeding, visit the Web site of the American College of Gastroenterology at *www.acg.gi.org/patients/gibleeding*.

Tamoxifen Eases Bipolar Disorder—Faster

Husseini K. Manji, MD, director, mood and anxiety disorders program, National Institute of Mental Health, Bethesda, Maryland.
Gary S. Sachs, MD, director, bipolar clinic and research program, Massachusetts General Hospital, and associate professor, psychiatry, Harvard Medical School, Boston.
Bipolar Disorders, online.

The breast cancer drug tamoxifen helps control the manic phase of bipolar disorder, and it works faster than many standard medications used to treat the chronic mental illness, a new study has found.

Symptoms of bipolar disorder, which affects nearly six million American adults, can be disabling. They include profound mood swings, from depression to the manic phase, during which people can become overly excited and energetic but also irritable, before they plunge into depression again.

"One of the problems with existing treatments for bipolar disorder is they seem to have this long period before they start to work," explained Husseini K. Manji, MD, senior study author and director of the US National Institute of Mental Health's mood and anxiety disorders program.

Current treatments sometimes take weeks to become effective, Dr. Manji said, "and that obviously creates a huge problem." When patients are in the manic phase, particularly, not getting relief fast enough from medication may mean they need to be hospitalized, he noted.

THE STUDY

Dr. Manji and his colleagues gave eight patients experiencing a manic episode tamoxifen, while another eight received a placebo. No one knew which drug they were getting. After three weeks, 63% of those on tamoxifen had reduced symptoms of mania, compared to just 13% of those on a placebo. The tamoxifen group responded by the fifth day of treatment.

HOW IT WORKS

Dr. Manji and his colleagues studied tamoxifen because they knew that standard medications used to treat mania are known to lower the activity of an enzyme—called protein *kinase C*, or *PKC*—that regulates activities in brain cells. This enzyme is believed to become overactive when bipolar disorder patients experience a manic episode.

Tamoxifen also blocks PKC, but does it more directly than some bipolar drugs, according to the researchers.

For the study, Dr. Manji said, "we started with 20 milligrams [of tamoxifen] a day. It was increased each day, usually up to 100 milligrams a day. Literally, at day five we saw this significant anti-mania effect," he said, adding that with standard medications it would have taken three weeks to see results. "If we had something that would nip mania in the bud, it might save people from being hospitalized and getting sedating agents."

A new bipolar drug would not be tamoxifen itself, he said, but rather another medicine that mimics what tamoxifen does in the brain. The development of such a drug would probably take at least five years before it could be approved for marketing, he said.

EXPERT REACTION

Gary S. Sachs, MD, director of the bipolar clinic and research program at Massachusetts General Hospital and associate professor of psychiatry at Harvard Medical School, called the results "encouraging."

"I wouldn't say this study proves that tamoxifen works faster than standard [treatment,]" Dr. Sachs said, since a head-to-head comparison was not done. But, while not definitive, "the study has important findings," he said.

info To learn more about bipolar disorder, visit the Bipolar World Web site at *www.bipolarworld.net*.

Warning! You Should Never Mix Medications

Cynthia Kuhn, PhD, professor in the department of pharmacology at Duke University School of Medicine, Durham, North Carolina, and codirector of Brainworks, a Duke program that develops education programs about the brain. She has studied the effects of alcohol, drugs and hormones on brain development and is a coauthor of *Buzzed: The Straight Facts About the Most Used and Abused Drugs from Alcohol to Ecstasy.* W.W. Norton.

The office of the chief medical examiner of New York City reported that the death of 28-year-old actor Heath Ledger was caused by a combination of prescription drugs—two narcotic pain relievers combined with antianxiety medication and sleep aids.

The use of multiple drugs is inherently risky. The FDA has identified thousands of potential drug interactions, many of which are minor. Serious problems tend to occur when patients take two or more drugs that affect the same body system. Each of the drugs used by Ledger, for example, can potentially affect cellular receptors that regulate breathing. Taken together, they had additive effects—the combination was more powerful than the effects of any one of the drugs taken alone.

According to the federal Substance Abuse and Mental Health Services Administration, nearly 600,000 emergency room visits in 2005 (the most recent year for which data is available) involved prescription or over-the-counter drugs or supplements.

Caution: The risk for drug interactions is highest among the elderly. They tend to use the most drugs, and their bodies metabolize (break down) drugs more slowly than younger adults.

HOW INTERACTIONS HAPPEN

Patients who use medications appropriately —taking the prescribed doses for only particular conditions and regularly reviewing drug use with a physician—are unlikely to have serious problems.

Main risks: Different drugs prescribed by more than one doctor...using drugs to treat conditions for which they weren't originally prescribed (many people stockpile leftover drugs and use them later, possibly for unrelated conditions)...or using a drug that was appropriate initially but might be dangerous when combined with drugs a patient has subsequently started taking.

Protect yourself by frequently updating a list of the drugs and supplements you take. Review the list with every doctor at every office visit and whenever a new drug is prescribed.

Most common dangerous drug interactions...

OPIOID PAINKILLERS/SEDATIVES

Opioid painkillers, such as *hydrocodone* and *oxycodone*, have powerful effects on the central nervous system. Even on their own, they can suppress breathing when taken in high enough doses. The risk is much higher when they're combined with sedating drugs, such as those used to treat anxiety or insomnia. These include the benzodiazepine class of medications, such as *diazepam* (Valium) and *alprazolam* (Xanax).

Many people take these drugs in combination. For example, someone might take alprazolam for chronic anxiety, then add hydrocodone following an injury. The drugs often are prescribed by different doctors who don't know the patient's drug history.

What to do: Never combine prescription painkillers and sedatives without your doctor's knowledge and approval.

WARFARIN/ANTIBIOTICS/NSAIDs

The blood thinner *warfarin* (Coumadin) is notorious for interacting with other drugs. It has a narrow "therapeutic index," the difference between a helpful and a toxic dose. Drugs that increase the effects of warfarin can lead to uncontrolled bleeding.

Many antibiotics and antifungal drugs, including *erythromycin, ciprofloxacin* and *ketoconazole*, are broken down by the same liver enzyme that metabolizes warfarin. Taking warfarin and any of these drugs together may deplete the enzyme, leading to higher levels of warfarin in the body.

What to do: If you have an infection, your doctor can prescribe an antibiotic that is less likely to interact with warfarin. Antibiotics that are less likely to cause an interaction include *penicillin, amoxicillin, ampicillin* and *tetracycline*.

Caution: Warfarin may cause gastrointestinal bleeding when combined with aspirin, ibuprofen or other nonsteroidal anti-inflammatory drugs (NSAIDs). If you take warfarin and need a painkiller, *acetaminophen* (Tylenol) might be a better choice.

MULTIPLE ANTIDEPRESSANTS

Patients who combine selective serotonin reuptake inhibitor (SSRI) antidepressants, such as *fluoxetine* (Prozac) and *sertraline* (Zoloft), or who combine an SSRI with another type of antidepressant may experience *serotonin syndrome*, a rare but potentially fatal reaction.

Many antidepressants increase brain levels of serotonin, a chemical produced by some neurons (nerve cells). Patients who combine antidepressants or take too much of one can accumulate toxic levels of serotonin. This can cause dangerously elevated blood pressure, known as a *hypertensive crisis*.

Serotonin syndrome usually occurs when patients switch from an SSRI antidepressant to a monoamine oxidase inhibitor (MAOI), an older type of antidepressant, without allowing time for the first drug to wash out of the body.

What to do: Follow your doctor's instructions exactly when discontinuing an antidepressant. Most of these drugs have to be tapered—slowly decreasing the dose over a period of weeks—before starting a new drug.

Caution: Combining an MAOI drug with an appetite stimulant, such as *sibutramine* (Meridia), also can cause serotonin syndrome.

VIAGRA/NITRATES

Men who take nitrate drugs (such as *nitroglycerine*) for heart problems should never take *sildenafil* (Viagra) without a doctor's supervision.

Viagra and similar drugs for treating erectile dysfunction cause blood vessels to relax. Nitrate drugs do the same thing. Combining them can cause a dangerous drop in blood pressure.

What to do: Men who take nitrates for heart problems can talk to their doctors about safer alternatives for treating erectile dysfunction, including vacuum devices or penile injections.

ACETAMINOPHEN FROM MULTIPLE PRODUCTS

Taken in excessive doses, the pain reliever acetaminophen can cause liver damage.

Main risk: Combining acetaminophen—for treating arthritis pain, for example—with unrelated products (such as cold/flu remedies) that also contain acetaminophen.

What to do: When using acetaminophen, don't exceed the dose listed on the product label—and check labels to ensure that you don't take another product that contains acetaminophen simultaneously.

Boost Your Medicine's Healing Powers

Leo Galland, MD, director, Foundation for Integrated Medicine, New York City. He is also creator of the Drug–Nutrient Workshop, a nutritional and dietary software tool for analyzing interactions among drugs, foods and supplements (*www.nutritionworkshop.com*). His most recent book is *The Fat Resistance Diet*. Broadway. *www.fatresistancediet.com*. Dr. Galland is a recipient of the Linus Pauling Award.

I f you're among the millions of Americans taking medication for pain, asthma or allergies, hypertension, high cholesterol or depression, research shows that you may be able to maximize the benefits…curb the side effects…and maybe even lower the dosages of your drugs by combining them with the right supplements.

Important: Consult your doctor before adding a supplement to your drug regimen. Some supplements can interact adversely with medications—for example, some research shows that fish oil can reduce the time it takes for blood to clot and should be used with caution by people taking a blood thinner, such as *warfarin* (Coumadin).

Supplements (available at health food stores) to consider using if you are taking any of the following…

ANTIDEPRESSANT

Supplement with: 1,000 milligrams (mg) to 2,000 mg daily of *eicosapentaenoic acid* (EPA), an omega-3 fatty acid found in fish oil. (Ask your doctor which dosage is right for you.)

What it does: Omega-3s are believed to enhance the ability of the brain chemical *serotonin* to act on the nervous system. In a recent British study, when depressed patients who were taking a prescription antidepressant, such as *fluoxetine* (Prozac) or *sertraline* (Zoloft), added 1,000 mg of EPA to their daily regimen for 12 weeks, they reported significantly less depression, anxiety and suicidal thoughts, as well as improved sleep, libido and energy.

Most standard fish oil supplements contain only 200 mg to 300 mg of EPA, so you'd need up to 10 capsules daily to get the recommended 1,000 mg to 2,000 mg of EPA. If you don't want to take that many capsules, take liquid fish oil—in an amount equal to 1,000 mg to 2,000 mg daily of EPA.

Helpful: To avoid "fishy-tasting" burping (the most frequent complaint), try taking the capsules on an empty stomach with a large glass of water. Some people also find that this unpleasant aftertaste is less likely to occur with liquid fish oil.

Also try: 500 micrograms (mcg) daily of folic acid, which promotes proper functioning of the nervous system. Low levels of folic acid have been linked to depression.

Harvard Medical School researchers report that depressed patients who had achieved remission with fluoxetine were 13 times more likely to relapse during a six-month period if they had low blood levels of folic acid.

Caution: Supplemental folic acid may mask a vitamin B-12 deficiency, which can lead to nerve damage. Take a 500-mcg to 1,000-mcg B-12 supplement daily to prevent worsening of a B-12 deficiency.

NONSTEROIDAL ANTI-INFLAMMATORY DRUG

Supplement with: 350 mg of *deglycyrrhizinated licorice* (DGL), three times daily.

What it does: Studies show that DGL may reduce or prevent the gastrointestinal (GI) inflammation, bleeding and ulcerations caused by aspirin and other nonsteroidal anti-inflammatory drugs (NSAIDs)—both prescription and over-the-counter.

Caution: Whole licorice extract also protects the stomach, but it contains *glycyrrhetinic acid,* which even in small doses may raise blood pressure. Stick with DGL.

Also try: 1,000 mg to 2,000 mg daily of vitamin C (in two divided doses) and 7 grams (g) of powdered glutamine (one heaping teaspoon dissolved in water, three times daily). Studies suggest that taking 1,000 mg of vitamin C twice daily may help prevent aspirin-induced inflammation of the small intestine.

Meanwhile, the amino acid glutamine, long used to help heal ulcers, may decrease the intestinal toxicity of other NSAIDs.

ASTHMA OR ALLERGY DRUG

Supplement with: 1,000 mg daily of *gamma-linolenic acid* (GLA) and 500 mg daily of EPA.

What it does: GLA, an omega-6 fatty acid derived from evening primrose oil or borage oil, may inhibit production of *leukotrienes,* molecules that trigger inflammation and constriction of the bronchial airways. The asthma drug *montelukast* (Singulair) also works by inhibiting leukotrienes.

Important: Most omega-6 fatty acids (including those found in many processed foods) *increase* inflammation, unless they're balanced by sufficient amounts of anti-inflammatory omega-3s. GLA, however, is an anti-inflammatory, but at high doses—and in the absence of omega-3s—it can become inflammatory. The recommended 500 mg of EPA daily creates an optimal balance of omega-6s and omega-3s.

Also try: Quercetin, a bioflavonoid derived from red onions, apples and other foods. In laboratory studies, quercetin has demonstrated antihistamine and anti-allergenic properties. Clinical trials are needed, but given its safety, I often recommend quercetin to my asthma and allergy patients. Try using 500 mg to 600 mg, twice daily, of quercetin—taken on an empty stomach for maximum benefit—as an adjunct to your antihistamine and/or GLA.

BLOOD PRESSURE DRUG

Supplement with: 1,000 mg of *arginine,* twice daily.

What it does: Arginine (also called L-arginine) is an amino acid used by the body to produce nitric oxide (NO), a molecule that helps keep blood vessels flexible and able to dilate—both of which stabilize blood pressure. Legumes (such as lentils, black beans and kidney beans) and whole grains (such as brown rice) contain some arginine, but you'll need a supplement to get the 2,000 mg daily that is recommended for blood vessel health.

Caution: Because some research has shown that arginine can be dangerous for people who have suffered a heart attack, it should not be used by these individuals. If you have the herpes simplex virus and want to take arginine, you may need to add 1,500 mg daily of lysine, another amino acid. The virus grows in the presence of arginine but is inhibited by lysine.

Also try: 100 mg daily of *Pycnogenol*. This plant extract appears to enhance NO synthesis in blood vessels. In a recent placebo-controlled trial, Chinese researchers found that hypertensive patients who took 100 mg of Pycnogenol daily for 12 weeks were able to significantly lower their dose of a calcium channel blocker, a popular category of blood pressure drugs.

STATIN

Supplement with: 100 mg daily of coenzyme Q10 (CoQ10).

What it does: Cholesterol-lowering statins deplete the naturally produced molecule coenzyme Q10—this depletion may lead to muscle damage.

Researchers at Stony Brook University in Stony Brook, New York, found that patients taking statins who added 100 mg of CoQ10 daily for one month reported a 40% reduction in severity of muscle pain, a common side effect of statins.

CoQ10 also may prevent oxidation of LDL "bad" cholesterol—an unfortunate side effect of statins that occurs to LDL cholesterol particles not eliminated by the drug.

Also try: Fish oil that contains 1,500 mg of EPA and 1,300 mg of *docosahexaenoic acid* (DHA) daily. Studies show that these essential fatty acids raise HDL "good" cholesterol and lower dangerous blood fats known as triglycerides—making EPA and DHA a valuable adjunct to statins, which mainly target elevated LDL cholesterol.

Warning! Side Effects Of Taking Supplements With Common Drugs

George T. Grossberg, MD, the Samuel W. Fordyce Endowed Chair in Geriatric Psychiatry in the department of neurology and psychiatry at St. Louis University School of Medicine in St. Louis, Missouri. He is the author, with Barry Fox, PhD, of *The Essential Herb-Drug-Vitamin Interaction Guide*. Broadway.

Most doctors warn their patients about the potential dangers of combining medications, but few take the time—and some are not well-informed enough—to offer guidance on the harmful effects of taking certain vitamins and/or herbs with prescription drugs.

New study: Among 132 pharmacists surveyed, 47% had seen a patient with a suspected side effect from a vitamin-drug or herb-drug interaction, according to research published in an issue of *The Annals of Pharmacotherapy*.

Hidden danger: The problem is particularly common among Americans over age 65, who comprise 14% of the US population but take 40% of all drugs, vitamins and herbs.

Older people also are more sensitive to the side effects of vitamin–drug or herb–drug interactions due to changes in metabolism and the brain.

HARMFUL INTERACTIONS

When some vitamins and/or herbs are taken with certain drugs, the supplement can...

•**Weaken** the effectiveness of the drug.

Example: The herb astragalus, which is used to boost immunity, may reduce the immunosuppressive effects of such drugs as *cortisone* (Cortone).

•**Strengthen** the effectiveness of the drug, causing a type of drug overdose.

Example: Black cohosh, an herb used to control the symptoms of menopause, can lower blood pressure.

If taken with an antihypertensive medication, it can cause *hypotension* (severely low blood pressure) with symptoms such as dizziness and fatigue.

VITAMIN–DRUG INTERACTIONS

Vitamins that are among the most likely to cause dangerous interactions with drugs…*

•**Vitamin A** promotes immunity, proper bone growth and healthy skin. It also plays a role in night vision and the growth and maintenance of cells of the gastrointestinal tract.

Recommended Dietary Allowance (RDA): 2,300 international units (IU) for women…3,000 IU for men.

Supplemental vitamin A may interact with drugs including: The anticoagulant warfarin—vitamin A can increase the risk for bleeding and bruising.

•**Vitamin B-6** is involved in digestion, the production of red blood cells and the maintenance of a healthy brain and nervous system.

RDA: 1.3 milligram (mg) for all adults ages 19 to 50…1.5 mg for women over age 50…1.7 mg for men over age 50.

Supplemental vitamin B-6 may interact with drugs including: *Amiodarone* (Cordarone), taken for heart arrhythmias—B-6 may increase skin sensitivity to sunlight…*carbidopa and levodopa* (Sinemet), taken for Parkinson's disease—B-6 may interfere with the medication's effectiveness…*theophylline* (Elixophyllin), taken for asthma—B-6 may increase the risk for seizures induced by theophylline.

•**Vitamin C** is important for immunity and helps the body manufacture and repair blood vessels, skin, muscles, teeth, bones, tendons, ligaments, hormones and neurotransmitters.

RDA: 75 mg for women…90 mg for men.

Supplemental vitamin C may interact with drugs including: The bloodthinners *heparin* (Hepalean) or *warfarin* (Coumadin), taken for cardiovascular disease—vitamin C may reduce the effectiveness of these drugs.

•**Calcium** helps build strong bones and assists in wound healing, blood clotting, cellular metabolism and muscle contraction.

Adequate intake (AI): 1,000 mg for adults ages 19 to 50…1,200 mg for adults over age 50.

Supplemental calcium may interact with drugs including: Digitalis drugs, such as *digoxin* (Lanoxin), which improve the heart's

*Multivitamins or individual supplements containing nutrients that exceed the RDA may cause interactions.

strength and efficiency—calcium can decrease digitalis levels…*aminoglycoside* antibiotics, especially *gentamicin* (Alcomicin)—calcium can increase the risk for kidney failure.

HERB–DRUG INTERACTIONS

Herbs that are among the most likely to cause dangerous interactions with drugs…

•**Valerian,** a mild sedative, is used to treat insomnia and anxiety.

Lowest effective dose: 400 mg, up to two hours before bedtime.

Valerian may interact with drugs including: A selective serotonin reuptake inhibitor (SSRI), such as *sertraline* (Zoloft), or tricyclic antidepressant, such as *desipramine* (Norpramin)—valerian can cause excessive sedation, depression and mental impairment.

•**Grapeseed extract** is rich in powerful antioxidants called *procyanidolic oligomers* (PCOs). It is used to treat high blood pressure, heart disease, varicose veins and macular degeneration.

Lowest effective dose: 75 mg daily.

Grapeseed extract may interact with drugs including: A blood-thinning medication, such as aspirin or warfarin—grapeseed extract can increase the risk for bleeding and bruising.

•**Yohimbe** is an African herb that improves blood flow. It is sometimes prescribed for men who have erectile dysfunction.

Lowest effective dose: 5.4 mg daily.

Yohimbe may interact with drugs including: The allergy medication *phenylephrine,* found in over-the-counter products, such as Vicks Sinex Nasal Spray, or in prescription drugs, such as *promethazine hydrochloride* (Phenergan)…or the asthma medication *albuterol* (Proventil)—yohimbe can cause a potentially dangerous increase in heart rate and blood pressure.

•**Apple cider vinegar** is a popular folk remedy that has been used to treat arthritis, high blood pressure and leg cramps.

Lowest effective dose: One tablespoon daily.

Apple cider vinegar may interact with drugs including: Medication for congestive heart failure and/or high blood pressure, such as digoxin, *furosemide* (Lasix) and *hydrochloro-thiazide* (Microzide)—apple cider vinegar can increase the risk for *hypokalemia* (low potassium levels), which can further complicate heart disease.

•**Evening primrose oil** delivers high levels of *gamma-linolenic acid* (GLA), an essential fatty acid. It is used to treat premenstrual syndrome, hot flashes, high blood pressure (during pregnancy) and rheumatoid arthritis.

Lowest effective dose: 540 mg daily.

Evening primrose oil may interact with drugs including: Antiseizure medications, such as *clonazepam* (Klonopin)—evening primrose oil can lower the effectiveness of such drugs, making a seizure more likely.

HOW TO STAY SAFE

You can take vitamins and/or herbs safely if you use them with the supervision of your primary care physician. Talk to your doctor first.

Helpful: Take a bottle of the supplement to your next appointment so your doctor determine whether it is likely to cause adverse interactions with any of your medications. Or call your doctor and read the supplement's ingredient list to him/her. Also, check the Web site of the National Institutes of Health's Office of Dietary Supplements, *www.ods.od.nih.gov*, for information about vitamins and herbs that interact with prescription medications.

Safest approach: The lower the dose of the vitamin and/or herb, the less likely it is to interact with a drug.

Generic Drug Dangers

Joe Graedon, a pharmacologist, and Teresa Graedon, PhD, consumer advocates who specialize in health issues related to drugs, herbs and vitamins. Their syndicated newspaper column "The People's Pharmacy" is widely distributed in the US and abroad, and they cohost an award-winning radio talk show. They are coauthors of 12 books, including *Best Choices from The People's Pharmacy*. Rodale.

Generic drugs cost 30% to 80% less than their brand-name counterparts, but most people feel safe taking them because the FDA requires that both types of medications provide the same active ingredients and level of effectiveness.

Recent development: A survey found that about 25% of 300 doctors throughout the US don't believe that generics are chemically identical to brand-name drugs…nearly one in five believe that generics are less safe…and more than one in four believe that generics cause more side effects.

So what's the truth about generic drugs?

WHAT PATIENTS SAY

Since 1976, when our book *The People's Pharmacy* was originally published as a consumer guide to drug and health information, thousands of patients have contacted us about their experiences with medications.

In the last few years, we've received hundreds of letters and E-mails—most of them complaints—about generic drugs, including pain relievers, antidepressants and blood pressure medicines. The number of such complaints has increased dramatically in that time.

What we've learned: Some patients who switch from a brand-name to a generic drug report a decline in effectiveness—for example, blood pressure that isn't controlled as well or a worsening of depression. Others report having a rash or other types of allergic reactions, probably due to one of the inactive "filler" ingredients in generic drugs. There also seem to be problems with the timed-release mechanism of some generics.

Example: We've heard more than 100 complaints about a generic version of the long-acting antidepressant Wellbutrin XL. At least one manufacturer's timed-release generic formulation appears to be different from the brand name—and may be releasing too much of the drug too quickly (known as "dose dumping"). This would explain many of the side effects, such as headaches and anxiety, that some people tell us they experience when they take the generic drug, but not the brand-name version.

We've contacted the FDA about the complaints regarding this generic drug, and we're also working with an independent laboratory to analyze this formulation.

IS THE FDA DOING ENOUGH?

Drug companies must apply to the FDA to sell generic versions of drugs. To gain FDA approval, a generic drug must contain the same active ingredients as brand-name medications and meet the same criteria for such factors as quality, strength and purity. *Possible problems with generic drugs...*

•**Periodic checks for impurities.** The FDA monitors generic drugs, testing for such things as proper dosing and active ingredients. But the agency only checks a few hundred tablets and capsules among the brand-name and generic products a year—out of a total of more than *three billion* prescriptions.

•**Infrequent inspections.** The FDA is supposed to inspect each US drug manufacturing plant every two years—but lacks the resources to meet that requirement.

•**Overseas manufacturing.** An enormous percentage of drug ingredients and raw materials for drugs (primarily generic and over-the-counter) come from India, China and other countries where quality assurance is not as rigorous as in the US—and where drug counterfeiting has been a problem.

Trap: Overseas plants are inspected much less frequently than those in the US. Without testing, there's no way to tell whether drugs and drug ingredients derived from these plants have impurities—or come in "subtherapeutic" doses (for example, a drug labeled as 10 milligrams (mg) may be only 6 mg).

STAYING SAFE

Most of the evidence for problems with generic drugs is based on anecdotal reports. However, research published in *Neurology* in 2004 reported that people with epilepsy who switched from the brand-name form of the antiseizure drug *phenytoin* (Dilantin) to the generic form of the drug began to have higher-than-expected rates of seizures.

Investigators found that in many patients, blood levels of the active ingredient had dropped by 30%.

Even so, patients should not give up on generic drugs. The cost savings can be considerable...and there's no evidence so far that the majority of generic drugs will cause problems for most patients. *Patients using generic drugs should simply take extra precautions...*

•**Stick with one manufacturer.** This is particularly important if you're taking a drug with a *narrow therapeutic index* (NTI), such as the anticoagulant warfarin, the antipsychotic *lithium* or the anticonvulsant *carbamazepine*. NTI drugs, which typically require periodic blood tests to measure blood levels of the medications, have a very thin margin between an effective dose and a toxic dose.

If you're taking a generic form, ask your pharmacist for the name of the manufacturer—and request that the pharmacy stick with that company, if possible, to avoid variations between products.

•**Track your numbers.** Many conditions, such as hypertension or high cholesterol, don't cause obvious symptoms.

The best way to tell whether a drug is working is to monitor your numbers—by taking daily blood pressure readings, tracking blood-sugar levels and keeping track of cholesterol levels with frequent blood tests at your doctor's office.

Important: Ask your doctor to give you copies of your test results.

Check them periodically to make sure that you're maintaining adequate control—particularly if you've recently switched from a brand name to a generic, or the reverse.

•**Trust your instincts.** Some medications affect the body in subtle ways. A patient taking a thyroid drug, for example, might feel slightly run-down if it isn't working exactly the way it should, even if test results appear to be normal. *Pay attention.* If you've switched to a generic and notice a difference—either in effectiveness or side effects—tell your doctor.

•**Do a "challenge, rechallenge" test.** If you suspect that a generic drug isn't working the way it should, write down changes in how long the drug works and side effects.

Then, ask your doctor to switch you to the brand-name equivalent, and see if there's improvement—in most cases, it will be apparent in about two weeks. Under the close supervision of your doctor, repeat the test, going back and forth until you have a clear idea which drug is more effective for you.

•**Report problems to the FDA.*** The FDA can analyze generic drugs to determine if they contain the stated amount of active ingredient. When reporting a drug to the FDA, ask your pharmacist to provide you with some basic information. You will need the name of the manufacturer, the lot number and exactly when the drug was dispensed to you.

If you'd also like to report problems with generic drugs to us, go to The People's Pharmacy Web site, *www.peoplespharmacy.org*.

info The US Food and Drug Administration has an Office of Generic Drugs. For further information visit their Web site *www.fda.gov/cder/ogd/*.

■ ■ ■ ■

"Generic Equivalent" vs. "Generic Alternative" Drugs

Generic equivalent has a specific legal definition. It means a non-brand-name product is identical in active ingredients to a brand-name product.

Example: The cholesterol-lowering drug *simvastatin* is the generic equivalent of Zocor.

A "generic alternative" is a medication in the same class that is not chemically identical to the brand name.

Example: If you are taking the statin Lipitor, you cannot yet buy a generic equivalent, because Lipitor is still under patent protection. Instead, if your doctor agrees, you could try the less expensive simvastatin, which is not chemically identical to Lipitor—in which case you would be using a generic alternative.

Larry Sasich, PharmD, MPH, FASHP, acting chair, department of pharmacy practice, School of Pharmacy, Lake Erie College of Osteopathic Medicine, Erie, Pennsylvania. He is coauthor of *Worst Pills, Best Pills*. Public Citizen.

*Go to the FDA Web site, *www.fda.gov/medwatch*, or call 888-463-6332.

Three Common Drugs That Send Seniors to the ER

Daniel Budnitz, MD, medical officer, US Centers for Disease Control and Prevention, Atlanta.
Knight Steel, Maryland, chief of geriatrics, Hackensack University Medical Center, New Jersey.
Annals of Internal Medicine.

Side effects from just three drugs are responsible for one-third of all US emergency room visits by senior citizens who had adverse reactions to medications, a new study found.

In a two-year period, the blood thinner *warfarin* (Coumadin), the diabetes drug *insulin* and the heart drug *digoxin* (Lanoxin, Digitek) caused about 58,000 emergency room visits a year in those 65 and older, the researchers found. The major problem is that it's hard to determine the correct dose for each drug, said study lead author Daniel Budnitz, MD, a medical officer with the US Centers for Disease Control and Prevention (CDC).

"It's challenging," he said, "and it takes work between the patient and physician to get the dose just right."

THE STUDY

The researchers looked at several surveys of emergency room visits from 2004 and 2005. The study findings are published in *Annals of Internal Medicine.*

Dr. Budnitz and his colleagues undertook the study to determine the danger posed to senior citizens by a long list of drugs that have been deemed "potentially inappropriate" for use in the elderly.

Forty-one drugs are on the list of potentially inappropriate drugs for the elderly, called the Beers criteria. But they accounted for just 3.6% of a total of about 177,000 annual emergency room visits.

Warfarin, insulin and digoxin posed many more problems. (Digoxin is also on the Beers list, but it's only listed as a potential problem if taken in certain situations.)

Warfarin, often prescribed to heart patients, prevents blood clots by thinning the blood, but can cause excessive bleeding if the blood becomes too thin. Insulin treats diabetes but can sometimes cause blood sugar levels to drop to dangerous levels. And digoxin, a long-used drug, can cause a variety of problems from nausea to potentially dangerous heart rhythm disturbances.

IMPLICATIONS

In some cases, there aren't good alternatives to these three drugs, although some doctors consider digoxin to have outlived its usefulness, the study authors noted.

Doctors can monitor the levels of all three drugs with blood tests, Dr. Budnitz said. Simple finger-prick blood tests allow testing of blood sugar levels, and similar tests measuring clotting ability are now available in some clinics for people taking warfarin, he said.

The study results are "a reminder that doctors and patients need to work on doing the best job we can managing these medicines," Dr. Budnitz said. "The answer isn't to take away medications."

Dr. Knight Steel, head of geriatric medicine at Hackensack University Medical Center in New Jersey, said the study results aren't really surprising. Doctors have long known the risks of the three drugs in question, he said.

info To learn more about the health risks that drugs can pose to the elderly, visit the Duke University Health System Web site, *www. dukehealth.org/HealthLibrary/News/7994.*

Survive Prostate Cancer With Statin Drugs

Michael J. Zelefsky, MD, professor, radiation oncology, Memorial Sloan-Kettering Cancer Center, New York City.

Eric Horwitz, MD, clinical director, radiation oncology, Fox Chase Cancer Center, Philadelphia.

American Society for Therapeutic Radiology and Oncology annual meeting.

Men who were taking statins to lower their cholesterol had a 10% greater chance of being cured of prostate cancer by radiation therapy 10 years after diagnosis, a new study finds.

It's an "intriguing and very interesting finding," but falls short of supporting statin use for all prostate cancer patients, said study author Michael J. Zelefsky, MD, a professor of radiation oncology at Memorial Sloan-Kettering Cancer Center in New York City. "But I would encourage men to see their internist and get on the medications if their blood cholesterol warranted it," he said.

THE STUDY

Dr. Zelefsky reported on 871 men given radiation therapy for prostate cancer between 1995 and 2000. The five-year relapse-free survival rate for the 168 men taking statins was 91% while the 10-year survival rate was 76%. That compares to 81% and 66%, respectively, for those not taking the drugs.

POSSIBLE EXPLANATIONS

"There have been some reports of a lower risk of developing prostate cancer for those men who have been on statins," Dr. Zelefsky said, but the possible mechanisms by which the drugs might help prevent the disease or cure it are unknown.

"There was a suggestion made of a possible added benefit by an interaction between the drug and radiation," he said. "Or does it have its own independent effect? That is possible as well."

MORE STUDIES SUPPORT LINK

Two recent reports have linked statin use with a lower risk of developing prostate cancer. One study, from the University of Alabama, Birmingham, found a decline in prostate cancer death rates that was most notable among white men who used statins.

Another study, from Duke University Medical Center, found lower blood levels of prostate-specific antigen (PSA), a potential marker of the cancer, among men taking statins.

CLINICAL TRIAL NEEDED

Dr. Zelefsky noted that these studies suggesting a beneficial effect of statins on prostate cancer, might fuel doctors to undertake a randomized, controlled trial, which is the best way to corroborate such an effect.

Eric Horwitz, MD, clinical director of radiation oncology at the Fox Chase Cancer Center in Philadelphia, said he agreed with Dr. Zelefsky's call for a tightly monitored clinical trial. "There has been great success in running these large tests, and I'm sure it can be done."

A study on statin use in prostate cancer prevention or treatment should center on men at higher risk. In other words, Dr. Zelefsky said, "older men with a family history."

There is "no significant downside" to statin use in such studies because the drugs have a low rate of adverse side effects, he said.

As it is, many men diagnosed with prostate cancer are already taking statins, and there is no reason for them to stop, Dr. Horwitz said. "This report is reassuring because of the overlap."

info For more on prostate cancer, visit the National Cancer Institute Web site, *www. cancer.gov* and click on "Prostate Cancer."

■ ■ ■ ■

Millions Taking Drug That Doesn't Work

Zetia—and a pill that contains it, Vytorin—failed to slow the accumulation of plaque in arteries.

Result: Millions of patients may be taking a drug that doesn't benefit them.

Going forward: Discuss with your doctor whether Zetia or Vytorin is the best therapy for you, or if you should take a more standard statin therapy.

Steven Nissen, MD, chairman, department of cardiovascular medicine, Cleveland Clinic, Ohio.

■ ■ ■ ■

Statin Lowers Dementia Risk by Nearly 50%

Researchers who analyzed medical data on more than 700,000 users of *simvastatin* (Zocor) found that the cholesterol-lowering drug was associated with a reduction in incidence of Alzheimer's disease and Parkinson's disease by nearly 50% in people age 65 or older who had taken statins for at least seven months. No similar results were found in study subjects taking the statins *lovastatin* (Mevacor) or *atorvastatin* (Lipitor).

Theory: Simvastatin's beneficial effect may be due to its ability to enter the brain and reduce both inflammation and cholesterol. More research is needed, but if you take simvastatin to lower cholesterol, a brain-protective effect may be an added benefit.

Benjamin Wolozin, MD, PhD, professor of pharmacology, Boston University School of Medicine.

■ ■ ■ ■

Don't Forget: Statins Can Cause Memory Loss

Cognitive problems are the second most common side effect of the cholesterol-lowering drugs, after muscle pain and weakness. Despite recent evidence linking statins with the prevention and treatment of Alzheimer's disease, people taking Lipitor, Zocor, Pravachol, Mevacor and other statins have reported a variety of cognitive disturbances, including slowly developing memory problems, disorientation, confusion and, in some cases, temporary complete amnesia lasting for hours or days. Generally, these memory problems disappear with time, but in some people, they can last for years. This side effect is not widely known.

Self-defense: Talk with your doctor about the benefits and risks of taking statins to lower cholesterol.

Julian Whitaker, MD, director, Whitaker Wellness Institute, Newport Beach, California, and author of *Dr. Julian Whitaker's Health & Healing. www.drwhitaker.com.*

■ ■ ■ ■

New Patch Treats Alzheimer's

People with mild-to-moderate Alzheimer's disease can now get help from a skin patch. The patch—recently approved by the FDA—contains *rivastigmine* (Exelon), a drug previously available only in capsule form and as an oral solution. The patch delivers the drug continuously throughout the day and causes fewer gastrointestinal side effects, such as nausea and vomiting, than the oral forms.

William Thies, PhD, vice president, medical and scientific relations, Alzheimer's Association, Chicago.

■ ■ ■ ■

Hypertension Drugs May Fight Alzheimer's

In experiments on mice genetically at risk for Alzheimer's, seven of 55 hypertension drugs tested slowed the buildup of beta-amyloid proteins, which form plaque in the brains of people with Alzheimer's. A study on humans has not yet been planned.

Giulio Maria Pasinetti, MD, PhD, Mount Sinai School of Medicine, New York City, and leader of the mouse study, published in *The Journal of Clinical Investigation*.

Low-Dose Aspirin Best Way to Reduce Heart Disease

Charles Campbell, MD, director of the Coronary Care Unit at the University of Kentucky's Gill Heart Institute and an assistant professor of medicine, both in Lexington. Dr. Campbell was lead author of an article on aspirin in the *Journal of the American Medical Association*.

Studies show that taking aspirin daily can lower heart attack risk by 33% and reduce your combined risk for heart attack, stroke and cardiovascular death by 15%.

Despite these well-established cardiovascular benefits, doctors disagree on the optimal dose of aspirin—about 60% favor one 81 milligrams (mg) dose daily (often referred to as "low-dose" or baby aspirin), while about 35% recommend 325 mg daily (a standard-sized tablet).

What's new: At the University of Kentucky, researchers analyzed 11 major clinical trials comparing different aspirin doses in 10,000 patients with cardiovascular disease (CVD) and found that 75 mg to 81 mg daily prevents heart attacks and strokes as well as higher-dose (325 mg) aspirin does—in some cases, even better—with fewer reports of gastrointestinal bleeding.

HOW ASPIRIN WORKS

Aspirin helps guard against heart attack and stroke by inhibiting the effects of *cyclooxygenase-1* (COX-1), an enzyme that blood platelets require for coagulation (clotting). Aspirin's effect on this enzyme helps prevent the formation of clots that might choke off oxygen to the heart or brain.

Aspirin also inhibits *cyclooxygenase-2* (COX-2), a related enzyme that helps regulate pain and inflammation, such as that caused by arthritis. However, aspirin is a much more effective blood thinner than anti-inflammatory—it typically requires eight times as much of the drug to relieve pain and swelling as it does to reduce heart attack and stroke risk.

My advice: Enteric-coated aspirin should not be used to protect against heart attack or stroke. It has not been well studied for this purpose. The coating may allow aspirin to pass undigested through the stomach, possibly limiting its clot-inhibiting powers.

WHO SHOULD TAKE ASPIRIN?

The potential for gastrointestinal bleeding problems and other side effects means that aspirin should be used only by people who need it.

My advice: If you have a 10% or greater risk of having a heart attack within 10 years, consult your doctor about aspirin therapy. To learn your heart attack risk, ask your doctor or go to the Web site of the American Heart Association (*www.americanheart.org/riskassessment*).

If you're a man over age 40 or a woman over age 50 with atherosclerosis (fatty buildup in the arteries)…high cholesterol (total of 200 mg/dL or higher)…diabetes…or a first-degree relative (parent or sibling) with heart disease, you are among those who may benefit from aspirin therapy. Do *not* begin aspirin therapy without consulting your doctor. A previous heart attack or stroke also means you should discuss aspirin therapy with your doctor.

HEART ATTACK PROTECTION

Aspirin can be a lifesaver if taken during—and for up to 30 days following—a heart attack, reducing your risk of dying by up to 23%.

My advice: If you think you are having a heart attack, first call 911, then chew 325 mg of aspirin immediately to help prevent the worsening of blood clots.

Caution: Aspirin should be avoided by people who are allergic to it and by those who have a bleeding disorder or asthma that is exacerbated by aspirin.

Important: Chewing 325 mg of aspirin (or four baby aspirin) before swallowing it can cut the absorption time from 60 minutes for an aspirin swallowed whole to 15 to 20 minutes. Never use enteric-coated aspirin for heart attack symptoms—the coating prevents rapid absorption in the stomach.

Caution: Do not take aspirin if you think you are having a stroke. Testing is necessary to determine whether a suspected stroke is caused by a blood clot or bleeding, which could be worsened by aspirin.

ASPIRIN RESISTANCE

Not everyone who takes aspirin experiences a reduction in heart attack and stroke risk. What's more, none of the dozen or so "aspirin-resistance" blood tests that measure a person's platelet response to aspirin is particularly reliable, according to research done to date.

My advice: Skip the aspirin-resistance tests, and ask your doctor about taking 81 mg of aspirin daily if you are at increased risk for heart attack or stroke.

IBUPROFEN AND ASPIRIN

A study by University of Pennsylvania researchers showed that *ibuprofen* (Advil, etc.) can block aspirin's blood clot–fighting activity —especially if the ibuprofen is taken before the aspirin and/or multiple times daily. Short-term use of ibuprofen (for a couple of days or less) is unlikely to interfere significantly with aspirin.

My advice: If you're relying on aspirin to prevent a heart attack or stroke, avoid long-term ibuprofen use. If you have arthritis or another chronic, painful condition, talk to your doctor about taking supplements of *glucosamine* (promotes cartilage formation) and chondroitin sulfate (promotes cartilage elasticity)…using *acetaminophen* (Tylenol) at the dosage prescribed by your doctor…or receiving steroid injections.

ASPIRIN'S OTHER BENEFITS

Research suggests that aspirin may also…

•**Prevent adult-onset asthma**. Among 22,000 men enrolled in the Physicians' Health Study, those who took 325 mg of aspirin daily for nearly five years were 22% less likely to develop asthma than those who took a placebo.

•**Reduce the risk for enlarged prostate** by up to 50%, possibly by fighting urinary tract inflammation, according to a recent Mayo Clinic study.

•**Curb cancer risks.** Of 22,507 postmenopausal women participating in the Iowa Women's Health Study, those who took aspirin once weekly were 16% less likely to develop cancer over a 12-year period than nonaspirin users. Other studies suggest that regular aspirin use may reduce the risks for skin, prostate, pancreatic and breast malignancies.

•**Improve longevity**. Aspirin may be a good preventive medicine overall. Cleveland Clinic researchers who tracked 6,174 adults for three years found that those taking aspirin daily were 33% less likely to die during that period, with the greatest benefits realized by people who are age 60 or older, unfit and/or diagnosed with pre-existing coronary artery disease.

NSAIDs Protect Against Parkinson's Disease

American Academy of Neurology news release.

Taking over-the-counter pain medicines called nonsteroidal anti-inflammatory drugs (NSAIDs) may reduce the risk for Parkinson's disease, according to a study by researchers at the UCLA School of Public Health in Los Angeles.

THE STUDY

The study included 579 men and women (half with Parkinson's disease) who were asked if they'd taken aspirin or NSAIDs, such as *ibuprofen* (Advil), once a week or more for at least a month at any time in their lives.

Those who took two or more pills (either aspirin or a non-aspirin NSAID) a week for at least a month were classified as regular users, while those participants who took fewer pills were non-regular users.

RESULTS

Compared to non-users and non-regular users, regular users of non-aspirin NSAIDs reduced their risk of Parkinson's disease by as much as 60%, the study found. Women who were regular users of aspirin reduced their risk of Parkinson's by 40%. This effect was especially noticeable in those who were regular users of aspirin for more than two years.

The study was published in an issue of the journal *Neurology*.

EXPERT COMMENTARY

"Our findings suggest NSAIDs are protective against Parkinson's disease, with a particularly strong protective effect among users of non-aspirin NSAIDs, especially those who reported two or more years of use," said study co-author Angelika D. Wahner, PhD. "Interestingly, aspirin only benefited women. It may be that men are taking lower doses of aspirin for heart problems, while women may be using higher doses for arthritis or headaches."

"Given our results and the growing burden of Parkinson's disease as people age, there's a pressing need for further studies explaining why these drugs may play a protective role," she said.

info We Move, a Web site that provides information on movement disorders, has more about Parkinson's disease. Visit *www.we move.org* and click on "Parkinson's Disease."

■ ■ ■ ■

Wow! Aspirin Fights Cancer

When researchers followed 22,507 women age 55 or older for an average of 10 years, they found that women who took aspirin at least once weekly were 16% less likely to develop cancer than those who never used aspirin.

Theory: Aspirin inhibits an enzyme that promotes inflammation, which is believed to contribute to the development of cancer.

If you already take aspirin for heart health: Cancer prevention may be an additional benefit.

Caution: Because aspirin can cause gastrointestinal bleeding, ask your doctor about the benefits and risks of aspirin therapy.

Jon O. Ebbert, MD, associate professor of medicine, Mayo Clinic College of Medicine, Rochester, Minnesota.

New Test Means Better Treatment for RA Sufferers

Eric L. Matteson, MD, MPH, chair of the department of rheumatology and pulmonary and critical care medicine at Mayo Clinic College of Medicine in Rochester, Minnesota. His research interests include the proteins and genetic mechanisms responsible for inflammation and rheumatoid arthritis. He recently served as the American College of Rheumatology drug safety subcommittee liaison.

Even though most people associate rheumatoid arthritis (RA) with joint pain, this is not always the most serious part of the disease. Unlike osteoarthritis (the more common, wear-and-tear form of arthritis), RA is accompanied by *systemic* inflammation that can affect not only the joints, but also the eyes, lungs and the heart.

Latest development: Research presented at the recent annual meeting of the American College of Rheumatology (ACR) suggests that adding a blood test to the criteria now used to diagnose RA will allow more patients to receive prompt treatment, greatly reducing their risk for joint destruction as well as inflammatory damage to other parts of the body.

What you need to know…

A PROMPT DIAGNOSIS

When doctors diagnose a person with RA, they look for several criteria, including morning joint stiffness that lasts for more than an hour… symptoms affecting three or more joints (such as those in the hands, feet and hips)…and a positive blood test for an antibody known as *rheumatoid factor.*

Among the changes proposed by the ACR is a recommendation for anti-CCP testing. This blood test, which is becoming more widely available, measures levels of *anti-cyclic citrullinated peptide* (anti-CCP) antibodies. Anti-CCP is a more accurate indicator of RA than the antibody rheumatoid factor, which can be elevated by other conditions, such as liver disease.

WHAT IS RHEUMATOID ARTHRITIS?

Rheumatoid arthritis (RA) is an inflammatory disease that causes pain and swelling in the joints, especially those in the hands and feet. The exact cause of RA is unknown, but it has been linked to a malfunctioning immune system that attacks the body's own tissues. RA is the second most common form of arthritis (after osteoarthritis), affecting 2.1 million Americans.

TREAT AGGRESSIVELY

RA cannot be cured, but people who start RA drug therapy within a year of the initial diagnosis typically have better remission rates (having no symptoms and no sign of disease progression over a period of one year) than those treated later.

Sobering: Joint destruction occurs in nearly 100% of patients who rely solely on over-the-counter (OTC) pain relievers, such as aspirin and *ibuprofen* (Advil). In contrast, those who use standard RA treatment favored by doctors—prescription medications known as *disease-modifying anti-rheumatic drugs* (DMARDs)—suffer less joint destruction and require up to 50% less joint surgery, including joint replacement.

Main drugs for RA…

•**Nonbiological DMARDs.** These drugs, including *methotrexate* (Rheumatrex), *leflunomide* (Arava) and *sulfasalazine* (Azulfidine), are equally effective, although individual patients may respond to one drug better than another.

Drawbacks: The immune-suppressing effect of these drugs helps control RA but also may increase the risk for infection, as well as some cancers, such as lymphoma (cancer of the lymph nodes).

Self-defense: Patients taking a nonbiological DMARD should get recommended vaccinations—such as those for the flu and hepatitis A and B—and ask their doctors about routine cancer screenings.

•**Biological DMARDs.** These drugs include *etanercept* (Enbrel), *adalimumab* (Humira) and *infliximab* (Remicade). They are made from living cells and interfere with signaling from a cell protein that triggers the inflammatory response associated with RA.

Biological DMARDs are newer than the nonbiological DMARDs and have not been used and tested as long. There's some evidence that biological DMARDs may be more effective at stopping disease progression—but many patients get comparable results with the older drugs.

Drawbacks: Biological DMARDs cost $12,000 to $62,000 a year, compared with about $1,500 to $2,000 a year for the nonbiological DMARDs. Both types are covered by Medicare. Some private insurers cover both as well.

Warning: Some biological DMARDs also can increase the risk for infection—as well as certain cancers, such as lymphoma.

REDUCING CARDIOVASCULAR RISK

In a study presented at the ACR meeting, researchers compared 553 RA patients with 574 people without RA. People in both groups were free of cardiovascular disease at the beginning of the study. A decade later, patients in the RA group were *twice* as likely to have had a serious cardiovascular event, such as a heart attack or heart failure.

Why: The chronic inflammation caused by RA irritates the linings of blood vessels, stimulates the accumulation of plaque and increases the risk for clots.

Important: RA patients need to be extra vigilant about reducing cardiovascular risks—by not smoking, reducing cholesterol, controlling blood pressure and body weight, and staying active. Patients who start therapy with DMARDs promptly have a lower cardiovascular risk—in part because they're less likely to need cortisone or other artery-damaging drugs.

NUTRITIONAL THERAPY

In some patients, the inflammation-fighting omega-3 fatty acids in fish oil supplements relieve pain about as well as OTC painkillers. The supplements also can reduce kidney or arterial inflammation linked to RA.

Recommended dosage: 3,000 milligrams (mg) daily of combined *eicosapentaenoic acid* (EPA) and *docosahexaenoic acid* (DHA).

Caution: Fish oil may increase the effects of blood-thinning drugs.

Long-term therapy with methotrexate can deplete levels of folic acid, a vitamin that plays a role in the formation of red blood cells and the metabolism of amino acids. Patients using this drug should ask their doctors about taking a folic acid supplement—typically, 1 mg daily.

Also important: Because the inflammation associated with RA can promote the breakdown of bone that accompanies osteoporosis, RA patients should consult their doctors about osteoporosis prevention and bone-density testing.

info To find a rheumatologist near you, contact the Arthritis Foundation, 800-283-7800, *www.arthritis.org*...or contact the American College of Rheumatology, 404-633-3777, *www.rheumatology.org*.

■ ■ ■ ■

New Approach to Bone-Density Drugs

In a recent study, bone mineral density (BMD) was found to have stopped declining and, in some cases, to have increased in women who took the osteoporosis drug *alendronate* (Fosamax) for five years and then stopped. Women with a low risk for fractures (who have not had fractures or whose BMDs are only moderately low) may be able to discontinue use of bone-building drugs after five years.

Dennis M. Black, PhD, professor, department of epidemiology and biostatistics, University of California at San Francisco, and leader of a study of 1,099 women, published in *Journal of the American Medical Association*.

■ ■ ■ ■

New Drug Could Save Your Life

An osteoporosis drug given after hip fracture cuts chances of another fracture and lowers the risk for death. Patients given *zoledronic acid* (Reclast) within 90 days of surgery for a hip fracture had a 28% reduction in death rate and were 35% less likely to suffer another fracture in the next two years. Among elderly patients who fracture a hip, 15% to 25% die within a year—so wide use of Reclast, which is given by injection, could save many lives. Other drugs similar to Reclast—such as Fosamax, Actonel or Boniva and known as bisphosphonates—may have similar benefits. Ask your doctor for details.

Kenneth W. Lyles, MD, professor of medicine, vice chair for clinical research, Duke University School of Medicine, Durham, North Carolina.

■ ■ ■ ■

Drug That's Two Times Better Than Fosamax!

People who have low bone-mineral density should consider *teriparatide* (Forteo) for bone building instead of Fosamax, says Kenneth Saag, MD, MSc. Forteo more than doubles bone density compared with Fosamax. (Side effects are similar.) It also may be a better choice for patients who have had fractures or who have osteoporosis caused by long-term steroid use. Forteo is given by injection once a day by a health professional or you can be shown how to do it yourself. It is covered by insurance under specific circumstances.

Kenneth Saag, MD, MSc, professor of medicine and epidemiology, division of clinical immunology and rheumatology, University of Alabama at Birmingham, and leader of a recent study comparing Forteo and Fosamax, published in *The New England Journal of Medicine*.

■ ■ ■ ■

Bone-Density Drugs May Cause Osteonecrosis in Some

Some patients who take *alendronate* (Fosamax) or its close cousin *risedronate* (Actonel) develop *osteonecrosis of the jaw*, a bone disease. It often is discovered after a tooth extraction or other dental surgery. The jawbone may fail to heal properly, causing pain, infection, loose teeth or other problems. Bones elsewhere in the body are not affected.

The risk for developing osteonecrosis is low, and much lower than the risk for a bone fracture because of untreated osteoporosis.

However: People who use Actonel or Fosamax, especially those on chronic steroid therapy, such as for rheumatoid arthritis or asthma, should consider stopping it for several months before and after oral surgery.

Salvatore L. Ruggiero, MD, DMD, associate professor of oral surgery, School of Dental Medicine, State University of New York at Stony Brook, and an oral surgeon at the New York Center for Orthognathic and Maxillofacial Surgery, West Islip, New York.

Good News on Heartburn Drugs from the FDA

Teleconference with Paul Seligman, MD, MPH, associate director, Office of Safety Policy and Communication, Center for Drug Evaluation and Research, US Food and Drug Administration.

Philip O. Katz, MD, chair, gastroenterology, Albert Einstein Medical Center, Philadelphia.

US Food and Drug Administration news release.

AstraZeneca news release.

A US government review of the popular heartburn drugs *omeprazole* (Prilosec) and *esomeprazole* (Nexium) found no evidence of increased heart risks, according to health officials.

The announcement followed a three-month safety review after reports of possible heart risks emerged from two preliminary studies. But detailed data from both studies, plus another 14 studies, showed no heightened risk associated with long-term use of the drugs, US Food and Drug Administration officials said.

Paul Seligman, MD, MPH, associate director of the FDA's Office of Safety Policy and Communication at the Center for Drug Evaluation and Research, told reporters that the agency "had completed our safety review, and our current assessment is that studies do not show a risk for heart attack or heart-related problems."

BACKGROUND

Prilosec and Nexium are drugs known as proton pump inhibitors, which treat the symptoms of gastroesophageal reflux disorder (GERD) and conditions caused by excess stomach acid. Prilosec is also available over-the-counter to treat frequent heartburn.

AstraZeneca says more than 1 billion patients worldwide take the drugs, according to *Bloomberg News*.

PRELIMINARY FINDINGS

The British pharmaceutical company Astra-Zeneca makes both drugs. The company gave the FDA findings from two small, preliminary trials that were designed to test the effectiveness of the drugs, compared with surgery, for severe GERD.

During the trials, some cardiac "events" were seen among study participants, hinting that long-term use of Prilosec and Nexium could increase the risk of heart attack, heart failure and heart-related sudden death, the FDA said at the time.

LONG-TERM STUDIES

Because of these concerns, AstraZeneca gave the FDA more detailed data from the two initial studies as well as findings from 14 other studies —one 14 years in length—that compared the drugs with a placebo.

The more complete data showed that patients taking Prilosec had a lower risk of heart problems than patients taking a placebo. And findings from the ongoing Nexium trial found no difference in heart problems between patients taking the drug and those undergoing surgery for GERD, the FDA statement said.

CONCLUSION

According to the FDA, "Based on everything now known at the agency, the reported difference in the frequency of heart attacks and other heart-related problems seen in the earlier analyses of the two small long-term studies does not indicate the presence of a true effect."

And it added, "FDA recommends that health care providers continue to prescribe, and patients continue to use, these products as described in the labeling for the two drugs."

GOOD NEWS

Philip O. Katz, MD, chairman of gastroenterology at Albert Einstein Medical Center in Philadelphia, agreed that these drugs are safe and that patients shouldn't hesitate to use them.

"This is altogether good news," Dr. Katz said. "It is reassuring to physicians and the public, who are using these drugs on a widespread basis, that this is not deemed to be an issue."

HIP FRACTURE RISK

However, Dr. Seligman said the FDA continues to investigate whether the drugs increase the risk for hip fracture. A report in the *Journal of the American Medical Association* found that people 50 and older who took Prilosec or Nexium had a 44% higher risk of hip fracture than people not taking these drugs.

info For more information on GERD, visit the About GERD Web site at *www.about gerd.org*.

Four Out of Five Infants Are Prescribed Unnecessary Drugs

Vikram Khoshoo, MD, PhD, pediatric gastroenterologist, Pediatric Specialty Center, West Jefferson Medical Center, New Orleans.

David Keljo, MD, pediatric gastroenterologist, and director, Inflammatory Bowel Disease Center, Children's Hospital of Pittsburgh, University of Pittsburgh Medical Center.

Pediatrics.

Doctors may be overprescribing anti-reflux medications to infants, recent research suggests.

Reflux, which occurs when stomach contents reflux, or back up, into the esophagus, is common in infants. In fact, more than half experience reflux symptoms during the first three months of life, according to the US National Institute of Diabetes and Digestive and Kidney Diseases. Symptoms of reflux include spitting up, vomiting, coughing, feeding difficulty and irritability.

The study found that fewer than one in five babies given anti-reflux medications, which work by lowering levels of stomach acid, actually had elevated acid levels. That means four out of five infants included in the study likely didn't need anti-reflux medications, and may have simply been experiencing normal infant regurgitation commonly referred to as "spitting up."

BACKGROUND

Study author Vikram Khoshoo, MD, PhD, a pediatric gastroenterologist at the Pediatric Specialty Center at West Jefferson Medical Center in New Orleans, and his colleagues reported that back in 1998 and 1999, infants with regurgitation made up about 14% of their referrals. About 40% of those babies were already on anti-reflux medication or on special easier-to-digest formula. But by 2006 to 2007, infants with regurgitation accounted for 23% of their referrals, and 90% were already on medications or special formula.

"We felt it was unlikely that the incidence had increased so suddenly," Dr. Khoshoo said.

THE STUDY

To measure whether or not these infants' symptoms were caused by acid reflux, the researchers conducted pH studies on 44 babies with persistent regurgitation. Babies who were already taking anti-reflux medication were taken off the drugs for seven to 14 days before the pH study. The average age of the babies was 18 weeks.

To complete a pH study, doctors must thread a wire down the nose and leave it in place for 24 hours, Dr. Khoshoo said, so it's not a test that would be practical to do on every child with regurgitation.

Of the 44 babies tested, only eight showed elevated pH levels, meaning they had excess levels of stomach acid. Anti-reflux medications would be indicated in these cases. However, 42 of the babies were already on such medications, meaning that many were taking a medication they didn't need.

MEDICATION SIDE EFFECTS

While these medications are generally considered safe, Dr. Khoshoo said there is some concern that they may affect calcium metabolism, and they've been associated with osteoporosis in older people who take them for long periods of time. Because infants are building new bones, this potential side effect is even more concerning, Dr. Khoshoo added.

EXPERT COMMENTARY

David Keljo, MD, is a pediatric gastroenterologist and director of the Inflammatory Bowel Disease Center at Children's Hospital of Pittsburgh. He said, "Reflux in babies is a tough issue, and I think the concerns in this study are well-raised. Babies may be cranky from reflux or from something else. The vast majority will outgrow their reflux whether we do anything or not."

Both Dr. Khoshoo and Dr. Keljo said these medications are probably overprescribed because parents want to do *something*, anything to try to stop their babies' regurgitation and irritability.

According to Dr. Khoshoo, "In the absence of red flags, such as a child who is not gaining weight, has feeding problems or a learned aversion to food, a chronic cough or recurrent respiratory problems or apnea, regurgitation may not require medication."

"Regurgitation won't improve with anti-reflux medications. Acid suppression will improve irritability and feeding problems, but it won't change spitting up. As long as the child is gaining weight and happy, and has no recurrent red flags, regurgitation is a laundry problem, not a medical problem," Dr. Khoshoo said.

WHAT TO DO

Dr. Khoshoo said that taking care not to overfeed your infant and making sure he or she is positioned so that their bodies are at least somewhat upright after eating would help to lessen reflux symptoms. Another critical thing parents can do, he said, is make sure that children aren't exposed to secondhand smoke, which can increase reflux symptoms.

Dr. Keljo said there are certain signs that indicate your baby should be evaluated by a specialist. If your child throws up blood or a substance that looks like coffee grounds, or if there's green in the vomit, see your child's doctor right away. Also, if your child isn't gaining weight or is even losing weight, if you can hear significant choking sounds, if there's a chronic cough or hoarseness that accompanies regurgitation, your child should see a gastroenterologist, he said.

info To learn more about acid reflux and how it affects babies, visit the Web site of the National Institute of Diabetes and Digestive and Kidney Diseases, *http://digestive.niddk. nih.gov,* and search "reflux in infants."

■ ■ ■ ■

Stomach-Acid Medicines May Cause Memory Problems

Stomach-acid medications can lead to mental decline, warns Malaz Boustani, MD, MPH. Mental decline can range from mild cognitive problems (such as confusion) to severe problems such as dementia.

Recent finding: People who used prescription and over-the-counter H2 blockers, such as Axid, Pepcid, Tagamet and Zantac, for more than two years were nearly two-and-a-half

times more likely to develop cognitive difficulties than people who had not used them.

Self-defense: Talk to your doctor about safer alternatives.

Malaz Boustani, MD, MPH, a geriatrician at Indiana University School of Medicine, Indianapolis, and leader of a study of 1,558 people, published in *Journal of the American Geriatrics Society.*

■ ■ ■ ■

Breakthrough for Crohn's Disease Treatment

Certolizumab pegol may be especially useful for patients who have stopped responding to *infliximab* or *adalimumab,* standard treatments for Crohn's disease. A severe inflammatory disease of the digestive tract, Crohn's affects an estimated 500,000 people in the US. Symptoms include abdominal pain, fever, nausea, vomiting, weight loss and diarrhea. Certolizumab pegol works by blocking *tumor necrosis factor,* which is a main cause of inflammation in Crohn's patients. The drug is administered through subcutaneous (under the skin) injections that patients can administer themselves. Ask your doctor for details.

William Sandborn, MD, gastroenterologist, Mayo Clinic, Rochester, Minnesota, and leader of a study of 662 adults with Crohn's disease, published in *The New England Journal of Medicine.*

■ ■ ■ ■

Birth-Control Pill Stops Menstruation

The Food and Drug Administration (FDA) approved Lybrel, which is taken daily to prevent pregnancy and ends monthly periods for as long as you take it. Unlike most other oral contraceptives, which use active pills for 21 days and sugar pills for the next seven, Lybrel contains only active pills, which are taken all 28 days.

Caution: Side effects include frequent irregular bleeding and spotting. Consult your doctor for more information.

Karen Mahoney, spokesperson, Center for Drug Evaluation and Research, US Food and Drug Administration, Rockville, Maryland.

Epilepsy Drug Holds Promise as Treatment For Alcoholism

Bankole Johnson, MD, PhD, chairman, Department of Psychiatry and Neurobehavioral Sciences, University of Virginia, Charlottesville.

J.C. Garbutt, MD, professor of psychiatry, University of North Carolina at Chapel Hill.

Journal of the American Medical Association.

A drug used to treat epileptic seizures could help alcoholics control their addiction, a study suggests. The drug, *topiramate* (Topamax), proved measurably better than a placebo at helping alcoholics stay away from heavy drinking, the study authors said.

"Not only is there an effective new treatment, but there's a medication that you can take at the time of crisis. You can start immediately when you need help," said study author Bankole Johnson, MD, PhD, chairman of the University of Virginia's Department of Psychiatry and Neurobehavioral Sciences.

For treatment, many alcoholics must rely on their own willpower, often with the help of groups like Alcoholics Anonymous. But some—about 3% to 4%, Dr. Johnson estimates—try to quit drinking with the help of prescription medications.

THE STUDY

In the new study, conducted between 2004 and 2006, Johnson and his colleagues recruited 371 alcoholics between the ages of 18 and 65. The participants, both male and female, received daily doses of topiramate or a placebo along with a brief weekly visit with a counselor.

Ortho-McNeil Janssen, the company that manufactures topiramate, funded the study.

RESULTS

Over 14 weeks, the percentage of heavy-drinking days per week dropped from 81.9% to 43.8% among those who took topiramate and from 82% to 51.8% among those who took a placebo.

Topiramate also led to a higher rate of achieving 28 or more days of continuous non-heavy drinking and 28 or more days of continuous abstinence, the researchers said.

The drug appears to work by cutting the craving for alcohol, according to Dr. Johnson.

DRAWBACKS

There are side effects with topiramate, Dr. Johnson said. The drug "can make you dizzy, give you headaches and the feeling of pins and needles in your fingers. Some people have difficulty naming words, which goes away after about a week."

The drug isn't cheap—it costs about $1,000 for three months, according to Dr. Johnson. In addition, patients do not see benefits for two to four weeks.

BENEFITS

Still, topiramate holds promise, Dr. Johnson said. "We're talking about a drug that will be many times better than what is currently available," he said. "And it doesn't require you to go to rehab."

J.C. Garbutt, MD, professor of psychiatry at the University of North Carolina at Chapel Hill, said the research on topiramate gives doctors another option when they treat alcoholism. Since the drug is already approved for use, doctors can prescribe it immediately.

Dr. Garbutt said it's still difficult for doctors to figure out which medication to prescribe to alcoholics. But "this gives you another one you can work with," he said.

Meanwhile, Dr. Johnson said, the next step is to study whether people can safely take topiramate for long periods of time.

info For more on alcoholism, visit the National Institute on Alcohol Abuse and Alcoholism Web site at *www.niaaa.nih.gov.*

■ ■ ■ ■

New Pill for Problem Drinkers

The drug *varenicline* (Chantix), which helps smokers kick the habit, could help heavy drinkers quit their addiction, too, according to a new study. Nicotine and alcohol act on the same locations in the brain. Varenicline blocks the release of dopamine in the brain's pleasure centers. Down the road, the drug might be prescribed for addictions to everything from gambling to painkillers.

Selena E. Bartlett, BPharm, PhD, director, preclinical development group, Gallo Research Center, University of California at San Francisco.

■ ■ ■ ■

Side Effects of Chantix

The stop-smoking drug, Chantix, may cause such side effects as suicidal thoughts, drowsiness, and aggressive and erratic behavior. The Food and Drug Administration, in cooperation with the drug's manufacturer, Pfizer, is investigating the reports of these side effects. It is not yet known whether the behavior changes are related to the drug itself or to nicotine withdrawal. Other options for people trying to quit smoking are nicotine replacement and *bupropion*, a non-nicotine medication. All medication treatments work better when combined with counseling programs.

Andrea King, PhD, associate professor of psychiatry, University of Chicago.

This Pain Med Won't Impair Driving

American Society of Anesthesiologists news release.

Moderate, long-term use of opioid pain medications, such as morphine, does not impair a person's driving ability, US researchers report.

BACKGROUND

Opioid pain relievers, a class of drugs used to treat moderate to severe pain, carry warning labels urging patients not to drive or operate heavy machinery while taking the medications.

Drivers under the influence of pain drugs are typically subject to the same laws and penalties as people who drink and drive.

NEW STUDY

A team at Rush University Medical Center in Chicago compared two groups of people—51 long-term users of oral morphine and 49 who weren't taking any pain medication. All the participants spent about 12 minutes in a driving simulator that measured deviation from the center of the road, weaving, number of accidents, and reaction time to unexpected events.

RESULTS

The average amount of weaving for both groups was 3.83 feet. The morphine group had 5.33 collisions, compared with 5.04 collisions for the control group. Average reaction time for the morphine group was 0.67 seconds, compared with 0.69 seconds for the control group.

IMPLICATIONS

The findings suggest that patients who require long-term pain medication may "become tolerant" to side effects that could potentially impair function, said researcher Asokumar Buvanendran, MD, an associate professor in the anesthesiology department at Rush.

According to Dr. Buvanendran, this study's findings suggest that patients on long-term pain medication may be able to live "like normal functioning people, without the stigma and limitations now associated with long-term pain medication use."

However, drinking even a small amount of alcohol while taking an opioid pain reliever can impair driving ability.

info For more information on pain medications, visit the American Academy of Family Physicians Web site, *http://familydoctor.org*, and search "chronic pain medicines."

7

Emotional Well-Being

Happiness *Is* in The Genes

The right genetic mix might lead to a lifetime of happiness, a new British study suggests. It all depends on your personality type.

"While it was known that around half the differences in happiness are related to genes, what we found was that those happiness-related genes are genes for personality, namely for being extroverted, emotionally stable and conscientious," said coresearcher Tim Bates, PhD, from the School of Philosophy, Psychology and Language Sciences at the University of Edinburgh.

Because personality is relatively stable, this new research helps solve what was otherwise a real puzzle, namely why people tend to show stable differences in happiness, Dr. Bates said.

"It turns out that if we want to understand happiness, we will need to understand personality," Dr. Bates said. "An important implication is that personality traits of being outgoing, calm and reliable provide a resource, we called it affective reserve, that drives future happiness."

THE STUDY

Dr. Bates' team collected personality and happiness information on 973 twin pairs. The researchers were able to identify evidence for genes tied to certain personality traits and genes that predispose people to happiness.

The researchers found that people who don't worry excessively and are sociable and conscientious tend to be happier, according to the report.

While happiness has a genetic component, about 50% of the difference in happiness between people results from relationships, physical health, and careers, Dr. Bates noted.

However, those lucky enough to have the right gene mix appear to have an extra supply

Tim Bates, PhD, School of Philosophy, Psychology and Language Sciences, University of Edinburgh, Scotland.

Sonja Lyubomirsky, PhD, professor, psychology, University of California, Riverside.

Psychological Science.

of happiness that they can use when times are tough, the researchers reported.

IMPLICATIONS

One expert thinks the study contributes to the understanding of happiness, because it shows that happiness and personality share some of the same genes.

"The results of this study are consistent with previous research on the genetic roots of happiness, which has shown that approximately 50% of the variance in individual differences in happiness is determined by genes," said Sonja Lyubomirsky, a professor of psychology at the University of California, Riverside.

The unique contribution of this study is the finding that happiness appears to have the same genetic roots as personality—both share genes, Lyubomirsky said. "This is intriguing, as we previously didn't know what the genetic component of happiness really represented," she added.

ADOPTING A "HAPPY PERSONALITY"

"If people want to raise their own levels of well-being, our best advice is that they practice the kinds of behaviors that characterize calm, conscientious, extroverts," Bates said.

"Try and be active and social, even if with just a few people. Practice the things you find emotionally challenging, maybe even keeping a diary to help you keep a sense of reality, and allow you to reflect on which strategies work, and which do not. Then set yourself small achievable goals, and work at them. Count your blessings—that's reflecting on what works in your life—keep a sense of humility and work for those things you really want," he said.

info For more on personality, visit the Web site of the American Psychological Association, *www.apa.org*. Under "Topics," click on "Personality."

■ ■ ■ ■

Breaking Up Is Easier to Do

Even though it is painful, breaking up is easier to do than most people realize.

Recent finding: Relationship breakups typically cause less distress than most people expect—and the unhappiness lasts for less time than predicted. Most people in a recent study were back to their prebreakup level of happiness within two months, even though they anticipated that it would take longer.

Paul Eastwick, PhD candidate, and Eli Finkel, PhD, psychology researchers, Northwestern University, Evanston, and coauthors of a study published on-line in *Journal of Experimental Social Psychology*.

Happy Marriages Help Women Ease Stress

University of California, Los Angeles, news release.

Coming home to a loving spouse and a good marriage helps working women shake off the stress of the day, new research confirms. Men, on the other hand, often drop their stress at the door when they come home, regardless of the state of their union, reported psychology researchers.

THE STUDY

Researchers at the University of California, Los Angeles, followed 30 married, parenting couples, with each partner employed in full-time jobs.

Over a three-day period, each of the 60 spouses completed a single survey about their satisfaction with their marriage and twice-daily questionnaires about their day. The researchers also took saliva samples four times a day (early morning, late morning, afternoon and evening) to test for *cortisol*, a hormone released by the body under stress.

RESULTS

"At least as far as women are concerned, being happily married appears to bolster physiological recovery from work," said lead author Darby E. Saxbe. "After a tough day at the office, cortisol levels dropped further among happily married women than less happily married ones. Less happily married women also showed a flatter daily pattern of cortisol release, suggesting that they are rebounding less well from everyday stress."

The researchers found that women who felt they were happily married saw a greater reduction in cortisol levels when they came home at the end of the work day than women who were less happily married. Cortisol levels in men dropped at the end of the day regardless of their satisfaction with their marriage.

The study appeared in *Health Psychology*.

IMPLICATIONS

Long-term elevated cortisol levels have been associated with a host of maladies, including depression, burnout, chronic fatigue syndrome, relationship problems, poor social adjustment and possibly even cancer, according to the researchers.

THEORY

The researchers suggested that women in happy marriages may have a more even balance of household responsibilities and may generally welcome an evening retreat from the world more than women in unhappy marriages.

CONCLUSION

This is the first study to examine daily cortisol levels with respect to marital satisfaction, said the researchers, who called for further research into the link between marriage and physical stress.

info For more on stress management, visit MedlinePlus at the US National Library of Medicine Web site, *www.medlineplus.gov.*

Panic Attacks May Raise Heart Attack Risk in Women

Jordan Smoller, MD, associate professor, psychiatry, Harvard Medical School, and assistant vice chairman, department of psychiatry, Massachusetts General Hospital, Boston.

Stephen Siegel, MD, cardiologist, New York University Medical Center, and clinical assistant professor, New York University School of Medicine, New York City.

Archives of General Psychiatry.

Postmenopausal women who have had at least one panic attack may be at greater risk for heart disease, stroke and even death, new research suggests.

The study found that older women with a history of panic attacks were four times more likely to have heart disease than women who hadn't had a panic attack.

"Women who reported at least one panic attack were at higher risk of having cardiovascular illness and death after an average of five years of follow-up. Even after controlling for other risk factors, a panic attack remained an independent risk factor on its own," said study author Jordan Smoller, MD, an associate professor of psychiatry at Harvard Medical School.

SYMPTOMS

Panic attack symptoms include a sudden feeling of fear, anxiety or extreme discomfort that's out of proportion to your current situation. Panic attacks may also be accompanied by a rapid heartbeat, sweating, chest pain, difficulty breathing, shaking, dizziness and a feeling that you might die.

Approximately one in 10 postmenopausal women has had at least one panic attack, according to the study.

THE STUDY

The research, published in *Archives of General Psychiatry*, included 3,369 postmenopausal women between the ages of 51 and 83. All of the women completed questionnaires about the occurrence of panic attacks in the previous six months.

A full-blown panic attack was one in which sudden fear was accompanied by at least four other panic attack symptoms. A limited panic attack was one in which fear was accompanied by one to three additional symptoms.

After an average 5.3 years of follow-up, the researchers collected information on heart disease, stroke and death from any cause. The researchers also adjusted the data to account for other known cardiovascular disease risk factors, such as weight, alcohol use, hormone use, high cholesterol, high blood pressure, age, diabetes and smoking history.

RESULTS

After adjusting for all those factors, the researchers found that full-blown panic attacks were associated with a fourfold higher risk for heart disease, nearly twice the risk for stroke, and a 75% increase in risk for death from any cause, compared to women who'd experienced no panic attacks.

Women who'd had limited panic attacks fared somewhat better. The adjusted risk for heart disease was 65% higher, stroke risk was more than doubled, and all-cause mortality was increased by 34%.

THEORIES

"Negative emotional states and psychiatric symptoms can be related to adverse medical outcomes," said Dr. Smoller, who is also assistant vice chairman of the department of psychiatry at Massachusetts General Hospital.

"Panic attacks may be having a direct effect on cardiovascular health—anxiety, panic and other negative emotional states have been related to changes in heart rhythm and changes in cardiac blood flow in previous studies.

It may be that stress hormones and other components of the 'fight-or-flight' reactions that accompany panic directly impact the cardiovascular system," he said.

EXPERT RECOMMENDATIONS

Stephen Siegel, MD, a cardiologist at New York University Medical Center, said the study definitely raises some interesting questions, but more research needs to be done to establish a definite link between panic attacks and cardiovascular health.

In the meantime, Dr. Siegel recommended that all women do whatever they can to reduce their cardiovascular disease risk factors. "Control all the known risk factors out there—hypertension, cigarette smoking, diabetes, elevated cholesterol," he said.

Exercise is another great—and proven—option, Dr. Siegel said. Not only does it improve your heart health by lowering blood sugar, blood pressure and cholesterol, but exercise can also help ease anxiety and depression, providing both a physical and psychological benefit.

info To learn more about panic attacks, visit the Web site of the Anxiety Disorders Association of America at *www.adaa. org*. Click on "Anxiety Disorders" and choose "Panic Disorder."

Lack of Sleep Awakens Uncontrollable Emotions

Cell Press, news release.

Ever get a little testy after a bad night's sleep? Scientists may now know why. A new study finds that a lack of sleep causes the brain's emotional centers to dramatically overreact to negative experiences.

A shutdown of the prefrontal lobe—a brain region that normally keeps emotions under control—is the reason for heightened emotional response in sleep-deprived people, said the researchers from Harvard Medical School and the University of California, Berkeley.

Reporting in the journal *Current Biology*, the team said its study is the first to determine, at the neural level, why lack of sleep can lead to emotionally irrational behavior and may help improve understanding of the link between sleep disruptions and psychiatric disorders.

THE RESEARCH

The study included 26 healthy people who were assigned to either a normal sleep group or to a sleep deprivation group, where they were kept awake for 35 hours. Afterwards, functional magnetic resonance imaging (fMRI) was used to measure the participants' brain activity.

RESULTS

"We had predicted a potential increase in the emotional reaction from the brain (in people deprived of sleep), but the size of the increase truly surprised us," said Matthew Walker of the University of California, Berkeley. "The emotional centers of the brain were over 60% more reactive under conditions of sleep deprivation than in subjects who had obtained a normal night of sleep."

He said it's almost as though lack of sleep causes the brain to revert "back to a more primitive pattern of activity, becoming unable to put emotional experiences in context and produce controlled, appropriate responses."

IMPLICATIONS

"This adds to the critical list of sleep's benefits," said Walker. "Sleep appears to restore our emotional brain circuits, and, in doing so, prepares us for the next day's challenges and social interactions. Most importantly, this study demonstrates the dangers of not sleeping enough. Sleep deprivation fractures the brain mechanisms that regulate key aspects of our mental health."

info For more information on how sleep works, visit the National Sleep Foundation Web site, *www.sleepfoundation.org,* and click on "How Sleep Works" under "Resources."

New Study May Mean Better Ways to Relieve Stress

Eric Nestler, MD, chairman, department of psychiatry, University of Texas Southwestern Medical Center at Dallas.

Vaishnav Krishnan, student, University of Texas Southwestern Medical Center at Dallas.

Thomas R. Insel, MD, director, US National Institute of Mental Health, Bethesda, Maryland.

Cell online.

Researchers have identified molecular mechanisms in the brain that may explain why some people are less vulnerable to the stress caused by difficult situations.

While the research was done with mice, the findings could eventually lead to better treatments for chronic stress, depression and the post-traumatic stress disorder suffered by troops in Iraq and other battlefields, said study coauthor Eric Nestler, MD, chairman of psychiatry at the University of Texas Southwestern Medical Center at Dallas.

BACKGROUND

"One important lesson we have shown even in previous papers is that a series of genetically identical animals respond differently to chronic stress," Dr. Nestler said. "Thirty to 40% seemed to be resilient and did not develop bad symptoms. The clinical implications are that the ability to identify mechanisms of resistance can help provide new and novel approaches to stress."

NEW STUDY

The key lies in a pair of molecules used by some brain cells to communicate with one another, said Vaishnav Krishnan, lead author of the report and a student in a University of Texas Southwestern Medical Center program that leads to simultaneous MD and PhD degrees.

"Under stress, vulnerable mice increase the frequency of nerve activity using the neurotransmitter dopamine," Krishnan said. "That subsequently causes release of a nerve growth factor called brain-derived neurotrophic factor (BDNF). Resilient mice overcome these changes by increasing the expression of molecules that prevent the release of dopamine."

A neurotransmitter is a molecule that sends signals from one nerve cell to another.

Mice in the experiments were so inbred that they were genetically identical. Then they were put under stress by being placed in the territory of larger, more aggressive mice. Some of the test mice adjusted well to the stress of the situation, while others avoided contact and showed submissive behavior.

The researchers then made detailed studies of two brain regions—the ventral tegmental area (VTA) and the nucleus accumbens (NAcc), which are part of the brain's reward area that promotes acts that aid in survival. They found that the excess BDNF production in vulnerable mice occurred in the VTA but not the NAcc region. Chemical signals sent by the protein from the VTA to the NAcc made the mice vulnerable to stress. Experimental compounds that blocked those signals turned vulnerable mice into resistant mice.

IMPLICATIONS

According to Dr. Nestler, the findings raise the possibility of "tools to develop things in the brain that encourage resilience, to help people with stress".

"We have always tried to understand the changes in the brain that lead to such things as the symptoms of post-traumatic stress disorder," Krishnan added. "This study shows we can increase our understanding and development of new therapeutic measures to overcome those changes."

But new therapies might not be easy to develop, Dr. Nestler said, since a decrease of dopamine or BDNF activity might be helpful in one part of the brain but harmful in another area.

Thomas R. Insel, MD, director of the US National Institute of Mental Health, which funded the research, said "What's exciting here is that it is important for resilience, being able to recover from a traumatic event," Dr. Insel added. "One of the great values of this work is to help us understand how mammals, including humans, might be able to recover from the traumas inherent in daily existence."

info For more about the role of stress in sickness and health, visit the Web site of the American Institute of Stress at *www.stress.org.*

■ ■ ■ ■

The Stress–Cholesterol Link

In a recent study of 716 men (average age 65), those who dealt well with stress (such as by directly addressing problems) had higher HDL "good" cholesterol levels than men who reacted to stress in negative ways (such as by blaming and/or isolating themselves).

Theory: Good coping mechanisms may decrease stress hormones, such as cortisol, thereby promoting healthful HDL levels.

Loriena A. Yancura, PhD, associate professor, department of family and consumer science, University of Hawaii at Manoa.

■ ■ ■ ■

Stress Promotes Gum Disease

High levels of stress, as well as anxiety, depression and loneliness, increase levels of the hormone *cortisol*. Cortisol inhibits the immune response, which can provoke periodontal tissue breakdown. Also, people under stress tend to neglect oral hygiene and increase nicotine and alcohol use.

Self-defense: Seek healthy ways to relieve stress—exercise, maintain a balanced diet and get plenty of sleep.

Daiane Peruzzo, PhD candidate, and Francisco Nociti, PhD, professor, department of periodontics, State University of Campinas, Piracicaba, Brazil, authors of a review of 14 studies, published in *Journal of Periodontology.*

Meditation for Women Who Hate to Sit Still

Judith Boice, ND, a naturopathic physician and acupuncturist in private practice in Montrose, Colorado. She conducts wellness seminars nationwide and is author of eight books, including *Menopause with Science and Soul: A Guidebook for Navigating the Journey.* Celestial Arts. *www.drjudithboice.com.*

Meditation is good for us—it can relieve tension by shifting brain activity away from the stress-prone right frontal cortex and into the calmer left frontal cortex. But some people have trouble finding time to meditate—or just can't seem to sit still.

Solution: Combine exercise and meditation through rhythmic, repetitive motions, such as walking, swimming or rowing. This way, you simultaneously strengthen the body and soothe the mind.

Bonus: "Meditation in motion" makes exercise easier, because while you do it, you won't be thinking about tired muscles or tasks that await after your workout. *Begin with walking meditation…*

•**Pick a spot.** Find a secluded outdoor area where you won't feel self-conscious…or even an empty hallway where you won't bump into furniture.

•**Begin walking.** Start slowly, focusing on the rhythm of your heels striking the ground and your toes pushing off. Keep your eyes open for safety, but don't get distracted by the sights around you.

•**Recite a mantra.** Choose or invent a rhythmic chant, such as "I am one with the world, I am filled with peace." Repeat it over and over, out loud or in your mind, melding its rhythm with the movement of your feet. I recommend not listening to music—it may distract you from your mantra.

•**Try to stay focused.** At first you may succeed for only a few minutes before thoughts of daily life intrude. Work your way up to a 30-minute session daily.

•**Meditate at the gym.** Once you've mastered walking meditation, try the technique while using a treadmill or elliptical machine or while swimming laps.

Resilience—The Key to A Happier, Stress-Free Retirement

Robert Brooks, PhD, a psychologist on the faculty of Harvard Medical School and in private practice in Needham, Massachusetts, *www.drrobertbrooks.com*. He is author or coauthor of many books, including *The Power of Resilience: Achieving Balance, Confidence and Personal Strength in Your Life*. McGraw-Hill.

By age 50 or 60, most of us have learned that life offers many hard knocks. The key to handling these jabs is resilience.

Resilience serves as a reservoir of emotional strength that can be tapped for everyday challenges, such as interactions with others, as well as life-altering events, such as a loved one's death or a financial setback. I see resilience as the ability to respond to tough situations with inner strength. *Steps toward developing that ability…*

LETTING GO

Substantial research shows that those who concentrate on what they have control over are more hopeful, more optimistic and more likely to enjoy life and withstand its hardships than those who focus on forces and issues beyond their control. *Examples…*

•**Sports.** Friends of mine who love participating in sports obsess about their deteriorating skills. When aging or injury wrecks their performance, they quit.

Solution: Recognize that few of us are as athletically fit at age 60 as we were at 40. I'm still jogging in my 60s. So what if I'm slower than I used to be? I'm not entering the Olympics.

•**Relationships.** If a relationship isn't working, avoid blaming others—you can't control them. Ask yourself, *What can I do to fix this?*

My private psychology practice includes marital therapy. Some couples complain that their long marriages are running dry because they don't feel the excitement or interest in each other that they used to. I always suggest that instead of waiting for their spouses to change, disgruntled partners should ask themselves, *How can I explain why I'm unhappy about what's going on in our relationship in a way that demonstrates my love and concern, and avoids finger-pointing?* and *Do I discuss our relationship only when I'm complaining about it, or do I make an effort to mention the good things, too?*

Negativity, a relentless drain, improves nothing, whereas bringing a positive attitude to daily communication can create an optimistic environment that feels open to change and embraces it.

Exception: For a person who is truly miserable in a marriage, ending it is often best.

Examples: Several months after a family friend in her early 60s left her husband of many years, my wife said, "I've never seen her so happy." My older brother, married for nearly 48 years, left his wife when he was almost 70. For him, it was the right decision.

One form of personal resilience is to know when to stop enduring unacceptable situations.

REMAIN CONNECTED

According to extensive research, the more connected people feel to something outside of themselves—a group, a cause, a religious belief—the longer they live. Feeling part of something larger than oneself supports a resilient mind-set.

As we age, especially in retirement, establishing new forms of connectedness is essential. What counts is the quality, not the quantity, of your relationships. Do you make an effort to be part of a social group? If you love backgammon, horseshoes or checkers, do you find partners and play? If you're religious, do you regularly attend services or a discussion group?

Those relocating in retirement should put "Make new friends" near the tops of their to-do lists. This is hard if you aren't used to befriending strangers—but as you seek people with similar interests, friendships will form naturally. Friends provide social support, and this builds resilience.

HELP OTHERS

Older people who help others tend to live longer, studies show. Contributing your time and talents states, "Because I'm on Earth, Earth is a better place."

I believe strongly that retirees should volunteer for a personally meaningful cause.

Example: Furthering a political or arts-related cause that you're passionate about.

Bonus: Contributing to society adds purpose to life, and strengthens meaningful ties to others, another key to building resilience.

STAY FIT

Our mental *and* physical lives are intertwined. To stay resilient physiologically and psychologically, eat a healthy diet and exercise. Any level is fine. When my legs give out and I can't jog, I'll walk or swim.

An Australian doctor who works with retirees has written that many feel like victims. As a result, they become victims. They say, "I can't lose weight because being overweight runs in my family," or, "I can't exercise because my joints hurt." Although genes play a role in our ability to stay fit, you may have more control over your fitness level than you think.

Nothing curtails an exercise regimen more swiftly than unrealistic goals.

Example: Mr. Whitaker had trapped himself into believing that unless he could institute a major change quickly, he was a failure. I helped him create an appropriate exercise-and-diet program with specific, achievable, short-term goals. He began with a one-mile walk—not the five miles he had envisioned—and met with a nutritionist whose sensible recommendations worked better than the starvation diets he had previously tried. You can start with a half-mile walk—or even less, and build up. You can start by cutting just 100 calories from your daily diet. The important thing is, start somewhere.

BE GRATEFUL—IN WRITING

It's easy to lose sight of gratifying aspects of life. To retain perspective, every day or two write down things for which you feel grateful. Feel free to repeat yourself.

My own list includes: "Four lovely grandchildren...my wonderful marriage...being able to follow my passion in my work."

The idea is not to deny or minimize the serious or sad things in life, but to remember the good parts. Once you've reminded yourself, reinforce what makes you happy. For me, that means visiting my grandchildren, being a good husband and working creatively to help others.

FOLLOW YOUR PASSIONS

Many new retirees find that for the first time they can follow their interests and passions.

Examples: My father-in-law took up golf after retiring from the police force...a friend who had always wanted to play the piano began lessons...my close friend Mickey started taking pictures of town events and quickly became a sought-after photographer.

Start something new or expend more effort on an activity you already perform. Loving what you do gives you a wealth of happiness, which, in turn, boosts your resilience.

Unlike Fine Wine, Crabby People Don't Age Well

Jason T. Newsom, PhD, associate professor, Portland State University School of Community Health, Oregon.

Janice Kiecolt-Glaser, PhD, director, division of health psychology, Ohio State University College of Medicine, Columbus.

Health Psychology.

There's new evidence that getting along with others is more than a key to pleasant human interaction. It also appears to be good for your health.

Researchers who analyzed a survey of nearly 700 older adults found that those who got along with their relatives, friends and neighbors were less likely to report health problems and physical limitations.

The findings don't prove a cause-and-effect relationship between social life and health. Still, "the take-home message is that conflict in your life may have important impacts on your physical health," said study lead author Jason T. Newsom, PhD, associate professor at the Portland State University School of Community Health in Oregon.

NEW STUDY

Dr. Newsom and his colleagues looked at the results of a multi-year national survey of people ages 65 to 90. A total of 666 people completed the survey, in which researchers asked them questions about their lives and their health.

Many of the questions were designed to reveal whether the study participants were prone to have "negative social interactions" with other people, Dr. Newsom said. The questions asked whether "people have interfered or meddled in your personal matters, have they acted unsympathetically or been critical of you. We asked them in a very general way," he said.

The survey didn't ask whether the participants were the instigators of negative encounters—by being crabby or cranky, for instance—or the victims of others who made their lives difficult.

The researchers found that those who reported more negative social encounters suffered greater declines in health.

IMPLICATIONS

"What we suspect is that there's some impact on the immune system, but there are other kinds of things that might be happening as well," Dr. Newsom said. "It may be that when there's a great deal of interpersonal conflict going on in someone's life, they're not able to take care of medical conditions as well."

The study authors noted that their research had limitations. It only looked at senior citizens and relied on their own estimates of their health status instead of physical examinations, for one, and only examined changes over two years.

EXPERT COMMENTARY

Janice Kiecolt-Glaser, PhD, director of the Ohio State University College of Medicine's Division of Health Psychology, said the new study came from "a group of excellent investigators." But, she added, she would like to have seen more analysis of whether the study participants were depressed.

"When people are blue, they tend to be overly sensitive to negative interactions, to feel that others are often unsympathetic—and then they behave in ways that tend to elicit even more negative behaviors from others," Dr. Kiecolt-Glaser said. "They're cranky and critical and cantankerous. If you're seeing the world through dark-colored glasses, you're more likely to focus on how unsympathetic or insensitive other people act toward you, and there's a big element of self-fulfilling prophecy."

info To learn more about conflict resolution, visit the office of Human Resource Development section at the Web site of the University of Wisconsin at *www.ohrd.wisc.edu/online training/resolution.*

Depression Linked To Bone Loss in Younger Women

Giovanni Cizza, MD, PhD, staff clinician, US National Institute of Diabetes and Digestive and Kidney Diseases, Bethesda, MD.
Archives of Internal Medicine.

Premenopausal women struggling with depression have lower bone mass than do non-depressed women in the same age range, a new study found. The bone loss was most pronounced in certain regions of the hip, which is troubling given that hip fractures are one of the most serious—and potentially fatal—consequences of osteoporosis.

The level of bone loss seen in the depressed women was the same or higher than that associated with other, established risk factors for osteoporosis, including smoking, low calcium intake and lack of physical exercise, the researchers said.

The findings could have implications for the prevention of osteoporosis, according to Dr. Giovanni Cizza, MD, PhD, senior author of the study who conducted the research while at the US National Institute of Mental Health. Dr. Cizza is now a staff clinician at the US National Institute of Diabetes and Digestive and Kidney Diseases.

BACKGROUND

A woman's bone mass peaks during youth, then thins after menopause. Previous preliminary studies had suggested that depression might be a risk factor for low bone mass in older women.

NEW STUDY

For this study, Dr. Cizza and his colleagues looked at 89 women with depression and 44 women without depression. The women ranged in age from 21 to 45. The depressed women were taking antidepressant medications.

Seventeen percent of the depressed women had thinner bone density in the femoral neck, a vulnerable part of the hip. Only 2% of non-depressed women, by contrast, had thinner bone in this area.

Twenty percent of depressed women also had low bone density in the lumbar spine, compared with 9% of the non-depressed women.

Blood and urine samples also revealed that the depressed women had lower levels of "good" anti-inflammatory cytokines, proteins secreted by immune system cells.

"The bad cytokines that may cause bone loss are higher," Dr. Cizza said.

RECOMMENDATIONS

It's not clear what role antidepressants might play, but by relieving the depression, the drugs may also help bone mineral density, the researchers said.

"Premenopausal women who have depression should be screened for low bone mass," advised Dr. Cizza.

"They should have a bone mineral density measurement, because osteoporosis is a silent condition. Until someone fractures, you don't know you have osteoporosis," he said.

info To learn more about bone health, visit the Web site of the National Osteoporosis Foundation, *www.nof.org*.

■ ■ ■ ■

Fat That Makes You Sad

In a recent study, researchers took blood samples from 43 people and found that those who had significantly higher levels of omega-6s (found in refined vegetable oils, such as corn oil) compared with omega-3s (found in cold-water fish, such as salmon or trout…walnuts…and flaxseeds) reported more symptoms of depression than those who had lower levels.

Theory: Omega-6s can cause chronic inflammation, which has been linked to depression. Omega-3s, on the other hand, have anti-inflammatory effects.

Self-defense: Eat at least two three-ounce servings weekly of cold-water fish or take a supplement containing omega-3s.

Janice Kiecolt-Glaser, PhD, professor and director, division of health psychology, Ohio State University College of Medicine, Columbus.

■ ■ ■ ■

Obesity Drug Is Linked to Depression and Anxiety

Overweight people who take *rimonabant* (Zimulti, Acomplia), which is prescribed to help obese people manage their weight, have twice the risk for severe depression and anxiety as overweight people who don't take the drug. Other side effects of rimonabant include suicidal thoughts, dry mouth and headache. If you take rimonabant and have these side effects, talk to your doctor about switching to a different weight-loss drug.

Arne Astrup, MD, head, department of nutrition, University of Copenhagen, Denmark, and leader of four studies of 4,105 people, reported in *The Lancet.*

Supplement That Works as Well as Antidepressant

Mark A. Stengler, ND, naturopathic physician in private practice, La Jolla, California…adjunct associate clinical professor at the National College of Natural Medicine, Portland, Oregon…author of many books, including *The Natural Physician's Healing Therapies* and coauthor of *Prescription for Natural Cures* (both from Bottom Line Books)…and author of the *Bottom Line/Natural Healing* newsletter.

Meghan's mother was at her wit's end. "I know teenagers are temperamental, but Meghan's moodiness seems extreme. Her irritability is affecting the entire family," she told me, casting a troubled glance at her 15-year-old daughter. When I asked Meghan about her health, the girl's sullen face and curt answers confirmed her mother's words.

First I considered whether Meghan's diet might be contributing to her ill temper. Because glucose is the primary fuel source for the brain, blood sugar imbalances can cause irritability. I recommended that Meghan include protein—eggs, legumes, whey protein shakes—with every meal. Because protein is absorbed into the bloodstream slowly, it stabilizes blood sugar levels. I also suggested that she eat more vegetables and fewer sweets to minimize blood sugar spikes. To provide the basic nutrients needed for a healthful balance of *neurotransmitters*—brain chemicals that influence mood—I advised that she take multivitamin and fish oil supplements daily.

Exercise would have increased production of neurotransmitters, but Meghan was unwilling. Because her symptoms were constant rather than cyclical, it seemed that the girl's irascibility was not linked to her menstrual cycle or other hormonal influences. I considered the herb St. John's wort, which can ease mild-to-moderate depression by prolonging activity of mood-boosting neurotransmitters—but Meghan had taken it previously without effect, so I opted against it. After a few weeks on the new diet, Meghan's mood improved slightly, yet clearly the problem was not resolved.

NEW TEST

I then learned about a new urine test that measures neurotransmitters, including *serotonin*, which has an antidepressant and calming effect...as well as *dopamine* and *norepinephrine*, which increase energy and motivation. No other type of neurotransmitter testing is available, so even though the urine tests were (and still are) in the investigational stage, I decided to try them. (Your doctor can get information from NeuroScience Inc., 888-342-7272, *www. neurorelief.com*.)

Results showed that Meghan had very low levels of serotonin. The cause is unknown but may be genetic. I did not want Meghan to take serotonin-boosting antidepressant drugs because these can cause anxiety, insomnia, nausea and liver damage. Instead, I prescribed the amino acid *5-hydroxytryptophan* (5-HTP)—which is converted in the brain into serotonin—taken daily in capsule form. This supplement is sold at health food stores, is appropriate for teens and adults, and occasionally causes nausea. It can be taken indefinitely and should not be used with antidepressant or psychiatric drugs.

Two months later, Meghan's mother was astonished at the transformation. She told me, "Meghan is even-tempered and polite once again. She has lots of energy, swims daily and does homework without complaint. The whole family is delighted with the change—and Meghan is, too."

■ ■ ■ ■

Loneliness May Raise Alzheimer's Risk

In a recent study, it was found that older adults who feel lonely are twice as likely to develop Alzheimer's disease as people who do not.

Self-defense: If loneliness is accompanied by symptoms of depression, consult a psychologist or psychiatrist.

Best: Maintain connections with others to safeguard your mental health.

Robert S. Wilson, PhD, researcher, Rush Alzheimer's Disease Center, Rush University Medical Center, Chicago, and leader of a study of 823 people, published in *Archives of General Psychiatry*.

■ ■ ■ ■

Is It Depression or Low Testosterone?

In two recent studies that looked at a total of 1,050 men with low levels of the hormone testosterone, those who received testosterone replacement therapy for three years, on average, had a 70% improvement in scores on a standard test used to diagnose depression.

Theory: *Hypogonadism* (low testosterone) can affect mood and result in depression. It can also cause fatigue, joint and muscle aches, and erectile dysfunction, all conditions that can, in turn, lead to depression.

Self-defense: If you're a man who experiences any or all of these symptoms, ask your doctor to assess your symptoms and check your testosterone level via blood tests. If you are diagnosed with hypogonadism, ask if testosterone replacement therapy is appropriate.

Caution: Men with prostate cancer, liver disease or high hematocrit (the volume of red cells in the blood) should not receive testosterone replacement therapy.

Lawrence Komer, MD, medical director, Masters Men's Clinic, Burlington, Ontario.

■ ■ ■ ■

Depressed? It Could Be Low Folate Levels

In a recent study people with low levels of the nutrient folate (folic acid) have as much as a 55% higher risk of depression.

Self-defense: Individuals who have a personal or family history of depression should have their blood tested for folate.

If levels are low: Eat folate-rich foods—breakfast cereals, leafy green vegetables, lentils, dried beans, liver and wheat germ—and take a daily multivitamin with 400 micrograms (mcg) of folic acid.

Mark A. Stengler, ND, naturopathic physician in private practice, La Jolla, California…adjunct associate clinical professor at the National College of Natural Medicine, Portland, Oregon…author of many books, including *The Natural Physician's Healing Therapies* and coauthor of *Prescription for Natural Cures* (both from Bottom Line Books)…and author of the *Bottom Line/Natural Healing* newsletter.

Not Your Teenager's Eating Disorder

Trisha Gura, PhD, author of *Lying in Weight: The Hidden Epidemic of Eating Disorders in Adult Women.* HarperCollins. Dr. Gura is a Knight Science Journalism fellow at Harvard University and Massachusetts Institute of Technology, both in Cambridge, Massachusetts, and a resident scholar at Brandeis University in Waltham, Massachusetts. *www.trishagura.com.*

One night, Katie ate a "stew" of leftovers —stale pasta, wrinkled grapes, half a can of refried beans and week-old slices of beef. Other nights, she gnawed on frozen food without defrosting it…or microwaved it and then ate it so fast that it scalded her mouth. Sometimes she ate from the trash can. Why?

Because, she thought, if she could make food repulsive or tasteless enough—or even dangerous enough—she might not binge again. Yet more often than not, the next night she would go on another binge—alone in her kitchen,

shoveling down food until she was painfully full…and completely disgusted with herself.

Katie may sound like a teenager in trouble. In fact, she's an adult—49 years old and suffering from binge-eating disorder (BED). Along with *bulimia* (bingeing that is followed by forced vomiting, overusing laxatives, excessive exercising or fasting) and *anorexia* (self-starvation), BED is one of three major eating disorders. Many people have never heard of BED—though it affects more than three times as many women as bulimia does and about four times as many as anorexia does. BED is widely unrecognized because people primarily binge alone, in ashamed secrecy.

Eating disorders afflict at least 10 million Americans, most of them female. While no exact figures are available, some treatment facilities report that the number of midlife women seeking help has tripled or quadrupled in the last five years. Among these women, as many as half may have BED.

HIDDEN PROBLEMS

In adult women, an eating disorder typically appears when a stressful transition—a divorce, a move, a parent's death—either triggers the recurrence of an adolescent eating disorder or launches a new one. In the face of intense or chronic stress, people are prone to return to familiar bad habits—and for many women, those involve food.

An eating disorder can have serious emotional and social consequences. A woman with BED or bulimia isolates herself because she is too embarrassed to eat in front of family or friends, so she stays home when others go out in order to be alone with her food. A woman with anorexia isolates herself because she doesn't want the temptation of being around food and she worries that others will notice how little she eats. Among women with eating disorders, self-loathing is common.

In addition, eating disorders carry grave health risks…

•**BED can lead to obesity,** with all the accompanying health problems, including increased risk for hypertension, high cholesterol, heart disease and stroke…diabetes…gallbladder disease...sleep apnea and respiratory problems ...and breast, endometrial and colon cancers.

•**Bulimia can cause nutritional deficiencies...**weakened immunity...erosion of tooth enamel, periodontal disease and inflamed salivary glands...muscle spasms...chronic constipation...pancreatitis...inflammation and possible rupture of the esophagus...permanent damage to the heart or kidneys...and electrolyte imbalances that can lead to heart failure and death.

•**Anorexia can lead to dehydration and malnutrition...**weakened immunity...infertility ...osteoporosis...damage to the heart and kidneys...and death from starvation.

HOPE FOR HEALING

It's never too late to develop an eating disorder—and it's never too late to seek help. Confide in your doctor, and ask for a referral to a mental-health professional.

Resource: The National Eating Disorders Association (800-931-2237, *www.nationaleatingdisorders.org*) provides referrals to doctors, counselors and residential treatment facilities in your area. *Approaches to treatment include...*

•**Cognitive-behavioral therapy (CBT).** There is more scientific evidence for the effectiveness of this therapy than there is for any other, particularly in treating BED and bulimia. CBT helps you to recognize the circumstances, emotions and thoughts that trigger a binge or other problem behavior, and then to change that behavior—for instance, by phoning a friend or going for a walk instead.

Referrals: National Association of Cognitive-Behavioral Therapists, (800-853-1135, *www.nacbt.org*).

•**Interpersonal therapy.** In one-on-one sessions with a psychologist or psychiatrist, you talk about your past and your relationships. Over time, you come to understand the underlying causes of your eating disorder so that it no longer controls you.

•**Adult in-patient treatment.** Some clinics offer programs specifically for women over age 30, including the Renfrew Center, with eight facilities on the East Coast (800-736-3739, *www.renfrewcenter.com*)...and Remuda Ranch in Wickenburg, Arizona, and Milford, Virginia (800-445-1900, *www.remudaranch.com*).

•**Support groups.** Meeting regularly with a group of adult women who also are combating eating disorders can provide a social network of sympathetic friends, practical advice for overcoming the problem and a sense of self-worth when you help another woman who is suffering.

Contact: Eating Disorder Referral and Information Center (858-792-7463, *www.edreferral.com*).

•**Medications.** Drugs appear not to be very effective in treating most eating disorders. However, if you also are depressed, antidepressant medication may help you feel more optimistic, which in turn may help you gain control over your eating. Ask your doctor or a psychiatrist about this option.

•**Creative endeavors.** An eating disorder keeps you isolated and secretive. Healing from such a disorder involves projecting your voice and personality into the community. Join a writers' group, take a class in art or dance, or get involved with an organization that advocates for a better world.

If one type of therapy does not help you, don't just give up—try a different approach. With the right help, you can recover.

Doctors Often Fail to Spot Suicidal Patients

Mitchell Feldman, MD, professor, medicine, University of California at San Francisco.

David Rudd, PhD, chair, psychology department, Texas Tech University, Lubbock.

Annals of Family Medicine.

Pointing to a disconnect between doctors and some of their patients in greatest need, a new study suggests that large numbers of physicians fail to spot symptoms that raise suicide risk.

US researchers recruited actresses to act as patients and visit physicians while showing signs of depression or a similar disorder.

Result: Only 36% of the doctors asked the "patients" about suicidal thoughts, the team found.

"There is often a window of opportunity for doctors to screen for suicidality and intervene appropriately, but, as we found, they frequently miss this opportunity," said study lead author Mitchell Feldman, MD, professor of medicine at the University of California at San Francisco.

BACKGROUND

According to Dr. Feldman, an estimated 2% to 7% of patients who visit primary-care physicians are thinking about suicide. In fact, as many as 75% of people who commit suicide visited a primary-care provider in the 30 days before killing themselves, the research shows.

Still, patients at risk for suicide rarely mention the topic directly to physicians, leaving it up to doctors to figure out what's going on.

"Remarkably little is known about the factors that influence whether primary-care physicians broach the topic of suicide with their depressed patients," Dr. Feldman said.

NEW STUDY

Researchers recruited 152 physicians from northern California and Rochester, New York to take part. All were told they would get unannounced visits by actors portraying patients who would tape-record their conversations.

A total of 18 actresses visited the doctors playing two types of patients—a person with major depression or a person with an "adjustment disorder," a catchall term encompassing a variety of mental problems. Some of the "patients" asked for medication.

RESULTS

Doctors were more likely to pursue the prospect of suicide if the "patients" said they had major depression or asked for medication. Doctors who had personal experience with depression were three times more likely to look into suicide.

POSSIBLE EXPLANATIONS

"Most physicians are not adequately trained to diagnose and treat mental and behavioral problems generally, and this problem is magnified with an issue like suicide that may evoke discomfort in some physicians who will then avoid the topic," Dr. Feldman said. "Some mistakenly believe that if they inquire about suicide, they will prompt the patient to consider it."

Dr. Feldman added, "I describe suicide as another of the Pandora's Box issues—like domestic violence—that doctors may avoid broaching for fear that once they bring it up, they will be unable to contain the patient's emotional responses. And, in addition, they will put themselves way behind schedule."

David Rudd, PhD chair of the psychology department at Texas Tech University, agreed with Dr. Feldman. Dr. Rudd, who's familiar with the study findings, blamed physician inaction on inadequate training, a fear of making things worse, and "anxiety and apprehension about handling suicidal crises."

RECOMMENDATIONS

What to do? Dr. Feldman said doctors need better education about suicidal patients, and patients need to know more about depression and feel comfortable asking for help. "We found that patients who make requests get more thorough and appropriate care including more inquiries about suicide from their physician."

info To learn more about suicide, visit the National Institute of Mental Health Web site, *www.nimh.nih.gov*. Click on "Health & Outreach" and then "Suicide Prevention."

■ ■ ■ ■

Suicides Are on The Rise Among Middle-Aged Americans

As of 2005 (the most recent data available), the number of suicides among people ages 45 to 54 was 16.5 per 100,000 people per year—the highest in 25 years. Experts don't know why suicide is increasing in this age group, but prevention programs tend to focus on suicide among teenagers and the elderly. If you think a loved one is contemplating suicide, contact the American Foundation for Suicide Prevention, 800-273-8255, *www.afsp.org*.

Mark Kaplan, DrPH, suicide researcher, Portland State University, Portland, Oregon.

■ ■ ■ ■

If You Fear Going to The Dentist...

Anxiety about going to the dentist is common, but fear shouldn't prevent you from keeping your teeth in good health.

The American Dental Association offers these suggestions to help ease anxiety at the dentist's office...

•**Talk to your dentist** or hygienist about your anxiety, so they can better understand and accommodate your needs.

•**Schedule appointments when you have plenty of time** and won't feel rushed, such as very early in the morning or on a Saturday.

•**Bring soothing music** to distract you during your appointment. This is especially helpful if the sounds in a dental office bother you.

•**Visualize yourself somewhere pleasant** —on a beach, with family or at a park.

Body Clock Can't Be Set to Daylight Saving Time

Till Roenneberg, PhD, Ludwig-Maximilians-University, Munich, Germany.
Louis Ptacek, MD, investigator, Howard Hughes Medical Institute, and professor, Department of Neurology, and director, Division of Neurogenetics, University of California, San Francisco.
Current Biology online.

Changing to daylight saving time may give people an hour more of sunlight, but it appears that their internal body clocks never really adjust to the change, German researchers report.

In fact, daylight saving time can cause a significant seasonal disruption that might have other effects on our bodies.

"When you change clocks to daylight saving time, you don't change anything related to sun time," explained lead researcher Till Roenneberg, PhD, of Ludwig-Maximilians-University in Munich. "This is one of those human arrogances

—that we can do whatever we want as long as we are disciplined. We forget that there is a biological clock that is as old as living organisms, a clock that cannot be fooled. The pure social change of time cannot fool the clock."

BACKGROUND

People's circadian rhythm—the body's internal clock—follows the sun and changes depending on where you live. It actually changes in four-minute intervals, exactly the time it takes for the sun to cross one line of longitude, Dr. Roenneberg explained.

"The circadian clock does not conform to the social change," Dr. Roenneberg said. "During the winter, there is a beautiful tracking of dawn in human sleep behavior, which is completely and immediately interrupted when daylight saving time is introduced in March," he said.

Daylight saving time may be one cause of what Dr. Roenneberg calls our lack of seasonality. By seasonality, he means that our internal clock is in tune with the natural change in light throughout the year. "This could have long-term effects," he said.

STUDY #1

Dr. Roenneberg's group collected data on the sleep patterns of 55,000 people in Central Europe. The researchers found that sleep time on days off work when daylight saving time took effect followed the seasonal progression of dawn under standard time, but not under daylight saving time.

STUDY #2

In another study, Dr. Roenneberg's group looked at the timing of sleep and activity for eight weeks during the change to daylight saving time in 50 people, taking into account each person's natural clock preferences, or "chronotypes," which range from morning larks to night owls.

For both morning larks and night owls, timing for sleep and peak activity easily adjusted when daylight saving time ended in the fall. However, it never adjusted to the return to daylight saving time in spring. This was especially true for night owls—those who stay up late and sleep late.

IMPLICATION

"If we didn't change to daylight saving time, people would adjust to dawn during the summer and again to dawn in the autumn," said Dr. Roenneberg. "But this natural adjustment is interrupted by daylight saving time," he said.

EXPERT COMMENTARY

"It is not surprising that when you change our time to respond to something other than the sun and daylight that different chronotypes are going to have a difficult time," said Louis Ptacek, MD, an investigator at the Howard Hughes Medical Institute and director of the Division of Neurogenetics at the University of California, San Francisco.

"Before artificial lighting, humans tended to live much more by the sun cycle," Dr. Ptacek said. "Whereas, now, people stay up all night and turn the lights on, which affects our biological clock. There is no question that we have been changing our clocks long before daylight saving time came along."

So, it's not surprising that daylight saving time affects our internal clock, Dr. Ptacek said. However, it is no more unnatural than our use of artificial light, he noted.

There is no reason to abandon daylight saving time, Dr. Ptacek added. "There may be societal benefits to daylight saving time, such as saving energy."

info For more information on circadian rhythms, visit the Northwestern University Web site at *www.northwestern.edu/cscb/about.html.*

When You May Have a Serious Illness...

Marjory Abrams, publisher, *Bottom Line* newsletters, Boardroom Inc., 281 Tresser Blvd., Stamford, Connecticut 06901.

Following two suspicious mammograms and an inconclusive ultrasound, I recently had a biopsy. Thankfully, it was negative, but the prolonged period of testing and then waiting for results was a very uneasy time. I had never before had to confront the real possibility of having a serious illness. I felt afraid of my body...that I had a hole inside me, where I had disassociated myself from my tumor. I am shocked at how much I cried.

Because so many people are in similar situations, I asked psychologist Neil Fiore, PhD (*www.neilfiore.com*), how to cope with the stress of being tested for cancer or another major disease. Thirty years ago, Neil was told that he had testicular cancer and had only one year to live. He strongly believes that his attitude about his body, which he wrote about in his book *The Road Back to Health: Coping with the Emotional Aspects of Cancer*, saved his life.

Here are some strategies that he recommends for the waiting period—and postdiagnosis, too...

•**Keep telling yourself that whatever the problem,** most of you is healthy, powerful and ready to fight disease.

•**Find out in advance what steps you should take if the test is positive.** Treatment decisions do not have to be made all at once, but knowing what may be immediately ahead of you makes the process more manageable and less frightening. As Neil explained, "The worrying mind needs to be heard, but it also needs a plan."

•**Use deep breathing and isometric exercises to destress.** Curl your toes, scrunch your face, tense your other muscles. Hold for a few seconds as you also hold your breath—and then let go of muscle tension as you exhale.

•**Rate your stress level from zero (none) to 10.** When you assign a number—say, a level of three to an unpleasant phone call—it tells your body that you don't need a full dose of stress hormones. Your body will quickly adjust the level of your stress response to the situation.

•**Express your emotions**. Releasing your emotions helps your immune system and has been shown to increase the number of white blood cells that fight infection and cancer.

Trying to deny your feelings in order to act cheerful may lower your immune response.

Write your feelings down in a journal, scream them in your car, sing the blues, dance them out...but get them out of your gut. Being honest and open with yourself will make it easier to cope with whatever fate throws your way.

Don't Let Grief Ruin Your Health

Phyllis Kosminsky, PhD, clinical social worker specializing in grief, loss and trauma at the Darien, Connecticut–based Center for Hope/Family Centers, a nonprofit organization that offers services to people coping with a life-threatening illness or the loss of a loved one. She also is in private practice in Pleasantville, New York, and Norwalk, Connecticut. She is author of *Getting Back to Life When Grief Won't Heal.* McGraw-Hill.

When someone close to you dies, it's natural to grieve. The ache may never go away entirely, but you gradually accept that your loved one is gone, and you find a new way for life to feel normal.

But for up to 15% of bereaved people, intense grief can linger for years or even decades. This so-called *complicated grief* is powerful enough to disrupt the bereaved person's ability to work, get along with others and/or to find much pleasure in anything. Although elements of depression are present, complicated grief also is marked by chronic and persistent yearning and longing for the deceased…and an inability to accept the loss.

Especially in older adults, complicated grief can go undetected by doctors and family members—or even the sufferers themselves. Regardless of age, the condition can contribute to chronic depression, drug and alcohol abuse and certain infectious diseases (by weakening the immune system). In people who have heart disease, the emotional stress created by complicated grief can worsen their condition.

HURT BUT HEALING

A person who is grieving is bound to experience feelings of sadness, emptiness, loss—and often anger. Physical symptoms are also common. You lack energy and feel fatigued. You may have trouble sleeping—or do nothing but sleep. You find it hard to concentrate and may even wonder about the meaning of life. Some people lose their appetites, while others eat uncontrollably. Headaches, digestive problems, and other aches and pains often occur.

These grief responses may actually serve a purpose. The psychological pain and physical symptoms force you to slow down, giving your mind and body the opportunity to heal.

Important: There's no fixed timetable for grieving. No one can say "you should be over it" in three months, six months or even a year. As long as the general trend is toward feeling better, it's normal to have ups and downs.

GRIEF CAN BE COMPLICATED

If painful feelings last for more than a few months—and don't seem to be getting better—something may have gone wrong with the grieving process.

Red flags: Thoughts of the lost person constantly intrude throughout the day…or you're simply unable to speak about your loss…or normal life seems impossible, and you feel you can't survive without the person.

Complicated grief is more likely to occur if your relationship with the person you lost was characterized by…

•**Dependence.** We all depend on those we love. But such dependence is excessive when you can't let yourself acknowledge that the person you need so badly is dead and no longer there for you.

•**Ambivalence.** Virtually all relationships have some degree of ambivalence. For example, it's common to love a parent for his/her strength and reliability, but resent that person's tendency toward harsh judgment. Even in the most loving of marriages, anger comes up from time to time. Recognizing our negative feelings toward the deceased person can trigger guilt, so we instinctively push away those thoughts. However, the negative thoughts invariably find their way back into our consciousness, until we acknowledge them.

Regardless of the nature of the relationship, a sudden or otherwise traumatic death can complicate the task of grieving. You relive the moment—or keep trying to push it out of your mind. Problems also arise when death follows an extended illness, triggering both grief and guilt-inducing relief that the person is no longer suffering—and perhaps that you no longer have to take care of him.

ALLOWING YOURSELF TO GRIEVE

Grieving involves experiencing your full range of emotions, including anger, resentment and relief as well as sadness. These feelings may be hard to bear, especially if you have no one with whom to share them. Most people find it helpful to have the emotional support of others.

What to do…

•**Don't isolate yourself.** Spend time with compassionate, understanding friends and family members who are willing to listen, and tell them how you feel.

If you need to talk more than these people are willing to listen, consider joining a grief support group. Meeting regularly with people who share a similar loss gives you the opportunity to express your feelings. Local hospitals, hospices and mental-health facilities can help you find a support group.

On-line support groups can be helpful if you live in a remote area, prefer not to deal with others face-to-face or lack transportation. To find an on-line support group, go to the Internet community GriefNet, *www.griefnet.org.*

•**Be active.** For many people, doing is better than simply talking. Volunteer work can be especially healing—helping others diverts you from your own sadness and is a powerful way to help yourself.

Physical exercise also is a potent mood-lifter, a general aid to mental health. Anything that gets you moving is a step in the right direction.

•**Take time to grieve.** Particularly if you have a busy schedule, spend five to 10 minutes a day in a quiet, private place where you feel safe and comfortable experiencing your grief. Focus on your feelings and on thoughts about the deceased. This way, if your grief intrudes during the day, you can remind yourself that you will have a chance to grieve at some point later.

WHEN TO GET HELP

If your own efforts to deal with grief aren't enough, a professional can help you find where and why you're stuck.

Consider therapy or counseling if you're showing signs of depression—you can't work, can't sleep, can't eat, can't get interested in anything or can't deal with other people. Ask your physician to direct you to a therapist or counselor with experience in dealing with grief. Or you can find a list of "thanatologists"—grief specialists—from

the Association for Death Education and Counseling, 847-509-0403, *www.adec.org.*

You also may want to consult your doctor about short-term use of medication to help you function in your day-to-day activities.

Best Ways Give Comfort

Joy Browne, PhD, clinical psychologist in New York City. Her internationally syndicated call-in radio show, *The Dr. Joy Browne Show,* is the longest-running of its kind (*www.drjoy.com*). She is author of many books, including *Getting Unstuck: 8 Simple Steps to Solving Any Problem.* Hay House.

Each year, I get hundreds of calls from people asking about the best way to comfort a friend or relative who has suffered a serious loss or setback. There are right things—and wrong things—to say and do at such times.

First, beware of well-meant but misguided words that spark resentment.

Examples: "I know how you feel" (the other person may think, *No, you don't*)…"It will all work out for the best" (*How could you possibly know that?*)…or "It's God's will" (*Who are you to say what God wants?*). So what should you say? Keep it simple—"I'm so sorry for your loss."

Don't let fear of saying the wrong thing keep you away. Realistically, one person can't take away another's pain. But showing up *in person* sends a clear message—"I care about you, and I'm here to help if there's anything I can do." Your presence can lighten the other person's sense of isolation—and you may find there *is* something concrete you can do to help.

I'm also a great fan of the hug. A touch communicates our caring well beyond our ability to verbalize. Whether or not you know what to say, a warm embrace brings a measure of comfort.

If it is impossible to visit in person, a phone call is better than nothing. Follow up with a note of condolence—handwritten, not E-mailed.

Miracles Do Happen

Joan Borysenko, PhD, cofounder and former director of the mind-body clinical programs at two Harvard Medical School hospitals, now merged as Boston's Beth Israel Deaconess Medical Center. Based in Boulder, Colorado, she runs workshops and conducts lectures on mind-body healing. An updated 20th anniversary edition of her 1987 best seller *Minding the Body, Mending the Mind* was just released. Da Capo. *www.joanborysenko.com.*

On occasion, a health problem that was expected to be permanent or fatal instead disappears without medical intervention. The limited research that has been done suggests that the reason why one person recovers when most others do not might have as much to do with the mind as the body.

Joan Borysenko, PhD, a former Harvard medical scientist who is a renowned expert in the field of mind/body healing, relayed these true stories of spontaneous healing...

MIND/BODY CURE

In 1985, Alice Epstein, a sociology doctoral student at the University of Massachusetts, was diagnosed with kidney cancer. One of her kidneys was removed, but it was no use—the cancer had spread to her lungs, and treatment was impossible. Epstein was told she had only a few more months to live.

With no way to treat the physical problem, Epstein and her psychology-professor husband decided to treat her mind. Epstein used meditation to reduce her stress, and psychotherapy to deal with the angry, unhappy component of her personality. Within six weeks, tests showed that her cancer was going into remission. Her progress slowed when she took time off from the intensive psychotherapy but resumed once the psychotherapy resumed. The cancer eventually disappeared. Epstein earned her PhD and is still alive today, more than 20 years later.

•**What may have happened.** Eliminating stress and anger will not cure every disease, but it can trigger a host of biochemical changes in the body—including providing a boost to the immune system. It is possible that Epstein's aggressive mental treatments played a role in her return to physical health.

A VISION IN LOURDES

Nearly 150 years ago, a teenage girl in Lourdes, France, reported seeing a vision of the Virgin Mary. Ever since, the waters in that area have been credited with healing powers. Most of these incidents involve cancer, multiple sclerosis and other diseases that occasionally go into remission, even without a visit to Lourdes.

The 1908 case of Marie Bire is more interesting. The 41-year-old French woman was blind as a result of optic atrophy—the degeneration of her optic nerve. According to medical science, it should not have been possible for optic nerves to recover from such a condition.

At Lourdes, the blind Bire attended Mass and received Holy Communion. Then, as the Blessed Sacrament in procession was passing the place where she sat, she suddenly regained her sight. Ten doctors examined Bire. They all found that her optic nerves were still withered but that she could see.

•**What may have happened.** We do not have to believe in divine miracles to believe that Bire's faith might have played a role in her recovery. Studies have found that depending upon the medical condition, between 30% and 50% of people respond to placebos. If you tell these people that you have given them painkillers, their brain activity will show that they actually feel less pain.

CONFIDENCE DESPITE THE ODDS

In 1975, Ian Gawler, a 24-year-old Australian veterinarian and decathlete, learned that he had bone cancer in his right leg. The leg was amputated, but the cancer reappeared later that year and spread throughout his body. In 1976, Gawler was given two weeks to live. No one had ever been known to recover from such an advanced case of this form of cancer. As a doctor, Gawler knew that the reasonable response was to prepare for death. Instead, he remained certain that he would recover. He focused on meditation, positive thinking and a natural diet.

Gawler did recover. He now runs The Gawler Foundation (*www.gawler.org*), which provides support for others suffering from serious illnesses. The foundation stresses healthy food, meditation and belief in recovery.

•**What may have happened.** We cannot simply imagine cancer away, but there is reason to think that believing in the desired health outcome might improve the odds that it will occur.

SURROUNDED BY LOVE

Fifty years ago, the outlook was bleak for those suffering psychotic hallucinations. Today's pharmaceuticals and cognitive behavior therapy were not yet available. Recovery was very rare.

That was bad news for one previously healthy 10-year-old girl growing up in the 1950s. Her nightmares had entered her waking life—she saw snakes, scorpions and headhunters. The girl believed that these tormentors were going to kill her family and that the only way she could stop them was to repeat obsessive-compulsive behaviors, such as scraping the inside of her mouth with her fingernails, reading books only upside down and backward, rereading each sentence three times and erasing everything she wrote three times before continuing. The girl eventually was pulled from school and lived each day in a landscape of terror.

For months, she prayed intensely for a cure. One day during these prayers, she suddenly felt surrounded by love and wisdom, as though she were being held in the arms of God. Her fear instantly disappeared, and she stopped her obsessive-compulsive behavior cold turkey. Within days, all of her symptoms were gone, never to return.

I was that little girl. The experience sparked my lifelong interest in psychology and spirituality.

•**What may have happened.** Most people with mental disorders cannot just pray their way to recovery. Still, it is worth noting that many people who experience spontaneous healing also experience a transformative spiritual episode similar to mine—a single moment when they feel aided by a loving, powerful outside force.

HOW TO USE YOUR MIND TO HEAL

Some things we can do when we are seriously ill that will benefit our overall health…

•**Do not let your mind be pulled into worry or into the past or the future.** Spend time each day doing something that makes you feel good and keeps you in the present, whether it is gardening, meditating or walking in nature.

•**Forgive any wrongs that have been done to you.** Letting go of anger and regrets can reduce stress and boost your immune system.

•**Have gratitude.** Before going to bed, be truly grateful for something that happened that day. Wasn't it wonderful when someone smiled at you? Soak up these positive feelings.

•**Imagine the health outcome that you desire.** Picture the disease disappearing from your body. If you have trouble visualizing a positive health outcome, begin by picturing other things that make you happy.

Why You'll Bounce Back Faster Than You Think

Nathan DeWall, PhD, assistant professor, psychology, University of Kentucky, Lexington.
Todd Kashdan, PhD, assistant professor, psychology, George Mason University, Fairfax, Virginia.
Psychological Science.

When thoughts of death intrude, the human mind isn't paralyzed with negativity or fear. Instead, the brain instinctively moves toward happier notions and images, a new study suggests.

The finding supports the belief that people are stronger, emotionally, when faced with their own or a loved one's death than they may have ever thought possible.

"It again speaks to how resilient humans are and how this tendency to cope with threats is some sort of indicator of mental health," said study coauthor Nathan DeWall, PhD, assistant professor of psychology at the University of Kentucky.

BACKGROUND

Humans are the only animals known to have a clear understanding that their life will end. On the surface, this knowledge could prove psychologically paralyzing—why compete, learn and grow if these achievements will end?

However, Dr. DeWall and other scientists believe that as humans developed an awareness of death, they also evolved what's been called the "psychological immune system."

During crisis, this mechanism tilts thoughts and attitudes toward the positive—even when the grimmest of events intervene. This mental shift is typically unconscious, Dr. DeWall said.

"That's why, when you ask people to predict how they'll respond to something negative, they usually say, 'Oh, it will be horrible, and it will last a long time,'" he said. However, studies don't bear that out—research involving people stricken with disease or disability show that people tend to bounce back emotionally much more rapidly than they would have expected.

THE STUDY

In their latest experiments, Dr. DeWall and colleagues first primed more than 100 healthy young adult volunteers to think about death as a reality. They asked them to imagine the process of their own death, as well as what it might be like to be dead.

Another group of young adults was asked to think about an unpleasant event—a trip to the dentist's office—but not death.

Immediately after the priming exercise, the researchers had all of the participants undergo standard word tests that tapped into unconscious emotional states. In one test, participants were give a word stem—"jo-" for example and asked to complete it to form a word (i.e., "job," "jog," "joy").

According to the researchers, individuals primed to think about death were much more likely than the other participants to choose the word "joy," compared to more neutral or negative words.

In another word test, the participants were offered a word and asked to pair it with one of two other words. One of the words was similar to the target word in its meaning, while the other word was more emotionally similar. For example, "puppy" might be paired with either "beetle" (another many-legged animal), or "parade" (not an animal, but fun, enjoyable, as puppies are).

Again, people primed to think about death were much more likely to choose "parade" over "beetle" compared to the other participants.

This suggests they unconsciously preferred the positive emotion embedded in that choice, the researchers said.

IMPLICATIONS

"People really don't know that they do this," Dr. DeWall said. "It's actually very counterintuitive. This picks up on the idea that when people are confronted with their own mortality, these sorts of concepts—positive emotion words—become readily accessible to them."

Another expert agreed that humans may be hardwired to "go to their happy place" when thoughts of death intrude.

"This is interesting work, because what it's really saying is that once you are primed with this idea that you're going to die, it sets off this automatic network," said Todd Kashdan, PhD, an expert in the psychology of positive emotions and an assistant professor of psychology at George Mason University, in Fairfax, Virginia.

The findings suggest that, in the face of death, one says, "I'm going to grab onto something that I know I can hang on to. It's not going to be negative things, I can't really hold on to that," Dr. Kashdan explained. "So, I'm going to focus on these positive things."

"These things are happening below the level of awareness," he added.

LONG-TERM OUTLOOK

Dr. Kashdan stressed that the Kentucky experiments focused on the very short term, however. Coping over the longer term may be much tougher, he said.

"What's going to happen to these people—not over the next few minutes but rather the next two weeks, six months? Do they end up reorganizing or shifting their life projects? There's research to show that for some people, it does, and for some people, it doesn't."

info For more information on the subject of positive psychology, visit the Web site of the University of Pennsylvania's Positive Psychology Center at *www.ppc.sas.upenn.edu*.

8

Family Health

Elective Cesareans Raise Risk of Breathing Problems in Newborns

Infants who are delivered by elective cesarean section are up to four times more likely to have breathing problems than babies born vaginally or by emergency C-section, says a Danish study published in the *British Medical Journal*.

THE STUDY

Researchers analyzed data on 34,000 births and found the 2,687 infants delivered by elective cesarean section had a nearly fourfold increased risk for breathing problems if they were delivered at 37 weeks' gestation, a threefold increased risk at 38 weeks' gestation and twice the risk at 39 weeks' gestation.

For example, 2.8% of infants delivered by intended vaginal delivery (which includes both vaginal delivery and emergency cesarean) at 37 weeks gestation had general respiratory problems, compared with 10% of infants delivered by elective cesarean section.

At 38 weeks, the rates were 1.7% versus 5.1%, and at 39 weeks, 1.1% versus 2.1%.

POSSIBLE EXPLANATION

The reasons why elective cesarean increases the risk for respiratory problems aren't clear. The study authors suggested that certain hormonal and physiological changes associated with labor are necessary for an infant's lungs to mature. These changes may not occur in infants delivered by elective c-section.

WHAT TO DO

Postponing elective cesarean section until 39 weeks gestation may greatly reduce the risk for breathing problems in infants, the researchers noted.

info For more information on cesarean sections, visit the Web site of the Nemours Foundation at *http://kidshealth.org/parent* and search "cesarean section."

BMJ Online First, news release.

■ ■ ■ ■

Unnecessary Cesarean Births Are Risky to Infants

B abies delivered via cesarean sections to women who did not require C-sections for medical reasons have twice the risk of dying within the first month as those born vaginally.

Safer: Have a C-section only if your doctor thinks it is necessary—not for convenience or to avoid the pain of vaginal delivery.

Marian F. MacDorman, PhD, statistician and senior social scientist, division of vital statistics, National Center for Health Statistics, Centers for Disease Control and Prevention, Atlanta.

Beware Baby Products Loaded with Chemicals

Sheela Sathyanarayana, MD, MPH, acting assistant professor, department of pediatrics, University of Washington, Seattle.
Jonathan Weinkle, MD, physician, Children's Hospital of Pittsburgh and University of Pittsburgh Cancer Institute's Center for Environmental Oncology.
American Chemistry Council statement.
Pediatrics.

M ore than 80% of infants tested in a new study had been exposed to phthalates, a potentially harmful group of chemicals used to make plastic softer and to help stabilize fragrance in personal care products.

Exactly what this means in terms of infant health isn't yet clear, however. Some animal studies have found these substances to be harmful to development, and one study on human infants found an association between exposure to a particular phthalate and male reproductive problems. Because the exact effects on the developing body aren't known, the researchers suggest limiting the use of products that contain these chemicals as much as possible. Baby lotion, baby shampoo and baby powder were all linked to phthalate exposure in the study.

"Right now, we still don't know the true long-term effects," said study author Sheela Sathyanarayana, MD, MPH, an acting assistant professor in the department of pediatrics at the University of Washington, Seattle. But, she added, it's probably a good idea to "decrease the amounts of products used, especially in newborns."

BACKGROUND

Phthalates are found in children's toys, infant care products, cosmetics, food packaging, vinyl flooring, blood storage containers and more, according to the US Centers for Disease Control and Prevention (CDC). Exposure to phthalates occurs when you use a product containing them, from breathing household dust containing phthalates, from medical treatments like dialysis that use products with phthalates, and from living near a manufacturing facility that uses phthalates, according to the CDC. Phthalates are banned from use in personal care products and in some toys in Europe.

THE STUDY

Researchers looked for nine different metabolites of phthalates in the urine of 163 infants born between 2000 and 2005. Testing the urine to look for evidence of phthalate exposure was necessary because manufacturers aren't required to disclose all phthalates in their products.

"Right now, manufacturers aren't required to label them, so it's difficult to know if you're using a product with phthalates," explained Dr. Sathyanarayana.

Researchers also questioned parents about which products they used on the babies.

THE RESULTS

Most of the infants studied—81%—had detectable levels of phthalate metabolites. Researchers found an association between higher levels of phthalate metabolites and the use of baby shampoo, lotion and powder. Diaper creams and baby wipes didn't appear to increase the concentration of phthalate metabolites in the urine, according to Dr. Sathyanarayana.

EXPERT COMMENTARY

"We believe that there is potential value in the study of metabolized phthalates. But we take great exception to any effort to draw unfounded conclusions that suggest human health risks are associated with the mere presence of very low levels of metabolized phthalates in urine," said Marian Stanley, manager of the Phthalates Esters Panel of the American Chemistry Council, a plastics industry trade group.

"With phthalates in particular, there's good research in multiple animal studies that these compounds can be harmful. It's interesting that industry is willing to accept animal studies to introduce new medication, but when something is found to be harmful, industry says, 'Well, those studies were just done on rats,'" said Jonathan Weinkle, MD, a physician at Children's Hospital of Pittsburgh and the University of Pittsburgh Cancer Institute's Center for Environmental Oncology. "If animals are useful models for things that are helpful, it's because their bodies are similar enough to ours. Animal models should be reliable for good and bad."

RECOMMENDATIONS

Both Drs. Weinkle and Sathyanarayana said that dose makes a difference. They recommend limiting the use of products containing phthalates if possible. They believe that the greater the exposure, the greater potential for harm. Dr. Sathyanarayana said that phthalates are often contained in fragrances, so a product that's fragrance-free may also be phthalate-free. There are products available that are labeled phthalate-free, she noted, but they're generally more expensive.

info For a database of safety ratings for cosmetics and personal care products, including children's products, visit the Environmental Working Group Web site, *http://cosmeticsdatabase.com*.

Nicotine in Breast Milk Shortens Baby's Nap Time

Monell Chemical Senses Center, news release.

Nicotine in breast milk disrupts babies' sleep patterns and shortens naps by one third, according to a new study,

"Infants spent less time sleeping overall and woke up from naps sooner when their mothers smoked prior to breast-feeding," said study lead author Julie A. Mennella, PhD, a psychobiologist at the Monell Chemical Senses Center, a nonprofit institute that researches the senses of taste, smell and chemical irritation.

Writing in the journal *Pediatrics*, Dr. Mennella and colleagues argued that these results should lead to further research on the impact of nicotine on infant development. Many women who quit smoking during pregnancy begin again while breast-feeding their infant, the researchers said.

"Because nicotine is not contraindicated during lactation, mothers may believe that smoking while breast-feeding will not harm their child as long as the child is not exposed to passive smoke. However, there has been very little research on either short- or long-term effects of nicotine delivered through breast milk," said Dr. Mennella.

THE STUDY

The team measured the feeding and sleeping patterns of 15 breast-fed infants over three and a half hours on two separate days. The infants were between two months and seven months old. All the mothers were current smokers who had abstained from smoking for at least 12 hours before the observation periods.

The mothers smoked one to three cigarettes before the first observation period and didn't smoke anything before the second period. On both occasions, the mothers breast-fed their infants on demand during the observation period. Following each feeding, the mothers laid the infants down in a cot or on the floor.

Researchers monitored the babies with an actigraph, a portable device that records sleep and activity. Levels of nicotine and cotinine, a chemical that is produced by the body from nicotine, were measured in breast milk samples provided by the mothers before each feeding.

THE RESULTS

Babies whose mothers smoked before the observation period napped for 53 minutes compared to 84 minutes of napping among babies whose mothers did not smoke. The 37% reduction in total sleep time was due to a shortening of the longest nap and to reductions in the amount of time spent in both active and quiet sleep.

Researchers noted that the infants consumed the same amount of breast milk during each observation period, suggesting that they tolerated the milk of women who smoked.

TIMING BREAST-FEEDING

Previous research by Dr. Mennella's team had shown that nicotine levels peak in breast milk 30 minutes to 60 minutes after smoking one to two cigarettes and are gone after three hours, suggesting that mothers can time their smoking and breast-feeding opportunities.

Additional research is needed to fully understand the impact of nicotine on infant development, Dr. Mennella said.

info To learn more about breast-feeding, visit the Centers for Disease Control and Prevention Web site, *www.cdc.gov/breastfeeding.*

■ ■ ■ ■

Smoking May Program Children to Smoke

Smoking during pregnancy may "program" unborn children to become smokers.

Recent study: Children whose mothers smoked while they were pregnant were three times more likely to begin smoking by age 14—and twice as likely to start after age 14—as children of women who did not smoke during pregnancy. Children of women who either never smoked or who quit during pregnancy but returned to smoking afterward were less likely to begin smoking.

Abdullah Al Mamun, PhD, senior lecturer, division of epidemiology and social medicine, University of Queensland, Herston, Australia, and leader of a study of 3,000 mothers and their children, published in *Tobacco Control.*

Even Tiny Babies Know Friend from Foe

Tracy Dennis, PhD, assistant professor, psychology, Hunter College, New York City.
Kiley Hamlin, doctoral student, developmental psychology, Yale University, New Haven, Connecticut.
Nature.

New research conducted at Yale University reveals that infants who have not yet learned language can still judge who is friend and who is foe. Babies as young as six months old prefer people who cooperate versus people who hurt, and this ability could be the foundation for moral thought and action later in life, say the Yale researchers.

"I think it is the first study that demonstrated that very young infants show some understanding of social cooperation," said Tracy Dennis, an expert on child development and assistant professor of psychology at Hunter College in New York City. "This is an important study."

BACKGROUND

Previous studies had showed that babies prefer physically attractive people, but there has been no data on whether babies judge people based on how they behave.

"We know babies evaluate others based on outside stuff, not necessarily inside stuff," said study author Kiley Hamlin, a doctoral candidate in developmental psychology at Yale University in New Haven, Connecticut. "We wanted to see whether or not babies, like adults, have evaluative mechanisms for other people based on behavior."

THE STUDY

Hamlin and her coauthors conducted a series of simple experiments to gauge whether 6- and 10-month-old infants preferred social individuals ("helpers") or antisocial individuals ("hinderers").

In one experiment, the infant watched a "climber" (basically a wood puppet with large eyes glued on to it) repeatedly try to climb a hill. On the third try, the climber was either given help or was pushed back down by a puppet.

The babies were then given the chance to choose (reach out and grasp) either the helper or hinderer puppet.

"Basically, we found very high rates of choosing of the helping character," Hamlin said.

IMPLICATIONS

One question is whether the babies are learning the behavior, or if it's something innate. The authors argue for the latter.

"Our results suggest that infants have a pretty advanced evaluating system that doesn't need much outside input to develop. It develops at a very early age, by six months," Hamlin said. "They are learning lots of stuff by six months, however, we know that it's incredibly unlikely that parents are explicitly teaching them anything about this. The fact that they can pick up on it by six months suggests that it's an important skill."

In fact, being able to distinguish between friend and foe could be an important survival skill. "It's important to tell who is going to be helpful, who is going to be threatening," Hamlin noted.

EXPERT COMMENTARY

"Even though these authors make a good argument that very young infants don't have a lot of time to learn, even some basic observation of people cooperating might be enough to make some learning take place," Dennis said. "It's important, but it's a study that people are going to debate about."

info To learn more about the stages of development during a child's early years, visit the Web site *www.childdevelopmentinfo. com* and click on "Development."

Can Sleep Make Kids Thinner?

Julie Lumeng, MD, assistant research scientist, University of Michigan Center for Human Growth and Development, and assistant professor, department of pediatrics and communicable diseases, C.S. Mott Children's Hospital, Ann Arbor, Michigan.

Stephen Sheldon, MD, director, Sleep Medicine Center, Children's Memorial Hospital, and professor of pediatrics, Northwestern University Feinberg School of Medicine, Chicago.

Pediatrics.

New research has uncovered a strong connection between a child's weight and the amount of sleep that child gets.

Sixth-graders who averaged less than 8.5 hours of sleep a night had a 23% rate of obesity, while their well-rested peers who averaged more than 9.25 hours of sleep had an obesity rate of just 12%, according to a new study.

"We found that children who got less sleep were more likely to be obese," said the study's lead author, Julie Lumeng, MD, an assistant research scientist at the University of Michigan Center for Human Growth and Development.

Dr. Lumeng said that even after compensating for other factors, such as the home environment, the link between less sleep and heavier weight was still apparent.

THE STUDY

The new study included 785 children who were in third grade at the start of the trial. Parents were interviewed about their children's sleep habits when the youngsters were in third grade and then again when they were in sixth grade. The researchers also measured the children's height and weight. Obesity was defined as having a body mass index, or BMI, (a ratio of weight to height) higher than the 95th percentile for age and gender, according to Dr. Lumeng.

The researchers also took into account maternal education, race, the quality of the home environment and parenting skills to see if those factors affected a child's weight.

Eighteen percent of the children were obese in sixth grade. No matter what a child weighed in third grade, too little sleep correlated with being obese in sixth grade. In addition, short sleep duration in sixth grade also correlated with excess weight in sixth grade, according to the study.

Third-graders who got less than nine hours and 45 minutes of sleep a night had an obesity prevalence of about 20%, while those who got more than nine hours and 45 minutes of sleep had obesity rates of about 12%, Dr. Lumeng said.

Those who were short-changing sleep in third grade had 40% higher odds of being obese in sixth grade. Moreover, sixth-graders who weren't getting enough sleep were 20% more likely to be obese, compared to their well-rested counterparts.

POSSIBLE EXPLANATIONS

Dr. Lumeng said there are three likely reasons why sleep might affect weight. First, if children don't get enough sleep at night, they'll be less likely to run around and get exercise during the day. Second, when kids are tired, they're more irritable and may reach for junk food to help regulate their mood. And, finally, what Dr. Lumeng called a "hot area for future research" is the possible connection between sleep and fat metabolism. She said there have been studies done with adults that have shown that a lack of sleep may disrupt the secretion of hormones involved in appetite and metabolism, such as leptin and insulin.

EXPERT COMMENTARY

Stephen Sheldon, MD, director of the Sleep Medicine Center at Children's Memorial Hospital in Chicago, said he would have liked to see sleep studies so the researchers could have known more about the quality of sleep these children were getting, such as how much REM (rapid eye movement) sleep did they get and how fragmented was the sleep?

Dr. Lumeng said the researchers weren't able to find a statistical association between quality of sleep and obesity. But, she said that without a lab-based sleep study, it's difficult to objectively assess the quality of the sleep being evaluated. There may well be an association that this study wasn't able to uncover.

SLEEP RECOMMENDATIONS

The bottom line is that "pediatricians and parents really need to start paying closer attention to sleep-wake habits. In this society, we put a premium on being awake, and that premium may hurt us in the long run. Sleep may be as important as food to our health and well-being," said Dr. Sheldon, who's also a professor of pediatrics at the Northwestern University Feinberg School of Medicine.

Both Drs. Lumeng and Sheldon recommend trying to keep a consistent sleep schedule. Bedtimes and wake times are both important—for children and adults. Sheldon said it's usually OK to vary your sleep times a little bit on the weekend, about an hour or so, but, he cautioned, "Letting you child sleep till noon or mid-afternoon is inviting trouble."

Dr. Lumeng also recommended that children not have a television in their bedroom, because it can make it more difficult to fall asleep.

info To read more about the connection between overweight and sleep, visit the Web site of the National Sleep Foundation, *www.sleepfoundation.org,* and search "Overweight and Overtired."

Kids Can Get Sleep Apnea, Too

Daniel Lewin, PhD, director, pediatric behavioral sleep medicine, Children's National Medical Center, Washington, D.C.

Ann Halbower, MD, medical director, pediatric sleep disorders program, Johns Hopkins University Children's Center, Baltimore.

The interrupted sleep, snoring, and nighttime breathing troubles associated with sleep apnea don't just affect adults—kids can get the condition, too, experts say.

In fact, sleep apnea has recently been linked to lowered childhood IQ scores and an increase in learning problems. Obstructive sleep apnea, the most common form, occurs when the muscles in the back of the throat relax, causing airway obstruction, suspension of breathing and frequent nighttime awakenings.

BACKGROUND

Daniel S. Lewin, PhD, director of pediatric behavioral sleep medicine at the Children's National Medical Center in Washington, D.C. believes that about 2% to 3% of children ages two-and-a-half to five may have obstructive sleep apnea.

In up to 75% of cases, the condition can be cured by removal of the tonsils and/or adenoids, the experts point out. However, as the number of overweight or obese children increases, the number of pediatric sleep apnea cases may also rise, Dr. Lewin said. Fat deposits in the upper airway can contribute to breathing obstruction.

And that could mean more trouble in school for affected children, added Ann Halbower, MD, medical director of the pediatric sleep disorders program at the Johns Hopkins University Children's Center in Baltimore.

THE STUDY

Dr. Halbower evaluated 31 children—ages 6 to 16—19 of whom had untreated severe sleep apnea. MRI scans showed that those children with sleep apnea had changes in two key brain regions associated with mental function—the hippocampus and the right frontal cortex.

The children with apnea also had altered ratios of three brain chemicals, possibly reflecting brain damage.

Those with apnea had lower average IQ test scores. "The control kids averaged 100 [considered average], the apnea kids 85," Dr. Halbower said. "That's a huge difference."

The study was published in the journal *Public Library of Science Medicine*.

Whether the damage is reversible or not is not known, Dr. Halbower said. She's continuing to study the problem.

WHAT TO LOOK FOR

Meanwhile, parents need to be alert to any symptoms of apnea in their children and seek help immediately, Dr. Halbower said.

What should parents look for? "Signs of disturbed breathing at night, including snoring, gasping, severe sweating, labored breathing, trouble sleeping at night," she said. "If they notice that, they should report it to their doctor and ask to have the child checked."

Other worrisome red flags, said Dr. Lewin, include the frequent need for a young child, under age 10, to sleep in. "Children who fall asleep at times other than their nap" should also be checked out, he said. "They might be sleep deprived or possibly have apnea."

TREATMENT WORKS

Luckily for most kids, a tonsillectomy and/or adenoidectomy can alleviate the problem. "If they can't get a surgical treatment, they should be on continuous positive airway pressure (CPAP) —a mask they can wear over the nose to give them air to breathe," Dr. Halbower said.

Dr. Lewin agreed. "Taking out the tonsils and adenoids cures about 75% of kids [with apnea]." For the others, he said, the airway pressure device can help.

info To learn more about sleep apnea, visit the Web site of the National Institute of Neurological Disorders and Stroke, *www.ninds. nih.gov* and search "sleep apnea" in the disorder index.

Omega-3s May Prevent Type 1 Diabetes

Jill Norris, MPH, PhD, professor, department of preventive medicine and biometrics, Barbara Davis Center for Childhood Diabetes, University of Colorado at Denver.
Stuart Weiss, MD, endocrinologist, New York University Medical Center, and clinical assistant professor, New York University School of Medicine, New York City.
Journal of the American Medical Association.

Children at high risk for developing type 1 diabetes might be able to prevent the disease by eating foods rich in omega-3 fatty acids, a new study suggests.

Researchers from the University of Colorado found that high-risk children with the highest omega-3 intake had up to a 55% reduced risk for type 1 diabetes.

"The kids with more omega-3 in their diets were about half as likely to develop type 1 diabetes than those with less," said study author Jill Norris, MPH, PhD, a professor in the department of preventive medicine and biometrics at the Barbara Davis Center for Childhood Diabetes at the University of Colorado at Denver.

BACKGROUND

Omega-3 fatty acids are found in fish, walnuts and certain plant oils, such as canola and olive. Omega-3 fatty acids have anti-inflammatory properties and are believed to help reduce the incidence of heart disease.

Type 1 diabetes is an autoimmune disease in which the body mistakenly attacks the islet cells in the pancreas. The islet cells produce insulin, which regulates blood sugar levels. In past research, scientists discovered that Norwegian children who were regularly given cod liver oil supplements, which are rich in omega-3 fatty acids and vitamin D, had a lower incidence of type 1 diabetes. It wasn't clear, however, whether the vitamin D or the omega-3 was responsible for the reduced risk.

THE STUDY

To assess the affect of omega-3 fatty acids on the risk for type 1 diabetes, Dr. Norris and her colleagues recruited 1,770 children who were at high risk for developing type 1 diabetes, either because they had a family member with the disease or because they had genetic markers that put them at a higher risk for developing type 1 diabetes.

Parents began periodically reporting dietary intake when the children were a year old. The average age at follow-up was 6.2 years. During that time period, 58 children developed type 1 diabetes, according to the study.

The researchers found a 55% reduced risk for diabetes in those who reported consuming the most omega-3 fatty acids.

Because self-reported dietary information isn't always the most reliable indicator of actual consumption, the researchers conducted an analysis that included 244 children and measured a biomarker of omega-3 consumption from the blood. In this subgroup, the researchers found that omega-3 fatty acid consumption reduced the risk for type 1 diabetes by 37%.

THEORY

Dr. Norris said the anti-inflammatory properties of omega-3s may be behind this potentially protective effect. "Inflammation is part of the very early process of diabetes," she explained.

"In type 1 diabetes, there is an inflammatory response that causes [islet] cell destruction, and it may be that omega-3 is a modulator of that inflammation," said Stuart Weiss, MD, an endocrinologist at New York University Medical Center. Dr. Weiss cautioned that this effect may not be permanent, however. "It may just be that omega-3s have delayed the onset of the disease, but the longer those cells function, the better."

MORE RESEARCH NEEDED

Dr. Weiss said he hopes the findings prompt a large, randomized, controlled study to confirm whether or not omega-3 consumption can truly prevent diabetes.

Dr. Norris said it's too soon to recommend that children, even those at high risk for diabetes, consume more omega-3s for the prevention of diabetes.

Dr. Weiss said that omega-3 fatty acids are often already part of a healthy diet since they're found in fish, fish oil and plant oils.

info To learn more about omega-3 fatty acids, visit the US National Library of Medicine Web site, *www.nlm.nih.gov/medlineplus.* Under "Drugs & Supplements" click on "Herbs and Supplements."

Dig into Better Eating Habits!

American Dietetic Association, news release.

Teens who eat dinner with their families on a regular basis are also more likely to eat healthy foods like fruit and vegetables as young adults, a new study shows.

These teens also go on to drink fewer soft drinks in adulthood, the study found.

THE STUDY

Reporting in the *Journal of the American Dietetic Association*, researchers at the University of Minnesota surveyed more than 1,500 students once during high school and again at age 20 about diet, social eating, meal structure and meal frequency.

The survey included questions about how often their family ate together, how much they enjoyed eating with family, if they ate on the run, and how often they ate breakfast, lunch and dinner.

RESULTS OF THE RESEARCH

Teens who reported eating family meals were more likely to report eating fruit, dark green and orange vegetables and key nutrients, and drinking fewer soft drinks.

The more frequently they ate family meals as teens, the more likely they were to eat dinner as adults, placing a higher priority on structured meals and social eating.

For women, eating with their family during adolescence meant significantly higher daily consumption of calcium, magnesium, potassium, vitamin B6 and fiber as adults.

Among males, eating with their family during adolescence resulted in eating more calcium, magnesium, potassium and fiber as adults.

info For tips on planning a healthy family meal, visit the National Dairy Council's Nutrition Explorations Web site, *www.nutritionexplorations.org*, and search "Meal Planning."

Are Food Additives Making Your Child Hyperactive?

David Katz, MD, MPH, director, Prevention Research Center, Yale University School of Medicine, New Haven, Connecticut.
The Lancet.

Some common food colorings and pre-servatives appear to increase the risk of hyperactive behavior among children, British researchers report. The link between food additives and hyperactivity has long been suspected, but this is the first study to show a direct connection.

The findings have already caused the British government's Food Standards Agency, which funded the study, to issue a warning to parents about food additives.

THE STUDY

Jim Stevenson, a professor of psychology at the University of Southampton in England, and his colleagues gave drinks containing additives to 297 children. The children were divided into two groups: 3-year-olds and 8- and 9-year-olds. The drinks contained artificial food coloring and addi-tives, such as sodium benzoate, a preservative.

These concoctions were similar to commer-cially available drinks. The amount of additives was similar to what is found in one or two serv-ings of candy a day, according to the report.

As a control, some children were given drinks without additives.

THE RESULTS

Over the six-week trial, Stevenson's team found that children in both age groups who drank the drinks containing additives displayed significantly more hyperactive behavior. These children also had shorter attention spans. How-ever, what specific additives caused which spe-cific behavioral problems is not known, the researchers said.

One of the additives, sodium benzoate, has been linked to cell damage in a previous study, and to an increased risk for cancer. Sodium ben-zoate is found in Coca-Cola, Pepsi Max and Diet Pepsi, and in many fruit drinks.

Other additives assessed in the study include a number of colorings—sunset yellow (E110), found in fruity drinks; carmoisine (E122), a red coloring often added to jams; ponceau 4R (E124), a red food coloring; tartrazine (E102), found in lollipops and carbonated drinks; quinoline yel-low (E104), a food coloring; and allura red AC (E129), and orange-red food dye.

IMPLICATIONS

"Although the use of artificial coloring in food manufacture might seem to be superfluous, the same cannot be said for sodium benzoate, which has an important preservative function. The implications of these results for the regula-tion of food additive use could be substantial," the researchers conclude.

FOOD ADDITIVE CAUTION

Based on these findings, the British gov-ernment's Food Standards Agency cautioned parents to be on the lookout for hyperactive behavior linked to food additives.

"Parents of children showing signs of hyper-activity are being advised that cutting out cer-tain artificial food colors from their diets might have some beneficial effects on their behavior," said the agency.

"However, we need to remember that there are many factors associated with hyperactive behavior in children. These are thought to in-clude genetic factors, being born prematurely, or environment and upbringing," said Dr. Andrew Wadge, chief scientist at the Food Standards Agency.

EXPERT COMMENTARY

According to David Katz, MD, MPH, director of the Prevention Research Center at Yale Uni-versity School of Medicine, "Attention-deficit hyperactivity disorder (ADHD) is an increas-ingly common problem, and theories abound to account for that. Among them is the notion that food additives induce hyperactivity."

Despite this apparent connection, Dr. Katz cautioned that the increasing number of chil-dren with ADHD cannot be blamed on food additives alone.

"No one factor is solely responsible for ris-ing rates of ADHD," Dr. Katz said. "Along with the hazards of a highly processed food sup-ply, children are getting less and less physical activity as a means of dissipating their native rambunctiousness."

Insights about the causes of ADHD should help parents implement preventive strategies, which are urgently needed, Dr. Katz noted. "A healthful, unadulterated diet and regular physical activity seem like a good place to start."

info For more information on food additives, visit the Web site of the US National Library of Medicine at *http://medlineplus.gov.* Click "Medical Encyclopedia," then on "F" and choose "Food Additives."

The A-B-Sees!
Good Vision Means
Better Test Scores

University of California, San Diego, School of Medicine, news release.

Preschoolers with poor vision significantly improved their test scores within six weeks of consistently wearing prescription glasses, a recent study shows.

"It has been theorized that when young children have early vision problems that are undiagnosed and uncorrected, their development and performance in school are impacted," said Stuart I. Brown, chairman of ophthalmology and director of the Shiley Eye Center at the University of California, San Diego, School of Medicine. "This study shows that children with vision impairment do perform below the norm in visual-motor coordination tests, and that they catch up quickly once they are given corrective lenses."

THE STUDY

The study, published in the *Archives of Ophthalmology,* followed 70 children, ages 3 to 5. Half the children had normal vision and half were diagnosed with ametropia, an abnormal refractive eye condition, such as astigmatism, leading to poor vision.

The children took two standardized tests that relate directly to future school performance —the Beery-Buktenica Developmental Test of

Visual-Motor Integration (VMI) and the Wechsler Preschool and Primary Scale of Intelligence-Revised (WPPSI-R).

RESULTS

The vision-impaired children scored significantly lower on both tests, demonstrating reduced ability of the brain to coordinate the eyes with the hands, the researchers said.

The vision-impaired children were then provided with prescription glasses and monitored with the assistance of their families over six weeks to ensure that they wore their glasses consistently.

Upon retesting, the VMI scores of the children with vision problems were at the same level as the scores of the children with normal eyesight. The WPPSI-R scores did not show the same dramatic improvement, but the researchers speculated that the test might not be as sensitive to changes in visual-motor integration skills tested by the VMI tool. The researchers are following the children to test whether the WPPSI-R scores change further over time.

"Amazingly, this is the first controlled study of preschool children to show the cognitive disadvantage preschool children have when they are farsighted and/or have astigmatism, as well as to show the benefit of early intervention with glasses," said study coauthor Barbara Brody, MPH, director of the Center for Community Ophthalmology at the Shiley Eye Center.

info For more on vision in preschool children, visit the Web site of the American Optometric Association at *www.aoa.org.* Under "Eye Health Topics," choose "Good Vision Throughout Life," and then "Preschool Vision."

■ ■ ■ ■

20% of Kids Who Wear Glasses Don't Need Them

Nearly one in five children wear glasses that they don't need.

Reason: Optometrists and ophthalmologists who usually treat adults may diagnose children as farsighted, but many children outgrow farsightedness without glasses.

Best: Take children to a pediatric ophthalmologist, who will be more familiar with children's eye problems.

Sean P. Donahue, MD, PhD, associate professor of ophthalmology, pediatrics and neurology, Vanderbilt University School of Medicine, Nashville, and lead author of a study of 102,508 preschoolers, published in *Journal of the American Association of Pediatric Ophthalmology and Strabismus.*

Depressed Moms' Kids at Higher Injury Risk

BMJ Specialist Journals, news release.

Young children of depressed mothers are at heightened risk for behavioral problems and injury, new research shows.

THE STUDY

A team at Cincinnati Children's Hospital Medical Center looked at two years of data on more than 1,100 mother/child pairs taking part in the National Longitudinal Study of Youth.

During the study period, 94 of the children (all under age 6) suffered injuries serious enough to require medical attention. Two-thirds of the injuries occurred at home.

Children of mothers who had persistently high scores on measures of depression symptoms were more than twice as likely to be injured as children of mothers with low scores of depression symptoms.

The study also found that children (especially boys) of mothers with high depression scores were much more likely to have behavioral problems and to "act out."

The researchers concluded that every one point increase on a mother's depression score (on a scale of 0 to 60) was associated with a 4% increased risk for injury and a 6% increased risk for behavioral problems in children.

That held true even after the researchers took into account a number of major factors, such as household income, health insurance coverage and level of education.

The study was published in the journal *Injury Prevention.*

IMPLICATIONS

Depression in mothers may increase the risk of behavioral problems in children and, in turn, boost youngsters' risk of injury, said the study authors, who added that depression in mothers may also result in less supervision of children or increased number of injury hazards in the home.

info For more information on women and depression, visit the Web site of the National Institute of Mental Health, *www.nimh. nih.gov*, and search "depression: what every woman should know."

■ ■ ■ ■

Depressed Mothers, Troubled Kids

Children whose mothers are depressed are three times more likely to develop anxiety, behavioral disorders and serious depression than kids whose mothers are not depressed.

Good news: Children improve when their mothers' treatment for depression is successful.

Myrna Weissman, PhD, professor of epidemiology and psychiatry, College of Physicians and Surgeons of Columbia University, New York City, and leader of a study of 151 mother-child pairs, published in *The Journal of the American Medical Association.*

■ ■ ■ ■

Kids Can Get Kidney Stones, Too

Painful kidney stones typically occur in middle-aged adults, but they are being seen more often now in children.

Possible reasons: Drinking too little water...consuming too much sodium...eating a lot of chocolate or nuts or drinking a lot of tea (both herbal and regular) all of which are high in oxalate, a substance that is commonly found in kidney stones.

Self-defense: Be sure your child has about eight eight-ounce glasses of liquids a day—as much as possible from water. Limit sodium in children's diets by cutting back on processed meats, frozen meals, fast food, packaged snack foods and convenience foods.

Alicia M. Neu, MD, clinical director of pediatric nephrology, Johns Hopkins Children's Center, Baltimore.

■ ■ ■ ■

Trick to Getting Kids To Take Medicine

Help a child swallow bad-tasting medicine by first giving him/her a sticky food, such as applesauce or pudding. The food helps prevent the bad taste from coming through.

Alternative: Give the child a drop of honey or a chocolate chip before the medicine.

Deborah Kristeller Moed, early childhood teacher, mother of two children and a Bottom Line/Personal subscriber.

Sweet! Honey Beats Meds At Soothing Kids' Coughs

Ian Paul, MD, MSc, director, pediatric clinical research, Penn State College of Medicine, Hershey.

Charlotte Jordan, project manager, research, National Honey Board, Firestone, Colorado.

Archives of Pediatrics and Adolescent Medicine.

With many children's cough syrups being pulled from the market because they don't work, an old folk remedy may work just as well or better, researchers report. *The remedy:* Honey.

In a study of kids having trouble sleeping because of cough, a research team at Penn State College of Medicine compared the effectiveness of a little bit of buckwheat honey before bedtime versus either no treatment or dextromethorphan (DM), the cough suppressant found in many over-the-counter cold medicines.

"Honey provided the greatest relief of symptoms compared with the other treatments," concluded lead researcher Ian Paul, MD, MSc, Penn State's director of pediatric clinical research.

BACKGROUND

An FDA advisory board recently recommended that over-the-counter cough and cold medicines not be given to children under six years of age because of a lack of effectiveness and potential for side effects.

"With honey, parents now have a safe and effective alternative to use for children over age one who have cough and cold symptoms," Dr. Paul said.

Some cough medicines tout honey on their labels, Dr. Paul noted, but they actually contain artificial honey flavor. Dr. Paul cautioned that real honey should never be given to children younger than one because of the rare risk of infantile botulism.

THE STUDY

In the study, 105 children ages two to 18 were given honey, artificial honey-flavored DM or no treatment about a half-hour before bedtime.

Dr. Paul's group found that honey was more effective in reducing the severity and frequency of nighttime cough compared with DM or no treatment. Honey quieted the cough enough to allow the children to sleep.

Moreover, DM was not much better at reducing cough than no treatment, the researchers found.

Dr. Paul's team used a dark honey in their trial. Whether other honeys would be equally effective is not known, Paul said.

Some of the children were hyperactive for a short time after being given the honey, Dr. Paul said. However, children who received honey slept better and so did their parents, the researcher noted.

HONEY AS MEDICINE

Honey has been used for centuries to treat upper respiratory infection symptoms, such as cough. In addition, honey has antioxidant and antimicrobial effects, and also soothes the back of the throat, Dr. Paul noted. "The World Health Organization has cited honey as a potential therapy," he said.

Charlotte Jordan, a project manager of research at the National Honey Board, believes the finding confirms what your grandmother told you.

"This is a really exciting finding," she said. "For a long time it's been considered folk medicine to use honey when you have a cough or a cold. It's exciting to have a scientific study to back that up."

Honey should not be given to children under the age of 12 months.

info For more information on children's cough, visit the Web site of the Nemours Foundation at *http://kidshealth.org/parent* and search "cough."

■ ■ ■ ■

Beware! Antibiotics Increase Asthma Risk in Kids

Infants given broad-spectrum antibiotics for respiratory tract and ear infections are more likely to develop asthma later in childhood.

Recent finding: A child who gets four or more courses of such antibiotics during the first year of life is 50% more likely to develop asthma by age seven than a child who receives no such antibiotics.

Reason: Unknown.

Self-defense: Avoid use of broad-spectrum antibiotics during a child's first year unless it is deemed necessary.

Anita Kozyrskyj, PhD, associate professor, faculty of pharmacy, University of Manitoba, Winnipeg, Canada, and leader of an analysis of data on more than 13,000 children, published in *Chest*.

Natural Treatments Best For Ear Infections

Mark A. Stengler, ND, naturopathic physician in private practice, La Jolla, California...adjunct associate clinical professor at the National College of Natural Medicine, Portland, Oregon...author of many books, including *The Natural Physician's Healing Therapies* and coauthor of *Prescription for Natural Cures* (both from Bottom Line Books)...and author of the *Bottom Line/Natural Healing* newsletter.

When a patient has an earache, he/she (or the parent, if the patient is a child) often asks for an antibiotic, thinking that the drug will alleviate the pain and cure the infection. But the American Academy of Pediatrics advises against prescribing antibiotics for mild-to-moderate ear infections in patients age two and older.

Reasons: Overuse of the drugs contributes to the rise in antibiotic-resistant bacteria...antibiotics reduce beneficial intestinal flora, interfering with digestion and immunity...and ear infections are caused mostly by viruses or occasionally by fungi, neither of which respond to antibiotics.

Natural treatments are more effective than antibiotics for reducing pain and hastening recovery from ear infections.

Evidence: In a German study of 131 children with ear infections, one group of children received conventional antibiotics, decongestants and fever-reducing medicines, while the rest were treated with homeopathic remedies. On average, children treated with homeopathy experienced two days of pain after treatment began and required four days of treatment... and 71% were free from recurrent infection in the year that followed. Children treated with conventional drugs had three days of ear pain and required 10 days of treatment (the standard length of antibiotic treatment)...and only 57% remained free from recurrence.

Antibiotics do not prevent complications, either. A study in the *British Medical Journal* analyzed data from 3.36 million episodes of respiratory tract infections, from which ear infections commonly develop.

Results: Serious complications from ear infections were rare...and antibiotics prevented complications for only one person out of every 4,000 who took the drugs.

I consider antibiotics when a patient has pus in the middle ear (seen during an exam)...has a fever of 104°F or higher for more than 24 hours or any fever for more than 48 hours...has rapidly worsening symptoms...or does not respond to natural treatments within two days.

The natural treatments below work well for most bacterial and viral ear infections. For mild pain, try eardrops alone. If pain is moderate to severe or does not ease after one or two applications of eardrops, use all three remedies. Therapies generally are safe for adults and children of all ages. Products are sold in health food stores.

•**Garlic/mullein/St. John's wort eardrops** relieve pain and have antibacterial and antiviral effects. Hold the capped bottle under hot water until warm…then place three drops in the affected ear three to four times daily. Do not use if the eardrum is ruptured (indicated by pus in the ear).

Try: Eclectic Institute Ear Drops (800-332-4372, *www.eclecticherb.com*).

•**Homeopathic chamomilla** (from the chamomile plant) reduces pain and fever.

Dosage: Two 30C potency pellets four times a day.

•**Echinacea/goldenseal herbal formula** strengthens the immune response. Use as directed, typically four times daily. For children, choose an alcohol-free product.

Pain relief: Run one facecloth under hot water and another under cold water to make compresses. Hold the hot compress over the ear for two minutes, then switch to the cold compress for 30 seconds. Repeat twice. Do in the morning, midday and evening for two days to reduce congestion and draw healing immune cells to the area.

■ ■ ■ ■

Warning: Hospitals Often Give Adult Drugs to Children

Most drugs given to children in hospitals are not approved for use in pediatric patients. In fact, very few medications have gone through testing to prove that they are safe and effective for children.

Result: Nearly 80% of hospitalized children get drugs not specifically approved for people their age. This sort of off-label use is most common with central nervous system drugs, such as morphine.

Self-defense: Parents should always ask about interactions with other medications and what is known about the effects of any drug given to their children.

Samir S. Shah, MD, infectious diseases physician, Children's Hospital of Philadelphia, and leader of an analysis of the medical records of more than 355,000 children, ages 18 or younger, admitted to 31 US hospitals during 2004, published in *Archives of Pediatrics & Adolescent Medicine*.

■ ■ ■ ■

Chicken Pox Vaccine— Take Two

Two doses of the chicken pox vaccine are needed for protection against the disease. The first dose should be given when a child is 12 to 15 months old. The second dose is given at four to six years of age.

People 13 years old or older who haven't had chicken pox or the vaccine should get two doses four to eight weeks apart.

When children receive only a single dose, 15% to 20% of them are not protected against chicken pox. If your child got only one dose—or if you received only one as a child—arrange for the second dose.

People who had chicken pox are at risk of developing shingles, which occurs later in life and is caused by the same herpes virus that causes chicken pox.

A separate vaccine against shingles is recommended for adults age 60 and older. Ask your doctor for details.

Mona Marin, MD, medical epidemiologist in the National Immunization Program, Centers for Disease Control and Prevention, Atlanta.

■ ■ ■ ■

Better Flu Prevention For Kids

Flu nasal spray is more effective than flu shots for young children. According to a new study, the spray is 55% more effective in protecting children under age five than the shots are.

Likely reason: The weakened but live viruses in the nasal spray (influenza shots contain dead viruses) stimulate an extra immune reaction in the nose and throat. The spray recently was approved for use in children ages two to five. Research has not shown a similar boost in effectiveness among adults.

Samuel Katz, MD, Wilburt C. Davison Professor and chairman emeritus of pediatrics, Duke University Medical Center, Durham, North Carolina, and former president of the American Pediatrics Society.

■ ■ ■ ■

Meningitis Vaccine a Must

Meningitis vaccine is now recommended for all children ages 11 to 18 and may be given to children as young as age two who are at high risk for bacterial meningitis or have been exposed to the disease. The meningococcal vaccine protects against bacterial meningitis and a related bloodstream infection—rare conditions in the US, but ones whose symptoms (stiff neck, fever, low blood pressure and rash) can develop quickly and may lead to death within just hours. Meningitis can be spread by coughing, sneezing and kissing. Living in a communal setting, such as a nursing home or a college dormitory, increases the risk. The vaccine costs about $89 and is usually covered by insurance.

Jon S. Abramson, MD, immediate past chairman, Advisory Committee on Immunization Practice of the CDC, Atlanta, and professor, department of pediatrics, Wake Forest University School of Medicine, Winston-Salem, North Carolina.

■ ■ ■ ■

Girls More Susceptible To Concussions

Teenage girls who play sports are more susceptible to concussions than teenage boys who play the same sports.

Recent finding: High school girls who play soccer sustained concussions 68% more often than boys did. Girls who play basketball sustained concussions 193% more often than boys.

Also: Concussion symptoms, including dizziness, lethargy and concentration problems, take longer to resolve in girls.

Dawn Comstock, PhD, principal investigator, Center for Injury Research and Policy, Nationwide Children's Hospital, Columbus, Ohio, and leader of a study of data from 100 high schools and 180 colleges in the US, published in *Journal of Athletic Training.*

■ ■ ■ ■

Nearly Half of US Teens Mutilate Themselves

Forty-six percent admit to cutting or burning their bodies…biting themselves…or picking at their skin to draw blood. Self-injury is glorified in some movies, songs and Web sites. Teens who do it say it gives them a sense of control over their lives…or that the physical pain distracts them from mental or emotional distress.

More information: Go to *Selfinjury.com,* or call 800-DONT-CUT.

Elizabeth E. Lloyd-Richardson, PhD, assistant professor of psychiatry and human behavior, Brown Medical School and The Miriam Hospital, both in Providence, and leader of a survey of 633 high school students, published in *Psychological Medicine.*

Too Much Estrogen A Big Problem… For Both Sexes

Mark A. Stengler, ND, naturopathic physician in private practice, La Jolla, California…adjunct associate clinical professor at the National College of Natural Medicine, Portland, Oregon…author of many books, including *The Natural Physician's Healing Therapies* and coauthor of *Prescription for Natural Cures* (both from Bottom Line Books)…and author of the *Bottom Line/Natural Healing* newsletter.

A little-known yet increasingly common health problem—for men and women— is excess estrogen. Though estrogen usually is thought of as a female hormone, men also produce it. When a person's estrogen levels are too high, the condition is called *hyperestrogenism*. This hormonal imbalance affects one in five people. It most commonly develops after age 50 but can affect younger adults and even children. Hyperestrogenism contributes to numerous and disparate health problems, from headaches to weight gain to cancer.

CAUSES: BIOLOGICAL

In women, estrogen is produced primarily in the ovaries. It plays many roles in the reproductive process, cognition and bone formation. Production drops dramatically at menopause. In men, small amounts of estrogen are created as a by-product of the metabolism of *testosterone,* a hormone produced in the testes. Estrogen's main role in men is to strengthen bones.

Various biological factors contribute to hyperestrogenism…

•**Excess weight.** Fat cells contain the enzyme *aromatase*, which stimulates estrogen production. Being just 5% over an appropriate weight increases hyperestrogenism risk.

•**Impaired liver function.** When the liver's detoxifying capabilities are compromised—by poor diet, excessive alcohol use, genetics or exposure to pollutants—the organ can't properly metabolize estrogen.

•**Sluggish bowel activity.** Normally, about 80% of excess estrogen is eliminated via stool. When bowel function is slow—for instance, due to insufficient dietary fiber—waste products linger in the colon, so estrogen is reabsorbed into the bloodstream.

•**Hormone therapy.** Birth control pills or estrogen therapy (in women) or testosterone therapy (in men) can increase hyperestrogenism risk.

•**Low thyroid hormone.** If the thyroid gland does not function well, metabolism slows.

•**Prescription medications.** The breast cancer drug *tamoxifen* binds with cells' estrogen receptors, leaving estrogen stranded in the bloodstream. The ulcer medication *cimetidine* (Tagamet) interferes with estrogen metabolism and increases estrogen activity.

•**Nutritional deficiencies.** The liver needs sufficient amounts of vitamins B-6, B-12, C and E as well as magnesium to function well and eliminate excess estrogen.

•**High sugar consumption.** Eating excess sweets raises blood sugar, causing the body to excrete more magnesium. Because this mineral is involved with estrogen detoxification, less magnesium means more risk for hyperestrogenism.

•**Diet high in dairy foods.** Cow's milk—even the organic kind—contains naturally occurring estrogen.

•**Stress.** The hormone *cortisol*, released at times of stress, makes cells more receptive to estrogen. It also interferes with the estrogen-modulating hormone *progesterone*, allowing estrogen to dominate.

CAUSES: ENVIRONMENTAL

Man-made substances that have estrogen-like effects are called *xenoestrogens*. These include *benzene* in car exhaust…*phthalates* in some plastics…*polychlorinated biphenyls* (PCBs) in electrical equipment…*polybrominated biphenyls* (PBBs) in flame retardants…and pesticides, such as *dichloro-diphenyl-trichloroethane* (DDT). Though PCBs and DDT were banned in the 1970s, they degrade slowly and still exist in water, plants and animals.

Estrogen-like hormones often are added to livestock feed to fatten up the animals—when we eat this meat, we ingest the hormones. When estrogen-elevating drugs are excreted by patients, they enter our drinking water supply and accumulate over time.

It is naive to believe that environmental pollutants do not affect humans. *Examples…*

•**One study investigated girls born in the 1970s in Puerto Rico.** Participants who showed signs of early breast development—as young as age seven—had higher blood levels of phthalates than did girls whose breasts budded at the normal age of 10.

•**Emory University researchers found that girls breast-fed by mothers** who had high blood levels of PBBs during pregnancy began to menstruate 12 months earlier, on average, than did girls whose mothers had lower PBB levels during pregnancy.

SELF-DEFENSE STRATEGIES

Excess estrogen can contribute to myriad health problems, from the bothersome to the life-threatening. It even may be linked to cognitive problems. A recent study of 2,974 Japanese-American men, ages 70 to 91, revealed that high levels of *estradiol* (an estrogen) were associated with an increased risk for cognitive decline and Alzheimer's disease.

To diagnose hyperestrogenism, a doctor may order tests of saliva and/or urine samples collected over 24 hours, to detect "active" estrogen (the amount attached to cell receptor sites and therefore problematic). Blood tests may be used—but they are less accurate, because they do not measure active estrogen.

If you are diagnosed with hyperestrogenism—or if you want to lower your risk for developing it—follow the guidelines below.

•**Eat a high-fiber diet.** Get 30 grams of fiber each day to improve liver and bowel function.

Good choices: Broccoli, cauliflower, brussels sprouts, buckwheat, brown rice, flaxseeds and whole grains.

•**Choose organic produce and grains,** which are largely free of pesticides. They ease the workload on the liver, helping it get rid of excess estrogen.

•**Select meats from grass-fed livestock.** These animals were not given feed laced with hormones, so their meat is free of extra added estrogen.

•**Opt for plant milks,** such as organic almond milk and rice milk, instead of milk from cows.

•**Drink purified water.** To remove xenoestrogens, install an under-sink reverse-osmosis water-filtration system (sold at home-improvement stores) at home.

Economical: Filters that are affixed to faucets. Brita or Pur are popular brands.

•**Consume alcohol only in moderation,** if at all, to optimize liver health.

•**Take daily multivitamin/mineral supplements.** Teens and adults should use a formula that includes magnesium at 400 milligrams (mg) to 500 mg...vitamin B-6 at 25 mg to 50 mg...vitamin B-12 at 50 micrograms (mcg) to 2,000 mcg...vitamin C at 500 mg to 1,000 mg...and vitamin E at 200 international units (IU). Children should take an age-appropriate formula.

People who test positive for or have many symptoms of hyperestrogenism should also...

•**Supplement with *indole 3 carbinol*.** This phytonutrient, extracted from broccoli, supports liver function.

Daily dosage: 400 mg in capsule form.

•**Take calcium d-glucarate.** Found naturally in apples, cherries, grapefruit, broccoli and alfalfa, this nutrient helps the liver.

Daily dosage: 2,000 mg.

Supplements are sold in health food stores. Indole 3 carbinol and calcium d-glucarate have

not been studied in children and should not be used by women who are pregnant or breast-feeding—otherwise they are safe and can be taken indefinitely.

SIGNS OF EXCESS ESTROGEN

Estrogen overload contributes to numerous health problems. If you have any of the conditions below, ask a holistic doctor if hyperestrogenism could be to blame.

•**In women...**
- •Endometriosis (uterine lining overgrowth)
- •Fibrocystic breast disease
- •Hair loss
- •Menstrual cycle irregularities
- •Premenstrual symptoms (moderate to severe)
- •Ovarian cysts or ovarian cancer
- •Uterine fibroids or uterine cancer

•**In men...**
- •Bloating
- •Breast enlargement
- •Irritability
- •Migraine headaches
- •Prostate enlargement (moderate to severe) or prostate cancer
- •Sperm count reduction

•**In both sexes...**
- •Aging prematurely
- •Body fat increases
- •Breast cancer
- •Dementia
- •Muscle atrophy
- •Sexual dysfunction
- •Weight gain

•**In children...**
- •Breast tissue excesses (in boys)
- •Undescended testicles (in boys)
- •Premature puberty (in girls)

The Best Natural Cold Remedies

William Schaffner, MD, an infectious disease specialist and vice president of the National Foundation for Infectious Diseases, Bethesda, Maryland. He is chair of the department of preventive medicine at Vanderbilt University Medical Center, Nashville, Tennessee.

Pharmacies stock hundreds of cold and cough remedies, including natural treatments and preventives, such as zinc and vitamin C. But which ones really work?

One proven way to prevent colds is to wash your hands frequently. You don't have to be around people who are coughing or sneezing to get sick—a person can be ill with a cold for 24 hours before symptoms start.

Best: Assume that you've been exposed—and wash your hands before viruses have a chance to enter the mucous membranes in your nose, eyes or mouth. If you are unable to wash your hands, use waterless hand sanitizers containing alcohol instead.

Unfortunately, not all cold preventives and remedies are so effective. *Here's the real story about common cold remedies…*

ECHINACEA

A recent study published in *The Lancet* analyzed the findings of 14 previous studies and reported that the herb echinacea reduced the risk of catching a cold by 58% and also shortened the duration of a cold. Yet previous research, including a large study published in *The New England Journal of Medicine*, found that echinacea doesn't make a significant difference.

A number of factors might explain the conflicting results. It's possible that some, but not all, cold viruses are susceptible to echinacea. Also, because the US Food and Drug Administration doesn't regulate herbal products, the doses and quality of echinacea—and even the species—may vary from study to study, affecting results.

My conclusion: Echinacea might have a minor effect on cold treatment and prevention, but the evidence is too weak to recommend it. It is one of the safer herbs, though, so apart from the modest expense, there is no downside to trying it.

VITAMIN C

More than 35 years ago, Nobel prizewinner Linus Pauling suggested that large doses of vitamin C—1,000 milligrams (mg) or more daily—could prevent a cold. Research since then has been inconsistent. Some studies indicate that vitamin C can reduce the duration and severity of cold symptoms and possibly aid in prevention. Other studies find no benefits.

Latest finding: Researchers looked at 30 previous clinical studies, which included a total of 11,350 participants. They concluded that vitamin C does not prevent colds. However, they also noted that patients with colds who took at least 200 mg of vitamin C daily did experience a slight reduction in cold symptoms and duration.

My conclusion: Vitamin C appears to reduce cold symptoms, but the improvement is so modest that many people won't notice the difference. Higher doses do not appear to help… and taking more than 200 mg daily increases the risk of kidney stones and diarrhea.

Important: Drink two extra glasses of water daily when taking vitamin C. It helps prevent kidney stones and moistens mucous membranes, which is helpful for reducing cold symptoms.

ZINC LOZENGES

Despite their unpleasant taste, zinc lozenges were popular in the 1990s. Early studies indicated that they could significantly shorten the duration of colds. Newer evidence, however, has shown that they probably are not effective. Other forms of zinc, including zinc-treated nasal swabs, are still being investigated.

My conclusion: Zinc lozenges are not effective for cold treatment or prevention.

DECONGESTANTS

Oral, long-lasting decongestants (which contain *pseudoephedrine*), such as Sudafed, and short-acting nasal sprays (which contain *oxymetazoline*), such as Afrin, work in a similar fashion. By shrinking blood vessels in the nose and sinuses, they reduce congestion, but they can cause side effects, including insomnia and the "jitters," in some people. They also occasionally cause an increase in blood pressure. Using them for more than a few days often results in rebound congestion—inflammation of the mucous membranes that increases stuffiness.

My conclusion: Decongestants don't shorten the duration of colds, but they are very effective at reducing stuffiness—the sprays work almost instantly. To limit side effects, use them for no more than 72 hours at a stretch.

COUGH SUPPRESSANTS

Most over-the-counter (OTC) cough suppressants contain *dextromethorphan*, a chemical that is supposed to suppress the cough reflex but that doesn't work all that well. Suppressants that contain *codeine* are far more effective, but they are available only with a prescription. Doctors prescribe cough suppressants for a dry, nagging cough, particularly if it's keeping you up at night. You do not want to suppress a productive cough, which can help remove mucus from the airways.

My conclusion: OTC cough suppressants give only modest relief. Stronger drugs, available by prescription, are a better choice for people with serious, persistent coughs.

ANTIHISTAMINES

They're a common ingredient in combination cough and cold remedies. Antihistamines dry mucous membranes and provide some relief from sneezing and/or a runny nose. However, their main effect is to block the effects of *histamine*, a chemical that's produced by allergies, not colds.

My conclusion: Don't take antihistamines for colds. They don't work. In fact, they can thicken cold secretions and make symptoms worse.

STAYING WARM

Will being cold cause you to get a cold? A few years ago, a study published in *Family Practice* found that 29% of volunteers who were chilled (they submerged their feet in icy water for 20 minutes) caught a cold, compared with less than 10% of participants in a "warm" group.

Study flaw: The two groups of volunteers weren't confined in one place after the experiment, so there was no way to tell if people in both groups were exposed equally to cold viruses later.

Earlier studies conducted in England did control for exposure. Volunteers were either chilled or not, then deliberately exposed to the same number of cold viruses. These studies showed that cold temperatures had no effect on the incidence of colds.

My conclusion: Staying warm will not prevent a cold.

■ ■ ■ ■

Ugh! Hidden Bacteria

Mouth guards often harbor bacteria, yeasts and molds that can cause serious health problems, including oral sores, difficulty breathing, nausea, vomiting and diarrhea. Rinsing or scrubbing mouth guards (worn overnight for problems such as teeth grinding) does not kill these microorganisms. Researchers are working to develop effective disinfection.

Self-defense: Use a disposable mouth guard ($1.50 to $2 apiece at a pharmacy or sporting-goods store), and toss after a week of use.

R. Thomas Glass, DDS, PhD, is professor of dental medicine at Oklahoma State University Center for Health Sciences, Tulsa. He is lead author of a mouth-guard study published in *General Dentistry*.

Ways to Stop a Scar

James Spencer, MD, clinical professor of medicine in the department of dermatology at Mount Sinai School of Medicine, New York City. He is a spokesperson for the American Academy of Dermatology and director of Spencer Dermatology Skin Surgery Center in St. Petersburg, Florida. *www.spencerdermatology.com*.

If you have a shallow wound—a skinned knee, a paper cut, a minor burn—new skin grows back, filling the injured area with fresh tissue that is virtually identical to the original.

If a wound has a depth of one-half inch or more—piercing the skin's outermost layer (the *epidermis*) and penetrating the dermis beneath it—the repair won't be perfect. To heal a deeper wound, your body relies on *collagen*, an elongated protein that provides structural support, like girders in a building—which often results in a scar.

Here's how to prevent scars and minimize the ones you have…

TYPES OF SCARS

Scars are categorized by shape…

•**Indented**—typically caused by acne or chicken pox.

•**Hypertrophic.** These red, thick scars stay within the boundary of the wound but rise above the skin's surface.

•**Keloid.** The scar tissue is raised but also pours out beyond the outline of the wound, over the surrounding skin.

Many factors can affect how a scar develops, including…

•**Age**—younger skin tends to heal more vigorously, producing larger scars.

•**Skin color**—keloids are more common among dark-skinned people.

•**Location**—tighter skin, such as that along the jawbone, makes a scar more visible.

•**Size of wound**—larger wounds typically produce larger scars.

PREVENTING SCARS

Proper self-care after sustaining a wound is crucial in either preventing a scar or achieving the smallest, least noticeable scar possible.

Important: Many people believe that a dry, uncovered wound heals best, but scientific studies show that keeping a wound moist is ideal for minimizing the scar as a wound heals. *What to do…*

•**Apply an over-the-counter antibiotic ointment.** Use enough to moisten the wound. This will also help prevent infection, which may create a deeper wound that is more likely to scar.

•**Cover the wound.** Use a bandage of some kind. Hundreds of products are available. Choose one that you find comfortable and easy to use.

•**Keep the wound covered until it's healed.** Change the ointment and covering every day or two. When showering, remove the bandage and replace with a clean one after the shower.

•**Don't pick at the wound.** Don't squeeze acne bumps, scratch mosquito bites or dig at scabs—you may increase the chances of a scar.

•**Try massage.** Just after healing is complete, if there is a scar, cover it with petroleum jelly and massage it gently but firmly with the tips of your fingers for 10 minutes or so every day for one to two months. This will soften the scar and help minimize its appearance.

•**Ask your doctor about silicone sheeting and gels.** Although scientists don't know why it works, applying a bandage like sheet of silicone gel can help stop a new scar from becoming hypertrophic or keloidal, or it can help reduce an old scar. For new scars, the sheeting should be applied about one week after the injury or removal of sutures.

MINIMIZING EXISTING SCARS

Many medical treatments may minimize an old scar—but none can completely remove it. A dermatologist and/or a plastic surgeon can recommend the best treatment(s) for the scar you have. *Here, the most effective ways…*

•**Keloid and hypertrophic scars.**

•Pulsed dye laser. Although many types of laser treatments are available (and widely advertised) for scar reduction, the pulsed dye laser (PDL)—which focuses ultrashort pulses of high-energy yellow light on the scar—is the gold standard. It can remove redness, flatten the scar and relieve itching (which often accompanies a scar). Two or three treatments are typical, once every one to two months.

•Cortisone injections. Injecting *cortisone*—a synthetic version of a hormone produced by the adrenal gland—can shrink and flatten a scar. (How it works is unknown.) Typically, three or four injections are needed, every two to four weeks.

•Interferon. The immune system produces this protein when battling viruses, bacteria and other infectious agents. When injected, it can flatten a scar and reduce redness. The number and timing of injections are the same as for cortisone.

•Aldara. A keloid scar can be surgically removed, but it's a risky procedure—chances are 50-50 it will grow back, perhaps even larger. Aldara cream is an immune response modulator that stimulates the production of interferon. Applied after surgery, it may help keep a keloid from returning. It is best for surgically removed keloids.

- **Indented scars.**

  - Laser resurfacing. This intense treatment employs the high-energy light of a carbon dioxide laser, which literally burns off the layers of damaged skin, creating an even, smooth surface. The procedure often requires local anesthesia and takes about a week to heal. The skin may remain red for months.

  - Fillers. Made from a material such as collagen, a filler is injected with a fine needle two to three times over three months into one or more indented scar areas, temporarily lifting the area. It typically takes more than one treatment to see results, which last six to eight months. Popular fillers include Dermalogen, Restylane, Hylaform, Cosmoderm, Cymetra and Artecoll.

- **Other scars.**

  - Surgical scar revision. The body has skin tension lines—creases where wrinkles form, such as where the nose meets the cheek. Scars falling along a tension line are less prominent than scars at an angle to a line. In this technique, the doctor surgically repositions the scar so that it falls within a tension line.

  Best for: Wide or long scars, scars in prominent places (such as the forehead) and scars with irregular, rather than straight, patterns.

- Botox. The muscle-paralyzing toxin, used cosmetically to relax wrinkles, also can minimize scars from forehead wounds.

  Recent study: Injections of Botox around a forehead wound from injury or surgery improved the appearance of the wound six months later by 20%, compared with noninjected wounds.

  Best for: Scars on the forehead.

WHAT DOESN'T WORK

- **Mederma.** This over-the-counter topical gel, made from onion extract, often is recommended as a way to minimize new or established scars.

  Recent study: Dermatological surgeons at Harvard Medical School studied 24 surgical patients, treating half of their scars with onion extract and the other half with petroleum-based gel. There was no difference between the two areas in appearance, redness or size of scar.

- **Vitamin E.** In a study conducted at the University of Miami reported in *Dermatological Surgery*, dermatologists found no difference in scarring of wounds treated with or without topical vitamin E.

9

Heart Disease

Global Warming May Trigger Rise in Heart Deaths

oaring temperatures and high ozone levels work together to boost death risks from heart disease and stroke, researchers report. Global warming —which brings more heat and more ozone— may further increase the number of people who die of cardiovascular events.

"Temperature and ozone are strong factors in cardiovascular mortality during June to September in the United States," noted the study's lead author, Cizao Ren, PhD, from the Department of Epidemiology in the School of Medicine at the University of California, Irvine. "Temperature and air pollution combine to affect the health of large populations," he added.

Dr. Ren expects the problem will get worse as the earth becomes hotter. "The increases in

both temperature and air pollution will have a strong affect on health," he said.

THE STUDY

His team based its findings on data on nearly 100 million people living in 95 different areas across the United States. The data was collected from June to September, the hottest time of year.

Four million deaths from heart attacks or strokes occurred during the study period. Dr. Ren's team compared death rates against changes in temperature during one day.

STUDY FINDINGS

The higher the ozone level, the greater the risk for cardiovascular death attributable to high temperatures, Dr. Ren's team concluded.

Ozone levels ranged from an average of 36.74 parts per billion to 142.85 parts per billion, while daily temperatures ranged from 68 to around 107 degrees Fahrenheit.

Cizao Ren, PhD, Department of Epidemiology, School of Medicine, University of California, Irvine.

George Thurston, PhD, associate professor, environmental medicine, New York University, New York City.

Occupational and Environmental Medicine online.

When the ozone level was at its lowest, a 10-degree increase in temperature was associated with about a 1% increase in deaths from heart disease and stroke.

However, when the ozone level was at its highest, there was a more than 8% increase in deaths from heart disease and stroke per 10-degree increase in temperature, Dr. Ren's group found.

EXPLANATION

Ozone is a pollutant strongly linked to weather conditions, particularly the amount of ultraviolet light in the atmosphere.

Ozone is generated by a reaction between airborne nitrogen oxides, volatile organic compounds, and oxygen in sunlight.

Exposure to high levels of ozone can affect the airways and the autonomic nervous system, making people more susceptible to the effects of temperature changes, the team explained.

EXPERT AGREES

"This paper reinforces what we know—that both temperature and ozone affect health, even to the extent that they affect mortality," said George Thurston, an associate professor of environmental medicine at New York University.

Global warming will increase both temperatures and pollution, Thurston added, because higher temperatures are conducive to the production of ozone. "This will be a growing problem," he said.

For the general public, the study raises questions about pollution and climate change, Thurston noted.

"The health effects may be even worse than thought," he said. "There are health benefits to reducing climate change."

Cutting back on the use of fossil fuels will help, Thurston pointed out. "Reducing fossil fuel combustion will reduce climate change and pollution," he said.

"We have seen the problem, and it's fossil fuel combustion. Now, all we have to do is come up with an alternative," Thurston concluded.

info For more information on heart disease, stroke and pollution, visit the American Heart Association Web site at *www.american heart.org* and search "air pollution."

Diesel Fumes Raise Risk of Heart Problems

American Heart Association annual meeting.

Exposure to diesel exhaust increases clot formation and blood platelet activity, boosting men's risk for heart attack and stroke, a small study has found.

THE STUDY

The volunteers—20 healthy men, ages 21 to 44—were first exposed to clean, filtered air (as a control) and then to diluted diesel exhaust at 300 micrograms per meter cubed (mcg/m3)—comparable to the amount breathed in by a person beside a busy street.

Tests conducted on the blood of the volunteers at two hours and six hours after exposure to diesel exhaust revealed a 19.1% to 24.2% increase in clot formation and an increase in activation of blood platelets (which play a major role in clotting) at two hours after diesel exhaust exposure.

LINK TO HEART ATTACK

"The study results are closely tied with previous observational and epidemiological studies showing that shortly after exposure to traffic air pollution, individuals are more likely to suffer a heart attack," said study lead author Dr. Andrew Lucking, a cardiology fellow at the University of Edinburgh in Scotland.

"This study shows that when a person is exposed to relatively high levels of diesel exhaust for a short time, the blood is more likely to clot. This could lead to a blocked vessel resulting in heart attack or stroke," he said.

EXPERT ADVICE

Based on the findings, people with existing cardiovascular disease shouldn't exercise in areas where there's heavy traffic, Lucking added.

info To learn more about air pollution and health, visit the Web site of the American Academy of Family Physicians at *http://family doctor.org* and search "pollution."

Anxiety Raises Men's Coronary Risk Up to 40%

Biing-Jiun Shen, PhD, assistant professor, psychology, University of Southern California, Los Angeles.

Gregg C. Fonarow, MD, professor, cardiology, University of California, Los Angeles.

Journal of the American College of Cardiology.

Older men who suffer from chronic anxiety substantially increase their risk of having a heart attack, say researchers in a recent study.

While stress has been linked to an increased risk for heart problems, this is the first time that chronic anxiety has been identified as a risk factor also.

"There is an independent contribution of anxiety that can predict the onset of a heart attack among healthy older men," said lead researcher Biing-Jiun Shen, PhD, an assistant professor of psychology at the University of Southern California in Los Angeles.

Even after accounting for anger, hostility, depression and type A personality, anxiety still predicted the onset of a heart attack, Dr. Shen said. "The relationship between anxiety and heart attack cannot be explained by depression, hostility or type A personality."

THE STUDY

In the study, Dr. Shen's group collected data on 735 men who participated in the Normative Aging Study, which assesses medical and psychological changes associated with aging.

Each of these men completed psychological testing in 1986 and had no heart problems at the time. The men were followed for an average of 12 years.

During follow-up, the researchers discovered men with chronic anxiety had a 30% to 40% increased risk for heart attack. Those with the highest levels of anxiety on psychological testing had an even higher risk for heart attack.

The risk posed by anxiety remained even after the researchers adjusted their data to account for standard cardiovascular risk factors, health habits, and negative psychological and personality traits, Dr. Shen said.

THEORY

Exaggerated response to acute and chronic stress in anxious individuals may trigger a number of pathways that increase the risk of developing coronary artery disease and being stricken with a heart attack, said Gregg C. Fonarow, MD, a professor of cardiology at the University of California, Los Angeles.

Whether treating anxiety reduces the risk of heart attack isn't known, Dr. Shen said. "But the implication is there," he added. "It is something that doctors can look out for." Dr. Shen's team is hoping to study that possibility.

In addition, it isn't known if women are also at risk for heart attack from chronic anxiety, Dr. Shen noted.

EXPERT REACTION TO STUDY RESULTS

Dr. Fonarow agreed that psychological factors play a significant role in the risk for having a heart attack.

"Psychological characteristics including anxiety, anger, hostility and type A personalities have been associated with increased risk of heart attack in a number of prior studies, and this study again shows that chronic anxiety appears to raise an individual's heart attack risk," said Dr. Fonarow.

"An important finding of this study is that anxiety not only represents an independent risk factor for heart attack but may also explain the associations between heart attack risk and other psychosocial risk factors," he explained.

SELF-DEFENSE FROM DR. FONAROW

"Highly anxious individuals should be aware they may face an increased risk of a heart attack and take proactive steps under physician supervision to control those cardiovascular risk factors which are modifiable, including blood pressure, lipid levels, activity level and weight," Dr. Fonarow added.

info For more on anxiety disorders, visit the Web site of the Anxiety Disorders Association of America, *www.adaa.org.*

Help Your Heart: Heal Heartache Now!

Robert De Vogli, PhD, lecturer, social epidemiology, University College London, England.
Frank A. Treiber, PhD, vice president, research, Medical College of Georgia, Augusta.
Carol Shively, PhD, professor, pathology, Wake Forest University School of Medicine, Winston-Salem, North Carolina.
Annals of Internal Medicine.

Clashing with those you are closest to can literally bring on a heap of heartache. So finds a British study that linked constant bickering to a heightened risk of cardiovascular disease.

When the researchers accounted for other heart risk factors, such as depression or smoking, "negative close relationships" boosted the risk of coronary events by a third, according to a report in the *Archives of Internal Medicine.*

BACKGROUND

"Previous research in this area focused more on philosophy," said lead researcher Robert De Vogli, PhD, a lecturer in social epidemiology at University College London. "It was assumed that if you were married, you were more likely to be healthy. It was well established that social relationships are important for health."

But more recently, Dr. De Vogli said, "research has focused on the *quality* of social relationships, rather than on their quantity—emotional support and social support, what kind of interactions you have with this partner."

THE STUDY

Approximately 9,000 British civil servants filled out questionnaires on up to four close relationships, with most attention paid to the primary relationship. Two-thirds of the time that relationship was with a spouse.

The participants were also asked about the emotional and practical support they received from that person. They were then followed for more than 12 years, with data collected on the incidence of heart disease events in the group.

THE RESULTS

Any increased heart risk found in the study appeared unrelated to either the participant's sex or social position. And it was not related to the social and emotional support given to an individual, the team found.

Instead, "it is possible that negative aspects of close relationships are more important for the health of individuals because of the power of negative close relationships to activate stronger emotions (worrying and anxiety) and the consequent physiological effects," according to this particular researchers.

THEORY

The impact probably comes from increased activity of the sympathetic nervous system (which becomes more active during times of stress), explained Frank A. Treiber, PhD, vice president for research at the Medical College of Georgia, who has also done research on this particular issue.

"A lot of my work has to do with things such as family relationships, risk factors for hypertension, kids from dysfunctional families," Dr. Treiber said. "They are more reactive to stress, which makes their hearts work harder."

EXPERT COMMENTARY

What is different about this study is that the participants defined the closeness of the relationship, noted Carol Shively, PhD, a psychologist who is also professor of pathology at Wake Forest University School of Medicine in Winston-Salem, North Carolina.

In previous studies, those definitions came from outside, usually on the basis of the marital status of the participants, she said.

According to Dr. Shively, "This captures much more closely what is the importance of social relationships to ourselves." That importance has to do with "the emotional quality as perceived by the person who is recording the relationship," she said.

The new report on the British study "does add another piece to the puzzle," Dr. Treiber said. The link between negative relationships and cardiovascular problems "has held up really well across a 12-year follow-up," he said. Still, more work is needed to determine if the same link exists in social groups other than British civil servants, Dr. Treiber noted.

COPING WITH STRESS

It's possible that the cardiovascular impact of negative relationships can be lessened by counseling and training, Dr. Treiber said. "I would say that the family doctor could evaluate the situation and get people referred to someone who would teach them how to cope with stress".

info For more information on coping with stress, visit the Web site of the American Psychological Association, *www.apahelpcenter. org/articles* and click on "Health & Emotional Wellness."

Anniversary of Parent's Passing Can Trigger Death

American College of Cardiology, news release.

The anniversary of the death of a parent can trigger sudden death—especially in men—according to research presented at the American College of Cardiology's annual meeting.

Sudden death, usually caused by lethal arrhythmia (irregular heartbeat), occurs unexpectedly and often within one hour of the onset of symptoms, the researchers found.

"We've all known close family members who have died within hours, weeks, months or years of each other," said the lead investigator of the study, Dr. Ivan Mendoza from Central University of Venezuela in Caracas.

"Physicians should be aware that mental stress, such as the anniversary effect, may induce sudden death in susceptible individuals," he added.

THE STUDY

Researchers evaluated a series of 102 documented sudden deaths of individuals between the ages of 37 and 79, 70% of whom died from coronary artery disease, the study found.

In 12% of the cases, the death occurred on the anniversary date of the death of a parent —seven occurred on the father's, five on the mother's, one on the anniversary of both when they died on the same date.

Roughly one-third died at a similar age as the parent, the study showed. And nearly 80% of those who died suddenly under the anniversary effect were male.

POSSIBLE EXPLANATION

The reason for this is not understood, but may reflect gender differences in response to stressful situations, said coinvestigator Dr. Juan Marques, also from the university.

According to Dr. Mendoza, patients may be especially vulnerable if they have a history of heart attack, family history of sudden death or coronary disease, and cardiovascular risk factors such as high cholesterol, high blood pressure, diabetes, smoking, obesity or a sedentary lifestyle.

info To learn more about sudden cardiac death, visit the Web site of the American Heart Association, *www.americanheart.org*, and search "sudden cardiac death."

Seven Signs of Heart Disease Most Women Ignore

Nieca Goldberg, MD, a cardiologist and pioneer in women's heart health. Her New York City practice, Total Heart Care, focuses primarily on caring for women (*www.niecagoldberg.com*). Dr. Goldberg is clinical associate professor of medicine and medical director of the New York University Women's Heart Program. She is author of *The Women's Healthy Heart Program: Lifesaving Strategies for Preventing and Healing Heart Disease.* Ballantine.

The following statement is shocking but true—even though heart disease is thought of mostly as a "man's disease," it kills more than one-third of American women. Hard to believe? Consider these facts…

•**Heart disease is the number-one killer of women in the US.**

•**Women age 40 and older who have a heart attack** are more likely than men of the same age to die within one year.

•**Women ages 40 to 69 are more likely than men** in the same age group to have a second heart attack within five years of the first attack.

One problem, say researchers, is that women aren't treated as aggressively for heart disease as men. That's because many doctors—and nearly nine out of 10 women—still don't recognize the extent and severity of women's heart disease.

What can you do to protect yourself? What are the risk factors that so many women are unaware of or do not properly manage?

REDUCING YOUR RISK

Understanding your personal risk factors for heart disease is crucial. Your family history, of course, cannot be changed. If a parent or sibling has heart disease, your own risk is increased. Because women typically suffer heart attacks later in life than men do—possibly because of the estrogen that helps protect them until menopause—if your mother was relatively young (under age 60) when she had a heart attack, you are at even greater risk.

However, you can do something about all the other risk factors. The personal habits and metabolic measurements, such as cholesterol, that make a heart attack or stroke more likely are the same for women and men. Most people do not realize, though, that there are several risk factors that threaten women more than men.

What women need to know to protect themselves from the likelihood of a heart attack…

•**Diabetes.** Extra blood sugar (glucose) in the bloodstream may damage arteries. For unknown reasons, this increases heart disease risk for women more than for men.

What to do: Diabetes is most likely to develop in midlife. If you are over age 45, ask your doctor for a *fasting blood glucose test*, which can detect diabetes. The test should be repeated every three years, or annually if you have a risk factor for diabetes—for example, if you have a family history of the disease or if you are overweight.

Diet, exercise and glucose-lowering medication, such as *metformin* (Glucophage), are effective for controlling diabetes and thus lowering heart disease risk.

•**HDL cholesterol.** This is the "good" cholesterol that carries harmful fat away from the arteries. Healthy HDL levels in women are 50

milligrams per deciliter (mg/dL) or higher, versus 40 mg/dL or higher for men. Increasing HDL by 10 mg/dL may reduce heart disease risk by 42% to 50% in women.

•**Triglycerides.** High levels of this type of blood fat may increase the risk for heart disease by 32% in men—and 76% in women. The reason for this disparity is unknown.

What to do: Anyone over age 20 should have a *fasting lipoprotein profile*. This blood test measures HDL and triglycerides, along with LDL "bad" cholesterol and total cholesterol. If results are normal, retest every five years.

If any of your levels are abnormal, treatment typically includes dietary changes, regular exercise and, if necessary, a statin drug, such as *lovastatin* (Mevacor) or *simvastatin* (Zocor) or the B vitamin niacin to increase HDL.

Caution: Niacin can be dangerous for some. Do not use it without consulting your doctor.

•**Smoking.** While most women know that smoking raises the risk for lung disease, many do not realize that it also triples a woman's risk for heart disease. In women under age 44, smoking is the most common risk factor for heart disease.

What to do: Stop smoking. After one year, your risk for heart disease will be halved. After 10 years, your risk for stroke will be the same as that of a lifelong nonsmoker. Ask your doctor about nicotine replacement treatments (patches, chewing gum) and other measures that can help you quit.

•**Excess weight.** Extra body weight causes an elevation in blood triglycerides. It is especially risky when fat is concentrated around the belly area, because abdominal fat releases hormones and other biochemicals that can increase blood sugar and lower HDL.

What to do: With a measuring tape, measure your waist just above the navel and your hips at the widest part. Divide your waist measurement by your hip measurement.

Example: If your waist is 30 inches and your hips are 40 inches, your waist-to-hip ratio is 0.75.

If your waist-to-hip ratio exceeds 0.8, you are at increased risk for heart disease. Work with your doctor to establish realistic diet and exercise goals to help you lose weight.

•**Anger.** Anger increases levels of stress hormones that may make arteries more vulnerable to cholesterol buildup. It also raises blood pressure. In our culture, women are taught to hold in their anger—a practice that may be particularly damaging to the heart, according to research. *Healthy ways to deal with anger...*

•Practice relaxation techniques, such as deep breathing, meditation and biofeedback. These strategies also can help reduce heart-damaging chronic stress.

•Try to avoid situations that you know trigger your anger, such as waiting in long lines or saying yes to too many responsibilities.

•Exercise—it helps distract you from and dissipate anger.

•Think honestly about what you can and cannot control. Try to accept your limitations.

•Talk to a behavioral psychologist, who can help you develop ways to handle your anger.

•**Lack of support.** Studies show that women who are not in supportive environments—at home, at work or both—have higher blood pressure and higher rates of heart disease. *Important types of support to cultivate...*

•Emotional support—someone you can trust with your most intimate thoughts, anxieties and fears, and who trusts you.

•Social support—someone you enjoy spending time with.

•Informational support—someone you can ask for advice.

•Practical support—someone who will try to help you out in a pinch.

■ ■ ■ ■

Kidney Problems Can Signal Heart Disease

Kidney disease can be a sign of heart disease, says Peter A. McCullough, MD, MPH. Because the heart pumps blood to the kidneys to be filtered, the health of these two organs is interrelated. Two simple tests that can measure kidney health also indicate heart health—*estimated glomerular filtration rate* (GFR) and *urine-albumin-to-creatinine ratio.* Most insurers cover the costs.

Self-defense: If your doctor doesn't order them as part of your annual physical, ask him/her to do so.

Peter A. McCullough, MD, MPH, chief of preventive medicine, Beaumont Health Center, Royal Oak, Michigan, and leader of a study of more than 37,000 people, published in *Archives of Internal Medicine.*

■ ■ ■ ■

Warning: Heart Attack Linked to Flu

An analysis of autopsy reports for nearly 35,000 people who died from heart disease over an eight-year period showed that the risk of dying from a heart attack increased by one-third during weeks of flu epidemics, compared with non-epidemic weeks.

Theory: Influenza causes inflammation, which can loosen plaques (fatty deposits) in coronary arteries and cause heart attacks.

If you have heart disease: Ask your doctor about getting an annual flu shot when the vaccine becomes available (usually in October or November).

Mohammad Madjid, MD, senior research scientist, Texas Heart Institute, Houston.

■ ■ ■ ■

Better Way to Calculate Heart Attack Risk

Age, sex, blood pressure, cholesterol level and smoking are commonly used to estimate heart attack risk. But up to 20% of female heart attack patients do not have high cholesterol or blood pressure and/or smoke.

New tool: Researchers studied 24,558 healthy women age 45 and older and devised a more accurate risk score that factors in blood levels of the inflammation marker C-reactive protein and parental history of a heart attack before age 60. Women can assess their heart attack risk at *www.reynoldsriskscore.org.*

Paul M. Ridker, MD, MPH, director, Center for Cardiovascular Disease Prevention, Brigham and Women's Hospital, Boston.

Rheumatoid Arthritis Affects Your Heart, Too

Hilal Maradit Kremers, MD, research associate, Mayo Clinic Department of Health Sciences Research, Rochester, Minnesota.

Hayes Wilson, MD, chief, rheumatology, Piedmont Hospital, Atlanta, and medical adviser, Arthritis Foundation, Atlanta.

American College of Rheumatology annual meeting, Boston.

People diagnosed with rheumatoid arthritis (RA) run a greater risk of developing heart disease. But that risk can be spotted and hopefully modified by employing the same criteria used to identify heart-disease risk in the general population, a new study suggests.

RA is characterized by inflammation of the lining of the joints and, over time, can lead to joint damage, severe pain, and immobility. Risk factors for heart disease include high blood pressure, high cholesterol, older age, and family history of cardiovascular illness. People diagnosed with rheumatoid arthritis (RA) should be screened using those risk factors as soon as possible following their diagnosis of RA, the study authors said.

BACKGROUND

"We need to know how can we predict which patients with RA are at a higher risk than others, so that we can then put more effort into the prevention of heart disease in these people," said lead researcher Hilal Maradit Kremers, MD, a research associate with the Mayo Clinic Department of Health Sciences Research in Rochester, Minnesota. "In our study we attempted to do just that, by using a typical cardiovascular risk profile to predict heart disease among these patients."

The study findings follow a 2005 Mayo Clinic report that suggested that the increase in heart disease risk among RA patients may be due to the systemic inflammation brought on by the disease, which, in turn, prompts arterial plaque to form blood clots.

According to the Arthritis Foundation, rheumatoid arthritis is a chronic and often disabling disease with no known cause or cure. It affects just over 2 million Americans. Treatments—such as nonsteroidal anti-inflammatories, analgesics and physical therapy—focus primarily on controlling pain and limiting inflammation and joint destruction.

THE STUDY

Dr. Kremers and her colleagues set out to predict the onset of heart disease over the course of a 10-year period among more than 1,100 people, approximately half of whom had just been diagnosed with RA. The patients were 57 years old, on average, and nearly three-quarters were women.

The patients were evaluated on standard indicators for heart disease risk, as detailed by the American Heart Association. The indicators included: gender; having a family history of heart disease; having diabetes; and/or being black. Patients were also examined for other risk factors, such as high cholesterol and high blood pressure. Risky lifestyle habits—including smoking, lack of exercise, and being overweight—were also considered, the researchers said.

Based on the risk-assessment scores, the researchers assigned the patients to one of five different risk categories for heart disease—ranging from very low to very high risk. Then the patients were tracked for an average of 12 to 14 years, during which time all incidents of heart attack, heart failure, heart surgeries, and cardiovascular-related deaths were noted.

THE RESULTS

The researchers found that while 85% of the RA patients between the ages of 50 and 59 had an intermediate or high risk for developing heart disease within 10 years of diagnosis, just 27% of comparable non-RA patients did. Among patients between the ages of 60 and 69 at the start of the study, 100% of the RA patients had an intermediate or high risk for heart disease, compared with 79% of non-RA patients.

When looking at just "high risk" among the 60 to 69 age group, the difference was even more dramatic—85% for RA patients, compared to just 40% for non-RA patients.

SELF-DEFENSE

In light of the findings, the Mayo researchers are encouraging doctors to conduct heart-disease assessment screenings similar to the ones used in the study for each of their RA patients. These screenings should be done as soon as possible following an RA diagnosis and prevention strategies put into place, the researchers said.

"By doing the things that we already know, such as measuring blood pressure, blood sugars, and cholesterol—all the standard things that we look at for the general population—we can help identify the risk for a major cardiovascular event among the RA population," Dr. Kremers said.

EXPERT COMMENTARY

Hayes Wilson, MD, chief of rheumatology at Piedmont Hospital in Atlanta, said he endorsed the Mayo researchers' work.

"Anything that helps us characterize and categorize risk factors helps us in the treatment of the disease," he said. "And, until we can figure out what the smoking gun is, hopefully this advice will help us prevent cardiovascular disease or related diseases by helping RA patients better appreciate the risks they face."

info For more information about rheumatoid arthritis, visit the Arthritis Foundation Web site, *www.arthritis.org*.

Heart Attack Alert— What to Do Before the Ambulance Arrives

Richard O'Brien, MD, a spokesman for the American College of Emergency Physicians. He is a clinical instructor in the department of medicine at Temple University School of Medicine in Philadelphia and an emergency physician at Moses Taylor Hospital in Scranton, Pennsylvania.

Would you know what to do if a loved one lost consciousness and stopped breathing?

Each day, about 900 Americans die after suffering these classic signs of sudden cardiac arrest (an abrupt cessation of the heartbeat), usually resulting from a heart attack. About 80% of cardiac arrests occur at the victim's home.

Cardiopulmonary resuscitation (CPR) has long been used to try to keep a cardiac arrest victim's blood circulating until emergency medical help

arrives. But CPR is difficult for nonprofessionals to master—and many laypeople administer it incorrectly.

Latest development: A study recently published in *The Lancet* found that when CPR was performed by bystanders, the use of continuous chest compressions alone resulted in better outcomes for cardiac arrest patients treated outside the hospital than the use of mouth-to-mouth resuscitation along with chest compressions.

The American Heart Association (AHA) says that more research is needed before general CPR guidelines are likely to change. However, the AHA does recommend that bystanders use compressions-only CPR if they are unable or unwilling to do mouth-to-mouth breathing.

Emergency physician Richard O'Brien, MD, discussed this and other new approaches to this potentially life-saving procedure...

WHO NEEDS HELP?

It should be assumed that anyone who suddenly loses consciousness and stops breathing requires immediate assistance. *What to do...*

1. Call for help. Ask someone to call 911 immediately. Do it yourself, if no one is available.

2. Determine whether the victim is unresponsive. Gently nudge and/or talk to the victim to see whether he/she is unconscious, rather than intoxicated or asleep.

3. Check breathing. Put your hand on the person's chest to feel for breathing movements... or put your ear close to the victim's nose and mouth and listen for breathing. Spend five to 10 seconds checking for normal breathing in an adult or for the presence or absence of breathing in an infant or child. (Gasping breaths that can occur in adults are uncommon in infants and children.) If an adult is breathing normally or a child is breathing at all, do not perform CPR—wait for help to arrive. Otherwise, continue following these steps.

4. Ask for a portable defibrillator. If you're in a public place—an airport, supermarket, etc.— yell that you need a defibrillator. When applied to the victim's chest, this device automatically analyzes the heart's rhythm (electrical activity), determines if an electric shock is needed and delivers the appropriate jolts. If a defibrillator shock is given within five minutes of cardiac arrest, the average survival rate is better than that offered by CPR. If a defibrillator is not immediately available, begin chest compressions.

DO NOT CHECK THE PULSE

Until recently, first-aid instructors taught would-be rescuers to check for a pulse before starting CPR.

New guideline: The AHA now discourages checking for a pulse in an unconscious victim. That's largely because untrained bystanders come to an incorrect conclusion when checking for a pulse in about 35% of cases.

GIVING CHEST COMPRESSIONS

If the victim is age nine or older, put the heel of one of your hands in the center of the person's chest between the nipples (at the "nipple line")…place your other hand on top…and push down one-and-a-half inches to two inches.

For a young child (ages one to eight), use one or both hands and press down at the nipple line about one-third to one-half the depth of the chest.

For infants, use two fingers and press on the breastbone just below the nipple line, one-third to one-half the chest depth.

Important: Allow the chest to completely *recoil* between compressions. Pressing down pushes blood out of the heart. During the recoil, the heart sucks in blood. Victims need about 100 chest compressions per minute.

Remember: When chest compressions are given, the goal is not to "restart" the victim's heart, but to improve his chances of survival until medical personnel can provide advanced life support, including defibrillation and intravenous drugs (such as *epinephrine*).

RESCUE BREATHING

Before starting mouth-to-mouth resuscitation, tilt the victim's head back slightly and lift the chin toward your face. Take a normal breath before giving a rescue breath, which should last up to one second and make the victim's chest rise.

New guideline: After giving two rescue breaths, immediately begin chest compressions, using a ratio of 30 chest compressions for every two ventilations (rescue breaths).

To view a video of these basic steps, go to *http://depts.washington.edu/learncpr/index.*

html, the Web site of the University of Washington School of Medicine.

info CPR classes are offered by the American Heart Association (800-242-8721, *www.americanheart.org*) and the American Red Cross (202-303-4498, *www.redcross.org*).

First 90 Days After Stopping Plavix Are the Most Dangerous

P. Michael Ho, MD, PhD, cardiologist, Denver VA Medical Center and assistant professor of medicine, University of Colorado.
Deepak Bhatt, MD, associate director, Cleveland Clinic Cardiovascular Coordinating Center.
Journal of the American Medical Association.

New research finds that the first three months after heart patients stop taking the clot-preventing drug *clopidogrel* (Plavix) are the most dangerous.

"This is the first study to make this observation," said P. Michael Ho, MD, PhD, a cardiologist at the Denver VA Medical Center and lead author of the report. "We need more studies to confirm it, and see whether and why there is an increase in adverse events after stopping."

The study does not address the issue of how long Plavix may safely be taken, said Dr. Ho, who is an assistant professor of medicine at the University of Colorado. The current recommendation is that it should be used for nine months after a heart attack and 12 months after a stent is implanted to help an artery stay open.

"We looked at people who took different lengths of clopidogrel treatment," Dr. Ho said. "We found a twofold increase in risk in the 90-day period after stopping for those who took it less than six months or greater than nine months. For those who took clopidogrel longer than 12 months or 15 months, we could not calculate the increased risk because we did not have enough patients."

THE STUDY

Dr. Ho and his colleagues assessed the incidence and timing of death or acute heart attacks in 3,137 people discharged from 127 VA hospitals. The patients were taking Plavix after an acute coronary event, such as a heart attack. The average time of Plavix treatment was 302 days.

Analysis found the incidence of adverse events was higher in the 90 days after the medication was stopped than in the 91 to 180 days after cessation.

"This is going to get a lot of attention, both from doctors and the medical community at large, because clopidogrel is such a widely used drug," said Deepak Bhatt, MD, associate director of the Cleveland Clinic Cardiovascular Coordinating Center.

The finding "follows common sense, but no one has actually shown this before in a large group of patients," Dr. Bhatt said.

IMPLICATIONS

The results appear to support the view that longer therapy with clopidogrel is better but does not completely answer that question, he said. "The very necessary next step is to figure out whether longer duration is better in a randomized, controlled trial."

Such a controlled trial would meet the gold standard for medical research. The newly reported study was observational, Dr. Ho noted, meaning that it examined what was happening in medical practice without attempting to single out factors affecting the results.

RECOMMENDATIONS

A decision on whether or when to stop clopidogrel treatment must be made on a case-by-case basis, Dr. Ho said. "The final decision should be left to provider and patient. They have to weigh the risk of discontinuing clopidogrel against the risk of abnormal bleeding if it is continued. The clinician needs to weigh the risk and benefits for each individual patient."

Those making the decision should remember that the risk found in the study was "relatively small," Dr. Ho said. Among the more than 3,000 cases studied, there were 163 adverse events in the 90 days after drug treatment stopped, 57 in the following 90 days, and 26 in the third 90-day period.

info To learn more about the benefits and side effects of clopidogrel, visit the Web site of the US National Library of Medicine at *http://medlineplus.gov*, and click on "Drugs and Supplements."

Take This Test Before Taking Blood Thinners

Raymond Woosley, MD, PhD, president, Critical Path Institute, Tucson, Arizona.

C. Michael Stein, MD, professor, medicine and pharmacology, Vanderbilt University, Nashville, Tennessee.

Dina Paltoo, PhD, MPH, Health Scientist Administrator, division of heart and vascular diseases, National Heart, Lung, and Blood Institute, Bethesda, Maryland.

New England Journal of Medicine.

Variations of a gene that determines a person's sensitivity to *warfarin* (Coumadin), an anti-clotting drug, are important in determining the initial doses of the medication, researchers report.

That information already is being put to medical use. The US Food and Drug Administration (FDA) changed the drug's labeling to say that doctors should consider a genetic test when first prescribing warfarin. "This test can save $1.1 billion in health care costs and 18,000 lives a year," said Raymond Woosley, MD, PhD, president of the Critical Path Institute, a private organization that is working with the FDA and the biotechnology industry on the subject.

BACKGROUND

The FDA estimates that 2 million Americans take warfarin to prevent potentially dangerous blood clots. Reasons range from implantation of an artificial heart valve to the abnormal heartbeat called atrial fibrillation.

But warfarin is a notoriously difficult drug to manage, especially at the start. Too much can lead to hemorrhages, and too little can allow clots to form. One individual may do well on 1.5 milligrams (mg) a day, while another may require 20 mg daily.

Some medical centers run elaborate tests to determine the starting dose, but "the standard way is to start with 5 milligrams, then titrate the doses according to blood tests that show the response to warfarin," said C. Michael Stein, MD, a professor of medicine and pharmacology at Vanderbilt University and leader of the study group.

THE STUDY

Two genes are known to affect the response to warfarin. One, designated CYP2C9, governs the metabolism of the medication, or how fast it is eliminated from the body. The other, designated VKORC1, governs sensitivity, or how the body reacts to a given dose of warfarin. The new study of 297 people starting warfarin therapy showed that variants of the sensitivity gene should be considered in the first prescription, Dr. Stein said.

TAILORING TREATMENT TO GENETIC MAKEUP

Dr. Stein is a leader in the new field of *pharmacogenomics* (the study of how genes affect a person's response to drugs), which hopes to tailor medical treatment to each individual's genetic makeup. The field has been made possible by the Human Genome Project, which has mapped the full human genetic makeup. That information has led the US government to sponsor programs on specific applications of pharmacogenomics and to a small but growing industry of companies developing and marketing genetic tests, such as one for warfarin sensitivity.

Several warfarin sensitivity tests are now available, costing perhaps $500 or $600, Dr. Woosley said.

IMPLICATIONS

"This is not something that changes the way doctors practice tomorrow," Dr. Stein said of the new study. "It is additional information on the relative importance of these two genes early in therapy which will refine the way that physicians use warfarin."

And the tests are useful only when warfarin treatment starts, Dr. Woosley said. They do not eliminate the need for periodic blood tests to make precise adjustments to warfarin dosage.

Nevertheless, said Dina Paltoo, PhD, MPH, the National Heart, Lung, and Blood Institute program director who oversaw the agency's funding of the study, "this can help physicians clarify what dose a patient should get, so it could reduce adverse drug effects, toxicity and bleeding."

Testing should be done because "these genetic variations are critically important in how warfarin affects each individual," Dr. Paltoo said.

info To learn more about pharmacogenomics, visit the Web site of the genome programs of the US Department of Energy, *http://genomics.energy.gov*. Under the heading "Medicine," click on "Pharmacogenomics."

Jump-Starting the Heart: What to Make Sure Your Doctor Knows

Paul S. Chan, MD, cardiologist, Saint Luke's Mid-America Heart Institute, Kansas City, Missouri.
Leslie A. Saxon, MD, FACC, chief, cardiology, University of Southern California, Los Angeles.
New England Journal of Medicine.

About a third of patients who suffer cardiac arrest in hospitals don't get a defibrillator-delivered shock to start the heart beating again within the two minutes recommended by the American Heart Association, a new study found.

This delay significantly reduces a patient's chance of survival, the study authors said.

"Until now, the recommendation for defibrillation within two minutes was based on expert opinion," said Paul S. Chan, MD, who led the study while at the University of Michigan and now is a cardiologist with Saint Luke's Mid-America Heart Institute in Kansas City, Missouri. "There were no clear standards established. This study helps support the two-minute recommendation."

Cardiac arrest is a too-common hospital problem. An estimated 750,000 patients experience cardiac arrest in US hospitals each year, the study authors said.

THE STUDY

Dr. Chan and his collaborators identified nearly 6,800 people who had cardiac arrest at 369 hospitals participating in the National Registry of Cardiopulmonary Resuscitation.

Overall, the response time seemed impressive, with defibrillation beginning an average of one minute after the heart stopped.

But defibrillation did not begin for two or more minutes in 2,045 cases, 30.1% of the total. Just 22.2% of that subgroup of patients survived to leave the hospital, compared to 39.3% of those who got early defibrillation, the study found.

"If we had the ability to look at all the hospitals across the country, the numbers probably would be worse," said Dr. Chan, referring both to the time defibrillation begins and chance of survival. "These are the better-performing hospitals, ones that issue quarterly reports."

Delayed defibrillation was more likely in hospitals with fewer than 250 beds; in hospital units where patients were not continuously monitored; for patients admitted with diagnoses other than heart disease; during "off hours" (nights and weekends); and for black patients, the study showed.

"But we found delays across all types of hospital beds and units," Dr. Chan said. It's not clear what can be done to speed up the response across-the-board in all hospitals, he added.

POSSIBLE SOLUTIONS

Monitoring all patients' heart function might make a difference, he said, "but we can only speculate because we don't have interventional trials to see if that would make a difference."

Changes in practice at some hospitals might also lead to improvements, Dr. Chan said. For example, some hospitals do not allow nurses who detect a problem to use a defibrillator—they must call a physician or a specially trained nurse instead, he said.

"We might make external defibrillators available to more units," Dr. Chan said. "That is one potential solution that might have a significant impact over time. And hospitals might set up emergency teams to intervene when there is a cardiac arrest code."

According to Dr. Chan, the effect of such measures will have to be tested in real life. Trials of rapid intervention teams are being planned.

CONTINUOUS MONITORING

A different approach to the problem is proposed by Leslie A. Saxon, MD, chief of cardiology at the University of Southern California—continuous monitoring of all hospitalized patients.

"We have to monitor them wherever they are," Dr. Saxon said. "They don't have to be in a specialized unit. We can go to an automated system with electrodes for rapid detection of heart arrhythmias (irregular heartbeat). The detection development devices are out there."

The study is important, she said, "because it points out a need in hospitalized patients. You've got to have these things [defibrillators] in every patient's room. Even the housekeeping person in the room can be trained to use them. I spend a lot of time thinking about ways to avoid sudden death."

info For more on defibrillators, visit the Web site of the Heart Rhythm Society, *www.hrsonline.org*, and search "defibrillators."

Defibrillators Work Even While Driving

Christine M. Albert, MD, director, Center for Arrhythmia Prevention, Brigham and Women's Hospital, Boston.
Bruce Wilkoff, MD, director of cardiac and tachyarrhythmia devices, Cleveland Clinic.
Journal of the American College of Cardiology.

The defibrillators that are implanted in people for instant correction of abnormal heartbeats pose no special risks for heart patients who drive, researchers report.

"What this confirms is what we already thought, that overall there is not a huge risk in this population," said study lead author Christine M. Albert, MD, director of the Center for Arrhythmia Prevention at Brigham and Women's Hospital in Boston.

BACKGROUND

About 50,000 defibrillators are implanted annually in the United States. Vice President Dick Cheney is one famous recipient of the device. There have been worries that the shock delivered by the device to correct an abnormal heartbeat might be dangerous for drivers, Dr. Albert said.

THE STUDY

The study included 1,188 people with a defibrillator, whose full name is implantable cardioverter defibrillator (ICD). The patients were followed for an average of 562 days, during which time the devices delivered a total of 193 shocks within one hour of driving—a rate of one shock for every 25,116 person-hours driving. None of the shocks resulted in an accident.

Overall, the study found that the incidence of having an ICD shock was not higher while a participant was driving. One oddity in the findings was that an ICD shock was twice as likely to be delivered during the 30 minutes after someone drove a car, Dr. Albert said, an indication of possible strains caused by driving.

"These data provide reassurance that driving by ICD patients should not translate into an important rate of personal or public injury," according to the researchers.

EXPERT COMMENTARY

"This is very strong evidence that our worries were not based on fact but were theoretical," said Bruce Wilkoff, MD, director of cardiac and tachyarrhythmia devices at the Cleveland Clinic.

But common sense factors into the safety issue of ICDs and drivers, Dr. Wilkoff added. "People who have frequent shocks tend not to drive in the first place." Twenty percent of the ICD recipients in the study did not drive at all, Dr. Wilkoff noted.

DRIVING RECOMMENDATIONS

Current guidelines say that someone who is given an ICD after experiencing a major arrhythmia—an irregular heartbeat—should not drive for at least one week after the implant. The one-week restriction also applies for patients who have not experienced an arrhythmia to allow for recovery from the surgery. Driving restrictions then should be decided during consultation with a physician, Dr. Albert said.

In practice, that works out to "don't drive when you're not feeling well," Dr. Wilkoff said.

info To learn more about ICDs, visit the US Food and Drug Administration Web site at *www.fda.gov* and search "implantable cardioverter defibrillators."

■ ■ ■ ■

Pacemakers Linked to Sleep Disorder

In a new study of 98 people who had pacemakers (implanted devices that regulate heartbeat), 59% of participants were found to have undiagnosed sleep apnea (temporary cessation of breathing while sleeping), a disorder that raises risk for cardiovascular disease.

Theory: Sleep apnea can lower blood oxygen levels, leading to cardiac disorders.

Self-defense: If your doctor has recommended that you have a pacemaker implanted, ask him/her to screen you for sleep apnea and recommend lifestyle changes, such as weight loss, and/or treatment, such as continuous positive airway pressure (CPAP), to prevent upper airway collapse.

Patrick Levy, MD, PhD, professor of physiology, University of Grenoble, Grenoble, France.

Heart Attack Prevention Update

Stephen R. Devries, MD, a preventive cardiologist and associate professor of medicine in the division of cardiology at the Center for Integrative Medicine at the Feinberg School of Medicine at Northwestern University in Chicago. He is the author of *What Your Doctor May Not Tell You About Cholesterol.* Warner Wellness.

Conventional medicine is very effective for treating existing and/or severe heart disease, but most doctors don't give nearly enough attention to prevention.

What you may not know: An estimated eight out of 10 heart attack deaths can be prevented—but *not* by focusing mainly on high cholesterol and prescribing powerful drugs, as most doctors do. With integrative heart care—which combines conventional medicine and alternative therapies—patients get much better results than either type of treatment can offer when used alone.

Problem: Too many doctors have not stayed up-to-date on a number of important heart disease risk factors that have been discovered only in recent years. *To protect yourself—or a loved one...*

•**Don't be fooled by a "normal" cholesterol reading.** A "normal" total cholesterol level is typically defined as less than 200 milligrams per deciliter (mg/dL). But one-third of patients with heart disease have cholesterol levels that *are* less than 200 mg/dL.

How does this happen? Total cholesterol is the combined total of LDL "bad" cholesterol...VLDL (very-low-density lipoprotein, also a "bad" cholesterol because high levels are linked to heart disease)...and HDL "good" cholesterol levels. Many people who have "normal" total cholesterol levels have dangerously low levels of the beneficial HDL cholesterol. HDL is responsible for removing LDL "bad" cholesterol from the arteries and carrying it to the liver for disposal. HDL also has antioxidant properties that can reduce arterial blockages (atherosclerosis).

Conversely, a total cholesterol reading that is 200 mg/dL or higher might be due to elevated HDL. These patients are less likely to get heart disease than those with the same total cholesterol level and a lower HDL level—but the standard cholesterol test would indicate that they are at increased risk.

Example: A 39-year-old woman I know had a total cholesterol reading of 125 mg/dL. Her doctor thought she was in great health—but her HDL was only 15 mg/dL, and she went on to develop coronary artery disease. (HDL should be at least 50 mg/dL in women...and at least 40 mg/dL in men.)

To raise "good" HDL: Ask your doctor about niacin. At doses of 1,000 mg to 2,000 mg daily, this form of vitamin B can increase HDL by 29%—that's more effective than the prescription drug *gemfibrozil* (Lopid), which is used to raise HDL.

Caution: Niacin at these doses can worsen gastroesophageal reflux disease and ulcers, elevate blood sugar, trigger gout (a type of arthritis) and cause liver irritation. Therefore, it should be taken only under a physician's supervision.

Helpful: To reduce flushing, a common side effect of high-dose niacin, take it with food. Do not take popular "flush-free" niacin—anecdotal

evidence suggests that it isn't as effective as standard types.

•**Don't settle for a traditional cholesterol test.** These tests measure levels of total, HDL and LDL cholesterol, along with blood fats known as triglycerides. Newer tests—which still aren't used by most doctors—look at cholesterol *subfractions*, blood fat measurements that may be more predictive of heart disease than total cholesterol, HDL and LDL alone. *Ask for a cholesterol test that looks at...*

•Lp(a). This is a particle that includes both LDL and a potentially dangerous blood-clotting chemical. People with an elevated Lp(a) are one-and-a-half times more likely to get heart disease than those whose level is normal.

Optimal Lp(a) level: Below 30 mg/dL.

Treatment: Niacin—500 mg to 2,000 mg daily—can lower Lp(a) by up to one-third.

Also helpful: Eating 10 walnuts daily will lower Lp(a) by up to 6%.

•**LDL size.** LDL particles are either small and dense or large and fluffy. Patients with a relatively high percentage of large particles are said to have *Pattern A* distribution. They're three times less likely to have heart disease than those with a higher percentage of small particles (*Pattern B*)—even when LDL readings are the same in both groups.

Treatment: If you have Pattern B distribution, fish oil may be beneficial because it can convert small particles into large ones.

Typical dosage: 1,000 mg to 4,000 mg of fish oil daily, from supplements containing at least 1,000 mg of combined *eicosapentaenoic acid* (EPA) and *docosahexaenoic acid* (DHA).

Caution: Fish oil can cause gastrointestinal upset and has a mild blood-thinning effect. It should not be used by patients who take the blood thinner *warfarin* (Coumadin) and should not be taken two weeks before and after any surgical procedure.

Exercise also decreases the concentration of small LDL particles. Aim for 30 to 60 minutes of aerobic exercise five to seven days a week.

•**Find out your high-sensitivity C-reactive protein (hs-CRP) level.** Hs-CRP is linked to higher rates of heart disease, yet few doctors test for it routinely. *Insist on it.* Elevated hs-CRP greatly increases heart attack risk, even in patients with normal cholesterol.

Optimal hs-CRP level: Below 1 mg/L.

Treatment: The cholesterol-lowering statin drugs, such as *atorvastatin* (Lipitor) or *simvastatin* (Zocor), can lower hs-CRP by up to 40%.

Also helpful: Weight loss (excess fat tissue, especially in the abdominal area, produces inflammatory chemicals that promote hardening of the arteries)…daily brushing and flossing (lowers risk for gum inflammation and dental infections, which are linked to heart disease)…exercise…and combining a statin drug with 1,000 mg to 4,000 mg of fish oil daily.

•**Take stress seriously.** Mainstream medicine greatly underestimates the effects of chronic stress on heart health. Patients with frequent stress maintain high levels of adrenaline and other potentially harmful chemicals and hormones that increase blood pressure and hs-CRP.

Treatment: Add stress reducers, such as exercise, yoga and/or meditation, to your daily schedule.

•**Consider supplements.** People without heart disease who have high blood pressure and mildly elevated cholesterol (requiring an LDL decrease of less than 25%) as well as those who can't tolerate prescription drugs may be good candidates for treatment with over-the-counter (OTC) supplements. *Use of the following supplements should be supervised by a physician—they have potential side effects and may interact with medications or other supplements…*

•Red yeast rice is an OTC product that can lower LDL by nearly 25%. Red yeast rice is helpful for patients with mildly elevated cholesterol (described above)…those who have experienced side effects from prescription statin drugs…or those who simply do not want to take a prescription statin.

Typical dosage: 600 mg twice daily. If stronger effects are needed, a maximum dosage of 1,200 mg twice daily.

Caution: Red yeast rice has the potential to cause liver and/or muscle irritation. Use it only under the supervision of a doctor, who can monitor its effectiveness and any side effects. Stop taking red yeast rice if you develop unexplained muscle aches or pain.

•Coenzyme Q10 (CoQ10) is a vitamin-like substance that's naturally present in cells. In supplement form, it lowers blood pressure and improves symptoms of heart failure. Important: Statins lower CoQ10 levels.

Typical dosage: 100 mg daily when taking statins…or 200 mg to 300 mg daily when taken for hypertension and/or congestive heart failure.

Caution: CoQ10 is a mild blood thinner, so it should not be taken by people on warfarin.

Regular Exercise Helps Fight Heart Failure

Sidney Smith, MD, past president, American Heart Association, and director, Center for Cardiovascular Science and Medicine, University of North Carolina School of Medicine, Chapel Hill.

Axel Linke, MD, assistant professor, medicine, University of Leipzig, Germany.

American Heart Association annual meeting, Orlando, Florida.

Exercise boosts the number of progenitor cells—immature cells that can divide into other cells to help repair tissue—in people with heart failure. Those cells in turn rebuild weakened muscle and blood vessels, researchers report.

According to two studies that were presented at the American Heart Association annual meeting in Orlando, Florida, that response can dramatically enhance patients' ability to move and work out.

"Both studies point to the beneficial effect of exercise on patients with heart failure," said Sidney Smith, MD, past president of the American Heart Association and director of the Center for Cardiovascular Science and Medicine at the University of North Carolina School of Medicine.

"These observations provide some understanding into the mechanisms that make exercise helpful," Dr. Smith said.

BACKGROUND

More than 5 million people in the United States have heart failure, a condition that affects the heart's ability to pump blood throughout the body.

However, researchers are beginning to understand that heart failure woes come not only from this pumping disorder, but also from changes in the legs and other parts of the body.

"The muscle of the leg starts to shrink, so there is less muscle mass," explained Axel Linke, MD, a coauthor on both studies and assistant professor of medicine at the University of Leipzig in Germany. "The endothelium and the vessels supplying blood to the muscles deteriorate, so they are less flexible—elasticity is reduced," he said. The endothelium is a layer of cells that lines blood vessels.

However, exercise opens up the vessels and improves their flexibility and elasticity.

STUDY #1

In the first study, investigators looked at whether exercise training could activate progenitor cells.

Fifty men with moderate-to-severe heart failure were randomized to receive either six months of exercise training under the supervision of a physician, or to remain inactive in a control group. Exercise consisted of riding a stationary bicycle at least 30 minutes a day (usually in two sessions).

At the end of six months, biopsies of the patients' quadriceps (thigh muscles) revealed that the number of progenitor cells in the exercise group increased by 109%, progenitor cells turning into muscle cells increased by 166%, and progenitor cells actively dividing to form new cells and repair damage to the muscle increased sixfold.

STUDY #2

For the second study, 37 men with severe heart failure were randomly assigned to receive three months of exercise or to remain inactive.

The exercisers experienced dramatic changes: Circulating progenitor cells increased 47%, progenitor cells beginning to mature into endothelial cells increased nearly 200%, and the density of capillaries (narrow blood vessels that connect small arteries with small veins) in skeletal tissue increased 17%. There were no changes in the control group.

When they began, the exercising patients had peak oxygen uptake in the range of other patients needing heart transplants. But regular exercise was linked to an average 35% increase in exercise capacity, giving the men about 75% of the capacity seen in healthy people of the same age.

"Your heart is like an engine with six cylinders, and when we started the exercise program in those patients, about 3.5 cylinders were just not working," Dr. Linke explained. "After three to six months of exercise training, two of the cylinders started working again."

"It's a tremendous improvement, and no medication is able to do it," he noted.

RECOMMENDATIONS

Patients with heart failure should only embark on an exercise regimen under the supervision of a physician, said Dr. Linke.

"We recommend exercise once a day for up to 20 minutes five days a week for patients with heart failure, said Dr. Linke. Ideally, an exercise program should be initiated in in-hospital conditions or an outpatient medical setting, so that individuals can be properly supervised, he added.

info For more information on how exercise and fitness can improve the lives of those with heart disease, visit the American Physical Therapy Association Web site, *www. apta.org.*

Is Alcohol Really Good For Your Heart?

University Health Network, news release.

Whether it's red wine or another spirit, the heart and blood vessels benefit slightly from one drink, but a second erases the positive effects, say Canadian researchers.

A study, published in the *American Journal of Physiology, Heart and Circulatory Physiology,* also raises more questions about the popular notion that red wine may be more effective against heart disease than other types of alcohol.

"We had anticipated that many of the effects of one ethanol drink would be enhanced by red wine. What was most surprising was how similar the effects were of red wine and ethanol. Any benefits that we found were not specific to red wine," said John Floras, MD, director of cardiology research at the Peter Munk Cardiac Centre at Toronto General Hospital.

BACKGROUND

Several population studies have shown light or moderate alcohol drinking may lower the risk of death and the development of heart disease. Many studies have also reported specific benefits of red wine.

The "French paradox," in which studies have found lower rates of heart disease, despite high-fat diets, in some European countries where red wine was consumed regularly, has also spurred interest in exploring whether red wine has special protective properties.

NEW STUDY

Researchers at the Canadian center conducted a real-time study of 13 volunteers who were given either 4 ounces of red wine, 1.5 ounces of ethanol or water at random at three separate sessions over two weeks. The volunteers were healthy, nonsmoking adults who were neither heavy drinkers nor total alcohol abstainers.

The wine, a moderately priced pinot noir, contained a high *t-resveratrol* content, a polyphenol compound found in plants, including red grapes, that exhibits antioxidant properties. Alcohol or substances in alcohol such as resveratrol may improve blood vessel function and also prevent platelets in the blood from sticking together, thus reducing clot formation and the risk of heart attack or stroke.

After one drink of either red wine or alcohol, blood vessels in the participant were more dilated, reducing the work the heart had to do. However, after two drinks, the heart rate, amount of blood pumped out of the heart, and action of the sympathetic nervous system (the part of the nervous system that is active during stress and is involved in regulating pulse and blood pressure) all increased. The ability of the blood vessels to expand in response to an increase in blood flow also diminished.

Increases in heart rate and sympathetic nervous system activity are recognized markers for hypertension, heart failure and sudden death.

IMPLICATIONS

Dr. Floras cautioned that this study measured the effects of these drinks on one occasion only. The effects of daily wine or alcohol intake may be quite different.

"Our findings point to a slight beneficial effect of one drink—be it alcohol or red wine—on the heart and blood vessels, whereas two or more drinks would seem to turn on systems that stress the circulation. If these actions are repeated frequently because of high alcohol consumption, these effects may expose individuals to a higher risk of heart attacks, stroke or chronic high blood pressure," Dr. Floras said.

The American Heart Association does not recommend that anyone start drinking alcohol to prevent heart disease. Reducing risk can be done using other methods such as exercise and following a healthy diet.

info For answers to frequently asked questions about alcohol and alcohol use, visit the Web site of the National Institute on Alcohol Abuse and Alcoholism, *www.niaaa.nih.gov/FAQs*.

Five Foods Proven to Prevent Heart Attacks

Bonnie T. Jortberg, RD, CDE, senior instructor, department of family medicine at University of Colorado at Denver and Health Sciences Center. She was program director of Colorado Weigh, a weight-loss and healthy-living program offered throughout the Denver metropolitan area. She is coauthor of *The Step Diet Book*. Workman.

Cardiovascular disease is still the number-one killer in America. It accounts for about 37% of all deaths, according to the American Heart Association.

Most of us know that a diet rich in fruits, vegetables and whole grains and low in saturated animal fats lowers the risk of heart disease. But certain foods have been shown to be particularly beneficial. Of course, no food is a magic bullet—you still need to exercise daily and maintain a healthy weight—but eating the recommended amounts of the following can go a long way toward preventing heart disease...

SPINACH

Like most fruits and vegetables, spinach is rich in vitamins and minerals. What makes spinach stand out for keeping the heart healthy is *folate*, one of the B vitamins. According to several studies, including an extensive report from the Harvard School of Public Health, folate helps prevent the buildup of *homocysteine*, an amino acid in the blood that is a major risk factor for heart disease and stroke.

How much: Two cups of raw spinach (about two ounces) has 30% of the daily value (DV) for folate...one-half cup of cooked spinach provides 25%. Frozen and fresh spinach are both good, but beware of canned spinach—it may have excessive amounts of salt. Too much salt increases blood pressure, and high blood pressure is another major risk factor for cardiovascular disease.

Alternatives: Asparagus. Four spears have 20% of the DV of folate. Also, many breakfast cereals are fortified with folate—check the labels.

SALMON

Salmon is rich in omega-3 fatty acids. Omega-3s reduce inflammation and make your blood less "sticky," which prevents plaque—fatty deposits—from clogging your arteries. Having unclogged arteries reduces the risk of heart attack and stroke.

How much: The American Heart Association recommends two to three three-ounce servings of salmon a week. Fresh or frozen, farmed or wild, is fine, but go easy on canned salmon, which may be high in salt.

Alternatives: Other cold-water fish high in omega-3 fatty acids include mackerel, lake trout, sardines, herring and albacore tuna. If you don't like fish, have one teaspoon of ground flaxseeds daily—sprinkle on cereal, yogurt or salads, and drink plenty of water to avoid constipation.

TOMATOES

Tomatoes are loaded with *lycopene*, a carotenoid that gives them their color. Lycopene reduces cholesterol in the body. Too much cholesterol can lead to atherosclerosis (hardening of the arteries), which decreases blood flow to the heart—and that can lead to heart attack and stroke.

Cooked and processed tomato products, such as spaghetti sauce and tomato juice, provide the greatest benefits. Researchers at Cornell University found that cooking or processing tomatoes boosts lycopene levels and makes lycopene easier for the body to absorb. Look for low-sodium or no-salt-added products.

If you like ketchup, another source of lycopene, buy an organic brand, made with pure cane sugar, not processed high-fructose corn syrup. Organic ketchup can contain up to three times as much lycopene as nonorganic brands, according to a study published by the United States Department of Agriculture. Other organic tomato products weren't studied, so it is not yet known if they're also higher in lycopene.

How much: One cup of tomato juice (about 23 milligrams, or mg, of lycopene) or one-half cup of tomato sauce (20 mg) daily. A medium raw tomato has 4.5 mg.

Alternative: Watermelon (one and a half cups of cut-up watermelon contain 9 mg to 13 mg of lycopene).

OATMEAL

Oatmeal is one of the best and most studied sources of soluble fiber. Soluble fiber absorbs water and turns to gel during digestion. It then acts like a sponge to absorb excess cholesterol from your body. That's good for your heart. Studies show that five grams (g) to 10 g of soluble fiber a day can reduce LDL "bad" cholesterol by about 5%.

Soluble fiber also helps remove saturated fat in your digestive tract before your body can absorb it. That's also good for your heart.

How much: One and a half cups of cooked oatmeal daily. This provides 4.5 g of fiber, enough to lower cholesterol. Rolled oats and steel-cut oatmeal work equally well to help lower cholesterol, but beware of flavored instant oatmeal—it is likely to have sugar added. Too much sugar in your diet increases the chance of inflammation, a risk factor for atherosclerosis. Sugar also can lead to weight gain, which is another risk factor for cardiovascular disease.

Alternatives: Kidney beans and brussels sprouts each have three g of soluble fiber per one-half cup, cooked.

POMEGRANATES

Pomegranates are loaded with *polyphenols,* antioxidants that neutralize free radicals, which can damage the body's cells.

Polyphenols help to maintain cardiovascular health by scooping up free radicals before they damage arteries.

These chemical substances also are believed to reduce LDL "bad" cholesterol. Red wine and purple grape juice are great sources of polyphenols, but pomegranates have amounts even higher.

How much: 1.5 ounces of concentrated pomegranate juice daily. This is the amount used in most studies. Look for products that are labeled 100% juice, or concentrated, with no added sugar.

Caution: Pomegranate juice may affect the metabolism of prescription drugs and may cause blood pressure to decrease too much when combined with certain blood pressure medications. Check with your doctor.

Alternatives: Red wine (no more than two five-ounce glasses a day for men and one for women) and purple grape juice (four to six ounces a day).

■ ■ ■ ■

Eat Citrus to Protect the Heart

In a study of nearly 35,000 women ages 55 to 69, researchers found that women who consumed the most *flavanones,* a flavonoid antioxidant found primarily in citrus fruits (such as grapefruit and oranges), had a 22% lower risk for death from heart disease than those who consumed the least.

Theory: Flavonoids help prevent blood clots and promote blood vessel health. If you take medication, ask your doctor whether citrus affects the drug's effectiveness.

Pamela Mink, PhD, MPH, senior managing scientist, Health Sciences, Exponent Inc., Washington, DC.

■ ■ ■ ■

Vitamin D Promotes Heart Health

In an analysis of six years of data on 12,644 people, researchers found that participants with the lowest blood levels of vitamin D had systolic (top number) and diastolic (bottom number) blood pressures that, on average, were 3 mmHg (millimeters of mercury, a unit of pressure) and 1.6 mmHg higher, respectively, than those with the highest vitamin D levels.

Theory: Vitamin D increases the elasticity of blood vessels, which promotes normal blood pressure.

Self-defense: Get 1,000 international units (IU) of vitamin D daily from food (such as milk) or supplements...or from 10 to 15 minutes of exposure to sunlight two to three times a week.

Robert Scragg, MD, associate professor of epidemiology, University of Auckland, New Zealand.

Weight Gain Big Trouble For Heart Patients

American Heart Association, news release.

Short-term weight gain can signal worsening outcomes for heart failure patients, a new study shows. Patients who gain as little as two pounds over the course of a few weeks may require hospitalization within the month, say heart researchers. Heart failure patients who gain more than 10 pounds are eight times more likely than heart failure patients with stable weights to need hospitalization.

Heart failure occurs when the heart cannot pump enough blood to meet the body's needs. Heart defects, certain viral infections, high blood pressure, scarring from previous heart attacks and coronary artery disease can all lead to heart failure. Weight gain may occur due to fluid buildup resulting from heart failure.

The study, published in *Circulation,* suggests that patients and their doctors may have several days or even weeks to control weight gain and avoid hospitalizations.

THE STUDY

The Yale University research team analyzed weight data and hospitalization records from 268 heart failure patients who were weighing themselves daily as part of a disease management program. The average age of the patients was 74. The researchers compared the data from half of the patients who were hospitalized with the half who were not.

THE RESULTS

The analysis showed that the hospitalized patients had gained more weight than their peers in the month before hospitalization. In the week before hospitalization, weight increased rapidly.

Doctors have known for some time that weight increase may be a sign of worsening heart failure, but the impact of the timing and amount of weight gain on hospitalization has not been studied before, the researchers said.

"We found that even small amounts of weight gain—as small as just over two pounds—predict hospitalization," said lead author Sarwat Chaudhry, MD, assistant professor of medicine at Yale University School of Medicine in New Haven, Connecticut. "We found that weight gain starts well before hospitalization, giving doctors and patients at least a few days to take steps to avoid the need for hospitalization."

People who gained an average of two to five pounds in the week before hospitalization were nearly three times more likely to need hospitalization than heart failure patients with stable weight. Those who gained five to 10 pounds were four and a half times more likely to need hospitalization, and those who gained more than 10 pounds were almost eight times more likely to require hospitalization for heart failure.

IMPLICATION

"Heart failure is the most common reason for hospitalization among Americans, and more Medicare dollars are spent for heart failure than for any other diagnosis," Dr. Chaudhry said. "Our data suggest that a simple bathroom scale could empower patients in managing their own disease and alert their physicians to early signs of heart failure decompensation (the failure of the heart to maintain adequate blood circulation). Ultimately, our data may help change the standard of care to prevent patients from being hospitalized, improve their quality of life and save precious health care resources."

The researchers noted that not all hospitalizations for heart failure occur after weight gain, but that monitoring weight daily can help patients with heart failure. The team is currently conducting a clinical trial to test whether daily weight measurement can help reduce rates of hospitalization for heart failure patients.

info To learn about living with heart failure, visit *http://familydoctor.org* and search "heart failure."

Help Your Heart with a Healthier Diet

Yunsheng Ma, MD, PhD, assistant professor, medicine, University of Massachusetts Medical School, Worcester, Massachusetts.
Alice Lichtenstein, DSc, Gershoff Professor, Friedman School of Nutrition, Tufts University, Boston.
Journal of the American Dietetic Association.

Having a heart attack is apparently not sufficient reason for most people to change to a heart-healthy diet, a new study finds. "We found that diet quality is poor after a coronary heart disease event," said study author Yunsheng Ma, MD, PhD, an assistant professor of medicine at the University of Massachusetts Medical School, in Worcester.

He warned, however, that patients' failure to eat healthier puts them at risk for another cardiac event.

"Coronary heart disease is the number one cause of mortality in Americans," the study noted. An estimated 13 million Americans have survived a heart attack or have coronary heart disease (CHD) symptoms, the researchers added.

THE STUDY

Dr. Ma's team surveyed 555 patients averaging 61 years of age, 60% of whom were men. All were diagnosed with coronary heart disease and had already experienced a heart attack, angina (chest pain) or arrhythmia (abnormal heart rhythm). The researchers queried the patients on their diets one year after they had undergone coronary angiography (a procedure to see how well blood is flowing through the heart) linked to some kind of coronary event.

RESULTS

According to the researchers, only 12.4% of the patients met the recommended consumption of vegetables. Similarly, only about 8% met daily fruit intake recommendations and just 8% were getting a heart-healthy amount of cereal fiber. Little more than 5% were limiting their intake of dangerous trans fats to recommended levels, the team said.

Compounding this, the researchers found that worst diets were associated with smoking and obesity. Poor diets were also closely correlated with lower levels of education.

RECOMMENDATIONS FOR A HEART-HEALTHY DIET

Research has confirmed that fruit and vegetable consumption is associated with a lowered risk for heart disease, the researchers noted. The American Heart Association currently recommends "an overall healthy diet" that is rich in fruits and vegetables, high-fiber foods and limited amounts of saturated fat and trans fats, with an eye to maintaining a healthy weight.

The study concluded that "it may be helpful for physicians and health care providers to refer CHD patients to behavioral interventions that include both diet and physical activity components, such as cardiac rehabilitation." Rehab by itself might not be enough, the study adds, urging consultation with registered dietitians to learn about how to make the necessary changes in diet.

Dr. Ma said that currently about 80% of patients do not go to rehabilitation after a coronary heart disease event, such as angina, arrhythmia or heart attack. But even if patients do enter rehabilitation, many of these programs do not include dietary modifications, he added.

EXPERT COMMENTARY

Alice Lichtenstein, DSc of Tufts University's Friedman School of Nutrition, helped to craft the American Heart Association's dietary recom-

mendations. She questioned whether the new study produced truly conclusive results, noting that the study subjects may have underreported their consumption of unhealthy foods. That's because the participants' mean calorie intake was a relatively healthy 1,775 calories but their average body mass index (a ratio of weight to height) was 30, which is in the obese range, Dr. Lichtenstein noted.

She said that instead of trying to calculate the exact amount of fat or saturated fat in their diet, it may be easier for people to simply concentrate on the types of healthy foods they should be eating—items such as fruits, vegetables, grains, beans and fish. Americans have a wide range of such foods to choose from, so "it is easier now to consume a diet consistent with a heart-healthy pattern than it's ever been before," Dr. Lichtenstein added.

info For more on heart-healthy eating, visit the Mayo Clinic Web site, *www.mayo clinic.com*, and search "heart-healthy diet."

■ ■ ■ ■

Time to Can the Soda!

Drinking just one 12-ounce soft drink a day—either regular or diet—increases the risk for metabolic syndrome by about 50%. Metabolic syndrome comprises at least three of the following symptoms—increased waistline…elevated blood pressure…elevated blood sugar levels…elevated triglycerides (a type of blood fat)…and reduced HDL (good) cholesterol. All of these symptoms are risk factors for heart disease and diabetes.

Vasan S. Ramachandran, MD, professor of medicine, Boston University School of Medicine, and leader of a study of 5,124 people, published in Circulation.

■ ■ ■ ■

Aortic Aneurysm: What Every Women Should Know

Abdominal aortic aneurysm (AAA)—which forms when a weak area of the aorta (the largest artery) expands or bulges—occurs four times more often among women who are or were smokers than among nonsmokers…and

3.6 times more often among women who have had a heart attack, heart bypass surgery or coronary angioplasty. Women who develop an AAA are more likely than men to die from internal bleeding if the aneurysm ruptures. AAA is usually detected during a routine checkup and confirmed with a noninvasive ultrasound. Surgery can repair an AAA before it ruptures.

K. Craig Kent, MD, chief of vascular surgery, New York Presbyterian Hospital, New York City, and author of a study of 17,540 people, published in *Journal of Vascular Surgery*.

■ ■ ■ ■

Aspirin Defense Ignored

Heart disease risk can be reduced by taking aspirin regularly. Yet only 41% of adults over age 40 use aspirin and only 33% say they have discussed aspirin use with their doctors. Regular aspirin use can prevent a heart attack in men and women who already have heart disease—and can reduce heart disease risk for people who have high cholesterol, diabetes and high blood pressure. Many doctors say the limited time they have available during office visits makes it difficult to discuss aspirin use and other preventive measures.

Self-defense: Ask your doctor about taking aspirin regularly to prevent heart disease.

Steven Weisman, PhD, head, global health care practice, Innovative Science Solutions, Morristown, New Jersey, and coauthor of a study of 1,299 adults, published in *American Journal of Preventive Medicine*.

Cutting-Edge Cure for Irregular Heartbeat

Jennifer E. Cummings, MD, director of electrophysiology research and a staff cardiologist in the Cleveland Clinic department of cardiovascular medicine, section of electrophysiology and pacing. She has authored or coauthored numerous scientific papers and textbook chapters on atrial fibrillation and other topics.

Atrial fibrillation (AF), the condition for which Vice President Dick Cheney was treated in late 2007, is the most common serious heart rhythm irregularity, affecting more than two million Americans.

WHAT IS ATRIAL FIBRILLATION?

Atrial fibrillation (AF) is a common heart problem that increases risk for stroke and heart failure. During AF, the heart's two upper chambers (atria) beat out of sync with the two lower chambers (ventricles), often triggering a rapid and irregular heart rate. Heart disease and high blood pressure are among the most common causes of AF.

Long considered a relatively harmless condition, AF has now been recognized by doctors as a serious health risk. It increases stroke risk five- to sevenfold and may eventually lead to heart failure (inadequate pumping action of the heart).

The standard treatments for AF are medications and procedures aimed at resetting the heart rhythm (electrical impulses in the heart that cause it to contract in a regular, rhythmic way) or controlling the irregular and accelerated heart rate that often characterizes the condition.

Latest development: Surgical techniques are now available for AF sufferers who need additional treatment to keep the condition under control.

What you need to know about AF...

ARE YOU AT RISK?

AF most commonly occurs in people age 60 and older who have high blood pressure and/or a history of cardiovascular disease, including previous heart attack, heart surgery or heart valve problems...or lung disease, such as emphysema.

An overactive thyroid...sleep apnea (temporary cessation of breathing during sleep)...stress (most often due to other illnesses or surgery)...ingestion of a stimulant, such as caffeine...or excessive use of alcohol are among the other possible causes of AF.

Important: At least 10% of AF patients have no obvious underlying risk factors. For many people with AF, the condition is "silent." When symptoms do occur, a fast heart rate (up to 175 beats per minute, rather than the normal rate of 60 to 100 beats per minute), fatigue, dizziness, chest discomfort (pressure, palpitation and/or pain) and/or shortness of breath are most commonly reported.

If you think you may have AF, see your primary care physician for appropriate tests, such as an electrocardiogram (ECG), a procedure that measures the electrical impulses produced by the heart...an echocardiogram (an ultrasound of the heart)...and blood tests that may show thyroid problems or blood chemistry abnormalities that can lead to AF.

TREATMENT OPTIONS

Treatment for AF focuses on the use of heart medication to restore normal heart rhythm and/or to control heart rate...and/or the use of *warfarin* (Coumadin) or some other blood thinner to reduce the risk for clots in the atria that can lead to a stroke.

Recent development: Because doctors have disagreed on whether control of heart rate or heart rhythm should take precedence, in 2006 the American Heart Association, the American College of Cardiology and the European Society of Cardiology jointly issued revised *Guidelines for the Management of Patients with Atrial Fibrillation* to help clarify the issue.

According to the new recommendations, patients age 70 and older with persistent AF (more than one episode) who have high blood pressure or heart disease are believed to benefit most when the heart rate is controlled (with a heart drug, such as a beta-blocker or calcium channel blocker). This is because older patients are at higher risk for stroke and therefore need more aggressive management of AF.

For people under age 70—especially those with recurrent AF and no underlying heart disease—heart *rhythm* control may be better. Drugs commonly prescribed to control heart rhythm, such as *propafenone* (Rythmol), *flecainide* (Tambocor) and *dofetilide* (Tikosyn), are generally effective for the short term. But their effectiveness tends to diminish over time, and they may cause serious side effects, including increased arrhythmias (irregular heartbeats), as well as thyroid, lung or liver problems.

For patients who continue to experience AF even while taking medication, electrical cardioversion (a quick burst of electricity to the heart to help restore its normal rhythm) may be necessary. It is a relatively safe procedure,

though it does require general anesthesia (for about five minutes). Often, patients undergo a couple of cardioversions over the course of a year, while also taking medication to control the heart rhythm.

However, cardioversion and medication are not a cure for AF. Also, many patients cannot tolerate the respiratory problems, vision difficulties, thyroid abnormalities and other side effects that can occur with long-term use of the drugs prescribed to manage the condition.

A SURGICAL CURE

A minimally invasive surgical procedure that doesn't simply control AF—but *cures* it—has become available in the US.

With the procedure, known as *ablation*, a heart surgeon or an electrophysiologist (a cardiologist who specializes in heart rhythms) makes tiny, strategic scars on the heart to block the misfiring electrical signals that occur with AF. Ablation can be performed either with devices attached to catheters that thread through veins leading to the heart, or through a small surgical opening in the side of the chest.

Tiny burns (about 1/25 of an inch long) are made on either the interior or exterior surface of the heart, typically using radio-frequency (low-voltage, high-frequency electricity) or cryothermy (freezing) tools.

When the burns heal, thin scars are left that effectively block the chaotic electrical signals that cause AF, allowing the heart to restore its normal rhythm. About 80% to 85% of patients with intermittent AF (episodes lasting seconds to hours) are cured after one ablation procedure...most of the other patients are cured after a second ablation.

As with any heart procedure, there is a small risk for stroke during the surgery, but serious complications (such as heart attack or perforation of the heart) occur in fewer than 2% of all ablations that are performed by experienced physicians.

For many patients, the small risks associated with ablation are more than outweighed by the benefit of being able to discontinue their medications, usually within a year of undergoing the procedure.

The FDA has not yet approved use of the devices to perform ablation on AF patients, so all such uses remain "off-label" (the term used to describe medical treatments not approved by the FDA). However, the American College of Cardiology and the American Heart Association list ablation as a treatment option for AF patients who don't respond to drug therapy.

The current lack of FDA approval means that some insurers may balk at covering the procedure, which costs about $25,000 to $50,000. It's also a technically challenging procedure, so smaller hospitals with limited staff and resources may not offer it.

Important: If you're considering ablation, ask your doctor for a referral to a hospital where a relatively high volume of these procedures is performed each year. Even if it means traveling, you'll be better off if you're treated by a physician who has had experience with the procedure.

■ ■ ■ ■

Wow! A New Kind of Heart Treatment

Heart patients who don't improve with medications and/or are not good candidates for surgery may want to consider *enhanced external counterpulsation* (EECP). This noninvasive procedure improves the ability of the coronary arteries to dilate, which promotes blood flow and can reduce chest pain caused by angina. With EECP, a series of inflatable cuffs (similar to blood pressure cuffs) are wrapped around a patient's legs. While the patient lies down, the cuffs are quickly inflated and deflated *sequentially* with each heartbeat, "milking" blood upward to the heart. The treatment lasts about one hour and is repeated three times a week for five weeks. It's not yet known if patients who undergo the procedure will have fewer heart attacks—but they have less chest pain and can more readily exercise without discomfort.

Caution: EECP is not recommended for patients with heart valve disease, thrombophlebitis (formation of blood clots and inflammation of the veins) or uncontrolled hypertension.

Richard A. Stein, MD, director of preventive cardiology, Beth Israel Medical Center, New York City.

Making Sense of Stents

Kirk Garratt, MD, associate director, division of cardiac intervention, and clinical director, interventional cardiovascular research, Heart Vascular Institute, Lenox Hill Hospital, New York City.

Charles Davidson, MD, director, cardiac catheterization laboratory, Northwestern Memorial Hospital, Chicago.

To stent or not to stent? Which type of the artery-opening device is best? When is heart bypass surgery smarter than getting a stent?

These are the questions many heart patients are left asking themselves and their doctors, as dozens of recent high-profile—and often conflicting—studies have compared the performance and safety of various types of coronary stents, narrow mesh tubes inserted to keep a narrowed blood vessel open.

But experts say a consensus on the safest and most effective use of the devices is slowly emerging.

For the majority of patients undergoing angioplasty to clear a blocked artery, newer, drug-coated stents are preferred over bare-metal ones, mainly because they reduce the risk of artery reclosure, cardiologists say.

And it may not matter which of the two established brands of drug-eluting stent you get—Boston Scientific Corp.'s *paclitaxel*-coated Taxus or Cordis Corp.'s *sirolimus*-coated Cypher.

"The truth appears to be that whatever differences exist between these two drug-eluting stents are so small that there's not a compelling reason to select one over the other," said Kirk Garratt, MD, clinical director of interventional cardiovascular research at Lenox Hill Hospital's Heart Vascular Institute, in New York City.

He said that in very special circumstances, a patient may be better suited for one type of drug-coated stent over another, "but for the average patient out there trying to make sense of this, he or she can be comfortable that whatever stent their doctor recommends is going to be a good choice."

BACKGROUND

Coronary stents were first developed in the mid-1980s, and, within a decade, the insertion of bare-metal stents to prop open narrowed vessels had become standard procedure for many patients at risk of heart attack.

However, the rate of artery reclosure (known as restenosis) after the insertion of a bare-metal stent was close to 30%. To circumvent that problem, researchers developed drug-eluting stents, which emit medicines that prevent restenosis. A majority of patients who need a stent now receive one of these devices, which cost about $2,000 each, double the price of a bare-metal stent.

In recent years, the Taxus and Cypher drug-eluting stents have dominated the field, and conflicting studies comparing their relative effectiveness appear regularly in major medical journals. A third drug-coated stent, Medtronic's *zotarolimus*-coated Endeavor, received US Food and Drug Administration approval more recently.

But even drug-coated stents aren't perfect. Soon after they gained widespread use, experts began to notice that rates of fatal or nonfatal blood clots were more likely in patients who received a drug-coated stent versus those who did not. This excess clotting risk was confirmed in later trials. For that reason, the FDA recommends that patients who receive drug-eluting stents be placed on dual anti-platelet therapy—typically *clopidogrel* (Plavix) and aspirin—for a year after they receive the device.

STENTS VS. BYPASS SURGERY

But are stents always the best option when arteries narrow or is bypass surgery sometimes a better choice?

In many cases, the answer to that question must still be decided on a case-by-case basis, the experts said. Studies suggest that in cases where only one vessel is blocked, stent placement (during angioplasty, a minimally invasive procedure in which a tiny balloon is inflated to open a blockage in an artery) may be a safer and equally effective option.

A study published in the *New England Journal of Medicine*, however, found that when multiple vessels are blocked, bypass might be a better choice. During this more invasive procedure, a healthy artery or vein from another part of the body is connected to the blocked coronary artery, and oxygen-rich blood is routed around the blockage.

"This is a really hazy issue," Dr. Garratt said. In more complex clinical situations, a surgeon must carefully weigh the pros and cons of each procedure before making a choice, he explained.

DRUG-ELUTING STENTS VS. BARE-METAL STENTS

If your cardiologist does suggest a stent, it will most likely be a drug-coated one.

The accumulated research is "uniformly very positive and has shown a benefit for drug-eluting stents" versus bare-metal stents in keeping arteries open, Dr. Garratt said.

Some patients will still receive bare-metal stents in certain scenarios, he noted. These would include people whose arteries are simply the wrong size for a drug-coated stent, for example. In other cases, patients may need to avoid the excess bleeding risk that comes with a year or more of anticoagulant therapy.

"This would include patients who are expected to need some surgical procedure in the next few months—maybe they want a hip replacement or they have a tumor that needs to be removed," Dr. Garratt said. "We don't want then to implant a product that requires them to stay on dual anti-platelet drugs for an extended period of time if we know that is coming."

For these types of reasons, bare-metal stents still make up 40% of the coronary stent market, said Charles Davidson, MD, director of the cardiac catheterization laboratory at Northwestern Memorial Hospital, in Chicago.

CHOOSING A DRUG-ELUTING STENT

When it comes to drug-eluting stents, the Taxus and Cypher models perform equally well, said Dr. Davidson. "If you look at the long-term clinical results and the short-term clinical results, they're very similar."

Many of the studies that have pitted the Taxus stent against its rival, Cypher, have been funded by the makers of either one of the devices, pointed out Dr. Davidson. Patients should "not put too much stock into what's been out in the press, some of which may have been biased in one direction or another, for whatever reason," he said.

IMPORTANT POST-SURGERY GUIDELINES

Instead, patients may want to focus on the steps they can take to ensure a long healthy life after receiving a stent.

"The most important thing that patients need to be aware of is that the anti-platelet therapy that is prescribed them by their physician needs to be adhered to," Dr. Davidson said. All too often, he said, patients either stop taking the anti-clotting drugs on their own or on the advice of a doctor who may not realize the patient has recently received a stent.

"That's where they have run into some real problems. Good communication and adherence to therapy is the number one thing they can do," Dr. Davidson said.

Positive lifestyle changes are also key, Dr. Garratt added. "The really dangerous thing is for patients to leave the angioplasty laboratory feeling like they have had their problem fixed, and then it's back to the cheeseburgers," he said.

"I think that happens all the time. We can fix them up temporarily with a stent, but if they go back to their old habits, new blockages will form, and they'll have the same risk of death and heart attack in the future."

Dr. Davidson concurred. He said the major cause of mortality after stent placement is a narrowing of another artery—not the one that received the stent.

"Remember, the angioplasty is only treating the most severe lesion, it's not treating the 50% blocked lesions that are very likely to go on and cause heart attacks," he said. "So, maybe with good lipid-lowering therapy, with healthy diets and exercise, severe blockages could also be prevented."

info To find out more about stents, visit the Web site, Angioplasty.org at *www.angioplasty.org* and search "stents."

■ **More from Kirk Garratt, MD...**

Device Makes Heart Surgery Possible for Weak Patients

There is a new device that makes heart surgery possible in patients who otherwise would be too weak to survive the procedure, reports Kirk Garratt, MD. *TandemHeart* is a temporary pumping device that takes over for the heart for up to two weeks, until the heart recovers from surgery. It is covered by Medicare and is available in 28 hospitals in the US. For more information, go to *www.cardiacassist.com*, and click on "Clinical Info."

10

Natural Remedies

Using Your Mind to Ease Irritable Bowel Syndrome

hen standard lifestyle adjustments such as dietary changes and drug therapy don't provide relief from the pain, bloating and other unpleasant gastrointestinal symptoms of irritable bowel syndrome, patients may want to try a different approach.

Recent studies show that using one's own thoughts, as taught in cognitive behavioral therapy, may help ease symptoms. Likewise, using hypnosis to visualize the pain and imagine it seeping away can be a powerful treatment strategy, too.

"Research indicates that the probability of achieving benefits is excellent with either approach, even for patients who haven't improved from the standard medical care," said Olafur S. Palsson, PsyD, a clinical psychologist and associate professor of medicine at the University of North Carolina at Chapel Hill's Center for Functional GI & Motility Disorders.

BACKGROUND

As many as 45 million Americans may have irritable bowel syndrome, or IBS, the International Foundation for Functional Gastrointestinal Disorders reports. Sixty to 65% of IBS sufferers are women.

In addition to pain and discomfort, people with IBS experience chronic or recurrent constipation or diarrhea—or bouts of both. While the exact cause of the condition isn't known, symptoms seem to result from a disturbance in the interaction of the gut, brain and nervous system, according to the Foundation.

Olafur S. Palsson, PsyD, associate professor, medicine, Center for Functional GI & Motility Disorders, University of North Carolina at Chapel Hill.

Jeffrey M. Lackner, PsyD, assistant professor, medicine, University at Buffalo School of Medicine & Biomedical Sciences, Buffalo, New York.

International Foundation for Functional Gastrointestinal Disorders, Milwaukee.

Doctors generally advise patients to avoid certain foods that may exacerbate symptoms. Several different medications may be recommended for relieving abdominal pain, diarrhea and constipation. But these approaches don't always provide adequate relief.

"For some people, medications and dietary changes are the perfect match, but most of our patients—the great, great majority of patients—have not responded to medications and dietary changes," said Jeffrey M. Lackner, PsyD, assistant professor of medicine at the University at Buffalo School of Medicine & Biomedical Sciences, and a behavioral medicine specialist whose research focuses on gastrointestinal disorders, particularly IBS.

For many patients, cognitive behavioral therapy, which uses the power of the mind to replace unhealthy beliefs and behaviors with healthy, positive ones, may be the answer. But, Dr. Lackner observed, very few facilities around the country specialize in this type of treatment. Recognizing this, he and his colleagues set out to devise and test a treatment program that IBS patients could administer themselves.

THE COGNITIVE BEHAVIORAL STUDY

Seventy-five women and men were divided into three groups. One group was placed on a "wait list" for 10 weeks while they monitored their symptoms. Another group received the standard treatment of 10 cognitive behavioral therapy sessions over weekly. The third group had once-a-month therapy sessions over four months and practiced relaxation and problem-solving exercises at home.

Not surprisingly, people on the wait list did not do well at all, while those in the weekly and monthly sessions showed significant improvement. "They said at the end of treatment they had achieved adequate relief from pain and adequate relief from bowel problems, and a significant proportion of patients said they improved their symptoms," Dr. Lackner explained.

While more studies are needed, the findings suggest that traditional and self-administered cognitive behavioral therapy both provide adequate relief and improve symptoms, said Dr. Lackner, who first reported the findings at a large meeting of GI professionals.

THE HYPNOSIS STUDY

Hypnosis may be another option. A pair of Swedish studies presented at that same meeting found that patients who received "gut-directed hypnotherapy" had significant improvement in symptoms compared with those who did not receive this intervention.

Hypnosis treatment has been reported to improve symptoms of the majority of treated IBS patients in all published studies, noted Dr. Palsson.

RECOMMENDATIONS

For patients who have tried the diet-and-drug regimen to no avail, Dr. Palsson said he would recommend either of these two psychological treatments.

"If a patient's main goal is substantial relief of bowel symptoms, hypnosis is probably the better choice," he said, for the research literature strongly suggests that it improves the gastrointestinal symptoms far more reliably.

On the other hand, he added, if a patient wants to cope better with the illness or improve mental well-being, then cognitive behavioral therapy is equally good or perhaps even the better treatment option.

info For more information on treating IBS, visit the Web site of the International Foundation for Functional Gastrointestinal Disorders, *www.iffgd.org*.

Rheumatoid Arthritis? Give Medication a Try

Elizabeth K. Pradhan, PhD, Center for Integrative Medicine, University of Maryland School of Medicine, Baltimore.

Stephen Lindsey, MD, head, rheumatology, Ochsner Health Systems, Baton Rouge, Louisiana.
Arthritis Care & Research.

For rheumatoid arthritis (RA) sufferers whose painful illness prompts depression, relief may come from the practice of an age-old technique already embraced by millions around the world—meditation.

Researchers found that a half-year exposure to meditation techniques helped patients with RA reduce their psychological distress by as much as one-third.

BACKGROUND

The research team, led by Elizabeth K. Pradhan, PhD, of the University of Maryland School of Medicine's Center for Integrative Medicine, based its conclusions on an analysis of a specific training course called "Mindfulness-Based Stress Reduction" (MBSR), which includes meditation and yoga exercises.

Dr. Pradhan and her colleagues said the MBSR concept of "mindfulness" is designed to guide patients to focus on the "here and now," while emphasizing the value of calmness, clarity, well-being and a compassion for oneself and others.

The Maryland researchers noted that prior studies had already shown that the MBSR course, in particular, seems to have a positive impact on the psychological symptoms of patients with conditions such as anxiety disorders, chronic pain, fibromyalgia, cancer and multiple sclerosis. Patients recovering from organ transplant surgery also seem to derive some benefit, the researchers said.

ARTHRITIS STUDY

For their study, Dr. Pradhan and her colleagues focused specifically on RA, an inflammatory form of arthritis that causes joint pain and damage. It was the first-ever analysis of MBSR and its impact on depression, general well-being and disease progression among RA patients, the researchers said.

Thirty-one patients were offered the meditation course over an eight-week period, followed by a four-month maintenance program. Another 32 patients did not participate but were told they would be offered free meditation training once the study was completed.

During the trial, all the patients (average age 54 years) continued to be treated by their regular doctor—and to take whatever medication they'd been taking before the study began.

At the start of the study, and two and six months later, all the patients completed questionnaires to assess depressive symptoms and psychological distress. Also, blood measures of inflammation were taken and an assessment of tender and swollen joints was done to evaluate current RA status.

THE RESULTS

By the two-month mark, both the meditation and the non-meditation groups had shown equal levels of improvement in terms of depression and emotional symptoms.

But by six months, there was a "significant" difference in perceived psychological distress between the two groups—those practicing meditation reported a 35% reduction in psychological distress.

The researchers emphasized, however, that the meditation had no impact on the progression and activity of RA disease itself.

IMPLICATIONS

Dr. Pradhan and her team concluded that the meditation technique offered RA patients a safe and appealing way to improve their sense of well-being, when offered alongside conventional medical care.

"There's a fair amount of emotional distress that accompanies RA in terms of stability, worrying about the future, worrying about the ability to take care of oneself, to keep a job, to say nothing about the daily pain," Dr. Pradhan said. "There's just a lot to deal with. So, I think this is a novel and innovative way to handle this emotional distress and one that hasn't been tried before, and we were happy to see that it did make a difference along those lines.

"It doesn't really change disease status. That didn't happen," she said. "But in terms of ability to cope with a chronic and debilitating condition, meditation did appear to be quite helpful. And there was really high satisfaction with the intervention. So, I think this bodes well for the future.

"The other thing I think is important to note about our study," Dr. Pradhan continued, "is that mindfulness meditation can be combined with any rheumatological therapy. It is truly complementary medicine in that sense, done in addition to pharmacological or other intervention. So, for physicians and patients who wonder what they can do to improve well-being beyond taking medications, this study offers evidence for a beneficial approach to dealing with the psychological distress of RA."

EXPERT REACTION

Stephen Lindsey, MD, head of rheumatology at Ochsner Health Systems in Baton Rouge, Louisiana, applauded Dr. Pradhan and her team for managing to get a scientific handle on a phenomenon he has observed throughout his practice.

"If someone is having stress and trouble with their arthritis, if you can somehow decrease the stress, you might be able to increase their function," Dr. Lindsey said. "And when you're meditating, you're trying to relax your body and get rid of the tension. It doesn't necessarily have to be a meditation scheme. It could be yoga, or Pilates, or a self-help course. But I'm in favor of using everything possible to help people, and this would be just one more way to help patients improve their lives."

info To learn more about meditation and arthritis, visit the Web site of the Arthritis Foundation, *ww2.arthritis.org* and search "meditation."

Yes, You Can Learn To Be Loving

Antoine Lutz, PhD, associate scientist, Waisman Center, University of Wisconsin-Madison.

Louis E. Teichholz, MD, medical director, complementary medicine, and chief, cardiology, Hackensack University Medical Center, New Jersey.

Public Library of Science One.

New research suggests that qualities the world desperately needs more of—love, kindness and compassion—are indeed teachable.

Imaging technology shows that people who practice meditation that focuses on kindness and compassion actually undergo changes in areas of the brain that make them more in tune to what others are feeling.

"Potentially one can train oneself to behave in a way which is more benevolent and altruistic," said study co-author Antoine Lutz, PhD, an associate scientist at the University of Wisconsin-Madison.

BACKGROUND

Recent brain-imaging studies have suggested that the *insula* and the *anterior cingulate cortices* regions are involved in the empathic response to other people's pain. But not much is known about how cultivating compassion might affect brain circuitry.

"The main research question was to see whether some positive qualities such as loving-kindness and compassion or, in general, pro-social altruistic behavior, can be understood as skills and can be taught," Dr. Lutz explained.

In the same way that training in sports, chess or music produces functional and structural changes in the brain, the Wisconsin researchers wanted to see if cultivating compassion through the practice of meditation also produced brain changes—suggesting that compassion could be viewed as a learned skill.

THE STUDY

The study followed 32 people, including 16 Tibetan monks and lay practitioners, who had meditated for a minimum of 10,000 hours throughout their lifetime (the "experts") and 16 control subjects, who had only recently been taught the basics of compassion meditation (the "novices").

Individuals in the control group were specifically instructed first to wish loved ones well-being and freedom from pain, then to wish such benefits to humankind as a whole.

The senior author of the paper, Richard Davidson, a professor of psychiatry and psychology at the University of Wisconsin-Madison and an expert on imaging the effects of meditation, has been collaborating with the Dalai Lama since 1992, studying the brains of Tibetan monks.

"We looked at whether there were any differences between experts and novices in generating compassion with the idea that a central practice in this tradition (of meditation) is to cultivate these positive emotions," Dr. Lutz said. "We wanted to see if there were any differences in the way the brain was reacting."

All participants were hooked up to a functional MRI both while meditating and not meditating.

During each state, the participants listened to sounds designed to produce responses—such as the negative sound of a distressed woman, the positive sound of a baby laughing and the neutral sound of background noise from a restaurant.

THE RESULTS

According to Dr. Lutz, when subjects were engaged in compassionate meditation, it altered activity in brain circuitry that was previously linked to empathy and perspective-taking or the capacity to understand other's intentions and mental states.

More precisely, the insula region showed greater activity, particularly in response to negative emotional sounds.

The monks especially showed the greatest level of activity in these areas of the brain when they heard the cries of the distressed woman, she said.

IMPLICATIONS

The study authors hope the findings might one day help with a range of problems, including reducing the incidence of bullying in schools or helping people with depression.

"The next step is to see if this works," Dr. Lutz said. "If it works, then it can be applied to selective populations—for instance, depressed people or, more broadly, in education."

EXPERT REACTION

"I think there's no question that people can benefit from these practices," said Louis Teichholz, MD, medical director of complementary medicine and chief of cardiology at Hackensack University Medical Center in New Jersey.

"I think the question is how easy is it to get trained enough so that it will make a clinical difference, and I don't think this study answers that," concluded Dr. Teichholz.

info For more information about meditation and health, visit the Web site of the US National Center for Complementary and Alternative Medicine, *http://nccam.nih.gov*, and search "meditation."

Music Gives Stroke Patients Note of Hope

Brain, news release.

Listening to music for a few hours a day can help boost a stroke patient's early recovery, according to Finnish researchers.

Their study of 54 patients who'd suffered a stroke of the right or left hemisphere found that those who listened to music for a few hours a day showed better improvements in verbal memory and focused attention, and had a more positive mood than those who listened to audio books or listened to nothing at all.

The study, published in the journal *Brain*, is the first to show this link between music listening and stroke recovery. The findings may prove useful in clinical practice, the researchers said.

THE STUDY

The two-month period of music therapy began as soon as possible after the stroke patients were admitted to the hospital. The patients, who made their own music selections, were followed and assessed up to six months after the stroke.

"We found that three months after the stroke, verbal memory improved from the first week post-stroke by 60% in music listeners, by 18% in audio book listeners and by 29% in non-listeners," said study author Teppo Sarkamo of the University of Helsinki and the Helsinki Brain Institute. "Similarly, focused attention—the ability to control and perform mental operations and resolve conflicts among responses—improved by 17% in music listeners, but no improvement was observed in audio book listeners and non-listeners. These differences were still essentially the same six months after the stroke."

Patients in the music listening group were less depressed and confused than non-listeners.

POSSIBLE EXPLANATIONS

The researchers said three neural mechanisms might be involved in how music helps stroke patients' recovery…

•**Improvements in alertness, attention, mood,** mediated by a part of the nervous system (known as the *dopaminergic mesocorticolimbic* system) that plays a role in pleasure, reward, arousal, motivation and memory.

•**Direct stimulation of the recovery of damaged areas of the brain.**

•**Simulation of mechanisms related to brain plasticity—**the ability of the brain to repair and renew its neural networks after damage.

RECOMMENDATIONS

"As a result of our findings, we suggest that everyday music listening during early stroke recovery offers a valuable addition to patients' care—especially if other active forms of rehabilitation are not yet feasible at this stage—by providing an individually targeted, easy-to-conduct and inexpensive means to facilitate cognitive and emotional recovery," said Dr. Sarkamo.

info For more information on stroke rehabilitation, visit the Web site of the National Institute of Neurological Disorders and Stroke, *www.ninds.nih.gov* and search "stroke rehabilitation."

The Music Cure

Barbara Reuer, PhD, founder and clinical training director of MusicWorx of California, a music-therapy consulting agency in San Diego. *www.musicworxofcalifornia. com*. She is past president of the American Music Therapy Association and has worked in medical and psychiatric settings for more than 30 years.

Music has been used for healing for thousands of years—and numerous recent studies confirm its healing powers. It can reduce pain and anxiety and improve blood pressure and breathing. It even can help infants in neonatal intensive care units gain weight faster. *Here's how you can use music to improve your mental and physical health…*

PAIN RELIEF

Music therapy can relieve pain and decrease the need for painkilling drugs. It seems to be most effective for short-term pain, such as during dental procedures, after surgery, etc. A study published in *European Journal of Anesthesiology* reported that postsurgical patients who listened to music required less morphine.

It also helps some types of chronic pain. A study published in *Journal of Advanced Nursing* found that listening to music for an hour a day reduced chronic pain by up to 21% and depression by up to 25%.

How it helps: People in pain can't focus on opposing sensations simultaneously. Listening to music helps block the perception of pain signals and reduces anxiety, which can heighten pain.

Recommended: When you're in pain, practice deep breathing while listening to a favorite piece of relaxing music. Ask your doctor to play calming background music during painful procedures. If a music therapist is available during the procedure, he/she might play music while guiding you through a visualization exercise (such as imagining a peaceful scene) or encouraging you to breathe more deeply.

HEART HELP

Music therapy is used in some coronary care units to lower blood pressure and heart rate. Music also lowers levels of stress chemicals (such as *cortisol*) that increase the risk for a heart attack.

Recommended: At least once a day, listen to music that you find relaxing. Pay attention to the melodies, rhythms and words…think about what the music means to you…and notice the physical signs of relaxation.

STROKE AND PARKINSON'S

A type of therapy called *neurologic music therapy* can help patients with neurological deficits that are caused by stroke, Parkinson's disease, etc.

Example: Parkinson's patients often walk with an uneven gait, which makes it difficult for them to get around and increases the risk for falls. With rhythmic auditory stimulation, therapists play music (or use a metronome) during walking exercises. This helps the brain stimulate skeletal muscles and coordinate movements, creating a more even stride.

The same technique is used with stroke patients, who often lose control of one side of the body. The unaffected brain hemisphere processes the music, "translating" the beat into physical movements. A music therapist, along with a physical therapist, can determine a patient's gait pattern and use music at certain tempos to help the patient improve his gait.

Singing is also helpful. Stroke patients who have lost the ability to speak sometimes can sing. A music therapist can use singing exercises to help patients recover speech skills.

DEMENTIA RELIEF

People with advanced Alzheimer's disease or other forms of dementia are often closed off in a private world. They may be confused and/or hostile. Playing music that was popular in their youth will sometimes make them more "present"…make it easier for them to remember the past…and will evoke a positive emotional response.

How it helps: The moments of lucidity provoked by music can reduce anxiety and make patients feel better. The sessions can be conducted when family members are present. This gives them a chance to reconnect, at least briefly, with loved ones.

BETTER BREATHING

In addition to listening to music, active music-making can be an effective component of music therapy. People who sing or play a wind instrument gain additional strength/flexibility in muscles in the chest wall. Improved muscle flexibility, called *elastance*, allows them to take deeper breaths with less fatigue.

Example: It's common for patients with asthma or chronic obstructive pulmonary disease (COPD) to take unusually shallow breaths. Singing or playing a wind instrument trains them to breathe more deeply…helps clear mucus from the lungs…and helps establish normal breathing rhythms. One study found that children who completed singing exercises had increased peak respiratory flow rates, a measure of lung health.

Recommended: Learn to play the harmonica. It's often used to help pulmonary patients exercise the chest-wall muscles and develop good breath control. Playing the harmonica requires a slow breath in and out, so it enables patients to focus on their breathing in a way that improves respiratory function. Harmonicas and instruction books can be found at most music stores.

EMERGING CLINICAL PRACTICE

There are now more than 70 four-year degree programs approved by the American Music Therapy Association (AMTA). There are about 5,000 board-certified music therapists who work in hospitals, pain clinics, hospice settings, etc. About 25% of music-therapy services are reimbursed by insurance plans.

How it works: A doctor, nurse or social worker may request music therapy for patients on a case-by-case basis. The therapist meets with the patient and assesses his/her needs. Is the patient depressed, in pain or anxious? Is he having trouble walking or breathing? The therapist then decides how the patient can benefit—physically and emotionally—from the treatments.

To find a music therapist, go to the AMTA site, *www.musictherapy.org*.

RESOURCES

Many music stores offer therapeutic music CDs and cassettes and may have a section labeled "health," "new age," "wellness," etc. Try to sample the music first to make sure you like it. Personal preference is important—if you find the music unpleasant, it won't be helpful to you. Good Web sites for therapeutic music include *www.rhythmicmedicine.com* and *www.inner peacemusic.com*.

Fight Cancer with a Pen

Carl Irwin, research administrator, West Virginia University, Morgantown.

Nancy P. Morgan, MA, writing clinician, and director, Arts & Humanities Program, Lombardi Comprehensive Cancer Center, Georgetown University, Washington, DC.

Sandi Stromberg, M.D. Anderson Cancer Center, Houston.

The Oncologist.

When 69-year-old Carl Irwin arrived at Georgetown University's Lombardi Comprehensive Cancer Center for treatment of lymphoma, he was handed a blank notebook and asked to write about how his cancer had changed him and how he felt about those changes.

Propped on a recliner chair, an IV in his left arm and a pen in his right hand, Irwin wrote about how he had confronted his cancer head-on from the first diagnosis, how he had assembled what he called an "advisory" team, and how he felt he had made the right choice by entering a clinical trial to try to treat his disease.

"It [writing] helped my confidence immensely," said Irwin, whose journaling was part of another trial being conducted at Lombardi, in Washington, D.C. "Sometimes my brain doesn't kick in till I write."

Previous research has uncovered physical and psychological benefits to so-called expressive writing among diverse groups of patients, including people with chronic illnesses, such as arthritis and asthma. Most of those studies were done in a controlled, laboratory setting.

The Georgetown study involved patients in an actual hospital setting.

"We were looking for feasibility," said Nancy Morgan, lead author of the study chronicling the Lombardi writing experiment. "Our goal was to try it in the real world."

THE STUDY

For the study, 63 patients with leukemia or lymphoma were asked when they arrived at the hospital to complete a 20-minute writing exercise as well as pre- and post-writing surveys and a telephone follow-up three weeks later.

Nearly half of the participants said writing had changed how they thought about their illness and led to improvement in their quality of life, while 35% said writing changed how they felt about the cancer. Sixty of the 63 people wrote "quite positively," Morgan said.

A software program helped the researchers analyze the writing for themes, words and phrases indicating how cancer had transformed the patients' lives.

But Morgan said she was most interested in what people had to say, how they felt about their experience with the disease.

"Basically, we were trying to stick to thoughts and feelings rather than the facts," she said. "Writing about facts doesn't get you anywhere."

BENEFITS OF EXPRESSIVE WRITING

"A lot of them wrote in the survey, 'I hate thinking about cancer but writing helped me process it and I feel better, it helped me create a script of things I want to say to my family,'" said Morgan, a writing clinician and director of Lombardi's Arts & Humanities Program.

They were saying they just couldn't deal and writing helped them deal," she pointed out.

Expressive writing has now been incorporated into the hospital's arts and humanities program and is part of general patient orientation.

During the orientation Morgan makes a presentation and hands out blank journals for participants to write in.

Some trial participants have incorporated the practice into their lives.

"I started writing updates for relatives and close friends. I still do, to this day," two years after the trial, Irwin said. "They just about always reply."

Sandi Stromberg teaches "Journaling: The Healing Power of Story," for patients and caregivers at M.D. Anderson Cancer Center in Houston.

"They say, 'I don't want to just sit here moaning about my cancer or my loved one's cancer,'" she said. "For cancer patients, the whole story becomes cancer. They forget they led perfectly normal, functioning lives before cancer."

Stromberg uses non-cancer related prompts such as "Write about your first car." Invariably, the patients want to share what they've written, and they bond strongly to each other.

"One time I had a man, I didn't think he would take part, and he did, and he started to cry," Stromberg recalled. "The woman next to him had the same cancer and was a four-year survivor. She put her hand on his wrist and said, 'I understand right where you are.' And he looked at her, and he said, 'Thank you,' with a big smile on his face."

info For more information on writing and health, visit the Web site of the University of Texas, *www.utexas.edu*, and search "writing and health."

The Eight Most Healing Herbs

David Hoffmann, a clinical medical herbalist based in Sonoma County, California, a fellow of Britain's National Institute of Medical Herbalists and one of the founding members of the American Herbalists Guild. He is the author of 17 books, including *Herbal Prescriptions After 50*. Healing Arts.

Anyone who has taken prescription drugs is well aware that these medications can not only be costly, but they also can cause a variety of uncomfortable or even dangerous side effects, such as excessive bleeding, headache, nausea and dizziness.

Recently reported problem: A study of 150,000 older adults (who are among the heaviest users of prescription medications) found that 29% were taking at least one inappropriate drug—including medications that were ineffective or even dangerous.

Often-overlooked alternative to drugs: Herbal medicine. Herbs should not be substituted for all prescription medications, but the careful use of medicinal plants can improve overall health and reduce or eliminate the need for some medications—as well as the risks for drug-related side effects.*

Common conditions—and the best herbal treatments…

CHRONIC BRONCHITIS

More than 5% of Americans suffer from chronic bronchitis (a mucus-producing cough that occurs on most days of the month at least three months of the year).

Best herbal treatment: Horehound (leaves and flowering tops). It relaxes the bronchi (airways that connect the windpipe to the lungs) and makes it easier to expel mucus.

How to use: Add 1 milliliter (ml) to 2 ml of horehound tincture (concentrated liquid) to 1 ounce of hot or cold water. Drink this amount three times daily during bronchitis flare-ups.

Important: Most herbs are available in various forms, such as dry leaf, capsules and powders,

*See your doctor before using medicinal herbs—especially if you take any medications, have a chronic medical condition or are pregnant or nursing.

but tinctures are convenient, among the quickest to be absorbed and have a long shelf life.

HEARTBURN

When acid from the stomach backs up into the esophagus, the result is often heartburn (a burning pain behind the breastbone).

Best herbal treatment: Marshmallow root. It coats and soothes the esophageal lining.

How to use: Make an infusion by adding one heaping teaspoon of powdered marshmallow root to a cup of cold water and letting it sit at room temperature for 12 hours. Drink the entire mixture when heartburn occurs. If you get heartburn more than three times a week, drink one infusion in the morning and another at bedtime until the heartburn eases. If you make more than one cup in advance, you can refrigerate the unused portion for 24 hours.

Important: Do *not* use hot water. It will provide only about one-fourth of the soothing *mucilage* (lubricating substance) of a cold-water infusion.

HYPERTENSION

High blood pressure (hypertension) is among the main causes of heart attack and stroke. Prescription medications usually are required for this condition, but herbal therapy can sometimes allow patients to take lower doses of blood pressure–lowering drugs.

Important: Check with your doctor before trying herbs for hypertension. Because the potential complications of hypertension are serious, everyone with this condition should be under a doctor's care.

Best herbal treatment: Hawthorn (berries). This herbal therapy dilates arteries (which allows more blood to circulate with less force)…and strengthens the cardiovascular system, in part by enhancing the activity of cells in the heart muscle. In Germany, hawthorn is widely recommended by doctors for cardiovascular disease.

How to use: Add 1 ml to 2 ml of hawthorn tincture to 1 ounce of hot or cold water. Drink this amount three times daily.

Alternative: Drink hot tea (two to three times daily) that combines hawthorn with linden flowers, an herb that has a mild antihypertensive effect. Such tea bags are available at most health food stores.

INSOMNIA

Stress, poor sleep habits and health problems that cause pain are common causes of insomnia (an inability to fall asleep or remain asleep).

Best herbal treatment: Passionflower (leaves or whole plant). Its depressant effect on the central nervous system helps promote restful sleep.

How to use: Add 1 ml to 4 ml of passionflower tincture to 1 ounce of cold water, or make an infusion by pouring one cup of boiling water over one teaspoon of dried passionflower and letting it sit for 15 minutes. Drink the entire tincture mixture or infusion at bedtime when you suffer from insomnia.

Caution: People who take drugs with sedative effects, such as certain antihistamines, antianxiety medications and insomnia supplements or drugs, should not use passionflower, which can increase these sedative effects.

IRRITABLE BOWEL SYNDROME

Alternating bouts of constipation and diarrhea are characteristic symptoms of irritable bowel syndrome (IBS).

Best herbal treatment: Yarrow (leaves and other parts that grow above ground) for the diarrhea phase…mugwort (leaves) for constipation. These herbs also are effective for episodes of diarrhea and constipation that are not related to IBS.

Yarrow contains *tannins*, substances that reduce the amount of water released by the intestinal lining. Mugwort is a bitter herb that promotes the intestinal contractions needed for bowel movements.

How to use: Add 1 ml to 2 ml of yarrow or mugwort tincture to 1 ounce of hot or cold water. Drink this amount three times daily when you have diarrhea or constipation.

OSTEOARTHRITIS

Age-related changes in the joints are the primary cause of osteoarthritis. Most patients can get temporary relief with pain relievers, such as *ibuprofen* (Advil), but these drugs often cause side effects, such as gastrointestinal bleeding.

Best herbal treatment: Black mustard (for external use) and meadowsweet (for internal use). A poultice of black mustard causes mild, temporary inflammation that stimulates circulation—good for muscle and/or joint pain.

How to use: Make a black-mustard poultice by grinding the seeds in a coffee grinder and mixing one-half cup of the mustard powder with 1 cup of flour. Add enough hot water to make a paste. Spread the mixture on a piece of heavy brown paper, cotton or muslin that has been soaked in hot water, then cover it with a second piece of dry material. Lay the moist side of the poultice across the painful area, leaving it on for 15 to 30 minutes once daily.

Caution: Consult a doctor before using the poultice on a young child, or on anyone who is age 70 or older or seriously ill.

Meadowsweet is a pain reliever that contains aspirin-like chemicals called *salicylates*.

How to use: Add 1 ml to 2 ml of meadowsweet tincture to 1 ounce of hot or cold water. Drink this amount three times daily until symptoms subside.

PERIODONTAL DISEASE

Bacterial buildup in the spaces between the teeth and gums leads to periodontal (gum) disease—the most common cause of tooth loss in older adults. Gum infection has been linked to an increased risk for heart attack and stroke. Regular dental care and cleanings (at least annually) are essential.

Best herbal treatment: Goldenseal and/or myrrh. Goldenseal acts as a topical antibiotic. Myrrh strengthens mucous membranes. Start treatment when you first notice gum tenderness and/or bleeding—the first signs of periodontal disease.

How to use: Mix equal amounts of goldenseal and myrrh tinctures. Use a very fine paintbrush to apply the mixture to the gum line. Leave it on as long as you can—the taste is unpleasant—then rinse your mouth with water and spit it out. Repeat two or three times daily.

SKIN DRYNESS

Declines in the activity of oil-producing glands make skin dryness a common complaint after age 50.

Best herbal treatment: Gentian. It's a bitter herb that stimulates the oil-producing exocrine glands in the skin.

203

How to use: Add 1 ml to 2 ml of tincture to 1 ounce of hot or cold water. Drink this amount three times daily, until your skin's condition improves.

Cayenne Conquers Cholesterol and More Spice Discoveries

David Winston, RH, a Washington, New Jersey–based registered herbalist and professional member of the American Herbalist Guild. He is the author of several books, including *Adaptogens: Herbs for Strength, Stamina and Stress Relief.* Healing Arts.

Researchers have now identified new health benefits for several popular spices. You may recognize the names of these spices, but the latest studies suggest uses that are not widely known. *Intriguing new research…*

CAYENNE PEPPER

•**Cholesterol.** Artery-clogging fatty buildups are created or worsened when cholesterol oxidizes, a biochemical process similar to metal rusting. Cayenne pepper (also known as chili pepper) contains a plaque-fighting antioxidant (capsaicin), which is also available in supplement form.

Newest research: When researchers asked 27 people to eat a diet that included cayenne-spiced chili or the same diet with no chili for one month, the chili group had much lower harmful cholesterol than those who did not eat chili. In addition to protecting cholesterol from oxidation, cayenne pepper also stimulates digestion and improves circulation—an important benefit for people with chronically cold hands and feet.

My recommendation: Use a cayenne-based hot sauce, to taste. I add it to a variety of foods, including chicken dishes and sandwiches.

Caution: In some people, cayenne causes digestive problems. If you experience stomach upset or anal irritation, use a milder hot sauce, cut back the amount or stop using it.

SAGE

•**Alzheimer's disease.** Herbalists and many doctors report that sage may help patients with mild to moderate Alzheimer's disease.

Newest research: Neurons of lab animals exposed to *amyloid beta* (the main constituent of harmful plaques in Alzheimer's) and sage leaves or *rosmarinic acid* (an active ingredient in sage) were less damaged than when the cells were exposed to amyloid beta alone. However, you cannot achieve this potential health benefit from the amount of sage used in cooking.

My recommendation: Drink sage tea.

What to do: Pour 8 ounces of boiling water over a tea strainer or tea ball that contains one-half teaspoon of ground sage. Let sit for 15 to 20 minutes. Drink 4 ounces twice a day. (Refrigerate any unused portion and gently reheat before drinking.)

Alternative: Use sage tea bags. Or add 20 to 30 drops of sage tincture to 1 ounce of water—drink this amount three times daily.

ROSEMARY

•**Cancer.** Laboratory studies of human cells show that rosemary may help prevent certain types of cancer.

Newest research: The rate at which human leukemia and breast cancer cells multiplied in a laboratory study was reduced when researchers exposed the cells to rosemary extract. More research is needed to confirm these benefits in human study subjects, but rosemary extract is safe to use in the meantime. Cooking with rosemary does not provide this potential health benefit.

My recommendation: Drink rosemary tea.

What to do: Pour 12 ounces of boiling water over a tea strainer or tea ball that contains one-half teaspoon of rosemary. Let sit for 15 to 20 minutes. Drink 4 ounces, three times a day. (Refrigerate unused tea.)

Alternative: Use rosemary tea bags. Or add 40 to 60 drops of rosemary tincture to 1 ounce of water—drink this amount three times daily.

HOW TO USE SPICES

The active ingredients in spices can eventually deteriorate after processing. For example, levels of antioxidants, known as carotenoids, in paprika drop by 75% after three months of storage.

My recommendation: Buy no more than a one-year supply of any spice you plan to use —and replace it annually. Keep your spices away from light, moisture and heat—for example, not near the oven. Consider buying whole rather than powdered spices, and grind them right before using, with a mortar and pestle or spice grinder. To tell whether a spice is rich in health-promoting compounds, smell and/or taste it—the richer the odor and flavor, the better the spice.

Put the Power of Aromatherapy to Work for You

Mindy Green, a practicing aromatherapist for more than 25 years. The Minneapolis-based coauthor of *Aromatherapy: A Complete Guide to the Healing Art* (Ten Speed) is a founding member of the American Herbalists' Guild.

A scented spray or candle may smell good, but true "aromatherapy" does much more. This ancient healing practice involves the therapeutic use of aromatic substances known as *essential oils* (highly concentrated extracts distilled from plants).

Some people scoff at the idea of using aromatherapy, but ongoing research has shown that essential oils are effective in treating a variety of common health problems.

How does it work? Smelling an essential oil releases neurotransmitters and other chemicals that affect the brain. When used topically, chemical constituents in essential oils are absorbed through the skin and enter the bloodstream, where they affect overall physiology, including hormones and enzymes.

AROMATHERAPY SAFETY

Essential oils are safe for most people. In rare cases, however, skin irritation can occur when used topically.

To check the sensitivity of your skin: Mix the essential oil you intend to use with a carrier oil and apply it to the inside of the crook of your arm or the side of your neck below the ear. (Never apply essential oil directly to your skin.) Check the area periodically over the next 12 hours to ensure that you do not experience itching or redness. If you do experience itching or redness, it is likely that you are reacting to that particular oil. Test another oil, using the same technique.

If you have a chronic medical condition, such as high blood pressure, heart disease or cancer, check with your doctor before using essential oils. Pregnant women and children should not use aromatherapy without first consulting a doctor. If an essential oil is accidentally ingested, call 911—the concentrated substances can be toxic if swallowed.

Store essential oils out of the reach of children—at room temperature and away from heat and light to preserve freshness and potency.

Best way to use topical therapy: Add five to 10 drops of essential oil to 1 ounce of a "carrier" oil, such as almond oil, which is odorless, and apply it to the affected part of your body. For a bath, add five to eight drops of essential oil mixed with a teaspoon of a carrier oil to a tub full of warm bathwater.

Best way to use inhalation therapy: Add three to six drops of essential oil to a basin of hot water (boil then cool slightly). Bend your head over the bowl and cover your head with a towel, creating a tent to trap the scented steam. Staying at least 12 inches away from the water source, inhale deeply for three to five minutes.

My favorite essential oils and their uses...

MUSCLE CRAMPS

•**Marjoram.** Add a mixture of marjoram and a carrier oil to your bath and soak for 20 minutes. Or massage marjoram oil and a carrier oil into the painful area as needed.

COUGH AND CONGESTION

•**Eucalyptus.** Rub a mixture of eucalyptus and a carrier oil onto your chest and back. The oils work via skin absorption and inhalation to ease coughs and congestion. For congestion, try inhalation therapy three times daily for five minutes each session.

Caution: Do not try this therapy during an asthma attack—it can exacerbate symptoms. If you don't get relief within a few days, see your doctor.

FATIGUE

•**Rosemary.** Add rosemary and a carrier oil to a warm bath and soak for 10 to 15 minutes as needed.

INSOMNIA

•**Lavender.** Add lavender and a carrier oil to warm bathwater and soak for 20 minutes before going to bed.

NAUSEA

•**Ginger and peppermint.** Mix two drops of ginger oil with one drop of peppermint oil and one tablespoon of a carrier oil. While lying on your back, gently massage the mixture onto the abdomen. When rubbing, follow the natural flow of intestinal movement—move your hand up the right side of your stomach, across the middle and down the left side. This is the way food normally moves through the large intestine. For even greater relief, also drink a cup of ginger or peppermint tea after the massage.

ESSENTIAL OIL BASICS

Essential oils are available at most health food stores and on-line.

Typical cost: $5 to $25 for a small (0.5 ounce) bottle. High-quality oils can be purchased from Aura Cacia, 800-437-3301, *www.auracacia.com* …The Essential Oil Company, 800-729-5912, *www.essentialoil.com*…or Oshadhi, 888-674-2344, *www.oshadhiusa.com*.

The Healing Power of Homeopathy

Mark A. Stengler, ND, naturopathic physician in private practice, La Jolla, California…adjunct associate clinical professor at the National College of Natural Medicine, Portland, Oregon…author of 16 books, including *The Natural Physician's Healing Therapies* (Bottom Line Books) and coauthor of *Prescription for Natural Cures* (Wiley)…and author of the *Bottom Line/Natural Healing* newsletter.

In this country, homeopathy is a source of controversy for medical practitioners and confusion for health care consumers. That's why I am providing this guide to homeopathic medicine, a therapy that aims to stimulate the body's own healing responses by using extremely small amounts of specific substances.

In my professional practice, I use homeopathy for one reason—it works. Before I get into the science, however, I want to share a personal story about the power of this healing therapy.

My first child was born prematurely, more than three months before he was due. His lungs were underdeveloped and he contracted life-threatening viral pneumonia. It was heartbreaking to see my baby boy with tubes down his tiny throat, as four pediatricians worked around the clock to save him. Though antibiotics do not work against viruses, the doctors administered intravenous antibiotics in case there also was a secondary bacterial infection. When my son's condition did not improve, the doctors seemed at a loss for what to do next.

At this point, I took matters into my own hands. I treated my son with homeopathic *Antimonium tartaricum*, a liquid solution derived from antimony (a metal) and potassium salts, which I rubbed onto his chest. Within one day, he had improved visibly. By the following day, my son was off the respirator and on his way to complete recovery.

THE HOMEOPATHY PRINCIPLE

Homeopathy was founded two centuries ago by the German physician Samuel Hahnemann, MD. It is based on the *law of similars*—the idea that "like cures like."

Underlying principle: The symptoms the body produces in response to illness, injury or stress are not extensions of the condition, but instead reflect the body's attempt to heal itself.

Homeopathy promotes healing by utilizing substances that mobilize the body's natural self-defense processes. For example, the same plant that causes an itchy rash also can cure that rash when given in very minute quantities. In conventional medicine, this principle underlies vaccination and allergy injections—which administer tiny amounts of a disease-causing or an allergy-provoking agent to stimulate the immune system to produce antibodies that protect against this same agent.

For uncomplicated health problems, such as occasional digestive upset or a cold, patients can be helped with simple, common homeopathic remedies sold in health food stores. For more complex problems, practitioners depend on a deep understanding of the individual patient's health status, an array of potent remedies and careful monitoring of the patient's progress.

THE PREPARATIONS

Homeopathy uses thousands of substances derived from plant, mineral or animal sources. Over many years, homeopaths have catalogued the physical and mental symptoms these substances can *cause* and, from this information, have created substances that *cure* these conditions.

Homeopathic remedies generally are safe for everyone, have no side effects when used properly, and are manufactured in accordance with standards set by the FDA.

SCIENTIFIC EVIDENCE

Researchers have been studying homeopathy for decades. Overall, studies show mixed results. This does not mean that treatments are ineffective, but rather that they are used in a holistic way not easily measured in conventional studies.

Reason: Drugs and nutritional supplements can be matched to specific problems and studied accordingly. For example, the drug *celecoxib* (Celebrex) and the natural supplement *glucosamine* (an amino sugar) both are used to treat osteoarthritis, so studies focus on their effectiveness against that particular disease. However, homeopathic treatment is highly individualized according to a patient's overall profile. If a patient has migraines, I select from among several dozen homeopathic remedies, taking into account the type and location of his/her migraines, how the weather affects him, his diet and exercise habits, etc. With so many variables influencing the choice of homeopathic remedy and the patient's response to it, I'm not surprised that study results sometimes are inconclusive.

Even so, more than 100 clinical trials have demonstrated homeopathy's benefits. Equally convincing, in my opinion, are the many reports I have received from patients who have been helped by homeopathic remedies—often after other treatments failed.

FINDING A HOMEOPATHIC PRACTITIONER

Homeopathy does not work for everyone. Some practitioners work with a limited number of substances that they have found especially effective—so if you do not get relief with a particular practitioner, try someone else.

In the US, homeopathy is practiced by many naturopathic physicians, chiropractors, nurses, dentists and some medical doctors. In most states, homeopaths are not licensed as such, and there are no national standards for training. However, the following organizations have stringent training requirements for members and offer on-line directories for finding practitioners in various areas.

•**The American Board of Homeotherapeutics** awards a *diplomate of homeopathy* (DHt) certification. A practitioner must hold an MD or a DO license, accrue 150 hours of education credits in homeopathy, and pass various exams (703-273-5250, *www.homeopathyusa.org*).

•**All naturopathic physicians** are educated in homeopathy. Those with the most extensive training are eligible to join the Homeopathic Academy of Naturopathic Physicians.

Referrals: American Association of Naturopathic Physicians (866-538-2267, *www.naturopathic.org*).

info For more information on homeopathy, contact the National Center for Homeopathy (703-548-7790, *www.nationalcenterforhomeopathy.org*).

■ **More from Mark A. Stengler, ND...**

Over-the-Counter Homeopathic Remedies

L ow-potency homeopathic remedies sold in health food stores are generally safe for all. They can be used in combination with other homeopathic remedies. Follow instructions on labels. Consult a doctor trained in homeopathy before using remedies if you have a serious illness...take medication...are pregnant or nursing...or if symptoms do not improve after 48 hours of use.

For this condition...	The remedy is...
Allergies, hay fever	Allium cepa
Arthritis pain	Rhus toxicodendron
Back pain	Rhus toxicodendron
Bee stings, insect bites	Apis

Bruising, swelling, sprains	Arnica
Cold sores	Rhus toxicodendron
Coughs, colds	Phosphorous
Earache	Chamomilla
Emotional distress, anxiety	Ignatia
Fever	Belladonna
Flu	Gelsemium
Hangover, heartburn	Nux vomica
Migraine	Belladonna
Muscle cramps, muscle spasms	Magnesia phosphorica
Nerve injury	Hypericum
Poison ivy	Rhus toxicodendron
Sore throat	Phosphorous
Skin rash, eczema	Sulphur
Stomach cramps, nausea	Nux vomica
Toothache, teething pain	Chamomilla
Urinary tract infection	Cantharis

■ ■ ■ ■

Fish Oil May Benefit Multiple Sclerosis Patients

Multiple sclerosis (MS) is a neurological disorder. Symptoms include weakness, pain and vision loss.

Recent finding: MS patients who took just over 2 teaspoons daily of fish oil containing omega-3 fatty acids had lower levels of an inflammatory blood protein that is often higher in MS patients.

Lynne Shinto, ND, MPH, assistant professor, department of neurology, Oregon Health & Science University, Portland, and principal investigator of a study presented at a meeting of the American Association of Naturopathic Physicians.

Tea and Mushroom Combo Slows Some Cancers

Federation of American Societies for Experimental Biology, news release.

A combination of the active ingredients in reishi mushrooms and green tea inhibited the growth of tumors and extended survival time of mice with sarcomas, two Chinese studies show.

Sarcomas are cancers of the bone, cartilage, fat, muscle, blood vessels or other connective or supportive tissue.

Both reishi mushrooms and green tea have long held a place in traditional medicine in Asia. Recent research has shown that both enhance the body's immune function, according to two new studies by researchers at the Pharmanex BJ Clinical Pharmacology Center in Beijing.

STUDY #1

Researchers injected mice with sarcoma cells and then gave them low, medium or high doses of a product called ReishiMax that contains high concentrations of the active components in reishi mushrooms, including polysaccharides and triterpenes, or a combination of ReishiMax and Tegreen, a product composed of 98% to 99% green tea polyphenols (plant chemicals that neutralize damaging free radicals in the body).

Result: The mice that received the combination treatment lived longer.

STUDY #2

Groups of healthy mice were given low, medium or high doses of ReishiMax or low, medium or high doses of a combination of ReishiMax and Tegreen. After 14 days of treatment, the mice were injected with sarcoma cells. The treatment then continued for another 14 days.

Result: Tumor development in the mice that received the combination treatment was less than in those that received only ReishiMax and 45% less than mice that received no treatment.

info For more information about sarcoma, visit the Web site of the Sarcoma Foundation of America, *www.curesarcoma.org*.

■ ■ ■ ■

Green Tea Combats Skin Cancer

Polyphenols, a type of antioxidant found in green tea, protect skin from the sun's damaging ultraviolet radiation and help prevent the formation of skin tumors.

Best: Drink five to six cups of green tea a day—the fresher, the better. Fresh green tea leaves have a light yellow or green color. A brownish hue indicates that the tea has undergone oxidation, which destroys antioxidants.

Tea bags and loose leaves are better than instant and bottled teas.

Santosh Katiyar, PhD, associate professor of dermatology, University of Alabama, Birmingham, and leader of a study of green tea and skin tumor development in mice, published in *The Journal of Nutritional Biochemistry*.

■ ■ ■ ■

Drinking Coffee Reduces Risk of Gout in Men

Men who drank four to five cups of coffee a day had a 40% lower risk for developing gout than men who drank no coffee at all.

Men who drank six or more cups daily had a 59% decreased risk.

Reason: Gout—which is a painful inflammatory disease characterized by attacks of arthritis—is caused by excessive buildup of *uric acid*.

Coffee tends to lower uric acid levels.

Hyon K. Choi, MD, associate professor, department of rheumatology, University of British Columbia, Vancouver, Canada, and Brigham and Women's Hospital, Boston, and leader of a study of 45,869 men, published in *Arthritis & Rheumatism*.

■ ■ ■ ■

Try Pomegranate Juice To Fight Prostate Cancer

Drinking 8 ounces of pomegranate juice daily increases the doubling time of *prostate specific antigen* (PSA) by more than 300% (more research is needed to determine why). The longer the doubling time, the slower the tumor growth.

Extra benefit: Pomegranate juice may slow the progression of breast, testicular and lung cancers, as well as help reduce blood pressure and protect against heart disease.

Kelly Morrow, RD, assistant professor of nutrition, Bastyr University, Kenmore, Washington.

Four Natural Ways to Ease Celiac Disease

Jamison Starbuck, ND, a naturopathic physician in family practice and a lecturer at the University of Montana, both in Missoula. She is past president of the American Association of Naturopathic Physicians and a contributing editor to *The Alternative Advisor: The Complete Guide to Natural Therapies and Alternative Treatments*. Time-Life.

The next time a waiter puts a basket of fresh bread on your restaurant table, think twice before you eat it. Experts believe that at least one out of every 100 American adults has celiac disease, a condition that can make sufferers ill after eating even a single slice of bread. The culprit is gluten—a type of protein found in wheat, barley, rye and, in some cases, oats that creates an autoimmune, inflammatory reaction in the small intestine. The usual symptoms are bloating and diarrhea, but some people also experience abdominal pain and/or constipation. In some cases, celiac disease causes only a blistery, itchy skin condition (*dermatitis herpetiformis*) or fatigue.

If you think you might have celiac disease, discuss it with your doctor. A diagnosis requires specific blood tests and, in some cases, an intestinal biopsy. If you do have celiac disease, your medical doctor will tell you to completely avoid gluten. This may sound like hard work, since gluten is in all sorts of things you might not suspect, such as many kinds of soy sauce, creamed soups and salad dressings. But it is definitely doable and gets easier as you learn where gluten-free products (even bread and pasta) are available—for example, in many health food stores and a growing number of restaurants.

Payoff: Once you start avoiding gluten, your celiac symptoms will disappear over a period of weeks and months. *Other steps to consider...**

•**Take supplements.** Inflammation in the small intestine interferes with the absorption of key nutrients. I advise my celiac patients to take a daily regimen that includes 5 mg of folic acid...800 international units (IU) each

*To minimize inflammation, follow the dietary advice indefinitely—and also continue to take the vitamin supplements to guard against a nutritional deficiency.

of vitamins E and D...25,000 IU of vitamin A ...and 2 mg of vitamin K.

Note: Vitamin K supplements should be avoided by patients taking *warfarin* (Coumadin) or another blood thinner. I also recommend taking a botanical formula that contains one or more of these herbs (in powdered form)—deglycyrrhizinated licorice root, slippery elm and marshmallow root. Follow label instructions and take until inflammatory bowel symptoms abate.

•**Eat healthful fats daily and fish twice a week.** Olive oil, avocado, soy milk and small portions of unsalted nuts (eight to 12) are good sources of healthful fat. (However, celiac patients should avoid peanuts, which can be hard for them to digest.) Fatty fish, such as salmon or halibut, is an easily digested protein source.

Warning: In people with celiac disease, high-fat dairy products, as well as fried foods, tend to worsen diarrhea.

•**Use plant-based enzymes.** Enzyme supplementation helps break down food and reduces post-meal bloating. Plant-based enzymes (available at natural food stores) are usually derived from pineapple or papaya, and they are safe for just about everyone unless you have ulcers or you are allergic to pineapple or papaya.

Typical dose: Take one or two capsules per meal.

•**Get support.** Avoiding gluten isn't easy, but you'll feel much better if you do. For more advice, consult the Celiac Sprue Association/ USA, 877-272-4272, *www.csaceliacs.org*.

■ ■ ■ ■

Biofeedback May Relieve Constipation

Biofeedback—which helps the mind to control involuntary body processes, such as blood pressure—can help with constipation if it is caused by rectal spasm or spasm of the pelvic muscles. In these cases of *dyssynergic defecation*—when muscles responsible for bowel movements don't work well due to a failure to relax pelvic floor muscles—biofeedback can retrain muscles to push more effectively. There is as yet no home-based biofeedback program— one is under development.

To find a doctor who works with biofeedback: Contact the Biofeedback Certification Institute of America (303-420-2902, *www. bcia.org*).

Other treatments include increasing consumption of dietary fiber...use of beneficial bacteria called probiotics...and consuming supplements called prebiotics, which help good bacteria grow to aid digestion. Probiotics and prebiotics are available in health food stores.

Leo Galland, MD, director, Foundation for Integrated Medicine, New York City. His latest book is *The Fat Resistance Diet*. Broadway. *www.fatresistancediet.com*. Dr. Galland is a recipient of the Linus Pauling award.

Tired? Gaining Weight? It May be Your Thyroid

Ellen Kamhi, PhD, RN, a board-certified holistic nurse and a clinical instructor at Stony Brook University's School of Medicine and New York Chiropractic College, Seneca Falls. As "The Natural Nurse," Dr. Kamhi addresses millions of Americans through radio and television programs. She is author of *Definitive Guide to Weight Loss* and coauthor of *The Natural Medicine Chest* (both from The Natural Nurse, 800-829-0918, *naturalnurse.com*). Dr. Kamhi develops herbal and nutritional products for Nature's Answer, Hauppauge, New York. *www.natures answer.com*.

Do you feel tired most of the time? Are you gaining weight for no apparent reason? A sluggish thyroid may be to blame. Though just 3% of all Americans suffer from an underactive thyroid, or *hypothyroidism* (sometimes referred to as a sluggish thyroid), as many as 10% to 15% of Americans have a subclinical (mild) hypothyroid condition. Because hypothyroidism often underlies other health conditions, the number of people who have the disorder may be even higher, perhaps as high as one in three.

Untreated hypothyroidism can lead to serious medical problems, including reduced immunity, high cholesterol and high blood pressure.

Recent finding: A study published in the July 2007 issue of *Archives of Internal Medicine* reported that even mild changes in thyroid function are associated with an increased risk for mortality in patients with cardiac disease.

The good news is that a sluggish thyroid often can be corrected naturally.

WHAT IS A SLUGGISH THYROID?

The thyroid, a butterfly-shaped gland in the lower front of the neck, produces hormones that help your body regulate your metabolism and keep your heart, brain, muscles and organs functioning normally. Hypothyroidism has several causes that can trigger a shortage in formation or utilization of thyroid hormones.

The risk for hypothyroidism increases with age, and being female puts you at even higher risk. According to the American Association of Clinical Endocrinologists, women are five to eight times more likely than men to have the condition. The risk for hypothyroidism increases if you have a family history of thyroid disease or if you have an autoimmune disorder, such as type 1 diabetes or rheumatoid arthritis.

SYMPTOMS

Symptoms of hypothyroidism include fatigue, depression, forgetfulness, weight gain, insomnia, intolerance to cold, constipation, dry skin, hair loss and/or chronic yeast infections.

For women, hypothyroid symptoms may include frequent and/or heavy menstrual periods. Also, symptoms commonly attributed to menopause, such as hot flashes and mood swings, can be signs of a sluggish thyroid.

If you regularly suffer from two or more hypothyroid symptoms over the course of several weeks or months, see your doctor. If your doctor suspects hypothyroidism, he/she will order a simple blood test that measures *thyroid stimulating hormone* (TSH) and "free" thyroxine (T4). An abnormally high level of TSH means the thyroid gland is asked to make more T4 because there isn't enough available. A "free" T4 index can effectively measure how much T4 is circulating in the blood and available for your body to use.

If your doctor doesn't discover a thyroid problem but you have many of the symptoms, visit a holistic practitioner who may have a better understanding of hidden thyroid issues.

NATURAL REMEDIES

Lifestyle changes can go a long way toward correcting a sluggish thyroid...

•**Consume natural sources of iodine.** If you're low in iodine, it can lead to a thyroid deficiency.

The best sources of iodine are iodized salt, sea vegetables, such as seaweed, as well as eggs and shellfish, including lobster, shrimp and crab.

You will need 100 micrograms (mcg) to 120 mcg of iodine a day. A 3-ounce serving of shrimp—or one egg—contains about 30 mcg.

Also, to ensure a healthy metabolism, eat a balanced diet that includes adequate amounts of protein (beef, poultry, fish, eggs and milk products, such as yogurt and cottage cheese), whole grains and plenty of vegetables. Whenever possible, opt for organic foods. Pesticides and herbicides have been linked to disorders of the thyroid.

•**Eat foods rich in vitamin E and selenium.** Studies reported in *Biofactors and European Journal of Endocrinology* indicate that vitamin E and selenium can revitalize an underactive thyroid.

Vitamin E can be found in various foods, including wheat germ, whole-grain cereals, nuts, avocados, green leafy vegetables and fish.

Try to consume a total of 400 international units (IU) per day. One tablespoon of wheat germ oil has 30 IU...one ounce of almonds has 10 IU.

Selenium is in seafood, liver, poultry, red meat and grains—aim for 200 mcg a day. A 4-ounce serving of most fish has 50 mcg to 75 mcg of selenium...4 ounces of turkey breast has 33 mcg.

•**Exercise.** The latest research on hypothyroidism suggests that thyroid dysfunction may be linked to stress. A study published in *Annals of the New York Academy of Science* found that exercise helps reestablish healthy thyroid function by decreasing the overall impact of stress. Aim for 30 minutes a day of any form of exercise.

Natural Ways to Increase Fertility

Mark A. Stengler, ND, naturopathic physician in private practice, La Jolla, California...adjunct associate clinical professor at the National College of Natural Medicine, Portland, Oregon...author of 16 books, including *The Natural Physician's Healing Therapies* (Bottom Line Books) and coauthor of *Prescription for Natural Cures* (Wiley)...and author of the *Bottom Line/Natural Healing* newsletter.

For three years, Sarah, a 36-year-old medical doctor, and her husband, Ray, had been trying to start a family—but each month brought disappointment. Conventional medical testing found no reason why she or her husband would be infertile (defined medically as being unable to achieve pregnancy after a year of unprotected intercourse). After in vitro fertilization failed, they consulted me.

First, we reviewed how to time sexual relations to maximize the chances of conception.

Optimal: One day before or on the day of ovulation, when an egg is released from the ovary. Sarah had been using an at-home urine test (sold in drugstores) that detects a surge in *luteinizing hormone*, indicating that ovulation is imminent. I recommended that she also pay attention to her cervical mucus, because fertility rises when there is an increase in its amount, slipperiness and stretchiness.

Some studies suggest that caffeine decreases female fertility, for unknown reasons. Also, regular and decaf coffee, as well as black and green tea, contain *tannic acid*, which may decrease sperm production. I advised Sarah and Ray to avoid coffee, cola, chocolate and tea (except herbal).

Wisely, Sarah had eliminated alcohol from her diet. Alcohol can sporadically halt ovulation (and contribute to birth defects). I suggested that Ray also avoid alcohol, because it can reduce sperm count and quality. I was pleased that Sarah's weight was normal. Being overweight raises levels of the hormone estrogen and may lead to irregular ovulation. Being underweight inhibits production of the hormones required to stimulate ovulation. I also was glad that neither partner smoked, because toxins in tobacco can damage eggs and sperm.

Sarah was unaware that nutritional and herbal therapies can help a woman get pregnant. I told her to take a daily multivitamin to guard against nutritional deficiencies that impair fertility. In addition, I suggested supplementing with the herb *Vitex* (chasteberry), which stimulates the pituitary gland to release luteinizing hormone...in turn increasing the ovaries' release of *progesterone*, a hormone that prepares the uterine lining for implantation of a fertilized egg.

A longstanding naturopathic treatment for female infertility is to enhance the level of thyroid hormone, because even a minor deficiency can prevent ovulation and increase the risk for miscarriage. Blood testing revealed that Sarah had a very low level of the most potent thyroid hormone, T3. I prescribed Armour Thyroid, a natural brand that contains T3 and other thyroid hormones found in the human body. Synthetic brands usually contain T4, the less potent form of the hormone.

Two months after her first visit, Sarah phoned and exclaimed, "I'm pregnant!" After congratulating her, I recommended that Sarah stop taking chasteberry, which was no longer needed ...continue her thyroid medication...and switch to a prenatal multivitamin that provided more folic acid, vitamin B-12 and iron. A few weeks later, Sarah came to my clinic again—this time, for morning sickness.

Acupuncture Zaps Surgical Pain

Tong J. Gan, MD, professor and vice chairman, department of anesthesiology, Duke University Medical Center, Durham, North Carolina.

Kenneth Levey, MD, director, New York Center for Pelvic Pain and Minimally Invasive Surgery, and clinical assistant professor, obstetrics and gynecology, New York University School of Medicine, New York City.

David P. Martin, MD, department of anesthesiology, Mayo Clinic, Rochester, Minnesota.

American Society for Anesthesiology meeting, San Francisco.

Powerful opioids taken after surgery can have powerful side effects, but new research finds that using acupuncture before and during an operation cuts a patient's need for the painkillers.

"From a pain perspective, you can reduce the amount of morphine that the patient uses and improve the quality of analgesia and pain control," said lead researcher Tong J. Gan, MD, a professor and vice chairman of anesthesiology at Duke University Medical Center, in Durham, North Carolina.

Morphine is a type of opioid, a category of potent painkillers that often produce side effects, such as nausea and vomiting.

THE STUDY

In the new study, Dr. Gan's team analyzed data taken from 15 small, randomized clinical trials looking at the use of acupuncture to reduce postoperative pain.

The analysis found that acupuncture received 30 minutes before and during surgery, could reduce common side effects of morphine experienced by eight out of 10 patients. It reduced post-op itchiness by 30%, nausea by 50% and dizziness by 60%, Dr. Gan said, in part because it lessened the need for morphine.

ACUPUNCTURE ALSO REDUCES URINARY RETENTION

One expert said Dr. Gan's finding that adjunctive acupuncture can reduce urinary retention by 3.5 times is especially important.

"The risk reduction is huge," said Kenneth Levey, MD, a clinical assistant professor of obstetrics and gynecology at New York University School of Medicine in New York City. Urinary retention is not only uncomfortable for the patient but the use of a catheter to relieve it increases the risk of infection, he said.

ACUPUNCTURE IN THE OPERATING ROOM

The studies also show that acupuncture could be of benefit following many types of surgeries, said Dr. Gan. Chinese acupuncture was the style used in the studies he reviewed, but similar effects would occur with other styles and whether needles, electrical or manual acupuncture were used, Dr. Gan speculated.

Adjunctive acupuncture is "not widely used because people need to be educated," Dr. Gan said. To use it, surgeons need training but they don't "need to know every acupuncture point.

Only a few are important points to relieve this discomfort."

Dr. Gan said he uses acupuncture in about 20% to 30% of the surgeries he's involved with. He said that few patients decline to use adjunctive acupuncture, and when they do it's usually because they have little knowledge of it.

Acupuncture "is becoming increasingly accepted by both physicians and patients," added David P. Martin, MD, an anesthesiologist at the Mayo Clinic in Rochester, Minnesota. He said the technique could be helpful whether it is used to lower morphine doses or other opioid painkillers, or whether it is used to relieve nausea.

He questioned, however, how widely acupuncture could be used during operations because "acupuncture needles tend to get in the way" in crowded operating room conditions.

"For optimum pain control with minimum side effects, opioids plus acupuncture are the way to go and hopefully will become more widely accepted," Dr. Levey added.

info For more information on acupuncture, visit the Web site of the National Center for Complementary and Alternative Medicine at *http://nccam.nih.gov/health/acupuncture.*

Acupuncture May Aid In Vitro Fertilization

Eric Manheimer, MS, research associate, Center for Integrative Medicine, University of Maryland School of Medicine, Baltimore.

Owen K. Davis, MD, co-director and associate professor, Center for Reproductive Medicine and Infertility, Weill Medical College of Cornell University, New York City.

Marshall H. Sager, DO, past president, American Academy of Medical Acupuncture, and acupuncturist, Bala Cynwyd, Pennsylvania.

British Medical Journal, online.

Women undergoing in vitro fertilization can increase their chances of becoming pregnant by up to 65% if they also have acupuncture, a preliminary study suggests.

About 10% to 15% of couples have difficulty conceiving, and many opt for in vitro fertilization (IVF), in which a woman's egg is fertilized in a laboratory and then transferred into her womb. There had been some evidence that acupuncture can increase the success rate of this procedure.

"Complementing the embryo transfer process with acupuncture seems to increase the odds of pregnancy by 65%, compared to sham acupuncture or no adjuvant treatment," said lead researcher Eric Manheimer, a research associate at the University of Maryland School of Medicine's Center for Integrative Medicine.

THE STUDY

Manheimer's team analyzed seven trials that included 1,366 women undergoing IVF. Each trial compared acupuncture given within one day of the embryo transfer, to sham acupuncture or no acupuncture.

The researchers found that women who had acupuncture increased their chances of becoming pregnant by 65% compared with women who had no acupuncture or sham acupuncture.

"This means that 10 women would need to be treated with acupuncture to result in one additional pregnancy," Manheimer said.

However, in studies where pregnancy rates were high, the benefit of acupuncture was small and non-significant, the researchers noted.

IMPLICATION

"Acupuncture may be useful adjuvant treatment in the IVF process," Manheimer said. "However, I think more studies are needed to confirm these findings, because they are still preliminary."

EXPERT REACTION

One reproduction expert cautioned that it's not clear if acupuncture improves the success of IVF. Studies show both that it does and doesn't work.

Owen K. Davis, MD, codirector and associate professor at the Center for Reproductive Medicine and Infertility at Weill Medical College of Cornell University in New York City is hopeful that future studies will support acupuncture's role in boosting pregnancy rates. Dr. Davis thinks a large, randomized study is needed to really answer the question.

"I don't think we can say conclusively that acupuncture is effective or is anywhere near being a standard care, but it's not something I would discourage someone from trying if they wanted to," he said.

One acupuncturist said the study findings bear out his own experience in using acupuncture to increase the success of IVF.

"I'm not surprised by these findings," said Marshall H. Sager, MD, past president of the American Academy of Medical Acupuncture. "I've done acupuncture for infertility and been successful a number of times."

Dr. Sager thinks all women undergoing in vitro fertilization can benefit from acupuncture. "I think you are increasing the chances of success," he said.

info For more information on acupuncture, visit the Web site of the American Academy of Medical Acupuncture, *www.medical acupuncture.org.*

■ ■ ■ ■

The Healing Wisdom of Tai Chi

Tai chi may help prevent shingles and other illnesses related to immunity.

Tai chi, the centuries-old Chinese martial arts practice, incorporates aerobic activity, relaxation and meditation.

It is easy to learn and can be practiced by older adults with physical limitations.

Recent study: People who practiced tai chi showed increased immunity to the virus that causes shingles.

This may be because tai chi decreases levels of the stress hormones that negatively impact immunity.

Bonus: Participants also experienced improved vitality, mental health, muscle strength and balance.

Michael R. Irwin, MD, Norman Cousins Professor, Cousins Center for Psychoneuroimmunology, University of California, Los Angeles, and leader of a study of 112 adults ages 59 to 86, published in *Journal of the American Geriatrics Society.*

Amazing! Massage Eases Pain as Well as Drugs

Daniel B. Hinshaw, MD, professor, surgery, University of Michigan, Ann Arbor and member of the palliative care team, VA Ann Arbor Health Care System.

Susanne Cutshall, RN, clinical nurse specialist, Mayo Clinic, Rochester, Minnesota.

Archives of Surgery.

A 20-minute evening back massage can help relieve the pain and anxiety that often follows major surgery, new research shows. "In patients getting massage, the acute response was equivalent to a [dose] of morphine, which was pretty remarkable," said study senior author Daniel B. Hinshaw, MD, professor of surgery and a member of the palliative care team at the VA Ann Arbor Health Care System in Michigan.

According to Dr. Hinshaw, the idea for the study originated years ago, when he would ask nurses to give elderly patients a massage to augment pain relief medication. "Over the years, I have been concerned about the kind of pain and suffering that surgeons produce," he said. "How could we improve pain relief and reduce suffering?"

THE STUDY

The massage trial included 605 veterans undergoing chest or abdominal surgery, randomly assigned to one of three groups. One group of 203 veterans received standard care, while another 200 got a daily 20-minute back massage. A third group of 202 got 20 minutes of individual attention but no massage. They were asked to quantify their feelings of pain and anxiety on a scale of 1 to 10.

"It's normal for a patient to have peak pain in the first day, which then declines," Dr. Hinshaw noted. But, according to the study, "The rate of decline was faster by about a day for patients in the massage group," he said. Patients also experienced short-term declines in anxiety following massage, the team found.

Dr. Hinshaw's team found no differences in longer-term patient anxiety, length of hospital stay or the amount of pain-relieving medication used among the three groups.

MASSAGE THERAPY OFFERED IN HOSPITALS

Massage will now become part of the post-surgical routine at the Ann Arbor facility and related VA facilities in the region, Dr. Hinshaw said. His group is exploring its use to reduce the incidence and length of delirium experienced after surgery. Delirium, which is difficult to treat, can often lengthen the time spent in the hospital after surgery, he noted.

A similar program of post-surgical massage has been in place at the Mayo Clinic in Rochester, Minnesota, for the past few years, said Susanne Cutshall, a clinical nurse specialist there.

"Ours is for cardiac surgery," Cutshall said. "We have a full-time therapist available. If there is a suggestion of back, shoulder or neck pain, the therapist can come and see them. Patients get a brochure about it before they come here, so they can ask for it."

The Mayo massage program "started about five years ago, when we were looking at pain medication," Cutshall said. "We stopped to listen to what the patients were saying about back, neck and shoulder pain. It seems to be muscular in origin."

A massage session at the Mayo Clinic can last from 20 minutes to 40 minutes, depending on what the patient might need, Cutshall said. "Most people, it helps. It may make the pain a little better, they might sleep better, they might be less anxious."

info For more information on massage therapy, visit the Web site of the Massage Therapy Foundation, *www.massagetherapy foundation.org.*

The Right Rub—How Massage Can Heal

Ben E. Benjamin, PhD, who maintains a private massage practice in Cambridge, Massachusetts. His books include *The Ethics of Touch* (Sohen Moe Associates) and *Exercise Without Injury* (MTI).

A good massage can be much more than just a relaxing treat. Research shows that a number of massage therapies can be used to alleviate various types of pain (such as headache, backache and knee pain), relieve chronic tension and boost immunity.

What you should know about the four most popular types of massage...

SWEDISH

Swedish massage uses a variety of movements, such as long, sweeping strokes as well as kneading strokes over muscles, to help move blood through the body. This increases circulation and gently reduces muscle tension.

Best used for: Mild insomnia, headache, anxiety, stress and muscle tension.

SHIATSU

Shiatsu—Japanese for "finger pressure"—uses acupressure points along pathways in the body (meridians) to move a form of energy known as "qi" (pronounced "chee"). Shiatsu aims to prevent disease with consistent and fluid movements that open channels of energy. Some massage therapists use their elbows, knees and feet in addition to thumb pressure, which may be very light or strong and deep.

Best used for: Headache, insomnia, low back pain, postoperative pain relief and depleted energy.

ORTHOPEDIC

Musculoskeletal pain occurs when a joint, muscle, tendon (tough bundle of fibers that attaches muscle to bone) or ligament (connective tissue that joins two bones at a joint) becomes swollen, inflamed and/or torn.

Even seemingly harmless activities, such as sleeping in an awkward position, bending in an unusual way or sitting at a computer for long periods, can cause the damage.

With orthopedic massage, a therapist uses his/her hands or fingers to end this pain-causing cycle by focusing on adhesive scar tissue that forms in response to the initial damage. Orthopedic massage can be mildly uncomfortable but should not be painful.

Best used for: Low back pain, knee pain, and strained muscles, tendons and ligaments.

MYOFASCIAL RELEASE

The *fascia* is a connective tissue that surrounds muscles, joints, nerves, blood vessels and internal organs. Ordinarily relaxed and pliable, fasciae develop adhesive scar tissue after an injury and become a source of tension.

Myofascial release (also known as deep-tissue work) involves a combination of deep and gentle pressure designed to affect not only the deeper structures of the musculoskeletal system, such as the spine and joints, but also the skin and muscles. To apply the desired pressure, the therapist may use his fingertips, knuckles or elbows.

Best used for: Fatigue, stiffness, recovery from a fall or accident and/or pain from chronic poor posture.

■ **More from Dr. Benjamin...**

Massage—What You Need to Know

Body massage is available at many health clubs and spas as well as medical centers and hospitals. Most massages last 30 to 60 minutes with prices ranging from about $50 to $150 per hour. Health insurance may cover massage therapy with a doctor's referral.

•**Massage is generally considered safe for most people.** However, massage should be avoided by people who have deep vein thrombosis, bleeding disorders, fever, varicose veins, osteoporosis, a recent fracture, open wounds or who have had recent surgery (unless approved by a physician).

Until recently, many medical experts warned cancer patients to avoid massage for fear of stimulating growth or spread of a malignancy. Now, this belief has been debunked and massage is generally considered safe for cancer patients, who often experience energy-boosting and/or stress-relieving benefits, but check with a doctor first. In some cases, it can damage tissue that is fragile due to radiation treatments and/or chemotherapy.

•**When selecting a massage therapist,** choose someone who is licensed by his/her municipality or state and certified by a national certifying agency. These qualifications will ensure that the practitioner has at least 500 hours of training. You can also seek a referral from the American Massage Therapy Association, 877-905-2700, *www.amtamassage.org*...or the Associated Bodywork & Massage Professionals, 800-458-2267, *www.abmp.com*.

11

Nutrition, Diet & Fitness

Women Need More Protein Than Men to Stay in Shape

Keeping yourself in good physical condition is more difficult for older women than men because it's harder for women to replace muscle that's lost naturally as they age, say US and British researchers.

BACKGROUND

Women are at particular risk for muscle mass decline, because they tend to have less muscle and more fat than men in early and middle age, which means they're already closer to the "danger" threshold of becoming frail when they're in their 50s and 60s, the researchers said.

The investigators noted that maintaining muscle is essential in reducing the risk of falls, one of the major causes of premature death in older adults. After age 50, people lose up to 0.4% of muscle mass per year.

THE STUDY

The study of 29 healthy women and men, ages 65 to 80, found that women were less able to use protein to build muscle mass—a key difference in the way women's and men's bodies react to food. This may be due to menopause-related hormone changes in women, said the researchers from the Washington University School of Medicine in St. Louis and The University of Nottingham in England. One possible culprit is estrogen, which is known to be needed to maintain bone mass.

The findings, published in *Public Library of Science One*, seem to fit with preliminary results showing that older women have less muscle-building response to weight training than older men. This difference is not apparent in younger women and men.

IMPLICATIONS

"Nobody has ever discovered any mechanistic differences between men and women in muscle

The University of Nottingham, news release.

217

loss before. This is a significant finding for the maintenance of better health in old age," and reducing demand on health care systems, according to Michael Rennie, a professor of clinical physiology at The University of Nottingham.

The findings of this new study suggest that it's important for older women to consume plenty of protein-rich foods, such as eggs, fish, chicken and lean red meat, and to do resistance training (lifting weights), the researchers said.

"Rather than eating more, older people should focus on eating a higher proportion of protein in their everyday diet. In conjunction with resistance exercise, this should help to reduce the loss of muscle mass over time. There is also a case for the beneficial hormonal effect of limited HRT (hormone replacement therapy), although this has to be balanced against the other risks associated with such treatment," Rennie said.

info For more information on healthy aging for older adults, visit the US Centers for Disease Control and Prevention Web site, *www.cdc.gov/aging*.

Supplement That Boosts Sperm Health

Brenda Eskenazi, PhD, professor, maternal and child health and epidemiology, director of the Center for Children's Environmental Health, School of Public Health, University of California, Berkeley.
Jamie Grifo, MD, PhD, director of reproductive endocrinology, New York University Medical Center, New York City.
Human Reproduction.

The benefits of the B-vitamin folate for women in preventing birth defects are well known, but new research suggests the nutrient also boosts sperm health.

Men with relatively low levels of folate had increased risk for sperm irregularities. Their sperm contained either too few or too many chromosomes, according to researchers at the University of California, Berkeley. These types of deficiencies can cause birth defects and miscarriages, the experts noted.

Folate is found in leafy green vegetables, fruit and beans, chickpeas and lentils. By law, breads and grains sold in the United States are now fortified with folate to help ward off birth defects.

BACKGROUND

"We looked at sperm to find different kinds of genetic abnormalities," said lead researcher Brenda Eskenazi, PhD, a professor of maternal and child health and epidemiology, and director of the Center for Children's Environmental Health at University of California, Berkeley's School of Public Health. "The abnormalities we looked at here were having too few or too many chromosomes," she said.

Human cells usually have two sets of 23 chromosomes. But "in sperm, you normally have one of each. Sometimes there are two and sometimes there are none of a particular chromosome," Dr. Eskenazi said.

If a normal egg was fertilized with one of these abnormal sperm, it could result in a birth defect, such as Down syndrome, Dr. Eskenazi said. "This can also result in an increase in miscarriage," she added.

The researchers looked at three specific chromosomes: X, Y and 21. "We saw an association between [male] folate intake and how many abnormal sperm there were, in terms of the chromosome number for these three different chromosomes," Dr. Eskenazi said.

THE STUDY

Dr. Eskenazi's group analyzed sperm from 89 healthy men. The researchers also asked the men about their daily consumption of zinc, vitamin C, vitamin E and beta-carotene as well as folate.

The researchers found that men who had the highest intake of folate had the lowest incidence of sperm abnormalities. In fact, men who had the highest intake of folate—722 to 1,150 micrograms a day—had a 20% to 30% lower frequency of several types of sperm abnormalities, compared with men who consumed lower amounts of folate.

The study findings are published in the journal *Human Reproduction.*

IMPLICATION

Up until now, birth-defect researchers have typically focused on women's diet in the period around conception, Dr. Eskenazi said. "Based on these data, maybe men, too, need to consider their diet when they are considering fathering a child," she said.

RECOMMENDATION

Although this study doesn't conclusively prove a link between folate and chromosomal abnormality, Dr. Eskenazi advises men who are thinking of becoming fathers to increase their folate intake, perhaps with a supplement or a multivitamin containing folate.

EXPERT REACTION

One expert agrees that healthy eating is linked to having healthy babies—even for men.

"This is another common-sense article that says good nutrition is associated with a better reproductive outcome," said Jamie Grifo, MD, PhD, director of reproductive endocrinology at New York University Medical Center.

info For more information on fertility, visit the Web site of the American Society of Reproductive Medicine, *www.asrm.org*, and select "For Patients."

What Your Doctor Won't Tell You About Nutrition

Lisa Hark, PhD, RD, director of the nutrition education program at the University of Pennsylvania School of Medicine in Philadelphia. She is coeditor, with Darwin Deen, Maryland, of *The Complete Guide to Nutrition in Primary Care*. Blackwell.

If you're like most Americans, you eat very few fruits and vegetables—for optimal health, the latest research calls for nine to 13 servings daily.

This dietary recommendation is linked to lower rates of serious diseases, such as cancer and heart disease, but few Americans learn about this from their doctors.

Why not? The most likely reasons are that few doctors receive training in how to counsel patients on nutrition, and office visits are often rushed. *Issues your doctor may not discuss—or even know about...*

NOT ENOUGH VITAMIN D

Adults age 65 and older have a greater need for dietary sources of vitamin D. In younger adults, most vitamin D is synthesized in the skin following sun exposure. Older adults, however, usually spend less time in the sun. What's more, their ability to synthesize vitamin D from sunshine declines.

A vitamin D deficiency increases the risk for *osteomalacia* (a condition that causes bone and muscle pain). Research shows that older adults who are vitamin D–deficient can improve muscle strength as well as reduce the risk for falls and fractures if they take a vitamin D supplement.

My advice: Get 1,000 international units (IU) of vitamin D-3 (*cholecalciferol*) daily from food and supplements. (Vitamin D-3 is the most potent form.)

Best food sources: Cold-water fish, such as salmon and mackerel, and milk.

Also: Get 10 to 15 minutes of sun exposure daily.

INADEQUATE B-12

A deficiency of vitamin B-12 is common in adults age 50 and older. It's usually due to an age-related decline in the production of gastric acid, necessary for vitamin B-12 absorption. Inadequate levels of vitamin B-12 can cause fatigue, loss of appetite and a form of anemia that, if not treated, leads to nerve damage and dementia.

A deficiency of folic acid (another B vitamin) can result in a similar type of anemia. If you take a folic acid supplement, it will correct the anemia but not if it is also due to a vitamin B-12 deficiency. In that case, your doctor may also prescribe a vitamin B-12 supplement.

My advice: Ask your doctor at least once a year for a blood test known as a complete blood count (CBC) to check for anemia. Specific blood tests to check for B vitamin deficiencies also may be recommended. In addition, tell your doctor about your diet, any supplements you take and your intake of alcohol, which can interfere with the absorption of many vitamins and minerals.

GLUTEN SENSITIVITY

Celiac disease occurs in people who react to *gluten*, a protein in wheat, barley and rye. Even trace amounts of gluten—in a single bite of bread, for example—can trigger the production of inflammatory chemicals, resulting in diarrhea, abdominal pain and/or bloating and other digestive symptoms.

Many celiac sufferers do not have the classic digestive symptoms of the disease. Instead, they may experience fatigue, headaches, and joint and muscle pain—symptoms doctors don't always associate with celiac disease.

My advice: If you have any of these symptoms and haven't been successfully treated, see an allergist or gastroenterologist. Ask about trying an elimination diet, in which all foods that contain gluten are completely avoided for two weeks. If you have celiac disease, symptoms usually will start to improve within that time.

WEIGHT AND WAIST SIZE

Obesity is among the primary modifiable risk factors for high blood pressure, diabetes and many other medical problems. But not all doctors pay adequate attention to this important health issue.

Shocking statistic: In a recent study of 12,835 overweight or obese patients, 58% said that they had never discussed weight with a primary care provider. When doctors do give weight-loss counseling, it *triples* the odds that patients will attempt to lose weight.

My advice: Determine your body mass index (BMI), a commonly used standard that is more closely associated with body fat than is body weight alone.* Aim for a BMI of 18.5 to 24.9 if you're age 65 or younger, and a BMI of 22 to 27 if you're age 66 or older. (A higher BMI is thought to help keep older adults healthy in the event of unintentional weight loss.)

Also, measure your waist circumference by wrapping a tape measure around your body at the midpoint between the tops of your hipbones and your lowest rib. (This point typically is at,

*BMI is calculated by multiplying your weight (in pounds) by 703, then dividing that number by your height (in inches) twice. For a free, on-line BMI calculator, go to the National Heart, Lung and Blood Institute Web site (www.nhlbisupport.com/bmi/).

or just below, the navel.) More than 35 inches in women or 40 inches in men indicates a high proportion of abdominal fat, which greatly increases the risk for heart disease, diabetes and certain types of cancer—even in patients of normal weight.

If you need help losing weight or maintaining weight loss or could benefit from basic dietary advice—ask your doctor for a referral to a registered dietitian.

TV AND DISEASE

Some doctors ask patients how much they exercise but rarely ask how much TV they watch. More than half of American adults watch more than two hours of TV daily—and even more on weekends.

Red flag: People who watch TV for more than two hours daily have an elevated risk for obesity, metabolic syndrome (a constellation of symptoms, including abdominal obesity, low HDL "good" cholesterol and high blood pressure) and cardiovascular disease.

My advice: Limit TV viewing to less than two hours daily—and don't eat while watching TV. Studies show that people tend to eat more while watching TV.

Caution: Even if you don't watch a lot of TV, you can be at higher risk for disease if you have a sedentary lifestyle that involves many hours of sitting while working at a desk or computer, for example.

Eight Great Reasons to Drink More Coffee!

Peter Martin, MD, professor of psychiatry and pharmacology, Vanderbilt University, Nashville, Tennessee.

According to the latest research, coffee is an extremely healthful drink. *Recent studies have found that coffee...*

•**Reduces risk for cardiovascular diseases such as heart attack.**

•**Helps the liver**—reducing risk for liver cancer (by up to 50%, in one study) and protecting against chronic liver disease, such as alcohol-related cirrhosis.

•**Reduces risk for Parkinson's disease** by as much as half.

•**Is the number-one source of antioxidants in the American diet**—ahead of fruits, vegetables, tea, wine and chocolate.

•**Contains a high level of soluble dietary fiber, reducing risk for gallstones** (by up to 25% in one study).

•**Contains elements that are known to help prevent colon cancer.**

•**Reduces soreness in muscles after exercising.**

•**Improves mental ability among seniors.** In one study, people over age 65 who drank coffee 30 minutes before a memory test scored higher than those who did not.

How much to drink: Experts suggest two to four cups a day, but many say there is no need to worry about an upper limit. In general, if you can sleep at night, you are not drinking too much. If you enjoy coffee, drink it.

■ ■ ■ ■

Tea Builds Better Bones

In a study of 1,500 healthy women (ages 70 to 85), hip-bone density was 2.8% higher in those who drank caffeinated or caffeine-free black tea, compared with people who did not drink tea. Tea drinkers consumed an average of three cups daily.

Theory: Flavonoid antioxidants in black tea may stimulate production of new cells that build bone.

Self-defense: Drinking black tea daily may help protect your bones as you age. If your doctor has advised you not to drink caffeine, opt for caffeine-free black tea.

Amanda Devine, PhD, senior lecturer, nutrition program, Edith Cowan University, Joondalup, Australia.

Technique Pulls Carcinogens Out of Fried Potatoes

Society of Chemical Industry, news release.

Soaking potatoes in water before frying cuts down on the formation of the suspected carcinogen *acrylamide*, says a new British study.

According to team leader Rachel Burch, of Leatherhead Food International, there has been much research done by the food industry on ways to reduce acrylamide in processed foods, but less so on foods cooked at home. "We wanted to explore ways of reducing the level of acrylamide in home cooking," she said.

BACKGROUND

Acrylamide is created when starch-rich foods are cooked at high temperatures, through frying, baking, grilling or roasting, according to background information in the study. Some research has suggested that acrylamide, which is found in a wide range of foods, may be harmful to health and may cause cancer in animals.

THE STUDY

Researchers found that simply soaking potatoes in water before frying could significantly reduce the formation of acrylamide and any health risks it may pose.

The researchers tried three different approaches. They washed raw french fries, soaked them for 30 minutes, and soaked them for two hours. This reduced acrylamide levels by up to 23%, 38% and 48%, respectively, when the fries were cooked to a light color.

It's not clear whether the same reductions could be achieved if french fries are cooked to a deep, dark brown, the researchers said.

The study was published in the *Journal of the Science of Food and Agriculture*.

info For more information about acrylamide, visit the World Health Organization's Web site, *www.who.int* and search "acrylamide."

Nutrition, Diet & Fitness

■ ■ ■ ■

Canned Veggies Better Than Fresh!

Canned vegetables can be as nutritious as their fresh counterparts. Vegetables are canned upon harvest, when nutrients are at their peak, so some canned varieties may have even more nutrients.

Best: To get a mix of essential nutrients, choose canned, fresh and frozen vegetables. Opt for low-sodium versions, or rinse canned produce to reduce sodium.

Christine Bruhn, PhD, specialist in the cooperative extension, food science and technology, University of California, Davis, and leader of a study of canned vegetables, published in *Journal of the Science of Food and Agriculture*.

■ ■ ■ ■

Sorry, Popeye—Spinach Isn't a Good Source of Iron

Spinach contains about as much iron as any green vegetable, but it contains *oxalic acid*, which prevents about 90% of the iron from being absorbed. Spinach is high in vitamins A and E, as well as many antioxidants, such as beta-carotene. Good sources of iron are clams, liver and fortified cereals. Also, consuming vitamin C at the same time as iron-rich foods can help increase iron absorption.

Reza Hakkak, PhD, chairman, department of dietetics and nutrition, University of Arkansas for Medical Sciences, Little Rock.

■ ■ ■ ■

Foods You Can Enjoy Even With Diverticular Disease

Researchers analyzed 18 years of dietary data for about 47,000 men, checking for development of complications from diverticulosis, including diverticulitis (infection of a diverticulum, or small pouch that forms in the colon). Consumption of nuts and popcorn—previously thought to aggravate the condition—did not lead to an increase in diverticular complications.

Theory: The anti-inflammatory properties of these foods may explain this effect.

If you have diverticulitis: Discuss your diet with your doctor.

Lisa L. Strate, MD, assistant professor of medicine, University of Washington, Seattle.

■ ■ ■ ■

Hidden Risk for Eye Disease

In an eight-year study of 3,977 people, those who ate the most carbohydrates with a high glycemic index (a measurement of how quickly a food boosts blood sugar levels)—such as cake, cookies and white bread—had a 40% higher risk for macular degeneration (a retinal disease that destroys central vision) than those who ate the least.

Theory: Such foods cause cellular damage to the retina (the light-sensitive membrane in the back of the eye).

Allen Taylor, PhD, director, laboratory for nutrition and vision research, Tufts University, Boston.

Foods That Trigger Deadly Inflammation

Leo Galland, MD, director, Foundation for Integrated Medicine, New York City. His latest book is *The Fat Resistance Diet*. Broadway. *www.fatresistancediet.com*. Dr. Galland is a recipient of the Linus Pauling award.

Most of us associate inflammation with the redness, pain, heat and swelling that accompany an injury or infection. This is part of the normal healing process. However, when the inflammatory process fails to turn itself off when it should, inflammation becomes chronic—and potentially quite damaging.

Chronic inflammation (CI) works slowly and silently at the cellular level.

One cause: Poor diet. This may trigger inflammation, which can impair immunity and contribute to artery damage and *insulin resistance* (the inability of the body's cells to effectively use the hormone *insulin* to regulate

222

blood sugar levels). These factors may increase the risk for heart disease, stroke, diabetes, osteoporosis, cancer and arthritis.

Despite these dangers, many people with CI go undiagnosed, in part because the symptoms are vague. Many doctors, not yet fully aware of CI, might not suspect inflammation. Only a blood test can confirm its presence. The best is the *high-sensitivity C-reactive protein* (hs-CRP) screening test, which detects levels of CRP, a marker for inflammation in the bloodstream. Health insurance often covers the cost.

WHAT NOT TO EAT

Avoid eating these common foods that produce inflammation…

•**Trans fats.** Trans fats are created by adding hydrogen to vegetable oil (a process called hydrogenation). Consuming trans fats may damage cells that line blood vessels, causing inflammation.

To do: Check labels and avoid foods with hydrogenated or partially hydrogenated vegetable oil (or aliases, such as shortening or margarine). Most commercial baked goods, such as cookies and crackers, and many fried foods contain such trans fats.

•**Omega-6 fatty acids.** Needed for good health, omega-6s are found naturally in meats, poultry, shellfish, milk, eggs, vegetable oils and some seeds. They are harmful only when eaten out of proportion to omega-3s, another essential fatty acid. A good ratio of omega-6s to omega-3s is three to one. The typical American diet has a ratio of up to 20 to one—which allows omega-6s to crowd out omega-3s, changing the body's metabolic processes and creating inflammatory chemicals.

To do: Boost your intake of foods rich in omega-3s.

•**Processed sugar.** Table sugar, candy, soft drinks and other sweets contribute to insulin resistance and extra pounds, both of which increase inflammation.

To do: Satisfy your sweet tooth with a wide variety of fruits.

Note: If you have diabetes, talk to your doctor before increasing fruit intake.

INFLAMMATION FIGHTERS

Work these into your diet…

•**Flavonoids.** These natural antioxidants (nutrients that neutralize harmful molecules called free radicals) inhibit inflammatory enzymes. They are prevalent in foods whose natural pigments give them a deep yellow to deep purple color—primarily fruits and vegetables.

To do: Aim for nine daily servings of intensely colored fruits and veggies a day, such as plums, eggplant (with skin) and red onions. Add unsweetened concentrated fruit juices (blueberry, pomegranate) to salad dressings and marinades.

•**Carotenoids.** These antioxidants are found primarily in produce that is yellow, orange or red. Particularly beneficial are carrots and tomatoes. Some green vegetables, such as spinach and broccoli, also are rich in carotenoids.

To do: Use a bit of olive oil or walnut oil to make salad dressing or sauté vegetables. The oil improves absorption of carotenoids by the intestine.

•**Omega-3s.** These fatty acids contain a potent inflammation-fighting component called *eicosapentaenoic acid* (EPA). Omega-3s are found in flaxseeds and flaxseed oil, walnuts, navy and kidney beans and leafy green vegetables. Fish is an excellent source, too.

To do: Increase your intake of the omega-3–rich foods above. Also, eat at least 12 ounces of fish a week, choosing types rich in omega-3s and relatively low in mercury—anchovies, conch, herring (fresh or pickled, not creamed), mackerel, salmon, sardines and sturgeon.

•**Fiber.** The more dietary fiber a person consumes, the lower her CRP levels tend to be. Best sources include beans, whole grains and vegetables.

To do: Go beyond your typical high-fiber favorites and try something new—whole-wheat pasta, bulgur (made from parboiled wheat grains), Swiss chard, yams.

•**Herbs and spices.** Garlic, onions, chives, ginger, turmeric, basil, parsley and cinnamon enhance the flavor of foods and also have anti-inflammatory properties.

To do: Use herbs and spices daily.

Healthful combination: Turmeric (a good source of flavonoids) plus black pepper, which increases turmeric's absorption.

The Food That Lowers Cholesterol 24%... In Just Five Weeks

Andrea Chernus, MS, RD, a registered dietitian, certified diabetes educator and exercise physiologist who maintains a private practice in New York City. She counsels patients on high cholesterol, diabetes, weight management and sports nutrition. She was formerly clinical nutritionist for Columbia University, New York City. *www. nutritionhandouts.com.*

If you're one of the millions of Americans with high cholesterol, chances are your doctor has told you what not to eat—high-fat meats and dairy, for example. But certain foods actually can lower your cholesterol and, in some cases, eliminate the need for cholesterol-lowering drugs. Regular intake of these foods can have a particularly powerful effect on reducing LDL—the "bad" cholesterol that damages arteries and other blood vessels. High LDL levels are associated with an increased risk for heart attack and stroke.

OAT BRAN, BARLEY AND MORE

Soluble fiber is present in plant-based foods in the form of gums and pectins. The National Cholesterol Education Program Adult Treatment Panel states that 5 to 10 grams (g) of soluble fiber daily can help to lower LDL by 5%.

A specific type of soluble fiber—*beta-glucan* (found in oat bran and barley)—has an even more potent cholesterol-lowering effect...

•**In a 2004 study, men eating 6 g of soluble fiber from barley per day** lowered their LDL cholesterol by an average of 24% in five weeks.

•**In a study published earlier this year, men given 6 g of beta-glucan in a fortified bread**—who also were following a low-fat diet and walking 60 minutes per day—experienced an average reduction in LDL cholesterol of 28%.

How it works: In the intestines, soluble fiber attaches itself to cholesterol and bile acids. Bile acids help with fat digestion. They are made from cholesterol, so when the body needs to make more bile acids, it pulls cholesterol from the bloodstream. The process of binding soluble fiber to bile acids forces the body to make more bile and use up cholesterol from the body's supply. Because fiber is not digested, it carries the cholesterol and bile acids out of the body, lowering the body's cholesterol.

Best sources of soluble fiber: Oat bran, oatmeal, barley, apples, citrus fruits, pears, kidney and lima beans, carrots, broccoli and brussels sprouts. Psyllium seed husks also are a good source and are found in some cereals, such as Kellogg's All-Bran Buds cereal.

Hot cereal made of 100% oat bran has about 3 g of soluble fiber per serving...plain oatmeal has about 2 g. Most cold oat-based cereals have one gram. Fruits and vegetables have 0.5 g to 1 g of soluble fiber per serving.

Beware: Commercially prepared muffins, pretzels and breads made with oat bran may not contain much soluble fiber. Also, some may be high in saturated or trans fats, sugars and sodium. As a rough guide, check the label to make sure oat bran is one of the first ingredients listed on the food label. (Soluble fiber does not have to be listed separately from total fiber.)

PLANT STEROLS AND STANOLS

Plant sterols (*phytosterols*) and plant stanols (*phytostanols*) are substances that block absorption of cholesterol. They are particularly high in vegetable oils and, to a lesser degree, in fruits, vegetables, nuts and seeds. More than 25 studies have proved their effectiveness in cholesterol reduction. *Examples...*

•**In a 2001 study, 155 adults with high cholesterol took in 1.5 g per day of plant sterols from margarine.** After six months, they had an average reduction in LDL cholesterol of 11% (and 9% reduction in total cholesterol).

•**In another study, 72 adults with high cholesterol took in 2 g per day of plant**

sterols from phytosterol-fortified orange juice. After eight weeks, their average reduction in LDL cholesterol was 12% (7% reduction in total cholesterol).

How they work: Plant sterols and stanols help block the absorption of dietary cholesterol and the reabsorption of cholesterol back into our intestinal tract. They compete with cholesterol for incorporation into mixed *micelles*, which are composite molecules that contain both water- and fat-soluble substances. In the body, micelles are used to carry fats through the bloodstream. When cholesterol is blocked from being absorbed and incorporated into these molecules, it is excreted from the body.

Best sources: To get a cholesterol-lowering dose from ordinary food, you would have to eat hundreds of calories worth of oils per day or bushels of fruits and vegetables. But researchers have isolated plant sterols and stanols, and food companies have incorporated them into "functional foods."

Until recently, only certain margarines contained these cholesterol-lowering ingredients, but food companies now have put them into lower-fat foods, such as yogurts, juices, breads and more. A dose of 2 g to 3 g of plant sterols and stanols per day has the greatest impact on lowering LDL cholesterol, reducing it by 6% to 15%. Higher doses of sterols and stanols are not more effective.

Foods containing effective amounts of plant sterols and stanols include Promise, Benecol and Take Control margarines…Minute Maid Heartwise Orange Juice…Nature Valley Healthy Heart Granola Bars…Hain Celestial Rice Dream beverage…Lifetime low-fat cheese…Orowheat whole-grain bread…and VitaMuffins.

The FDA now allows foods containing sterols and stanols that meet certain criteria to put a health claim on the label that they can help reduce the risk of coronary heart disease.

Beware: Margarines and juices are dense in calories. Check food labels to see how much you need to eat to obtain 2 g to 3 g of sterols and stanols.

If you're worried about calories, you can take sterol/stanol supplements. Generally, they are called beta-sitosterol or sitostanol. It is safe to use these supplements along with statin drugs for an additional cholesterol-lowering effect.

NUTS

People who are trying to lower cholesterol levels often eliminate nuts from their diets because nuts are high in fat and calories. But nuts contain mostly monounsaturated fats, which, when substituted for the saturated fats found in high-fat meats and dairy, not only can lower LDL levels but also boost HDL "good" cholesterol levels.

Studies have shown the greatest effect when nuts comprise 20% of one's total calories, which typically amounts to 1.5 to 3.5 ounces of nuts daily (about one-quarter to one-half cup).

On average, LDL cholesterol levels fall 8% to 12% when walnuts or almonds are substituted for saturated fats. HDL levels may increase by 9% to 20%. Other nuts, such as peanuts (technically a legume), pistachios and pecans, have been shown to lower cholesterol, but fewer studies are available on these varieties.

How they work: The exact mechanism of nuts' healthful effects hasn't been discovered yet, but nuts contain a combination of plant sterols, fiber and healthy fats.

Beware: Because nuts are high in calories, the trick is to substitute nuts for less healthful, high-fat foods, including cheese and meat.

■ ■ ■ ■

Lower Cholesterol with Soy Nuts

Women who substituted soy nuts (dry-roasted soybeans) for red meat for eight weeks had a 9.5% decrease in LDL (bad) cholesterol, reducing risk for cardiovascular disease, and a 5.1% decrease in blood sugar levels, lowering risk for diabetes, according to a recent study. These risk factors also improved when women substituted textured soy protein (imitation meat made from soy) for red meat.

Leila Azadbakht, PhD, department of nutrition, School of Health, Isfahan University of Medical Sciences, Isfahan, Iran, and leader of a study of postmenopausal women on the Dietary Approaches to Stop Hypertension (DASH) diet, published in *The American Journal of Clinical Nutrition*.

Important Fiber Facts Update

Len Marquart, PhD, RD, an assistant professor in the department of food science and nutrition at the University of Minnesota in St. Paul. He is coeditor of *Whole Grains and Health*. Blackwell.

The health benefits of dietary fiber have been so highly touted that few people know where the scientific evidence ends and the hype begins.

What you may not know: Scientists who have studied the link between fiber (in both foods and supplements) and health have sometimes found only modest benefits—or no benefits at all.

Reason: To get the optimal benefits of fiber, it must be combined with other healthful substances, such as the antioxidants, vitamins and minerals found in fiber-rich plant foods, including fruits, vegetables and whole grains.

That's why fiber supplements, in the form of powders, tablets and capsules, provide little overall health benefits, other than promoting bowel regularity.

Other important facts…

TYPES OF FIBER

Fiber has long been divided into two main categories…

•**Soluble fiber,** which dissolves in liquid, is found in such foods as oats, beans, psyllium (a plant-derived product) and citrus fruits.

•**Insoluble fiber,** which does not dissolve in liquid, is mainly found in grain products, such as whole wheat…most nuts…and vegetables, such as beets, brussels sprouts and cauliflower.

Now: The National Academy of Sciences discourages the use of the terms "soluble" and "insoluble"—partly because distinctions between the two types of fiber and their physiological effects aren't as clear-cut as scientists once thought. What's more, researchers have discovered subtypes of fiber, including beta glucan and arabinoxylan, both of which show promise for lowering both total and LDL "bad" cholesterol and reducing the risk for coronary artery disease.

DISEASE PREVENTION

Even though soluble fiber and insoluble fiber have different chemical properties and effects in the body, they both provide similar health benefits, such as reducing the risk for heart disease.

The latest research shows that everyone should get a mix of different fibers daily. Unfortunately, the average American's total daily fiber consumption is only about 15 g (the equivalent of one medium apple and one cup each of raspberries and cooked oatmeal). The recommended daily amount is 38 g for men up to age 50…and 30 g at age 51 or older. For women, it's 25 g up to age 50…21 g at age 51 and older.

Because the optimal mix of the different fibers has not been determined, all adults should eat a wide variety of foods that contain both soluble and insoluble fibers, such as grains, fruits and vegetables, including beans. *Latest research on fiber's health effects…*

•**Colon cancer.** In theory, fiber *should* prevent colon cancer by speeding the elimination of stools. The faster that stools—and the bile acids and other potential carcinogens that are present in stools—exit the intestines, the less risk of cell damage that can lead to cancer.

Scientific evidence: The research on the effects of dietary fiber on colon cancer and polyps (growths that often turn into cancer) is mixed. Some studies have shown no benefit—although it's possible that the levels of fiber in these studies, and the length of time the studies were conducted, may have been insufficient.

New theory: As fiber is broken down by bacteria in the colon, it creates substances called *butyrates*—short-chain fatty acids that "bathe" cells in the colon and are thought to reduce cancer risk.

Helpful: Eat at least five servings daily of fruits and vegetables, including several servings of legumes, such as pinto beans.

•**Constipation and other digestive problems.** Fiber not only decreases the time it takes for stools to exit the body (transit time), it also absorbs water in the colon, which increases the weight and size of stools, making them softer and easier to eliminate.

Scientific evidence: Researchers agree that people who consume the recommended daily

226

amount of fiber are far less likely to suffer from constipation than those who eat less. Fiber also reduces the constipation and diarrhea that can accompany irritable bowel syndrome.

Helpful: Eat three to six servings daily of high-fiber foods, such as bran cereals, whole-grain breads, brown rice, barley and whole-wheat pasta.

•**Diabetes.** There's very strong evidence that a high-fiber diet—particularly the fiber in whole grains—both reduces the risk of developing diabetes and improves insulin control in those who already have diabetes.

Scientific evidence: Research shows that people who eat the most whole grains (three servings daily) can reduce their risk of developing diabetes by 26%, compared with those who eat the least (less than one serving daily).

Helpful: Eat three to four servings daily of whole grains, such as brown rice, whole-grain crackers or bread. Grains that have been processed, such as those used in white rice and white bread, don't have the same benefits.

•**Heart disease.** Whole grains may promote blood vessel health and are rich in antioxidants, which may inhibit cellular damage. Whole oats and barley are rich in soluble fiber, including beta-glucans that help control levels of LDL cholesterol. The fiber binds to bile acids and pulls cholesterol out of the intestines and bloodstream. It's also thought to lower blood sugar and improve insulin sensitivity (the body's response to insulin)—both of which reduce the risk for heart disease.

Scientific evidence: People who eat whole grains and whole-grain breakfast cereals can reduce their risk for heart disease by 35% or more. Other studies have shown that the fiber in oat cereals can lower blood cholesterol by 5%, which results in about a 10% reduction in heart disease risk.

Helpful: Eat three servings daily of whole grains, such as oats and/or barley.

•**Obesity.** Fiber not only absorbs water in the stomach but also promotes a feeling of fullness (satiety)—causing people to consume fewer calories overall. High-fiber foods also appear to increase the body's production of cholecystokinin (CCK), a hormone involved in appetite control.

Scientific evidence: Studies at Harvard have shown that people who consume the most fiber are less likely to gain weight than those who get lower amounts. In one study, women with the greatest increase in fiber intake over 12 years had a 49% lower risk for major weight gain than did women with the lowest increase. An eight-year study of men found that for every 40 g per day of whole-grain and cereal fiber consumed, weight gain dropped by about one pound.

Helpful: Eat at least five servings daily of vegetables (including beans)…three servings of whole grains (including cereals, bread and brown rice)…and about four servings of fruits.

■ ■ ■ ■

Can Flaxseeds Prevent Heart Disease?

Claims that flaxseeds can prevent heart disease and cancer are not yet proven. But like other seeds and nuts, flaxseeds contain many healthful components, including lignan, which may have antioxidant properties, as well as fiber. Flaxseed oil contains omega-3 fatty acids, which may lower total cholesterol levels and LDL ("bad") cholesterol.

How to use flaxseeds: Grind flaxseeds in a coffee grinder. If you eat them whole, flaxseeds may pass through your body undigested and you won't benefit as much. Sprinkle ground flaxseeds on hot or cold breakfast cereals…stir a few tablespoons into muffin, cookie, waffle or pancake batter. Or use them to replace eggs in recipes—whip one tablespoon of finely ground flaxseeds with one-quarter cup of water to replace one whole egg.

Caution: Flaxseeds are high in fiber, so if you add flaxseeds to your diet, be sure to drink plenty of fluids to maintain normal bowel function. High doses of flaxseed oil from supplements are not recommended—they have no proven benefit and could interfere with some medications.

Suzanne Havala Hobbs, DrPH, RD, clinical assistant professor, department of health policy and administration, University of North Carolina, Chapel Hill.

Outrageous! Antacids Make Digestion Problems Worse

Andrew L. Rubman, ND, director, Southbury Clinic for Traditional Medicines, Southbury, Connecticut, *www.naturopath.org*. Dr. Rubman is contributing editor to the free E-letter *Bottom Line's Daily Health News* (*www.bottomlinesecrets.com*).

Healthy digestion is at the core of wellness—the nutrients in your food fuel your body and help build strong defenses against illness. But what is the key to healthy digestion? Believe it or not—despite all those TV ads you see about heartburn pills that "fight stomach acid"—it's *stomach acid* that you really need for healthy digestion.

What makes having acid in your stomach a good thing? Many of your body's digestive enzymes won't work properly unless they're in an acidic environment—and if your enzymes aren't working well, your digestion isn't working well either.

ENZYME BASICS

Enzymes are natural chemicals manufactured by the body and present in many foods to make some kind of chemical reaction happen faster. Digestive enzymes work by breaking down the chemical bonds in your food and releasing the nutrients so you can absorb them. Without the enzymes, proper digestion doesn't happen. *Three major types...*

•**Proteolytic enzymes digest proteins.** The major proteolytic enzyme is pepsin, which breaks down the complex bonds in protein like a rock crusher.

•**Lipolytic enzymes digest fats.** Lipase is a major enzyme in this category.

•**Amylolytic enzymes digest carbohydrates.** Amylase, a major enzyme in this category, is primarily found in saliva, where it starts digesting as soon as you start chewing.

In your stomach, pepsin is the primary digestive enzyme—the others play a much bigger role later, when the food moves on to your small intestine. You make pepsin in your stomach lining, but it starts out in a preliminary form called pepsinogen.

The acid connection: Only when pepsinogen encounters sufficient stomach acid does it get converted to pepsin so it can do its job. Not enough acid in your stomach can prevent you from digesting protein, or anything else, well.

NOT ENOUGH STOMACH ACID

Another naturally occurring and vital substance in the stomach is hydrochloric acid. By the time most people hit age 40, they no longer make as much hydrochloric acid as they used to. By then, most people aren't making enough to trigger proper pepsin production, and digestion and nutrient absorption begin to suffer. Low stomach acid can lead to trouble with gas and heartburn from incomplete breakdown of protein and other nutrients in the stomach.

The B connection: Animal protein is most people's major dietary source of B vitamins. When you don't digest it well, the B's aren't released to be absorbed—so you can start to run low on these vitamins. Serious consequences include anemia, poor healing, low resistance to illness and memory problems that can even resemble dementia.

Stomach acid production continues to drop gradually with stress and as you get older, to the point where many elderly people produce far less than they need for good nutrition.

What can you do to restore a good level of stomach acidity? My recommendations fall into two areas—better eating habits and acid-producing supplements.

EATING AND ENZYMES

How and what you eat has a lot to do with how well you digest it. *Some simple changes in the way you eat that can have a big positive effect...*

•**Chew more.** Digestion begins with your mouth. Chewing coats your food with saliva, which contains carbohydrate-digesting amylase. Chewing also breaks your food down into small pieces for better digestion.

What to do: Chew your food thoroughly. Consciously spend a little time on each mouthful.

Bonus: You'll enjoy your food more, feel more satisfied, and you'll probably eat less. If you need to lose weight, this is a painless way to do it—while improving your digestion at the same time.

•**Drink less.** Cut back on the liquids you drink while consuming a meal. When you chase your bites with sips, you dilute the acid in your stomach, and the enzymes themselves, which keeps them from working as well.

What to do: Limit the amount you drink during a meal. Skip sodas and drinks with caffeine. Sodas cause gassiness, and caffeine slows down your digestion of carbohydrates. Stick to plain water, a half hour after you finish eating.

•**Combine your foods carefully.** Different foods need different amounts of time to be fully digested. Simple carbohydrates, such as bread, pasta, rice, potatoes and sugary foods, are digested quickly. Complex carbohydrates—such as whole grains, beans and nuts—as well as proteins and fats, take longer. When you combine simple carbs with these complex foods, your stomach can empty too slowly, promoting fermentation (and growth of yeast) from improper carbohydrate digestion.

What to do: Eat *small* amounts of simple carbs along with more complex foods.

Example: Have only a small portion of French fries along with a steak and salad. Skip prepared desserts completely. For a sweet treat, have fresh fruit—but fruit is sugary, so wait at least an hour after finishing your meal or eat it a half hour before.

ENZYME SUPPLEMENTS

Even with dietary changes, if you're older than age 40, you're probably not making enough stomach acid for good digestion, and are likely to experience such symptoms as increased irregularity and intestinal gas. *I often prescribe the following effective, safe supplements to help restore healthy stomach acid levels...*

•**Betaine HCL.** This generic supplement (available at health food stores) works well to turn on the acid switch in your stomach. A 500-milligram dose just before each meal is often prescribed.

•**DuoZyme.** This combination supplement (available only through a health care practitioner) contains betaine HCL, pepsin and other enzymes that help increase stomach acid, combined with additional enzymes that help later in the digestive process.

•**Gastri-Gest.** Another combination supplement (available only through a health care practitioner), but made with plant-derived enzymes, Gastri-Gest helps increase stomach acid and also helps in the later phase of digestion.

Digestive enzymes can be helpful to nearly anyone older than age 40, particularly those who experience acid stomach, mild nausea, gas, irregularity and other digestive upsets. Often betaine HCL is prescribed for a few weeks. If symptoms still persist, DuoZyme or Gastri-Gest may follow. Both can help, but some people respond better to one or the other. Vegetarians and vegans will prefer Gastri-Gest, which doesn't contain animal products.

You'll probably need to take the supplements for a few weeks before you notice improvement. Digestive enzymes are generally very safe. But to avoid possible interactions, don't take them if you're taking an antibiotic or medication for an ulcer or other digestive problem, such as Crohn's disease. As with all medication, inform your doctor or other prescriber and follow his/her directions.

Intestines: Your Secret Weapon for Better Health

Gary B. Huffnagle, PhD, professor of internal medicine, microbiology and immunology at the University of Michigan Medical School in Ann Arbor. His research on probiotics has appeared in leading scientific journals. He is also the author of *The Probiotics Revolution.* Bantam.

The small and large intestines (gut) do most of the work involved in digesting the 20 tons of food that the average person consumes in a lifetime. This process involves trillions of bacteria—some of them harmful and others beneficial.

What you may not know: While the gut is most commonly associated with digestion, it's estimated that at least 60% of a person's immune system is located there. "Good" bacteria protect against the growth of harmful bacteria to help prevent infections, such as vaginal yeast infections and urinary tract infections.

Probiotic bacteria (a subset of good bacteria) also secrete substances that act on intestinal muscles and help regulate motility (the intestinal contractions that move food and waste through the intestine at the proper rate).

Because these good bacteria play a key role in preventing infections as well as keeping the digestive system functioning properly, "probiotics"—dietary supplements or foods that contain beneficial bacteria or yeasts similar to those found in the human gut—have become increasingly popular, particularly among people who take antibiotics.

Reason: Antibiotics kill not only harmful microorganisms that cause disease, but also the body's beneficial bacteria, sometimes leading to gas, cramping and such conditions as diarrhea. People who take antibiotics regularly may have permanent reductions in probiotic organisms unless they replenish the body's natural supply. For most people, the occasional use of antibiotics—such as a 10-day course—is unlikely to cause lasting problems.

WHEN SUPPLEMENTS HELP

Probiotics are live microorganisms. Two of the most beneficial types of probiotics—*Lactobacilli* and *Bifida* organisms—thrive in the naturally acidic environments of the stomach and small intestine.

Probiotics are often recommended for digestion (to help reduce such problems as gas, bloating, constipation and diarrhea), but they appear to be equally important—if not more so—for the immune system.

Probiotics in the intestine stimulate production of white blood cells known as regulatory *T cells*, which help fight inflammation associated with such disorders as eczema, seasonal allergies and inflammatory bowel disease (IBD), a condition in which the bowel becomes inflamed, often resulting in abdominal cramps and diarrhea.

Probiotics also help prevent and treat diarrhea related to *Clostridium difficile* infection.

There are many dozens of species of probiotic organisms. The most reliable probiotic formulations now available in the US are in capsule form. Most probiotic capsules should be refrigerated.

Two highly effective products are used primarily for digestive problems. *Use the one that most closely matches your symptoms...* *

• **Culturelle.** Studies over the past 30 years have shown that *Lactobacillus rhamnosus GG* (the active organism in this product) reduces the severity and duration of traveler's diarrhea, as well as diarrhea associated with antibiotic therapy.

Typical dose: One to two daily supplements (each containing 30 billion organisms), taken at the onset of diarrhea. Continue for one week after symptoms stop. To prevent antibiotic-related diarrhea, take the supplements during antibiotic therapy and for at least one week afterward.

Important: To ensure optimal effectiveness of the antibiotic, do not take it at the same time of day you are taking the probiotic.

• **Align** contains *Bifidobacterium infantis* 35624, an organism shown in studies to decrease symptoms of irritable bowel syndrome (IBS), a condition that causes diarrhea and/or constipation and other digestive problems.

Typical dose: One capsule (containing one billion live organisms) daily—taken indefinitely if symptoms are ongoing. If the bowel symptoms are associated with stomach flu, take the probiotic supplement during symptoms and continue for one week after they subside.

IMMUNE-BOOSTING BENEFITS

To ensure that your immune system is working at its best, it's a good idea to take probiotic supplements and/or to eat foods containing probiotics daily even if you don't have a particular condition that you're trying to treat.

To boost immunity, look for probiotic supplements and foods that contain the bacterium *Lactobacillus casei* or several probiotic bacteria strains.

My favorite multistrain supplements are Jarro-Dophilus EPS and Theralac. Follow the dosage instructions on the label.

Helpful: Probiotics are stimulated by soluble dietary fiber, so they're more likely to proliferate in the intestine when you also eat complex carbohydrates, such as legumes, vegetables and

*If you have an immune deficiency, talk to your doctor before taking probiotics.

whole grains. These foods contain "*pre*biotics," which provide the nutrition that probiotics need to multiply.

PROBIOTIC FOODS

In the last few years, food manufacturers have begun to promote probiotic-enriched foods, such as the low-fat yogurt Activia and the probiotic dairy drink DanActive (both by Dannon). These products contain the well-researched probiotic bacteria *Bifidobacterium animalis* and *L. casei*, respectively.

When these foods are bought in a grocery store and analyzed in a laboratory, they consistently contain about the same number of active organisms as listed on the labels.

Other probiotic food products...

•**Yogurt.**

Best choices: Foods with the "live and active cultures" seal from the National Yogurt Association. These products must contain 100 million live bacteria per gram at the time of their manufacture.

•**Aged cheeses,** such as cheddar or blue cheese, typically contain three billion to 10 billion organisms per serving. Generally, the longer amount of time a cheese is aged, the higher the probiotic load.

•**Kefir,** a type of fermented milk, usually has at least three billion organisms per serving.

Caution: Aged cheeses and kefir should be avoided by people who have food sensitivities to milk products.

Vitamin K—Why You May Need More Now

Sarah Booth, PhD, director of the Vitamin K Laboratory at the Jean Mayer USDA Human Nutrition and Research Center on Aging and a professor at the Gerald J. and Dorothy R. Friedman School of Nutrition Science and Policy, both at Tufts University in Boston. Dr. Booth has led or participated in more than 50 scientific studies on vitamin K.

V itamin K is the first nutritional supplement that most Americans ever receive. That's because newborns routinely get a shot of the nutrient—which is crucial for *co-agulation* (blood clotting)—to help prevent a severe and sometimes fatal bleeding disorder.

Discovered by a Danish scientist in 1934, the vitamin was dubbed "K" for "Koagulation" (the Danish spelling). But it wasn't until years later that scientists figured out *how* it works—by helping the liver manufacture several proteins that control blood clotting.

Latest development: Researchers are now discovering that vitamin K provides a wide variety of health benefits that extend well beyond blood clotting.

VITAMIN K FOR BETTER HEALTH

Vitamins C and E tend to get the most media attention, but recent findings on vitamin K's ability to help curb the development and/or progression of certain common medical ailments are worth noting. *Examples...*

•**Arthritis.** Research shows that low dietary intake of vitamin K may play a role in the development of osteoarthritis.

Scientific evidence: In a study published in the April 2006 issue of the journal *Arthritis & Rheumatism*, higher blood levels of dietary vitamin K were associated with a lower risk for osteoarthritis of the hand and knee.

•**Heart disease.** Vitamin K aids the function of the biochemical *matrix Gla-protein*, which helps prevent calcium buildup in plaque-filled arteries.

Scientific evidence: Researchers in the Netherlands studied more than 4,800 people over age 55. Compared with those with the lowest intake of vitamin K, those with the highest intake were 52% less likely to have severe calcification of the aorta, the major artery leading from the heart. The participants were 57% less likely to die of heart disease.

•**Liver cancer.** Cirrhosis of the liver, which occurs when alcoholism or infection with the hepatitis B or C virus results in scarred, abnormal liver tissue, can lead to liver cancer.

Scientific evidence: Studies of animal and human cells show that vitamin K may help control the progression of liver cancer. For example, in a study published in the *Journal of the American Medical Association*, Japanese researchers divided 40 women with viral cirrhosis of the liver into two groups. One group received vitamin K daily...the other did not. Two of the women in the vitamin K group developed liver cancer, compared with nine in the non-vitamin K group. Statistically, vitamin K lowered the risk for liver cancer by 80%.

• **Osteoporosis.** Vitamin K aids in the formation of *osteocalcin* (a protein that helps calcium bind to bone). This bone-strengthening process may help prevent and/or treat osteoporosis, the brittle-bone disease that afflicts more than 10 million older Americans—80% of them women.

Scientific evidence: Scientists at Harvard Medical School analyzed data on vitamin K intake and bone health in more than 70,000 women. Those with the highest dietary intake of vitamin K had a 30% decreased risk for hip fracture compared with those who had the lowest intake. Other studies show similar results for men.

In England, researchers analyzed data from 13 Japanese clinical trials that used large, pharmacological doses of vitamin K to treat osteoporosis. Overall, the vitamin reduced the rate of spinal fractures by 40% and hip fractures by 13%.

Latest development: Scientists at the University of Toronto, Tufts University and the University of Wisconsin have completed three clinical trials to determine whether nutritional doses of vitamin K can prevent bone loss in postmenopausal women. It is likely that researchers will present or publish their results within 12 months.*

ARE YOU GETTING ENOUGH?

The US government's recommended daily intake for vitamin K is 90 micrograms (mcg) for adult women...and 120 mcg for adult men. That level is high enough to prevent vitamin K deficiency, a rare condition that can lead to impaired blood clotting.

But is it high enough to keep your blood, bones and heart healthy? That's a question nutritional scientists are asking—but haven't yet answered.

However, scientists *do* know an easy, natural way to maximize your intake of vitamin K. It comes down to the classic maternal advice—eat your vegetables.

*To stay abreast of this research, go to the National Institutes of Health Web site, *www.clinicaltrials.gov.*

Green vegetables—leafy and otherwise—are among the best dietary sources of vitamin K.

Don't have a taste for kale or spinach? Don't worry. One-half cup of broccoli sautéed in olive oil gives you plenty of vitamin K. Or try a lettuce salad (using any type except iceberg) with a teaspoon of salad dressing that contains vegetable oil (some fat is needed for absorption of vitamin K). And don't worry about cooking—it doesn't destroy the vitamin.

Among vegetable oils, the richest sources of vitamin K (per two-tablespoon serving) are soybean oil (50 mcg) and olive oil (13 mcg).

Another good source of vitamin K: Mayonnaise (23 mcg).

Should you take a vitamin K supplement? Scientists don't have enough data at this point to recommend a dietary supplement of this nutrient for healthy adults.

IF YOU TAKE WARFARIN

Warfarin (Coumadin and Jantoven) is a widely used blood-thinning medication given to people who have had or are likely to develop an artery-blocking blood clot. Warfarin is often prescribed following a heart attack, stroke, blood clot in the leg (deep vein thrombosis) or a clot that has traveled to the lung (pulmonary embolism). The drug is also used in people who have an irregular heart rhythm (atrial fibrillation) or an artificial heart valve.

Warfarin works by decreasing the activity of vitamin K.

If you take warfarin: Don't eat dark, leafy green vegetables. The amount of vitamin K in these foods can vary threefold, depending on where they're grown. For example, a serving of spinach could contain 200 mcg of vitamin K...or 600 mcg. That's a significant difference in vitamin K intake for someone taking warfarin, who should not have large fluctuations in intake of this vitamin.

Instead, eat three daily servings of vitamin K–rich foods with lower but predictable amounts of the nutrient. That could include one-half cup of broccoli, one-half cup of green peas or six ounces of tomato juice. Other good choices of foods that contain relatively low amounts of vitamin K include asparagus and green beans.

To help determine the dose of warfarin that prevents blood cots from forming, doctors test the coagulation time—a measurement known as the International Normalized Ratio and Pro-thrombin Time (INR/PT). INR/PT is checked monthly, and the patient is instructed to main-tain a consistent dietary intake of vitamin K to avoid altering the effectiveness of warfarin.

info For more information on nutrients in food, visit the National Agricultural Li-brary at the US Department of Agriculture Web site, *www.nal.usda.gov*, and type the nu-trient name into the search box.

The Miraculous Healing Power of Nuts

Joy Bauer, RD, nutrition expert for *The Today Show* and Yahoo.com, with offices in New York City and West-chester, New York. She is a weight-loss columnist for *Self* magazine and coauthor, with Carol Svec, of *Joy Bauer's Food Cures*. Rodale. *www.joybauernutrition.com*.

Nuts are among the most healthful foods you can eat. Rich in nutrients, they can help prevent some of the most common —and most serious—diseases.

Example: In a long-running health study conducted by researchers at Loma Linda Uni-versity, participants were asked what foods they ate most often. Those who ate nuts five or more times a week were about 50% less likely to have a heart attack than those who ate them less than once a week.

FORGET THE FAT

Many Americans avoid nuts because they want to cut back on fat and calories. It's true that a single serving of nuts can have 20 grams (g) or more of fat and 180 to 200 calories, but most of the fats are healthful fats, such as omega-3 fatty acids and monounsaturated fat. Americans need to get more, not less, of these fats. As long as you limit yourself to a small handful of nuts daily—the recommended amount, unless oth-erwise noted—you don't need to worry about the "extra" calories.

Each type of nut contains a different mix of nutrients, fats and protective antioxidants, which can "neutralize" cell-damaging free radi-cals. People who eat a variety of nuts will get the widest range of benefits. Raw, toasted or roasted nuts are fine as long as they are unsalted.

Here's what nuts can do…

NUTS FOR THE HEART

All nuts are good for the heart, but the follow-ing nuts are especially beneficial…

•**Macadamia nuts.** Of the 21 g of total fat in a serving of macadamias, 17 g are monoun-saturated—the kind of fat that lowers a person's levels of harmful LDL cholesterol without low-ering levels of beneficial HDL cholesterol. Both the antioxidants and the monounsaturated fat in macadamias have anti-inflammatory effects that are important for curtailing arterial damage that can lead to heart disease.

•**Peanuts.** Actually a type of legume, not a true nut, peanuts contain 34 micrograms (mcg) of folate per one-ounce serving, a little less than 10% of the recommended daily amount. Folate is a B vitamin that lowers levels of *homocysteine*, an amino acid that damages arteries and in-creases the risk of heart disease.

Peanuts also are high in *L-arginine*, an amino acid that is converted by cells in blood vessels into nitric oxide. *Nitric oxide* improves circulation and may inhibit fatty buildups in the arteries.

•**Pistachios.** A 2007 study conducted by Penn State University found that pistachios low-er blood pressure. Men who added 1.5 ounces of shelled pistachios to their daily diets had drops in systolic pressure (the top number in a blood pressure reading) of 4.8 points. The antioxidants and healthy fats in pistachios relax blood vessels and allow blood to circulate with less force.

ALMONDS FOR BONES

Just about everyone needs more calcium, the mineral that strengthens bones and reduces the risk of osteoporosis. The recommended daily amount is 1,000 milligrams (mg). Almonds have more calcium than other nuts, with about 80 mg in 20 to 25 nuts. For people with lactose intolerance, who have trouble digesting dairy, a daily dose of almonds helps raise calcium to bone-protecting levels.

Blood pressure bonus: One serving of almonds has 98 mg of magnesium, about one-fourth the recommended daily amount. Magnesium, along with potassium and calcium, controls the relaxation and contraction of blood vessels and can help control blood pressure.

BRAZIL NUTS FOR PROSTATE

Brazil nuts are a superb source of selenium, with about 155 mcg in just two nuts. The recommended daily amount is 55 mcg. They're also high in vitamin E. One study—the Selenium and Vitamin E Cancer Prevention Trial—found that men getting selenium and vitamin E, alone or in combination, reduced their risk of prostate cancer by up to 60%. Selenium improves the ability of the immune system to recognize and destroy cancer cells in the prostate. Vitamin E is an antioxidant that also has been linked to reduced cancer risk.

Caution: People who get too much selenium may have decreased immunity. Because Brazil nuts are so high in selenium and calories (50 calories in two nuts), don't have more than two nuts daily. If you take a multivitamin that has more than 50% of the daily value of selenium, opt for one nut.

PECANS FOR THE EYES

The most serious eye diseases, including cataracts and macular degeneration, are caused, in part, by free radicals. The antioxidants in nuts and other plant foods fight free radicals to keep the eyes healthy.

A study conducted by the US Department of Agriculture (USDA) found that pecans are particularly rich in antioxidants. The National Eye Institute's Age-Related Eye Diseases Study reported that patients with macular degeneration who had adequate intakes of antioxidants were 29% less likely to experience disease progression than those who got lower levels.

Bonus for heart health: The vitamin E in pecans reduces the tendency of LDL cholesterol to oxidize and stick to artery walls. Pecans also are high in *phytosterols*—plant compounds that are similar to the active ingredients in cholesterol-lowering margarines, such as Benecol.

WALNUTS FOR MOOD

Apart from fish and flaxseed, walnuts are one of the best sources of omega-3 fatty acids. They're the only nut that contains *alpha linolenic acid* (ALA), a polyunsaturated fat that is converted to omega-3s in the body.

The omega-3s appear to help maintain healthy brain levels of *serotonin*, a neurochemical involved in mood. People who eat walnuts and/or two to three fish meals a week may experience a reduction in symptoms of depression.

Bonus for heart health: Omega-3s lower LDL cholesterol and triglycerides, another type of blood fat…increase HDL good cholesterol… inhibit blood clots in the arteries…and reduce arterial inflammation.

■ ■ ■ ■

The Brain Power Supplement

In a new study of 2,000 men and women (average age 72), those with the lowest levels of selenium had cognitive test scores equivalent to scores of someone who is 10 years older, compared with people with the highest levels of the trace mineral.

Theory: Selenium protects against free radicals, which can cause cellular damage in the brain.

Self-defense: Aim to get the recommended daily intake of selenium—55 micrograms (mcg) for adults—through foods, such as nuts, whole grains and seafood…and/or supplements.

Sujuan Gao, PhD, associate professor, division of biostatistics, Indiana University School of Medicine, Indianapolis.

Citrus Juice Squeezes More Antioxidants From Green Tea

Purdue University, news release.

Adding citrus juices or vitamin C to green tea may raise its antioxidant goodness, a new study suggests.

The antioxidants in question are called *catechins*, believed to be responsible for some of green tea's reported health benefits, such as reducing the risk of cancer, heart attack and stroke.

"Although these results are preliminary, I think it's encouraging that a big part of the puzzle comes down to simple chemistry," said lead author Mario Ferruzzi, assistant professor of food science at Purdue University in West Lafayette, Indiana.

THE STUDY

Using a laboratory model that simulates digestion in the stomach and small intestine, Ferruzzi tested green tea with a number of additives, including juices and creamers.

He found that citrus juice increased recoverable (absorbable) catechin levels by more than five times, while vitamin C (ascorbic acid) boosted recoverable levels of the two most abundant catechins by six and 13 times.

The findings were published in the journal *Molecular Nutrition and Food Research*.

POSSIBLE EXPLANATION

Citrus juices and vitamin C may interact with catechins to prevent degradation in the intestines, Ferruzzi said.

RECOMMENDATION

"If you want more out of your green tea, add some citrus juices to your cup after brewing or pick a ready-to-drink product formulated with ascorbic acid," he suggested.

Ferruzzi is currently conducting a study examining whether citrus juices and vitamin C increase catechin absorption in lab animals.

info For more information on green tea, visit the MedlinePlus Web site at *http://www.nlm.nih.gov/medlineplus* and type "green tea" in the search box.

■ ■ ■ ■

Magnesium Makes You Stronger

In a study of 1,138 men and women, participants with the highest blood levels of magnesium were stronger (based on tests for handgrip strength and power in leg muscles) than those with the lowest levels.

Theory: Magnesium is essential to the body's cellular energy production, thereby promoting optimal muscle performance.

Self-defense: To get the recommended intake of magnesium (420 mg daily for men age 31 or older…320 mg daily for women age 31 or older), eat such foods as dark green, leafy vegetables, navy beans and pumpkin seeds.

Ligia J. Dominquez, MD, researcher, geriatric unit, University of Palermo, Palermo, Italy.

■ ■ ■ ■

Chocolate Is Not a Health Food

Like red wine, fruits and vegetables, cocoa contains *flavonoids*, antioxidants that may reduce the risk for coronary artery disease—but most flavonoids are removed when the cocoa is processed and made into chocolate. Also, the added sugar and fat make chocolate—even chocolate that is marketed as good for you—a nutritional loser.

Best: If you like the flavor of chocolate, enjoy it sparingly.

Suzanne Havala Hobbs, DrPH, RD, clinical assistant professor, department of health policy and administration, University of North Carolina, Chapel Hill.

■ ■ ■ ■

Better Chocolate Choice

In a recent analysis of five studies involving 173 people, those who ate dark chocolate or other cocoa-rich products daily for two weeks had an average 4.7-point lower systolic (top number) blood pressure compared with those who ate white chocolate or other products without cocoa.

Theory: Cocoa is high in *procyanidins*, antioxidants that boost the body's production of nitric oxide, a chemical that relaxes blood vessels.

For healthy blood pressure: Substitute one-half ounce daily of dark chocolate for other high-calorie or high-fat desserts.

Dirk Taubert, MD, PhD, senior lecturer, University Hospital, Cologne, Germany.

New Study May Help People Stop Overeating

Brookhaven National Laboratory, news release.

A brain area linked to the desire to overeat has been identified, according to a new study published in *NeuroImage*. Treatments that target this region may help control chronic overeating, said the study authors.

THE STUDY

Researchers at the US government's Brookhaven National Laboratory used functional magnetic resonance imaging (fMRI) to observe how the brain responds to satiety messages delivered when the stomach is in various stages of fullness.

The researchers found that overweight people had less activation than normal weight people in a brain area called the left posterior amygdala when they were full. Overweight people were also less likely to report satiety when their stomach was moderately full.

"By stimulating feelings of fullness with an expandable balloon, we saw the activation of different areas of the brain in normal weight and overweight people," said study author Gene-Jack Wang, MD, of Brookhaven's Center for Translational Neuroimaging.

IMPLICATIONS

"These findings provide new evidence for why some people will continue to eat despite having eaten a moderate-sized meal," Dr. Wang said.

The study is the first to show "the connection of the left amygdala and feelings of hunger during stomach fullness, demonstrating that activation of this brain region suppresses hunger," Dr. Wang said. "Our findings indicate a potential direction for treatment strategies—be they behavioral, medical or surgical—targeting this brain region."

info For information about weight control, visit the Web site of the National Institute of Diabetes and Digestive and Kidney Diseases, *http://win.niddk.nih.gov.*

■ ■ ■ ■

Eat More Slowly to Cut Calories

Women ingested 67 fewer calories and felt more satisfied after taking 29 minutes to eat a meal than when they took nine minutes to consume the same meal.

Best: Savor meals by taking smaller bites… chewing thoroughly…pausing between bites… and consuming calorie-free beverages, such as water or unsweetened tea, with the meal.

Kathleen J. Melanson, PhD, RD, associate professor, nutrition and food sciences department, University of Rhode Island at Kingston, and leader of a study of 30 women, presented at the annual meeting of the Obesity Society.

■ ■ ■ ■

Exercise Is Not Enough to Take Off the Pounds

Exercise is not enough to take off the pounds if you spend a lot of time sitting. When people sit for long periods—doing desk jobs, using computers, playing video games, watching television or for other reasons—the body burns fat more slowly.

Result: People who sit too much have significantly greater risk for premature heart attack, diabetes and death.

Self-defense: In addition to exercising, it is important to stand up and move around as much as possible throughout the day—walk around the office, go up and down stairs, take a break from the computer and go outdoors, or do something else to get out of a seated position.

Marc Hamilton, PhD, associate professor of biomedical sciences, University of Missouri-Columbia, and leader of a study of the physiological effects of sitting, published in *Diabetes*.

■ ■ ■ ■

Being Fit Helps Even If You're Fat

Fitness beats thinness for promoting longevity. A recent study compared the effects of fitness and obesity on longevity by tracking 2,600 people over age 60 for 12 years.

Findings: People who were overweight or obese but judged physically fit by performance on a treadmill test had a lower death rate than those who had normal body weight but were not fit.

Importance: It's best to be fit and not overweight. But even if you are seriously overweight, just moderate exercise can greatly improve your health. Increasing fitness from the level of the "bottom fifth" to only the next-lowest fifth reduced mortality risk by 50%.

Steven Blair, PED, professor, department of exercise science and department of epidemiology and biostatistics, University of South Carolina, Columbia.

Sedentary Lifestyle Speeds Up Aging

JAMA/Archives journals, news release.

People who are physically active in their free time may be biologically younger than couch potatoes, a new British study suggests.

"A sedentary lifestyle increases the propensity to aging-related diseases and premature death. Inactivity may diminish life expectancy not only by predisposing to aging-related diseases, but also because it may influence the aging process itself," said study author Lynn F. Cherkas, of King's College, London.

The study was published in the *Archives of Internal Medicine.*

THE STUDY

The researchers looked at the physical activity levels, smoking habits and socioeconomic status of 2,401 white twins.

The researchers also collected DNA samples from participants, and examined the length of *telomeres*—repeated sequences at the end of chromosomes in white blood cells (leukocytes). Leukocyte telomeres shorten over time and may serve as a marker of a person's biological age.

Overall, the study participants had an average telomere loss of 21 nucleotides (structural units) per year. However, researchers noted, those who were more active in their leisure

time had longer leukocyte telomeres than those who were less active.

"Such a relationship between leukocyte telomere length and physical activity remained significant after adjustment for body-mass index, smoking, socioeconomic status and physical activity at work," said the study authors.

"The mean difference in leukocyte telomere length between the most active (those who performed an average of 199 minutes—just over 2½ hours—of physical activity per week) and least active (16 minutes of physical activity per week) subjects was 200 nucleotides," the researchers said.

Translation: This means that the most active subjects had telomeres the same length as sedentary individuals up to 10 years younger, on average.

POSSIBLE EXPLANATIONS

Oxidative stress damage caused to cells by exposure to oxygen and inflammation may be a factor contributing to shorter telomere length in sedentary people.

Stress has also been linked to telomere length. Exercise may reduce stress and its effect on telomeres and the aging process, the study authors suggested.

IMPLICATIONS

According to researchers, "The US guidelines recommend that an exercise regimen of 30 minutes of moderate-intensity physical activity at least five days a week can have significant health benefits."

"Our results underscore the vital importance of these guidelines. They show that adults who partake in regular physical activity are biologically younger than sedentary individuals," said the authors.

But more research is needed to confirm a direct link between physical activity and aging, the study noted.

info For more information about physical activity, visit the Web site of the Centers for Disease Control and Prevention, *www.cdc.gov.* Under "Healthy Living" click the option "Physical Activity."

Powerful Health Secret Your Doctor Doesn't Know About

Timothy McCall, MD, a board-certified internist and medical editor of *Yoga Journal*. Dr. McCall's articles have appeared in dozens of publications, including *The New England Journal of Medicine* and *The Journal of the American Medical Association*. He was a *Bottom Line/Health* columnist from 1995 to 2003 and is author of *Yoga as Medicine: The Yogic Prescription for Health and Healing*. Bantam. *www.DrMcCall.com*.

Yoga is one of the most underutilized and underrated medical therapies in the US. It's rare for American medical doctors to prescribe yoga—most are not knowledgeable about its wide array of health benefits.

What you may not know: More than 100 scientific studies have demonstrated that yoga can improve health problems ranging from heart disease to insomnia...diabetes to arthritis...and cancer to bronchitis.

As a medical doctor who has practiced yoga for over 12 years, I firmly believe that it is the most powerful system of overall health and well-being that I have ever seen. By promoting overall health, yoga increases the benefits you may derive from conventional and/or other alternative/complementary therapies—and may even eliminate your need for some medication.

WHAT IS YOGA?

Yoga is a holistic system of exercise and controlled breathing aimed at optimizing physical and mental well-being. Developed in ancient India, yoga poses stretch all muscle groups while gently squeezing internal organs—a practice that lowers blood pressure and respiratory rate and increases cardiac efficiency.

HOW YOGA HELPS

Studies suggest that a wide variety of health problems respond positively to yoga.

Landmark research: When 2,700 people suffering from a variety of ailments practiced yoga (for at least two hours a week for one year or longer), it helped 96% of those with back disorders...94% of those with heart disease...90% of those with cancer...90% of those with arthritis...88% of those with bronchitis or asthma...and 86% of those with diabetes.

What's responsible for all these salutary effects? Yoga, which is practiced by children as well as adults well into their 80s and 90s, helps with such a wide range of medical conditions because of its many different mechanisms of action. *Yoga can...*

•**Increase flexibility,** strengthen muscles, and improve posture and balance.

•**Boost immunity** by reducing levels of the stress hormone cortisol and increasing the circulation of *lymph* (a fluid rich in lymphocytes and other immune cells).

•**Enhance lung function** by using slower and deeper breathing that promotes oxygenation of tissues.

•**Strengthen bones and joints** and nourish the cartilage in spinal discs by improving range of motion and helping to deliver nutrients to the cartilage.

•**Condition the heart and circulatory system,** lower elevated blood sugars and artery-damaging high blood pressure...and improve levels of cholesterol and triglycerides.

•**Relieve pain** due to conditions such as arthritis, back problems, fibromyalgia and carpal tunnel syndrome, by reducing muscle spasms, improving the alignment of bones in joints and teaching people to separate pain from their emotional response to the pain.

•**Heighten brain function** by improving concentration, changing levels of neurotransmitters (brain chemicals) and activating an area of the brain (the left prefrontal cortex) that is correlated with reductions in anxiety and anger.

GETTING THE BENEFITS

There are a variety of ways to maximize the effectiveness and safety of yoga therapy. *My advice...*

•**Talk to your doctor.** Certain yoga practices are not recommended for people who suffer from specific medical conditions.

Example: People who have diabetic retinopathy (damage to the retina as a result of diabetes) should avoid upside-down poses, shoulder-stand or headstand, because these poses can increase pressure on the blood vessels in the eyes.

Helpful: When you visit your doctor, bring a book with photos of yoga poses that reflect the yoga style that you are considering. Since your doctor may not be aware of all possible contraindications, be sure to also discuss your concerns with your yoga teacher.

•**Choose the right type of instruction.** Yoga therapy ideally is tailored to the individual based on the evaluation of an experienced yoga teacher. While large group yoga classes can be great preventive medicine for people who are relatively fit and flexible, those with chronic medical conditions are usually better off working with a teacher privately or in a small group (two to four students). The cost of private lessons ranges from about $40 to $100 or more an hour. Group classes range from about $10 to $20 a session.

Helpful: If you're not sure whether a class is right for you, call or E-mail the teacher before you attend and explain your situation. If the class doesn't fit your needs, ask for a recommendation for another class or teacher.

•**Find an experienced teacher.** Some styles of yoga require teachers to undergo 200 to 500 hours of training to be certified. However, there is no universal accrediting organization.*

Warning: Some yoga teachers may have completed only a weekend training course to become "certified." Before attending a yoga class, ask the instructor how long he/she trained. (At least 200 hours is standard; 500 is better.)

•**Pay attention to your body.** If you experience sharp pain when you do a yoga posture, stop. If you perform a breathing exercise and feel short of breath, stop. In either case, tell the teacher as soon as possible—during or after the class.

•**Practice regularly.** The key to success with yoga is steady practice—once a day is ideal, even if it's only for 10 or 15 minutes. Yoga works well as part of an overall fitness program that includes aerobic exercise and strength training.

*To find a yoga instructor near you, go to the Web site of the International Association of Yoga Therapists, *www.iayt.org*.

Helpful: Set a goal for daily practice and make an appointment with yourself, just as you would make plans to meet a friend for lunch.

•**Be patient.** Most drugs work fast, but the longer you take them, the less effective they tend to become. Yoga is not a quick fix. But the longer you practice it, the more effective it tends to become. Yoga is slow—but strong—medicine.

That doesn't mean you won't see immediate results. It's a well-known fact among yoga teachers that people starting yoga make quicker progress than people who have been practicing for a long time. Just a little bit of added flexibility, strength and balance can make a huge difference in how you function day to day—by reducing back pain, for example, or helping you climb stairs more easily.

And some yoga techniques can help you instantly in stress-provoking situations, such as getting stuck in traffic.

Example: Counting silently, inhale for three seconds and exhale for six seconds, for a single breath. Take a few normal breaths, then repeat the first sequence, breathing smoothly. In a few breaths, you should start to feel calmer.

Even a Little Exercise Extends Men's Lives

Peter Kokkinos, PhD, director, exercise testing and research lab, cardiology department, Veterans Affairs Medical Center, Washington D.C.

Alice H. Lichtenstein, DSc, director, Cardiovascular Nutrition Lab, Gershoff professor of nutrition, USDA Human Nutrition Research Center, Tufts University, Boston, and former vice chair, nutrition committee, American Heart Association.

Circulation, online.

Even a moderate amount of exercise can dramatically prolong a man's life, new research on middle-aged and elderly American veterans reveals.

The government-sponsored analysis—the largest such study ever—found that a regimen of brisk walking 30 minutes a day at least four to six days a week was enough to halve the risk of premature death from all causes.

"As you increase your ability to exercise—increase your fitness—you are decreasing in a step-wise fashion the risk of death," said study author Peter Kokkinos, PhD, director of the exercise testing and research lab in the cardiology department of the Veterans Affairs Medical Center in Washington, D.C.

That conclusion applies more or less equally to white and black men, regardless of their prior history of cardiovascular disease. This evened the playing field, he said, giving him "great confidence" in the results, published in *Circulation.*

THE STUDY

Dr. Kokkinos and his team reviewed information gathered by the VA from 15,660 black and white male patients treated either in Palo Alto, California, or in Washington, D.C.

The men ranged in age from 47 to 71 and had been referred to a VA medical facility for a clinically prescribed treadmill exercise test. All participants were asked to run until fatigued, at which point the researchers then recorded the total amount of energy expended and oxygen consumed.

The numbers were then crunched into "metabolic equivalents," or METS. In turn, the researchers graded the fitness of each man according to his MET score, ranging from "low-fit" (below 5 METS) to "very high-fit" (above 10 METS).

THE RESULTS

By tracking fatalities, Dr. Kokkinos and his colleagues found that for both black and white men it was their fitness level, rather than their age, blood pressure or body-mass index, that was most strongly linked to their future risk for death.

Every extra MET point conferred a 14% reduction in the risk for death among black men, and a 12% reduction among whites. Among all participants, those categorized as "moderately fit" (5 to 7 METS) had about a 20% lower risk for death than "low-fit" men. "High-fit" men (7.1 to 10 METS) had a 50% lower risk, while the "very high-fit" (above 10 METS) cut their odds of an early death by 70%.

GOOD NEWS

"The point is, it takes relatively little exercise to achieve the benefit we found," noted Dr. Kokkinos. "Approximately two to three hours per week of brisk walking per week. That's just 120 to 200 minutes per week. And this can be split up throughout the week, and throughout the day. So it's doable in the real world."

Alice H. Lichtenstein, DSc, director of the Cardiovascular Nutrition Lab at Tufts University's USDA Human Nutrition Research Center in Boston, agreed.

"What this finding demonstrates is that levels of physical activity that should be achievable by anyone can have a real benefit with respect to risk reduction," she said.

"What's really important to understand is that you don't need special clothes, special memberships, special equipment," added Dr. Lichtenstein, who is also former vice chair of the American Heart Association's nutrition committee. "It's something everyone can engage in. And although we don't know from this research that this applies to women as well, there's no reason to suspect that it wouldn't."

 For more information on physical fitness, visit *www.healthierus.gov/exercise.html.*

Get More from Your Workout

Gerald Fletcher, MD, a specialist in preventive cardiology at the Mayo Clinic in Jacksonville, Florida. He is coauthor of the American Heart Association's exercise guidelines for the prevention and treatment of cardiovascular disease.

Serious athletes have long relied on an exercise technique known as "interval training"—alternating periods of intense (fast) physical activity with lighter (slow) activity—to improve their performance and endurance.

Latest development: A growing body of scientific evidence shows that interval training used in aerobic exercise—including walking, running, swimming, cycling or working out on exercise equipment—helps people of all fitness levels to optimize the health benefits of their workout routines, often within a matter of weeks.

In addition, I believe dividing workouts into three shorter sessions can boost the effectiveness of interval training further.

Specifically, interval training helps…

•**Provide more cardiovascular benefit.** Interval training enhances total oxygen consumption and physical fitness, leading to improved cardiovascular health.

•**Burn more calories—and body fat.** Research shows that the rise in calorie-burning metabolic activity that occurs during exercise continues for 10 to 15 minutes after stopping. By doing three short workouts per day instead of one long workout, for example, you can gain 30 to 45 minutes of post-exercise calorie burning, instead of 10 to 15.

•**Curb boredom.** Interval training adds variety to your workouts. Studies show that people who break their daily exercise into several sessions look forward to exercising more and are more likely to stick to their exercise programs.

DESIGN YOUR OWN PROGRAM

As a rule of thumb, a good interval training program includes exercising four to six days weekly. On days that you don't perform interval training, do resistance-training (strength-training) exercises to maintain your overall physical conditioning.

Important: Always check with your doctor before beginning a new exercise program—especially if you are over age 60 or have high blood pressure, heart disease and/or arthritis.

Here is a popular approach to interval training that can be adapted to any fitness level…

•**Three-a-Day Workout.** This workout is particularly recommended for beginning exercisers, people over age 65 and those who are exercising to lose weight. It consists of three interval-training sessions—performed, for example, in the early morning, before lunch and in the late afternoon—for a daily total of about 45 minutes.

Walkers/Runners: Warm up with three minutes of easy walking or jogging. Next, walk briskly or run at a moderate pace for four minutes…walk or jog slowly for two minutes…then walk briskly or run at a moderate pace for another four minutes. Finish with two minutes of easy walking. (You'll be exercising at a moderate pace when you become a little breathless, and your exertion level is somewhat hard. However, if you can't talk easily while exercising, you're working too hard.)

Cyclists: Warm up with three minutes of easy cycling. Next, cycle at a moderate level of effort for four minutes…cycle at an easy pace for two minutes…then cycle at a moderate level for another four minutes. Finish with two minutes of easy cycling.

Exercising in a gym: Warm up with three minutes of walking or easy jogging. Next, exercise on a treadmill, exercise bike, elliptical trainer or rowing machine for four minutes at a moderate level of effort (equivalent to walking three miles per hour, or a 20-minute mile pace)…then walk or jog slowly around the gym or outside for two minutes. Switch to a different piece of equipment, and exercise for another four minutes at a moderate level of effort. Finish with two minutes of easy walking.

Swimmers: Warm up with three minutes of easy swimming. Next, swim one length of the pool (backyard or Olympic-sized) at a moderate level of effort (becoming a little breathless)…then swim one length of the pool at a slow pace. Repeat this pattern twice, for a daily total of three times. Finish with two minutes of easy swimming.

Four Ways to Better Balance and Fewer Falls

Erik Peper, PhD, professor of holistic health and co-director of San Francisco State University's Institute for Holistic Healing Studies. He also was lead author of an article on preventing falls, published in *Biofeedback.*

Falls are a primary cause of injury, especially as we get older. Reduce the risk of falling—and the bone fractures that can result—with exercises that improve balance, strength and coordination. Before starting an exercise program, check with your doctor.

•**Strengthen core muscles** (in the abdomen and low back).

Equipment: Inflatable exercise ball, about $20 at sporting-goods stores.

To start: Holding on to a counter or other stable object, sit on the ball, feet flat on the floor. Rock gently side to side, then forward and back. Continue for one minute, and gradually increase to 10 minutes.

Advanced: Do the moves above while lifting one foot off the floor slightly and/or without holding on to anything.

●**Improve awareness and sensitivity.**

Helpful habit: To heighten the sensitivity of your feet, walk barefoot as often as possible—in your home or over a safe but slightly uneven surface, such as a lawn, beach or plastic simulated pebble mat.

Do anywhere: When you are walking, plan your path—step on each crack in the sidewalk or on alternating tiles of a linoleum floor. This trains you to notice obstacles in your path.

●**Build hip and leg strength.**

To start: Sit in a chair and lift one knee as high as is comfortable, hold for a count of three, then lower. Do 10 lifts with each leg.

Intermediate: Stand and hold on to a counter with one or both hands. Bending your leg, lift one knee as high as is comfortable and hold for a count of 10. Repeat 10 times, then switch legs.

Advanced: Standing and holding on to a counter, lift your left knee above waist height, then lunge forward with the left foot in an exaggerated step. Both knees will be slightly bent as your foot lands. Repeat 10 times, then switch legs. When mastered, do it without holding on.

Do anywhere: When walking, concentrate on pushing off with the big toe of the back foot. This improves the speed and coordination of your gait.

●**Gain confidence in movement.**

To start: Placing both hands on a wall at shoulder level, step back until your arms are almost straight. Lean slightly toward the wall until you begin to lose your balance (to simulate the start of a fall), then quickly step forward with one foot to prevent falling. Keep your hands on the wall for added security.

Advanced: Stand farther away from the wall to increase the tipping angle, with hands raised to shoulder level but not touching the wall. Lean forward and step quickly, as above. If necessary, catch yourself by gently placing your hands on the wall.

Do anywhere: Incorporate physical activity into your routine as much as possible.

Examples: Climb stairs two at a time…use a basket, not a cart, when you shop.

Illustrations by Shawn Banner.

■ ■ ■ ■

How Much Do You Sweat?

Figure out your sweat rate so you know how much water to drink when exercising. Weigh yourself naked before and immediately after exercising for an hour at the most intense level you would normally exercise. Convert the weight lost to fluid ounces.

Example: A one-pound (16-ounce) loss would mean you sweated about 16 ounces of fluid, and that you need to take in 16 ounces per hour of fluids while exercising. Most people need eight ounces of fluid for every 15 minutes of exercise.

From the American College of Sports Medicine.

■ ■ ■ ■

Exercise Cuts Men's Risk for Fractures

When researchers interviewed 2,205 men over a 35-year period, sedentary men were two-and-a-half times more likely to break a hip than were men who exercised or played sports vigorously at least three hours weekly. (Studies show similar results for women.)

Theory: Physical activity increases skeletal strength and muscle mass.

If you're sedentary: Ask your doctor to recommend an exercise program.

Karl Michaëlsson, MD, professor of surgery and epidemiology, Uppsala University, Sweden.

Putting on a Pedometer Helps Walkers Take Off Pounds

Caroline R. Richardson, MD, assistant professor, department of family medicine, University of Michigan Medical School, and research scientist, Health Services Research and Development Center, Ann Arbor Veterans' Affairs Medical Center, Ann Arbor, Michigan.

Alice H. Lichtenstein, DSc, director, Cardiovascular Nutrition Lab, and Gershoff Professor of Nutrition, USDA Human Nutrition Research Center, Tufts University, Boston, and former chair, nutrition committee, American Heart Association.

Annals of Family Medicine.

Just by strapping on a step-counting pedometer, overweight or obese "couch potatoes" who start a daily walking regimen can expect to lose at least a modest amount of weight—even in the absence of any special diet, new research reveals.

The review of data from nine studies found that patients who used a pedometer to track and motivate their walking achieved a loss of about a pound every 10 weeks.

"The main point is that pedometer-based walking programs are effective at getting people to walk more, and they do result in a modest amount of weight loss," said study lead author Caroline R. Richardson, MD, an assistant professor in the department of family medicine at the University of Michigan Medical School in Ann Arbor.

HOW PEDOMETERS WORK

Simple, inexpensive and pager-sized, pedometers are worn at the waist to automatically keep track of every step the wearer takes while walking, running, climbing, dancing or engaging in a variety of sports.

According to experts, pedometer users may gain some flexibility as they set exercise goals—for example, they can meet their target in a single daily outing or through several short outings spread across the day. In this way, pedometers may help encourage more people to exercise, fitness experts say.

But others question that theory.

THE STUDY

To help settle the debate, Dr. Richardson's team analyzed data collected in nine pedometer-based walking studies conducted between 1995 and 2006.

In each study, previously sedentary and overweight or obese patients were motivated to join a new walking program by using pedometers to monitor their total daily step counts.

Study size varied from 15 to 106 participants each, for a total of 307 participants. Almost three-quarters of the patients were women. Special diets were not included as part of the studies.

RESULTS

The researchers found what they called "remarkably consistent" results. With the exception of those participating in one of the studies, all of the enrolled patients ended up losing a small amount of weight by each study's end.

On average, participants lost about a tenth of a pound per week—an amount the authors described as "small but important." They noted that over the course of a year, this figure translates into an expected weight loss of five pounds.

Such weight loss resulted from an average step count increase of 2,000 to 4,000 steps (one to two miles) per day per participant over the course of each study.

Assuming a walking pace of three miles per hour, such increases were calculated to be the equivalent of an additional 20 to 40 minutes of walking per day.

Richardson and her colleagues also noted that the longer the program lasted, the greater the ultimate weight loss.

MORE HEALTH BENEFITS

Pedometer-based walking programs should confer significant health benefits beyond weight loss, including lowered blood pressure and a boost in cardiovascular health.

Those coping with type 2 diabetes or glucose intolerance may also reap related health rewards, Richardson's group noted.

"There are other things you can achieve as well," noted Dr. Richardson, who also serves as a research scientist in the Health Services Research and Development Center at Ann Arbor Veterans' Affairs Medical Center. "You can get stress relief, you may sleep better at night, and you may have an improved mood. And focusing your motivation on some of these other changes may help you stick with the program. And if you stick with walking, you may eventually get the weight reduction goal you're looking for."

EXPERT REACTION

Alice H. Lichtenstein, DSc, is director of the Cardiovascular Nutrition Lab in the US Department of Agriculture's Human Nutrition Research Center at Tufts University in Boston. She was encouraged but not surprised by the findings.

"There's something about a pedometer that makes a difference," said Dr. Lichtenstein, who is also a former chair of the American Heart Association's nutrition committee.

"Perhaps the pedometer is reinforcing behavior change," she speculated. "With some people, it gives them a goal. For others, it serves as a reminder. And, of course, anyone who's made a commitment to wear a pedometer has likely made some sort of internal commitment to stick with the exercise program. This is a way you can look and check and see how you're doing. And that's instant gratification."

info For more information on pedometer use, visit the Web site of the Division of Nutrition Research Coordination at the National Institutes of Health, *http://dnrc.nib.gov* and type "pedometer use" into the search box.

Walk This Way for Better Fitness

Danny Dreyer, a walking and running coach and nationally ranked ultra marathon runner based in Asheville, North Caroline, *www.chiwalking.com.* He conducts workshops and lectures at races and other events nationwide.

Chi (also spelled "qi" and pronounced *chee*) is the Chinese concept of a life force that animates all things. It is a type of energy that flows through your body and unites your body, mind and spirit. We all know that walking is good for us physically. But in

ChiWalking, you apply the principles of chi to the simple act of walking to achieve more than just a workout for your body—you also gain balance and alignment in your life.

ChiWalking is a way to get stronger and healthier without stress or strain and with very little chance of injury. Unlike power walking or race walking, it doesn't involve walking in an unnatural or competitive way. Anyone at any age or level of fitness can learn ChiWalking.

MOVEMENT IS THE KEY

ChiWalking uses good walking form to help you walk more efficiently with less wear and tear on the body. The beauty of ChiWalking is that you can feel the benefits quickly. Many people with knee and hip problems can still enjoy ChiWalking, because when your body is in alignment and moving correctly, there's far less impact on your joints. I've even taught ChiWalking to people who use canes or walkers.

The basic principle of chi is that it must flow freely through your body. If your body is misaligned or your joints and muscles are tight, the flow of chi will be blocked, just as a crimp in a hose blocks the flow of water. When the principle of chi is applied to walking, it teaches us to align our spines, engage our core muscles and relax everything else. The energy flows and walking becomes fluid and easy.

A fit mind in a fit body—isn't that what we all want as we grow older? By following five mindful steps as you walk, your whole being gets an enjoyable workout every time. You can also suit the type of walk you do to harmonize with your current mood and energy level. *Here are the five mindful steps to successful ChiWalking...*

MINDFUL STEP 1: GET ALIGNED

Body connection: Align your spine so that you stand tall and straight and have good posture while you walk. Stand with your feet hip-width apart and parallel...relax your knees a little...move your shoulders, hipbones and ankles into a vertical line. Your weight is now being carried by your bones, rather than your muscles, just as steel pillars support a skyscraper. Your muscles can now move more freely and easily.

Mind connection: The chi concept of "needle in cotton" applies here. Imagine a needle poked down through a ball of cotton. The needle is the thin, strong, straight line running through the center of the cotton. Think of your spine as the needle and your arms and legs as being as light as cotton. Gather energy in toward your spine and let your arms and legs relax. Get mentally aligned with your intentions for your walk.

MINDFUL STEP 2: ENGAGE YOUR CORE

Body connection: Your core muscles are the lower abdominal muscles that stabilize your pelvis when you stand, walk or run. They also hold your spine erect and help lift your legs. When your core muscles are strong, your body is stable. You can stand up straight easily and move your arms and legs easily. To engage your core muscles, level your pelvis—stand up straight in alignment, as described above, and then lift up on your pubic bone by using your lower abdominal muscles. This may take a little practice, but you'll soon learn to feel those muscles and get them to work.

Once you've got your posture aligned and your pelvis level, stand tall and tilt your upper body forward just a quarter of an inch. This will keep your upper body aligned and moving forward—which allows gravity to do most of the work as you walk.

Mind connection: Your inner core is your internal sense of self. When you engage your inner core, you feel grounded and centered. You have willpower when you need it.

MINDFUL STEP 3: CREATE BALANCE

Body connection: Imagine your body in the shape of a letter C—your spine is straight, your chin is down slightly, and your pelvis is rising slightly in front because you're lifting it slightly, as explained in Step 2. Your upper and lower body are in balance and ready to move forward.

Mind connection: Take a balanced approach to your walks, spreading them evenly across the week and never going beyond what your body tells you is right. As you get fitter, feel how your mind and body become more in balance with each other.

MINDFUL STEP 4: MAKE A CHOICE

Body connection: Choose to walk regularly, even on days when you don't really feel like it. Try to walk for at least 30 minutes on most days—but if you can't squeeze it in, even 15 minutes will improve your cardiovascular fitness and improve your outlook on life.

Mind connection: Overall, choose to create health. On a daily basis, choose the kind of walk you want. If you're feeling scattered or stressed, a slower, more meditative walk might be better than a fast cardiovascular workout.

MINDFUL STEP 5: MOVE FORWARD

Body connection: To walk, push your core ahead with each step, letting gravity move the rest of your body forward. Work with gravity—don't fight it. Listen to your body and move only as fast as is comfortable for you. Good form is more important than speed.

Mind connection: Now is the time for action and resolve. As you walk, focus your mind on maintaining good form. Bear in mind that each step is part of going forward with your quest for lifelong energy and health.

THE PRACTICE OF WALKING

By "practice" I mean walking as a regular, mindful activity that works to enhance your quality of life. When you make walking a regular practice, you raise it beyond just healthful physical exercise. It becomes a way to focus your energy and to channel your thoughts—because your chi is flowing freely.

Illustrations by Shawn Banner.

12

Pain Treatments

Chronic Pain Bad For the Brain

Chronic pain can disrupt the functioning of the brain and cause an array of problems such as disturbed sleep, depression, anxiety and difficulty making simple decisions, a recent US study finds.

THE STUDY

Researchers at Northwestern University's Feinberg School of Medicine in Chicago used functional magnetic resonance imaging (fMRI) to scan brain activity in people with chronic low back pain while they tracked a moving bar on a computer screen. They did the same thing with a control group of people with no pain.

THE RESULTS

In those with no pain, the brain regions displayed a state of equilibrium. When one region was active, the other regions calmed down. But in people with chronic pain, the front region of the cortex mostly associated with emotion "never shuts up," said study author Dante Chialvo, MD, a research associate professor of physiology at Northwestern.

This region remains highly active, which alters the connections of neurons to each other. The constant firing of neurons could cause permanent damage.

The study was published in *The Journal of Neuroscience*.

IMPLICATIONS

"We know when neurons fire too much, they may change their connections with other neurons or even die, because they can't sustain high activity for so long," Dr. Chialvo said.

"If you are a chronic pain patient, you have pain 24 hours a day, seven days a week, every minute of your life. That permanent perception of pain in your brain makes these areas in your brain continuously active. This continuous dysfunction in the equilibrium of the brain can

Northwestern University, news release.

change the wiring forever and could hurt the brain," Dr. Chialvo explained.

These changes "may make it harder for you to make a decision or be in a good mood or to get up in the morning. It could be that pain produces depression and the other reported abnormalities because it disturbs the balance of the brain as a whole," he said.

Dr. Chialvo said the findings show that, along with working out new ways to treat pain, it's also important to develop methods to evaluate and prevent disruption of brain function caused by chronic pain.

info For more information on chronic pain, visit the Web site of the American Academy of Family Physicians, *http://family doctor.org*, and search "chronic pain: how to get relief."

Sugar Water Eases Vaccination for Babies

Linda A. Hatfield, PhD, CNNP, assistant professor, public health services, Pennsylvania State University School of Nursing, University Park.

Kenneth R. Goldschneider, MD, director, division of pain management, Cincinnati Children's Hospital Medical Center, Ohio.

Pediatrics.

While a spoonful of sugar helps the medicine go down, a new study shows it may also ease the pain of vaccinations in infants.

According to study author Linda Hatfield, PhD, an assistant professor of public health services at the Pennsylvania State University School of Nursing in University Park, this paper is one of the first to study infants who have already left the hospital. Most previous studies were done on preterm newborns who, by circumstance, receive more shots.

BACKGROUND

The annual immunization schedule for healthy new arrivals in this world is daunting; infants and toddlers receive as many as 24 injections in the first two years of life. As many as five injections can be given to a child in a single visit.

But many parents are petrified at the prospect of seeing their child in pain.

"Some mothers say they've never heard their baby cry like that," Dr. Hatfield said. "They're reluctant to bring their sweet little children in."

There's also some indication that exposure to pain early in life might have long-term neurological effects.

THE STUDY

Dr. Hatfield and her colleagues randomized 100 two- and four-month-old infants to receive either oral sucrose or a placebo (sterile water) two minutes before routine immunizations.

Pain was assessed with a score that took into account crying, facial expression, body movement, behavioral indications and sleep.

Parents were asked not to swaddle or cuddle their child during the immunization as this could have had an effect on the experience of pain.

RESULTS

The sucrose group showed lower pain scores at five, seven and nine minutes after being given the solution and, by nine minutes, had a mean pain score 78.5% lower than that of the placebo group.

THEORY

Previous research has suggested a link between exposure to sucrose and release of the body's natural pain-relieving chemicals.

IMPLICATIONS

Is it a good idea to give sugar to young babies? Dr. Hatfield says the solution is so weak (only one-quarter sugar) that it's unlikely to have any effect on later weight problems and doesn't even raise blood sugar in the short-term.

And experts are hoping that a simple sugar-and-water solution will also ease parents' fears and boost immunization rates for infants.

"We're hoping this will encourage parents to get their children vaccinated," said Dr. Hatfield, "It's very simple, not very expensive. Babies leave the clinic just as they came in."

EXPERT REACTION

The strategy becomes one in an armamentarium of safer pain relievers for children.

"What's shaking out is a combination of things that can be used safely in pediatricians' offices that are useful to the child," said Kenneth R. Goldschneider, MD, director of the division of pain management at Cincinnati Children's Hospital Medical Center in Ohio. "Sucrose, swaddling, kangaroo care [direct, skin-to-skin contact with a parent], non-nutritive sucking [a pacifier with nothing on it], topical analgesics, use of thinner needles and proper injection site selection [are all] means to keep painful interventions from being overly stressful. None of them are perfect, but they are safe, and work at least reasonably well."

info For an up-to-date childhood immunization schedule, visit the Web site of the Centers for Disease Control and Prevention, *www.cdc.gov.* Click on "Healthy Living," then type "immunization schedule" into the search box.

Is It Really Ulcerative Colitis?

Leo Galland, MD, director, Foundation for Integrated Medicine, New York City. His latest book is *The Fat Resistance Diet.* Broadway. *www.fatresistancediet.com.* Dr. Galland is a recipient of the Linus Pauling Award.

Life changed quite suddenly for Judith at the age of 52, when she developed a serious episode of abdominal pain and diarrhea. Her doctor diagnosed food poisoning, and her pain resolved within three weeks, but the diarrhea continued. She soon found that most of the foods she loved, such as bread and fresh fruit, increased her bouts of diarrhea and caused uncomfortable swelling of her abdomen.

Her first gastroenterologist performed a colonoscopy (a test that uses a lighted tube to examine the lining of the colon). Finding extensive inflammation in her large intestine, he told her that she had ulcerative colitis (chronic inflammation and ulceration of the lining of the rectum and colon that leads to diarrhea, abdominal cramps and fever). Her doctor prescribed the anti-inflammatory drugs *sulfasalazine* and *prednisone* (a steroid), but Judith felt no better—perhaps somewhat worse. Her second gastroenterologist wanted to perform another colonoscopy and suggested treatment with a powerful drug used to treat autoimmune diseases, including ulcerative colitis. Concerned about possible side effects, she refused.

Frustrated by her doctors' inability to treat her condition, Judith started reviewing her own history to look for patterns. A decade earlier, she had found that eliminating sweets and dairy products from her diet had cured her lifelong eczema (inflammation of the skin that causes itching, blisters and redness), so she decided that this new disease might really be caused by eating the wrong food. Judith began to restrict her diet again. For the next year and a half, she lived on buckwheat, millet, sweet potatoes, lettuce, peas, carrots, chicken and lamb—foods she found that she could eat. She had no bloating, but she continued to experience diarrhea three to four times a day, was becoming seriously underweight and the quality of her life was severely impaired.

When Judith consulted me for a fresh opinion, my first impression was that the diagnosis of ulcerative colitis had been made perhaps too quickly, without taking into account all the features of her case that are not typical of this condition…

• **Sudden onset at the age of 52.** Ulcerative colitis usually begins at a younger age, although it may be triggered by an acute gastrointestinal infection, which is what happened in Judith's case.

• **Lack of response to anti-inflammatory drugs.** Most patients with ulcerative colitis will show at least partial improvement with medication, but Judith did not.

• **Intolerance to multiple foods.** Although many patients with ulcerative colitis experience intolerance to some foods, Judith was far more sensitive to a wide variety of common foods than most people.

Based on these inconsistencies, my first decision was to test Judith for a chronic intestinal infection using stool testing. During the past two decades, I have evaluated scores of patients with "ulcerative colitis." In all of these cases, I have found that thorough testing for an intestinal infection was crucial to identifying the root cause of the problem. About one-quarter of these patients tested positive for intestinal infection. In almost half of these cases, the intestinal infection was the real cause of their symptoms. In the other half, the diagnosis of chronic ulcerative colitis was correct, but the infection had produced an acute flare-up of symptoms. In either case, curing the infection relieved the symptoms.

Judith's lab results showed that she was infected with two intestinal parasites—*Entamoeba histolytica*, which causes a form of colitis that is very hard to distinguish from ulcerative colitis…and *Giardia lamblia*, which may cause severe food intolerance. Parasites are organisms that survive by living on or inside another organism. They generally enter the body via the mouth or skin—for example, through exposure to contaminated food or water.

After treatment with the appropriate antibiotics, Judith's diarrhea cleared up and her sensitivity to foods began to decrease. Six months later, she was able to eat a varied diet (she still avoids sweets and dairy products). A follow-up colonoscopy showed no evidence of inflammation in her large intestine.

Correct diagnosis: Intestinal parasites.

Lesson for all: Just because your illness has been given a name, it does not mean that its cause has been found. If you suffer from sudden gastrointestinal symptoms, such as diarrhea, pain, bloating and/or constipation, do not accept a diagnosis until you have been tested for parasitic infection.

New Study Brings Pain Relief for Osteoporosis Patients

Society for Interventional Radiology, news release.

In osteoporosis patients with spinal fractures, *vertebroplasty*—a procedure in which bone cement is injected into the area of a spinal fracture—provides significant pain relief and helps decrease disability, according to a new study.

BACKGROUND

Osteoporosis affects about 10 million Americans and causes about 1.5 million vertebral fractures each year, according to the US National Institutes of Health. Multiple vertebral fractures can cause chronic pain, disability, loss of independence, stooped posture and compression of the lungs and stomach.

Vertebroplasty involves injection of medical-grade bone cement into a fractured vertebra to shore up the fracture and provide pain relief. It's used to treat painful vertebral compression fractures that don't respond to conventional medical therapy with analgesics or narcotics.

THE STUDY

The study followed 884 patients for five years who were assessed before and after vertebroplasty. Their average pre-treatment pain score on an 11-point scale decreased from 7.9 before treatment to an average of 1.3 after treatment.

The patients' ability to manage everyday tasks such as washing and dressing was measured using the Oswestry Disability Questionnaire. The patients' scores went from an average of 69.3% a month before treatment to 18.8% a month after treatment, reflecting a lower level of disability.

IMPLICATIONS

"These data provide good news for physicians and osteoporosis patients. Many osteoporosis patients with compression fractures are in terrible pain and have a greatly diminished ability to perform basic daily activities, such as dressing themselves," said Giovanni C. Anselmetti, MD, an interventional radiologist at the Institute for Cancer Research and Treatment in Turin, Italy.

The study also found that vertebroplasty did not increase the risk for fracture in nearby vertebra.

"Osteoporosis patients remain susceptible to new fractures, which often occur in the contiguous vertebra to an existing fracture. Our large-scale study shows that vertebroplasty does not increase the risk of fracture in the level contiguous to previously treated vertebra and that these new fractures occur at the same rate as they would in osteoporosis patients who did not have vertebroplasty," Dr. Anselmetti said.

info For more information on vertebroplasty, visit the Web site of the American College of Radiology and the Radiological Society of North American, *www.radiologyinfo.org*, and search "vertebroplasty."

Best Ways to Repair That Aching Hip

William Macaulay, MD, professor of clinical orthopedic surgery, director of the Center for Hip and Knee Replacement and advisory dean of students at the College of Physicians and Surgeons, New York-Presbyterian Hospital at Columbia University, all in New York City.

For decades, people whose severe hip pain did not improve with painkillers and/or physical therapy had only one option—a hip replacement.

Now: A procedure that "resurfaces" worn-out hip joints rather than replacing them is available in the US. Known as *hip resurfacing*, the technique can be as durable as hip replacement with less pain during recovery and greater long-term mobility. Originally introduced in England in 1997, the Birmingham Hip System (one of the products used for hip resurfacing) was approved by the FDA in May 2006.

DO YOU NEED A BETTER HIP?

Osteoarthritis of the hip is the most common reason for hip pain. This disease occurs when the cartilage covering joint surfaces begins to wear out, causing pain and stiffness that can be so severe that sufferers limp and have difficulty climbing stairs, walking, standing and even sitting. Other causes of hip pain include rheumatoid arthritis and serious hip injury.

If you suffer from hip pain that does not improve with pain medication and physical therapy...interferes with activities that you enjoy, such as gardening or brisk walking...and/or disturbs your sleep, you may want to consider one of several surgical options.

A BREAKTHROUGH APPROACH

For several years, Americans who wanted to try an alternative to hip replacement have traveled to England, India or one of the other countries that have offered hip resurfacing. Now this procedure is available at more than 100 medical centers throughout the US.

With hip resurfacing, the round head of the femur (thighbone) is reshaped and covered with a metal cap about the same size as the natural femoral head. The reshaped head moves within a smooth metal socket that is implanted into the pelvic bone. Enough bone is left in place to allow for a future hip replacement, if necessary.

Hip resurfacing is a good option for patients age 55 and younger...people of any age who have relatively healthy bones or who are highly active.

Hip resurfacing may take slightly longer than the hour to hour-and-a-half required for a standard hip replacement surgery. The incision is often two to three inches longer than the six- to 12-inch incision required for conventional hip replacement, due in part to the limited maneuverability the surgeon has with most of the thighbone left in place. As with traditional hip replacement, a two- to three-day hospital stay is usually required following hip resurfacing, and healing is more than 90% complete within six to eight weeks. The procedure typically costs about $25,000 and is usually covered by insurance.

HIP REPLACEMENT OPTIONS

If you are not a candidate for hip resurfacing (due to age, osteoporosis or bone weakness), *total hip replacement* is an option. During this procedure, the surgeon makes an incision, removes the femoral head and replaces the ball-and-socket mechanism with an artificial implant that functions much like a natural joint.

A significant amount of bone is removed with hip replacement in order to insert a metal stem that attaches the synthetic ball-and-socket mechanism to the femur. If any part of the implant loosens in the future, this loss of bone makes a follow-up surgery more difficult.

Traditional hip replacement (as described above) is usually recommended for patients who are obese or very muscular. Recovery time is the same as that for hip resurfacing.

With a newer minimally invasive approach, the surgeon uses specially designed surgical instruments to place the hip implant. Minimally invasive hip replacement generally takes one-and-a-half hours, uses one-and-a-half- to three-inch incisions and requires a one- to two-day hospital stay. It is usually recommended for people who are thin. The recovery period is comparable to that for hip resurfacing and a traditional hip replacement. However, the minimally invasive procedure is controversial, because it has been associated with significant complications in some studies.

The same type of artificial implant is used with both procedures. Each procedure costs about $25,000, which usually is covered by health insurance.

INSTALLING HIP IMPLANTS

More than 300 types of hip implants are now available, as well as dozens of different techniques for installing them. *Main choices...*

•**Cemented.** The implant is attached to the bone of the thigh with an acrylic cement. The cement gives immediate strength and is extremely durable.

Recommended for: Patients with less-than-healthy bone, such as those with osteoporosis or osteoarthritis.

•**Uncemented.** The joint implants have a porous surface that allows the patient's natural bone to surround and grow into the implant.

Recommended for: Active patients with normal bone metabolism.

•**Metal/ceramic-on-plastic.** A metal or ceramic femoral ball (prosthetic head) is mated with a hard plastic (polyethylene) socket. It's one of the older configurations—proven to be durable and reliable.

Recommended for: Any patient.

RISKS AND RECOVERY

The main cause of hip-replacement failure is aseptic loosening (when normal bone loss occurs around the implant, causing the joint to separate). In this case, the hip replacement must be repeated. *Other risks...*

•**Deep vein thrombosis.** Blood clots can form in the leg veins—a life-threatening complication if a clot travels to the lungs. After the procedure, most patients are treated with blood thinners, such as *warfarin* (Coumadin), and advised to move their ankles up and down frequently (about 10 times at least three times daily), which helps prevent clots.

•**Uneven leg lengths.** In some cases, the leg on the side that was operated on will be slightly longer than the other leg. When this happens, a patient may need to wear a shoe with a slightly raised heel.

Important: Postsurgical exercise, including low-impact activities, such as walking or using an elliptical trainer, are among the best ways to stabilize the joint and maintain hip strength and/or flexibility.

Seven Easy Exercises To Ease Pain

Harris H. McIlwain, MD, a rheumatologist and pain specialist with Tampa Medical Group and adjunct professor at University of South Florida College of Public Health, both in Tampa. He is coauthor, with Debra Fulghum Bruce, PhD, of *Diet for a Pain-Free Life* (Marlowe) and *Pain-Free Arthritis* (Henry Holt).

If you have joint problems, simply opening a jar or climbing stairs can cause pain. It turns into a vicious cycle. It hurts to move, so you may stop exercising—yet moderate exercise eases joint aches and stiffness by increasing strength and flexibility and decreasing inflammation.

Solution: With your doctor's approval, try the exercises below.

Stretching makes joints more limber, prevents muscles from becoming short and tight, and protects against injury. Stretch gently, moving each joint to the maximum range of motion possible without causing unusual discomfort. Do these moves daily, working up to 15 repetitions of each.

•**Shoulder stretch.** Sit with back straight and clasp hands behind your head. Move elbows forward as if trying to get them to touch in front of your face. Hold five seconds. Next, move elbows back until they point out to the side...hold five seconds. This increases

251

shoulders' range of motion—making it easier, for instance, to style your hair.

•**Bathtub stretch.** Moist heat eases movement by increasing flow of blood, oxygen and nutrients to joints. During a warm bath or while seated on a shower stool, "circle" wrists by rotating hands, envisioning fingertips tracing the face of a clock. Next, circle ankles by rotating feet.

•**Finger flexion.** Bring the tips of your right thumb and forefinger together, making as round an "O" as possible...hold five seconds...repeat with other fingers. Switch hands.

Resistance training strengthens muscles that surround joints, easing pain by providing muscular support. Try these exercises three times weekly, building up to 15 repetitions of each.

•**Hand helper.** Hold a tennis-ball–sized foam (Nerf) ball in one hand...squeeze, hold five seconds, release. Switch hands.

•**Hip extension.** Lie facedown on a mat or bed, legs extended. Bend arms and turn head to one side, resting your cheek on the backs of your hands. Knees straight, raise your right leg until your ankle is eight to 12 inches above the mat...hold five seconds...lower. Switch legs.

•**Knee extension.** Sit in a chair, feet flat on floor. Raise your left foot, straightening knee completely so the leg is parallel to the floor... tighten knee and thigh muscles...hold five seconds...lower foot to floor and relax. Switch sides.

•**Foot and ankle strengthener.** Sit in a chair. Place your bare foot on top of a tennis ball on the floor. Bearing down slightly, roll the ball underfoot, using the muscles of the toes, arch and ankle to move the ball back and forth and side to side. Continue for 30 seconds. Switch feet.

Aerobic activity, such as walking, rowing and stair-climbing, burns calories and helps you lose excess weight that stresses joints.

For sore shoulders: Swim in a heated pool.

For problem knees and hips: Try biking or stationary cycling. Build up to five 30-minute sessions weekly.

Illustrations by Shawn Banner.

Dance to Avoid Arthritis

Women in their 70s who reported no stiff or painful joints at the start of a three-year study and who engaged in moderate exercise, such as dancing or brisk walking, for a little more than one hour a week reduced their risk of developing arthritis symptoms by 26%. Women who did at least two hours per week of moderate exercise reduced their risk by 46%.

Other good options: Tai chi, qigong, yoga and swimming.

Kristiann Heesch, DrPh, research fellow, School of Human Movement Studies, University of Queensland, Australia, and researcher on a study of 8,750 women, published in *Arthritis Research & Therapy*.

A Little-Known Supplement Relieves Arthritis Pain

Mark A. Stengler, ND, naturopathic physician in private practice, La Jolla, California...adjunct associate clinical professor at the National College of Natural Medicine, Portland, Oregon...author of many books, including *The Natural Physician's Healing Therapies* and coauthor of *Prescription for Natural Cures* (both from Bottom Line Books)...and author of the *Bottom Line/Natural Healing* newsletter.

On her first visit to me, 60-year-old Jenny said, "Every time I hear of a supplement that might reduce my arthritis pain, I try it—but I've gotten very little relief. I've almost given up on finding anything that works." I paid close attention as she named nearly a dozen supplements she had taken for the arthritis in her hips and knees. Then I mentioned one oral supplement that had not been on her list—*hyaluronic acid* (HA). "I've never even heard of it, but it's worth trying," Jenny said. Six weeks later, she walked nimbly into my clinic and reported a dramatic reduction in her pain and stiffness. She was surprised at this success—but I was not.

HA has been so effective for so many of my arthritis patients that I consider it an up-and-coming superstar among nutritional supplements.

WHAT IS HYALURONIC ACID?

A naturally occurring substance in the body, the HA molecule is formed by two sugars strung together in a long chain. HA is an essential component of the joints, skin, eyes and blood vessels (as well as the umbilical cord). HA deficiencies, which develop for reasons that are not well-understood, contribute to premature aging and disease in these tissues. As yet, there is no reliable test to measure HA levels.

HA is a key component of *synovial fluid*, the lubricating fluid in joint cavities. This fluid, which is secreted by a membrane that forms a capsule around the ends of bones, has two main purposes. First, it helps to minimize friction and prevent breakdown of the joints (like the oil used to lubricate moving car parts). Second, synovial fluid helps with shock absorption within joints. Cartilage is the main shock absorber, but it does not contain blood vessels—so synovial fluid transports the nutrients required for cartilage healing and regeneration, and removes waste products. In addition, HA is an actual component of cartilage and is required for healthy cartilage formation.

There are two main types of arthritis. *Osteoarthritis* is caused by the normal wear and tear of aging and/or by injury. *Rheumatoid arthritis* is an autoimmune disease in which the immune system attacks the body's own joint tissue and causes deterioration. As either type of arthritis progresses, the synovial fluid degrades, lessening its lubricating and shock-absorbing abilities …and cartilage breaks down and becomes inflamed. Supplementing with HA helps to counteract both of these effects.

THE FIGHT AGAINST ARTHRITIS

When I mention HA to patients, most say they've never heard of it. I expect this to change as news of HA's effectiveness spreads.

•**HA injections.** In 1997, HA injections were approved by the FDA for patients with osteoarthritis of the knee, and they now are being studied for use in shoulder, hip and ankle joints. Injectable HA products include Hyalgan, Supartz, Orthovisc and Synvisc.

HA injections go directly into the affected joint or joints…are done in a doctor's office using local anesthetic…take just a few minutes… and usually are given three to five times, each one week apart. Side effects include minor swelling, temporary pain, rash and/or bruising at the injection site. While not everyone who receives HA injections finds relief, for many people the painful symptoms of arthritis are noticeably reduced for up to six months (especially in the early stages of the disease), allowing patients to delay or avoid joint-replacement surgery.

For now, only a limited number of rheumatologists and osteopaths provide this therapy. HA shots cost about $230 each and may or may not be covered by insurance, depending on your policy. Fortunately, there is a promising alternative—oral HA.

•**HA oral supplementation.** With regard to HA's use as an oral supplement, the big question is whether it can be absorbed and used by the body when taken in capsule form. Critics of HA supplementation say that its molecular structure is too large to be absorbed in the digestive tract—yet several studies in the past four years have shown otherwise.

One of the first studies to demonstrate that HA is absorbed effectively into the bloodstream and the joints was presented at the 2004 Experimental Biology Conference. Researchers gave rats and dogs one oral dose of HA that was *radio labeled* (chemically joined with a radioactive substance), allowing it to be tracked with diagnostic imaging.

Result: HA was absorbed into the animals' bloodstreams and distributed to their joints. Although no similar studies have been done on people, I think it is logical to assume that HA's absorbability in humans may be similar to its action in animals.

Why am I keen on supplemental HA for arthritis? During the past year, several dozens of my patients with osteoarthritis and rheumatoid arthritis have taken nonprescription oral HA with good results. I have found that HA by itself can produce significant results—and in many cases, results are even better when HA is taken in combination with mainstay joint supplements, such as chondroitin, fish oil, glucosamine, *methylsulfonylmethane* (MSM) and/or *S-adenosylmethionine* (SAMe).

This is wonderful news, because HA often allows patients to reduce or discontinue pharmaceutical nonsteroidal anti-inflammatory (NSAID) drugs, such as *ibuprofen* (Motrin) and *naproxen* (Aleve). These drugs are associated with serious adverse side effects, including bleeding stomach ulcers, liver and kidney damage and increased risk for heart attack and stroke.

WHAT THE RESEARCH SAYS

HA is an example of a supplement that works well in the real world but has generated limited published data. Existing research mostly involves a patented HA product called BioCell Collagen II (714-632-1231, *www.biocelltechnology.com*), made from the sternal cartilage of chickens and used as an ingredient in various brands of HA oral supplements. One small study included 16 patients with osteoarthritis of the knee or hand who were taking COX-2 inhibitors or other NSAIDs. Eight patients took 1,000 mg of BioCell daily, while the other eight took a placebo. After two months of treatment, the group receiving BioCell reported significant improvement in pain, range of motion and swelling—whereas the placebo group showed no significant changes. One such product, sold at health food stores, is BioCell Chicken Sternum Collagen Type II, made by Premier Labs (800-887-5227, *www.premierlabs.com*).

Other oral products contain a type of HA called *sodium hyaluronate*, which is produced during microbial fermentation. While I am not aware of any human studies on this form of HA, animal studies suggest that it is safe and several of my patients have reported positive effects. One such product available in health food stores is Now Foods Hyaluronic Acid (888-669-3663, *www.nowfoods.com*). The recommended dosage is 100 mg twice daily. The Now Foods capsules, like brands that contain BioCell, can be used indefinitely, generally are safe and only rarely cause mild digestive upset.

■ **More from Mark A. Stengler, ND...**

Maximum Relief from Arthritis

For maximum relief from arthritis pain and inflammation, combine *hyaluronic acid* (HA) oral supplements or injections with other natural supplements described below. All are available in health food stores and, unless noted, generally are safe for everyone. Mild arthritis symptoms may respond to the lower end of the dosage range, while severe symptoms may require the higher dosage.

•**Chondroitin,** a substance derived from cow cartilage.

Dosage: 1,200 mg daily. Lower the dosage or discontinue use if you experience digestive upset, such as nausea.

•**Fish oil** in the form of *docosahexaenoic acid* (DHA) and *eicosapentaenoic acid* (EPA), combined.

Dosage: 1,000 mg to 2,000 mg daily.

Caution: Get your doctor's approval first if you take a blood thinner, such as aspirin or *warfarin* (Coumadin).

•**Glucosamine,** a substance derived from shellfish.

Dosage: 1,500 mg daily. Lower the dosage or discontinue use if you experience digestive upset, such as diarrhea.

Caution: Check with your doctor before using if you are allergic to shellfish...or if you have diabetes, because glucosamine may cause blood-sugar fluctuations.

•**Methylsulfonylmethane (MSM),** an organic sulfur compound.

Dosage: 2,000 mg to 6,000 mg daily.

•**S-adenosylmethionine (SAMe),** an amino acid-like substance.

Dosage: 600 mg to 1,200 mg daily.

How to use: For rheumatoid arthritis, take fish oil and MSM. For osteoarthritis, start with glucosamine and MSM...and if symptoms are not adequately relieved within two months, also take chondroitin, fish oil and SAMe.

■ ■ ■ ■

Best Options for Pain

Nonsteroidal anti-inflammatory drugs (NSAIDs) are good for mild-to-moderate joint pain. I typically prescribe *ibuprofen* (Advil, etc.) or *naproxen* (Aleve)—you can't tell in advance which will work better for an individual. Talk to your doctor about the best dosage for your situation. Don't rely on these drugs for more than a week at a stretch. When NSAIDs don't stop chronic pain, you must address the root cause of the pain.

Some patients tell me that their joints feel better when they take the supplements glucosamine and/or chondroitin sulfate, widely touted for this purpose. In fact, I feel there is no good evidence that these products build cartilage or have a statistically significant benefit for joint pain.

However, there is no evidence that these supplements are harmful (assuming you are not allergic)—so if a patient wants to try them or to continue using them, I don't object.

Beth E. Shubin Stein, MD, an orthopaedic surgeon and sports medicine specialist at the Women's Sports Medicine Center at the Hospital for Special Surgery and an assistant professor at Weill Medical College of Cornell University, both in New York City.

■ ■ ■ ■

Foods That Help Reduce Arthritis Pain

Vegetables, fruits and whole grains provide antioxidants that may ease the pain and swelling of arthritis, an inflammation of the joints. Also helpful are omega-3 fatty acids (found in cold-water fish, flaxseed and other foods), which the body converts to anti-inflammatory compounds. Eat eight to 12 ounces weekly of fish rich in omega-3s, such as salmon, mackerel and sardines. Limit polyunsaturated fats, such as corn oil and safflower oil, which are high in omega-6 fatty acids, substances converted in the body into compounds that promote inflammation. Also limit your intake of saturated fat, found primarily in meat and dairy products, because these unhealthy fats may increase inflammation.

Karen Collins, RD, CDN, nutrition adviser, American Institute for Cancer Research, Washington, DC.

Natural Remedies a Pharmacist Has in Her Own Medicine Cabinet

Suzy Cohen, RPh, a registered practicing pharmacist for nearly 20 years and author of *The 24-Hour Pharmacist*. Collins. Her syndicated newspaper column, "Dear Pharmacist," reaches more than 24 million readers. Based in Florida, she is a member of the Association of Natural Medicine Pharmacists and the American Holistic Health Association.

As a pharmacist for almost two decades, Suzy Cohen knows the importance of medication—but she also has learned to "think outside the pill" and recommend natural options that often are just as good or better at promoting health without the risk of dangerous side effects.

Here are the remedies she recommends most often. All are free of significant side effects unless otherwise noted, but always talk with your doctor before using any supplements.

TEA TREE OIL FOR WOUNDS

This oil kills germs, reduces pain and helps wounds heal more quickly. You can use it in place of antibiotic ointment for minor cuts, scratches and burns…to treat toenail fungus… and, when diluted, as a gargle to kill the germs that cause sore throat.

How it works: It's a strong antiseptic that kills bacteria as well as fungi.

How to use: Moisten a cotton ball or swab with one or two drops of the oil, and apply it to the area two to three times daily until it heals.

For a gargle for sore throat: Mix a few drops in a cup of water, gargle and spit it out.

Caution: Do not swallow it.

GINGER FOR NAUSEA

Studies have shown that ginger can relieve nausea—due to pregnancy, seasickness, etc.—as well as or better than over-the-counter drugs.

In one study, published in *The Lancet*, volunteers were given either ginger or Dramamine (a nausea-preventing drug), then were seated in a chair designed to trigger motion sickness. Those given ginger were able to withstand the motion 57% longer than those given the drug.

How to use: Put one teaspoon of peeled, grated fresh gingerroot in a cup of boiling water. Let it steep for 10 minutes, then drink (you can filter out the ginger if you want). Or chew and swallow a piece of crystallized ginger, sold in health food stores.

Caution: Ginger can increase the risk of bleeding when taken with blood-thinning drugs, such as *warfarin* (Coumadin).

RHODIOLA ROSEA FOR STRESS

This herb acts like a natural form of Valium by reducing physical and emotional stress. The supplement is made from the root of the Siberian plant.

How it works: Herbalists classify Rhodiola as an *adaptogen*, a class of herbs that "sense" chemicals in the body and either raise or lower them, according to need. It normalizes levels of brain chemicals that affect mood, such as *monoamines* and *beta-endorphins*, which help counter the effects of stress. Rhodiola also may increase *serotonin*, which enhances feelings of well-being.

How to use: During times of stress, take 100 milligrams (mg) of rhodiola rosea in capsule form, two to three times daily. It's best taken on a cyclical basis—two months on, two weeks off.

CALCIUM PLUS MAGNESIUM FOR CRAMPS

People who experience frequent and/or painful menstrual or muscle cramps often have a deficiency of calcium and magnesium.

How it works: Calcium and magnesium regulate the contraction and relaxation of muscles.

How to use: Before going to bed, take 500 mg to 600 mg of calcium, along with 150 mg to 200 mg of magnesium (using the chelate or glycinate forms—check the label). Combination formulas are easy to find and fine to use.

For menstrual problems, start 10 days before you expect your period to begin each month and continue until your period is complete.

GABA FOR INSOMNIA

Gamma-aminobutyric acid (GABA) is a neurotransmitter (mood-related brain chemical) that is naturally present in the body. It's taken in supplement form to reduce insomnia, as well as anxiety and depression.

How it works: GABA is an inhibitory neurotransmitter that slows activity in the brain and makes it easier to fall asleep.

How to use: Take 500 mg to 1,000 mg one hour before bedtime if you have trouble getting to sleep. If your problem is that you wake in the middle of the night and can't get back to sleep, take it then. Don't exceed recommended doses on the package. Do this for two weeks. If it doesn't help, talk to your doctor.

Caution: Combining GABA with prescription or over-the-counter sleep aids can cause excessive sedation.

CAPSAICIN CREAM FOR PAIN

Capsaicin is the chemical compound that puts the "hot" in chili peppers. It is effective for easing muscle aches, back and joint pain and nerve pain caused by the herpes virus (postherpetic neuralgia).

How it works: When applied as a cream, it causes nerve cells to empty their reservoirs of *substance P*, a pain-causing chemical. This results in less pain from the underlying disorder.

How to use: Start with a 0.025% concentration. Apply it two to three times daily—the initial burning sensation diminishes with continued use. If needed, you can always buy the stronger 0.075% concentration—but it's best to work your way up to this strength.

Caution: Wear latex gloves when applying capsaicin—and wash your hands thoroughly after using to prevent residual cream from getting into the eyes, nose, etc.

PROBIOTICS FOR DIGESTIVE DISCOMFORT

A healthy digestive tract contains trillions of bacteria, many of which have beneficial effects. These so-called "good" (probiotic) organisms promote digestive health, improve immunity and aid in the synthesis of B vitamins, among many other functions.

How they work: Probiotic supplements replenish beneficial bacteria and crowd out harmful organisms that can cause gas, bloating, diarrhea and other digestive problems.

How to use: Take a daily supplement of a least 10 billion organisms that contains a variety of living organisms, such as *L. bulgaricus,*

L. bifida and *B. longum.* Some yogurts contain these live active cultures, but avoid those that contain sugar or artificial sweeteners.

BIOTIN FOR CRACKED NAILS

The B vitamin biotin is the only nutrient that has been shown to improve nail health in generally healthy adults. People with a deficiency of biotin often have fragile nails that crack easily.

How it works: Biotin is absorbed by the nail matrix, the part under the fingernail where nail cells are generated.

How to use: Take 2,000 micrograms (mcg) to 4,000 mcg of biotin daily, as well as a B-complex supplement. Most people will notice an improvement in nail strength and thickness in one to two months.

No More Migraines

Mark A. Stengler, ND, naturopathic physician in private practice, La Jolla, California…adjunct associate clinical professor at the National College of Natural Medicine, Portland, Oregon…author of many books, including *The Natural Physician's Healing Therapies* and coauthor of *Prescription for Natural Cures* (both from Bottom Line Books)…and author of the *Bottom Line/Natural Healing* newsletter.

Using the word headache to describe a migraine is like referring to the space shuttle as an airplane. Technically, migraines are headaches, of course—but the suffering they cause far exceeds that of most other types. An estimated 30 million Americans, most of them between ages 15 and 55, get migraines. Women sufferers outnumber men three to one, and while the onset of menopause sometimes brings relief, it doesn't always. Fewer than half of migraine sufferers are properly diagnosed—instead, many are incorrectly told that their headaches stem from sinus problems or tension. Because treatments for other types of headaches do not alleviate migraines, millions of people suffer needlessly.

Standard treatment for migraines includes prescription drugs, such as *sumatriptan* (Imitrex), *zolmitriptan* (Zomig) and *rizatriptan* (Maxalt). These are intended to prevent, halt or ease migraines—but they do not work for everyone. Potential side effects include nausea, dizziness, diarrhea and sweating…and in rare cases, an increased risk for heart attack and stroke, perhaps due to blood vessel damage. When the drugs are discontinued, patients may get rebound headaches.

Good news: It is possible to reduce the frequency of migraines or prevent them by using natural, nutritional, drug-free substances.

GETTING THE RIGHT DIAGNOSIS

Migraines may be caused when arteries in the brain dilate abnormally and nerves that coil around the arteries are stretched. In response, the nerves release chemicals that cause painful inflammation and further enlargement of arteries, magnifying pain even more.

Migraine symptoms are distinct from those of other types of headaches. If you experience two or more of the following symptoms, you probably are dealing with migraines. *Migraine pain may…*

- **Occur on one side of the head.**
- **Last from four hours to as long as 72 hours.**
- **Pulsate or throb.**
- **Be triggered by certain situations or eating particular foods.**
- **Worsen during exertion,** such as when climbing stairs.
- **Be accompanied by nausea or vomiting.**
- **Be exacerbated by sound.**
- **Be accompanied by oversensitivity to light.**

About 20% of migraine sufferers experience *aura*, a visual disturbance that typically comes on 20 to 60 minutes before the onset of pain. Aura may be perceived as flashing lights, blind spots or wavy lines in the field of vision. It may be accompanied by facial tingling, muscle weakness and/or speech difficulties, such as slurring words or having trouble finding words. Aura occurs when certain nerve cells in the brain become temporarily hyperactive, triggering visual disturbances and tingling sensations…while in other nerve cells, activity is depressed, temporarily impairing vision, speech and muscle strength.

Another clue: Up to 80% of migraine sufferers have a family history of the condition—so if a close relative has migraines, you are more likely to get them, too.

If you suspect migraines, see a headache specialist or neurologist. He/she should take a detailed history that includes your migraine symptoms…pattern of attacks…other types of headaches you have…family history of headaches…and all of your medications. Many, such as hypertension drugs, birth control pills and nonsteroidal anti-inflammatory drugs (NSAIDs), can contribute to migraines. Hormone testing may be appropriate, as deficiencies of estrogen and/or progesterone (in women) or of thyroid hormone can lead to migraines. All of this information is vital, because no tests can definitively confirm a migraine diagnosis.

NATURAL WAYS TO PREVENT MIGRAINES

Numerous studies confirm the benefits of the vitamin-like *coenzyme Q10* (CoQ10)…*riboflavin* (vitamin B-2)…and the mineral *magnesium*. Taking just one of these three natural substances can decrease migraine severity and/or frequency by about half. In my experience, when patients regularly take all three, overall improvement can exceed 75%.

Theory: An abnormal lag in brain cells' energy production triggers the blood vessel dilation that leads to a migraine. These three nutrients support the *mitochondria*—structures in cells that convert oxygen and nutrients into chemical energy to power the cells' metabolic activities—helping them to work more effectively and thereby preventing migraines.

Daily prevention strategy: I suggest using all three of these substances if you get migraines once or more per month. Take them for four months. If you notice improvement, continue indefinitely. *Dosages and guidelines for people age 12 and up…*

•**CoQ10 at 100 mg three times daily.** Occasional side effects, such as mild heartburn or nausea, can be avoided by taking CoQ10 with meals.

•**Riboflavin at 400 mg once daily.** B vitamins work best when in balance with one another, so take an additional B complex or multivitamin.

•**Magnesium at 200 mg twice daily** (reduce dosage if you develop diarrhea). Least likely to cause loose stool is the magnesium glycinate form.

These supplements are sold in health food stores, are nontoxic, rarely have side effects and generally are safe. *Evidence that they work…*

•**CoQ10.** In a study published in the journal *Cephalalgia*, 31 migraine patients took 150 mg of CoQ10 daily. After three months, the number of migraine attacks fell, on average, from 4.85 to 2.81 per month…and duration of pain (measured in "migraine days") was significantly reduced. In another study, Swiss and Belgian researchers gave 42 patients a placebo or CoQ10 at 100 mg three times daily for three months. Migraine frequency fell by at least half in 47% of patients taking CoQ10, compared with 14% of the placebo group. CoQ10 users also had less nausea.

•**Riboflavin.** In a Belgian study, 55 migraine patients took either a placebo or 400 mg of riboflavin daily. Frequency and duration of migraines decreased by at least half in 59% of riboflavin users, compared with 15% of placebo users. Research suggests that combining riboflavin with *beta-blockers* (cardiovascular drugs sometimes prescribed for migraines) may be more effective at preventing migraines than either therapy used alone.

•**Magnesium.** Up to half of patients have a deficiency of magnesium during a migraine, as shown by testing of blood drawn during attacks. Oral magnesium supplementation may reduce the frequency and duration of migraines.

Possible reason: Upon exposure to a migraine trigger, excess calcium flows into brain cells, causing a sudden constriction of blood vessels…and magnesium supplementation combats this by normalizing the balance of minerals in the brain. In addition, intravenous (IV) magnesium can give fast relief from acute migraine symptoms. Although conventional doctors generally do not offer this therapy, some holistic practitioners do.

■ **More from Mark A. Stengler, ND...**

Beware These Migraine Triggers

In susceptible individuals, certain foods and/or situations can bring on migraines. To identify your triggers, keep a diary for four weeks, noting when your migraines occur and looking for patterns.

Common food culprits...

- **Alcohol,** especially red wine and beer
- **Caffeine and/or caffeine withdrawal**
- **Chocolate**
- **Cheese,** especially aged (Parmesan, Asiago)
- **Fermented foods** (miso, sauerkraut)
- **Monosodium glutamate** (a flavoring)
- **Nitrates** (a type of preservative)
- **Pickled foods** (dill pickles, olives)
- **Shellfish**
- **Wheat**

Situational triggers...

- **Changes in weather, altitude, time zone**
- **Dehydration**
- **Fatigue,** sleep problems
- **Glaring lights**
- **Perfumes,** powerful odors
- **Stress**

■ ■ ■ ■

Botox for Migraines?

When other treatments fail, some doctors offer injections of prescription *botulinim toxin* (Botox). This use of Botox is "off label"—meaning it is legal but the drug has not been FDA-approved for this purpose. Since the therapy is considered experimental, insurance generally does not cover it. If a clinical trial, now in its final stage, shows Botox to be effective against migraine, it may earn FDA approval within a few years.

Some evidence suggests that multiple Botox injections in the head and/or neck can reduce the severity and frequency of migraine attacks for three to four months by decreasing the release of certain chemicals from nerve endings. Cost varies widely, from $700 to $2,000 or more.

Alan M. Rapoport, MD, assistant clinical professor of neurology at the Yale University School of Medicine, New Haven, Connecticut. Founder and director emeritus of The New England Center for Headache in Stamford, Connecticut he has coauthored nine books on headache, including Conquering Daily Headache. BC Decker.

■ ■ ■ ■

New Treatment Cuts Migraine Attacks by 46%

Injections of local anesthetic can reduce the number and severity of attacks, reports Maria Adele Giamberardino, MD. Many migraine sufferers have trigger points in the neck that, when stimulated, elicit the same pain as their migraine attacks. In a recent study, anesthetic was injected into patients' trigger points four times over a two-month period.

Result: The number of attacks decreased by 46%, and the intensity decreased by 17%.

Maria Adele Giamberardino, MD, associate professor of internal medicine and director of the centers for headache and fibromyalgia, "G. d'Annunzio" University of Chieti, Chieti, Italy.

■ ■ ■ ■

Better Migraine Treatment

In two recent studies involving a total of 2,956 people, participants received pills containing the migraine drug *sumatriptan* (Imitrex) or the nonsteroidal anti-inflammatory drug *naproxen* (Aleve)...pills containing both painkilling drugs ...or a placebo.

Result: Those who took the combination pill reported better headache relief than those who took either drug alone or a placebo.

Theory: The drug combination targets several neural pathways believed to trigger migraines. A combination pill is under review by the FDA.

Jan Lewis Brandes, MD, assistant clinical professor of neurology, Vanderbilt University School of Medicine, Nashville.

■ ■ ■ ■

New Treatment for Cluster Headaches

In a recent study, 63% of attacks in patients who were given 10 mg of the migraine nasal spray *zolmitriptan* (Zomig) were significantly relieved in as little as 30 minutes.

Some patients had relief within 10 minutes. Just 5 mg eased pain in half of participants.

Cluster headaches are among the most painful form of headaches, and there are few FDA-approved treatments available.

Zolmitriptan's side effects include drowsiness, tingling and chest discomfort. Zolmitriptan is a triptan, a type of drug that should not be given to patients who have heart disease, high blood pressure or blood vessel problems.

Alan M. Rapoport, MD, assistant clinical professor of neurology at the Yale University School of Medicine, New Haven, Connecticut, founder and director emeritus, The New England Center for Headache, Stamford, Connecticut. He was leader of a study of 52 people, published in Neurology.

■ ■ ■ ■

Hypnosis for Pain Reduction

In a recent study of 200 women scheduled for breast cancer surgery, a psychologist treated one group with 15 minutes of hypnosis (including suggestions on how to reduce pain) within one hour prior to surgery, while the other group simply spoke with a psychologist about whatever they wished.

Result: The hypnosis group needed less anesthesia and reported less pain than the other group.

Theory: Hypnosis induces relaxation, which helps reduce pain.

To find a hypnotist: Contact the American Society of Clinical Hypnosis (630-980-4740, *www.asch.net.*)

Guy Montgomery, PhD, associate professor, Mount Sinai School of Medicine, New York City.

Back Pain Relief

Mark A. Stengler, ND, naturopathic physician in private practice, La Jolla, California...adjunct associate clinical professor at the National College of Natural Medicine, Portland, Oregon...author of many books, including The Natural Physician's Healing Therapies *and coauthor of* Prescription for Natural Cures *(both from Bottom Line Books)...and author of the* Bottom Line/Natural Healing *newsletter.*

Picking up a heavy box, you get a sudden stab of pain in your lower back—and now all you feel like doing is lying down. Or while sitting at your desk, you rub your aching back, thinking resignedly that it's time for surgery. If these scenarios sound familiar, don't be too hasty to follow through—or you may regret it.

Now we know: Bed rest for lower back pain (LBP) may do more harm than good...and surgery, once routine for certain lower back problems, is usually unnecessary.

LBP can result from an injury to muscles, tendons and/or ligaments that surround the spine. Or the problem can occur in the spine itself—for instance, misaligned vertebrae or a herniated disc (when the gel-like inner pulp of the disc between two vertebrae bulges out and irritates nearby nerves). Less frequently, LBP is due to nerve damage from an infection or tumor, osteoporosis (brittle bones) or problems with the kidneys or other organs.

LBP is called acute if it lasts several days to several weeks...and chronic if it lasts a few months or more. Acute LBP typically comes on suddenly, when an abrupt twist of the body or an attempt to lift something heavy leads to a muscle strain or spasm. Acute pain may ease quickly as the tissues heal, or it may persist due to tiny tears in the muscle and become chronic. When LBP is caused by a spine problem, discomfort usually grows as the condition gradually worsens. If back pain is severe or lasts for more than a week, see your doctor or a physiatrist (a physician specializing in physical medicine and rehabilitation). Typically the cause of LBP can be determined by a physical exam, X-ray and/or MRI.

PAIN RELIEF RIGHT NOW

Doctors used to think that the best treatment for acute LBP was strict bed rest—and this belief persists among the general population, though many studies show that bed rest delays recovery. Obviously, you should avoid exercising or lifting until pain eases significantly, but try to stay mobile.

To reduce pain and inflammation, apply a cold pack to the sore area for about 15 minutes out of each waking hour. After 24 hours, alternate the hourly 15-minute applications between cold and heat. Heat relaxes muscles and increases blood flow to the area. Continue until pain subsides.

Convenient: Instant single-use heat and cold packs that self-activate...or reusable microwavable heat packs and freezable cold packs (all sold at drugstores).

Also, consult a chiropractor for *spinal manipulation*—hands-on maneuvers that stretch and realign the spine and surrounding tissues, relieving pain.

Evidence: A study in the *Journal of Manipulative and Physiological Therapeutics* compared 93 LBP patients treated by chiropractors with 45 patients treated by family physicians. After one month, 56% of the chiropractic group felt better or much better, but only 13% of the other group experienced such improvement. To find a practitioner, contact the American Chiropractic Association (703-276-8800, *www.amerchiro. org*). If you have *spinal stenosis* (narrowing of the spinal canal), do not have spinal manipulation—it could damage the spinal cord.

In addition, consider acupuncture, which reduces muscle spasms and releases natural painkillers called *endorphins*...massage therapy, which relaxes tight muscles and increases blood flow to the sore area...and/or physical therapy, which uses exercises, hands-on maneuvers, heat and cold to promote healing.

SOOTHING SUPPLEMENTS

Various natural substances can alleviate back pain. All are sold at health food stores and, unless otherwise noted, generally are safe and can be taken until symptoms are gone. Use the lower end of each dosage range if you weigh less than 200 pounds, and the higher dosage if you weigh more or if relief has not been achieved within one week. Depending on the aggressiveness of the treatment you desire, these supplements can be used individually, in any combination or even all together.

To reduce muscle pain and inflammation...

•**Devil's claw,** an African root.

Dosage: For acute pain, take 800 mg three times daily of concentrated extract capsules (standardized to 1.5% to 3% harpagosides) for up to two weeks. For chronic pain, take 200 mg to 400 mg three times daily for up to eight weeks. Consult a doctor before using if you have diabetes. Do not use if you have an ulcer, heartburn, gastritis or gallstones...are pregnant or nursing...or take a blood thinner, such as aspirin or *warfarin* (Coumadin).

•**Protease (protein-digesting)** enzymes.

Dosage: Bromelain at 1,000 mg three times daily between meals.

Alternative: A combination enzyme formula, such as Wobenzym from Mucos Pharma (866-962-6996, *www.wobenzym-usa.com*). Take five to 10 tablets three times daily on an empty stomach. Do not use if you take a blood thinner or have an ulcer.

•**B vitamins.**

Dosage: Vitamin B-1 and vitamin B-6, each at 50 mg to 100 mg three times daily...plus vitamin B-12 at 250 micrograms (mcg) to 500 mcg three times daily.

To ease muscle spasms...

•**Methylsulfonylmethane (MSM),** an organic sulfur compound.

Dosage: 4,000 mg to 8,000 mg daily.

•**Magnesium.**

Dosage: 250 mg twice daily.

•**Calcium.**

Dosage: 500 mg twice daily.

To alleviate stiffness...

•**Rhus tox, a homeopathic remedy derived from poison ivy.**

Dosage: Two pellets four times daily of a 30C potency.

To soothe nerve pain...

•**St. John's wort oil.** Rub a few drops of this herbal oil over the affected area twice daily.

Natural supplements may take 24 hours or more to provide relief. In the interim, if pain is severe, also take an over-the-counter nonsteroidal anti-inflammatory drug (NSAID), such as aspirin, *ibuprofen* (Advil) or *naproxen* (Aleve). Or ask your doctor about prescription pain medication, such as hydrocodone with *acetaminophen* (Vicodin)…and/or a prescription muscle relaxant, such as *cyclobenzaprine* (Flexeril). Take these medications as briefly as possible to minimize the risk of side effects, such as ulcers, kidney disease and/or liver damage.

LONG-TERM HEALING STRATEGIES

Chronic LBP often results from poor posture, which misaligns the spine and weakens torso muscles. *These exercise regimens can help…*

•**Alexander Technique** teaches proper body mechanics and movement techniques.

Referrals: American Society for the Alexander Technique (800-473-0620, *www.alexandertech.org*).

•**Feldenkrais Method** is administered as one-on-one manipulation and/or group instruction in proper alignment.

Referrals: Feldenkrais Guild of North America (800-775-2118, *www.feldenkraisguild.com*).

•**Pilates targets supportive "core" muscles** of the torso.

Referrals: Pilates Method Alliance (866-573-4945, *www.pilatesmethodalliance.org*).

•**Yoga increases flexibility,** balance and muscle strength.

Referrals: International Association of Yoga Therapists (928-541-0004, *www.iayt.org*).

Surprisingly, LBP also may result from foot problems that lead to spinal misalignment—such as when arches are too flat or too high (so feet roll inward or outward) or when one leg is slightly shorter than the other. A podiatrist can provide supportive custom-made orthotic shoe inserts that promote proper alignment, allowing back muscles to heal.

■ **More from Mark A. Stengler, ND…**

When to Call 911

Back pain accompanied by certain other symptoms can signal a medical emergency.

Heart attack can cause back pain and…

•**Chest pain,** especially if there also is a crushing or squeezing sensation

•**Sweating**

•**Shortness of breath**

•**Nausea**

•**Pain that spreads into the jaw,** shoulders or arms.

Spinal injury can cause back pain and…

•**Weakness in the legs**

•**Numbness or tingling in the buttocks,** genital area or legs

•**Loss of bowel or bladder control.**

If you experience any of these symptoms in conjunction with back pain, call 911 and be specific—"I think I'm having a heart attack" or "I think I have a spinal injury." This is not the time to be stoic about back pain.

■ ■ ■ ■

Ouch! Sitting Up Straight Is Bad for Your Back

Despite the age-old belief that "sitting up straight" is good for your back, research shows that in reality it increases strain on the disks in your back. Hunching forward is bad for your back, too.

New study: The best sitting position for one's back is a 135-degree thigh-to-trunk angle with feet planted on the floor. This minimizes the strain on disks. The best way to achieve the 135-degree angle is by sitting on a wedge-shaped cushion with the thicker end under your tailbone to raise it slightly. But any position in which you open up the angle between thighs and back to reduce back strain and avert back pain—such as by leaning backward—is better than sitting with your legs and back at right angles.

Waseem Amir Bashir, MBCbB, MRCP, radiologist, University of Alberta Hospital, Edmonton, Canada.

■ ■ ■ ■

Drug Combination May Increase Bleeding

In an analysis of studies involving 153,000 men and women, those who took a selective serotonin reuptake inhibitor (SSRI) antidepressant, such as *fluoxetine* (Prozac), had twice the risk for upper gastrointestinal bleeding as those who did not take an SSRI. Those who took an SSRI and an oral nonsteroidal anti-inflammatory drug (NSAID), such as aspirin or *ibuprofen* (Advil, etc.), had six times the risk for bleeding as those who took neither drug.

Theory: The combination has a synergistic effect that increases the bleeding risk from each drug alone.

If you take an SSRI: Ask your doctor about taking painkillers other than NSAIDs, such as *acetaminophen* (Tylenol).

Sonal Singh, MD, assistant professor of internal medicine, Wake Forest University School of Medicine, Winston-Salem, North Carolina.

■ ■ ■ ■

Acid Reflux Can Cause Chest Pain

In a study of 31 emergency room patients (median age 46) who complained of chest pain, 57% had acid levels in the esophagus high enough to indicate gastroesophageal reflux disease (GERD). Heartburn is the most common symptom of GERD, but the disorder also can cause chest pain, hoarseness and chronic cough with or without heartburn.

If you have any of these symptoms: Ask your doctor if GERD is a possible cause.

Caution: If you suffer severe chest pain that does not go away within five minutes, seek immediate medical care to rule out a heart-related cause.

Julia Liu, MD, assistant professor, division of gastroenterology, University of Alberta Hospital, Edmonton, Canada.

How to Live Happily— Even If You're Sick

Arthur J. Barsky, MD, professor of psychiatry at Harvard Medical School and director of psychiatric research at the Brigham and Women's Hospital, both in Boston. He is coauthor (with Emily C. Deans, MD) of *Stop Being Your Symptoms and Start Being Yourself.* HarperCollins.

For nearly one out of every three Americans, chronic illness and/or pain is a way of life. Despite medical care, symptoms, such as arthritis pain, headache, back pain or serious fatigue, persist—often making sufferers miserable on a regular basis.

But why do some people become devastated by their health problems, while others lead full and satisfying lives despite them? It's never easy to live with a chronic ailment, but the degree to which it impacts your life is largely within your control. *Secrets to living better—despite illness...*

SHIFT YOUR FOCUS

Research shows that focusing on pain only makes it worse.

Important finding: Researchers divided people who had just had a tooth pulled into two groups—one group was told to rate their pain every 20 minutes, while the other group rated it only after two hours. Those who had been observing their pain regularly felt significantly more pain at the two-hour mark than those who had not.

Helpful: If you have a chronic health problem, carry a notebook and record each time you think about your symptom (you may be surprised how often this is)...what those thoughts are...and what you are doing.

After seven days, review the notebook. What were you typically doing when you frequently thought about your health problem? When you thought about it less often? The goal is to increase the amount of time you spend in activities that lead your focus away from the symptom. For example, if you don't think about your health problem when you spend time with friends, work in your garden or listen to music, schedule more time for such distractions.

Once you've determined the most effective distractions, do these activities for a while.

Then try this exercise: Focus intently on your symptom for five minutes and rate its severity on a scale of one to five. Then use a distraction (examples described above) for three to five minutes and rate your pain again. Keep track of the distractions that work best and incorporate them into your life.

RETHINK YOUR SYMPTOMS

Changing how you think about your ailment is key to minimizing its impact on your life. Distress is often caused less by the symptoms themselves than your worry about them.

Example: If you have worrisome, alarming thoughts about the symptoms of your illness or chronic condition, those thoughts can make your symptoms feel much worse. *Helpful...*

- **Recognize negative thoughts.**

You may think: "Now, besides my headache, I have ringing in my ears...I must have a brain tumor." These thoughts are bound to make your breathing shallow, your heart race and your muscles tense—all of which worsen the pain.

- **Replace catastrophic thoughts.** "I feel uncomfortable today, but these symptoms have occurred before. I still can work or run errands despite my headache. And tomorrow I'll probably feel a lot better."

- **Remember that minor symptoms come and go.** When you have a new, unexplained pain or discomfort elsewhere in your body, remind yourself that the vast majority of such symptoms get better by themselves.

Important: Tell your doctor about any new symptoms that concern you.

STOP DESTRUCTIVE BEHAVIORS

Common mistakes to avoid...

- **Constantly examining yourself.** Paying excessive attention to a medical problem will only make it feel worse. Prodding a lump or lesion repeatedly, for example, is likely to make it sore, increasing anxiety.

Solution: Ask your doctor how often you should be checking yourself.

- **Obsessively researching your problem.** Researching symptoms in a quest for reassurance or new answers usually adds to anxiety instead of reducing it—and certainly takes time away from more rewarding activities, such as hobbies or spending time with family.

Solution: Schedule an hour in the evening to do research in medical books or on-line. When you are able, gradually postpone the session. This will help you develop the ability to better control your anxiety. Then taper off the research time over the following weeks and months until the information you're gathering no longer amplifies your worries.

- **Giving up the things you love.** Chronic pain or fatigue leads many people to cut back on physical activities. But while acute pain is a signal that damage may be occurring, chronic pain may not necessarily be. In fact, inactivity usually weakens muscles and stiffens joints. The less you do, the less you'll feel like doing.

Solution: If there is something that you once enjoyed but have stopped due to your health problem, check with your doctor to see whether the activity is truly risky. If not, gradually add the activity back into your life.

Example: If you've given up golfing, start by taking out your old clubs and polishing them up. The next day, take a few practice swings outdoors. Over a period of weeks, get out to the driving range and then to the golf course.

ADJUST YOUR ATTITUDES

Your beliefs and attitudes can either magnify or minimize the impact of your physical problem. *Thoughts to watch out for...*

- **Why is this happening to me?** Feeling that you've been singled out for misfortune often transforms ordinary pain into misery. In reality, you're not alone—everyone gets sick at some point in his life. For help putting your troubles in perspective, consider joining a support group for people who have a similar ailment. Large hospitals and academic medical centers often sponsor such groups.

- **Good health is everything.** People who cope best with chronic symptoms understand that health is indeed precious—but it can't replace love, fulfillment, self-respect and wisdom. Health problems may make it more difficult to attain the things that make life most worth living—but usually such obstacles can be overcome.

13

Savvy Consumer

Dangerous Chemical Can Leach from Food Containers

nvironmental health organizations in the United States and Canada are calling for a ban on the use of the chemical bisphenol A (BPA) in baby bottles, toddler cups, water bottles and other food and beverage containers.

"This is cause for concern. All 19 polycarbonate bottles [investigated in the study] leached BPA when heated. This clearly shows that BPA is certainly leaching from popular and common consumer products," said Judith Robinson, special projects director with the Environmental Health Fund. "We're calling for an immediate moratorium on the use of BPA in all baby bottles, as well as all food and beverage containers. It's not necessary, and we're calling for an end to it immediately."

TWO STUDIES SHOW BPA LEACHES FROM BOTTLES

The call for a ban coincides with publication of a new study, "Baby's Toxic Bottle: Bisphenol A Leaching from Popular Brands of Baby Bottles," commissioned by the same group of organizations, showing that BPA leaches from popular brands of plastic baby bottles when the bottles are heated.

This study comes just days after another study found that exposing plastic bottles in general to boiling water can release BPA 55 times faster than normal.

RISKS OF BPA

There is concern in many quarters that BPA, an environmental estrogen, may pose some

Teleconference with Judith Robinson, special projects director, Environmental Health Fund.
"Baby's Toxic Bottle: Bisphenol A Leaching from Popular Brands of Baby Bottles."
David Carpenter, MD, professor, environmental health sciences, School of Public Health, State University of New York at Albany.
Steven Hentges, PhD, executive director, Polycarbonate Business Unit, American Plastics Council.

risk to development and reproduction, although it's unclear at what level that harm begins.

The fear has been that exposure to BPA can cause birth defects and developmental problems. Exposure to BPA has also been blamed for a variety of other problems, including cancer, diabetes, obesity and attention-deficit disorder.

David Carpenter, MD, a professor of environmental health sciences at the State University of New York at Albany School of Public Health, said BPA taken into the body before birth and in the early years of life could alter the ratio of sex hormones and affect development.

"It's absolutely obscene to use a substance that can make little boys less masculine and opens the chance that little girls will go on to develop breast cancer," he said.

PLASTICS INDUSTRY REACTION

A representative of the plastics industry, however, dismissed the alarm.

"The data that is presented has been known for years, " said Steven Hentges, PhD, executive director of the American Plastics Council's Polycarbonate Business Unit. "Most importantly, data of that type has been reviewed by government agencies around the world in their comprehensive reviews on BPA and, in every case, they reach a conclusion even after considering this kind of data that polycarbonate baby bottles are safe for use."

BABY BOTTLES TESTED

The new report tested six major brands of plastic baby bottles available at major retailers, including Walmart and Babies-R-Us, in the United States and Canada. According to the study, 95% of baby bottles on the market contain BPA.

The brands tested—which included Avent, Disney/The First Years, Dr. Brown, Evenflo, Gerber and Playtex—all leached BPA when heated. According to the study authors, these same levels of BPA caused a range of adverse effects in laboratory animals.

Among US bottles, the Dr. Brown brand had the highest level of leaching while Avent brand bottles had the lowest levels, the report said.

info For more information on BPA and to read the full study, visit the Web site of the Center for Health, Environment & Justice, *www.babystoxicbottle.org.*

Toy Magnets Can Attract Real Problems

Sanjeev Dutta, MD, assistant professor, surgery and pediatrics, Lucile Packard Children's Hospital, Stanford University.
Jill Eberle, San José, California.
Archives of Pediatric and Adolescent Medicine.

This is the story of a little boy who swallowed a magnet and then wound up in the hospital.

Actually, Braden Eberle, 4, of San José, California, swallowed two tiny magnets from his older brother's construction kit on two successive days.

After the first ingestion, he confessed to his mom, Jill Eberle, whose first reaction was that the magnet would pass through her son's system without a problem. "People swallow pennies of the same size every day," she said. "They're smaller than an eraser."

But by dinnertime on the day after Braden swallowed the second magnet, he developed stomach pains. His mother thought it was either the flu or the magnets. "The magnets never left my mind," she said.

The next morning, with Braden still in pain, the family's doctor told them to go straight to the emergency room. An X-ray revealed the two magnets were stuck together.

But not stuck together the way you would think. Each had been ingested separately and both were in different segments of the intestine.

"They were attracted to each other, with the wall of each segment they were in stuck together," said Sanjeev Dutta, MD, the pediatric surgeon at Good Samaritan Hospital who would operate on Braden later that day. "Because they were so powerful, the wall of the intestine was getting squeezed, squeezed, squeezed, and then it just necrosed, or kind of rotted away, and created a hole between the two."

Using minimally invasive laparoscopy, Dr. Dutta removed both magnets with three small incisions during a procedure that lasted two hours. Braden went home three days after the operation.

Dr. Dutta, who is also an assistant professor of surgery and pediatrics at Lucile Packard Children's Hospital of Stanford University (which provides pediatric surgical services to Good Samaritan), has co-authored an article on the episode, which is published in *Archives of Pediatric and Adolescent Medicine.*

MAGNET WARNING

About two weeks later, the US Consumer Product Safety Commission (CPSC) updated an earlier warning about magnet-containing toys. Several construction sets, similar to the one Braden played with, have since been recalled.

According to the CPSC, there has been at least one death attributed to magnet ingestion, and at least 19 children required surgery after they swallowed magnets or pieces of metal (that can get stuck to the magnet).

Many of today's toys contain "rare-earth" magnets. "It's a new type of magnet that's extremely powerful, many times more powerful than the magnets that we used to play with," Dr. Dutta explained.

Dr. Dutta wants to make sure that parents are aware of this risk. "It seems like such a benign thing," he said. "[But] these things look like candy to a 3-year-old."

"It all happened because of a *toy*," said Eberle. "I didn't comprehend it. It was surreal. He knew to run to us. That probably saved him. He knew to tell us that, thank God, or I would've thought it was the flu."

For her part, Jill Eberle started getting rid of all magnetic toys in her house, even the huge ones. But 10 months later, she is still finding the little pieces.

"They're stuck to the side of a wall or a computer table," she said. "They're not gone yet."

info For more information on magnet safety, visit the Web site of the US Consumer Product Safety Commission at *www.cpsc.gov* and search "magnet safety."

Pet Turtles Linked to Rise in *Salmonella* Infections

Julie Harris, PhD, Epidemic Intelligence Service Officer, US Centers for Disease Control and Prevention, Atlanta, Georgia.

Pascal James Imperato, MD, MPH, distinguished service professor, and chair, department of preventive medicine and community health and director, master of public health program, State University of New York Downstate Medical Center, New York City.

Morbidity and Mortality Weekly Report.

Small pet turtles were to blame for 103 cases of *salmonella* infection in the second half of 2007, mostly in young children, US health officials said.

But the true number of infections with the potentially fatal bacteria is undoubtedly much higher, officials added.

Even though the sale of small turtles has been banned in the United States since 1975, the number of these reptiles being purchased for children has been increasing, according to the US Centers for Disease Control and Prevention (CDC).

"This is a larger number of cases than we would usually see," said Julie Harris, PhD, a CDC Epidemic Intelligence Service Officer. "We haven't documented such a large number of cases before associated with turtle exposure."

No deaths have been reported, but the infections led to the hospitalization of dozens of children, the CDC said.

The number of turtles owned by Americans has almost doubled in the last five years to more than 2 million, according to Dr. Harris, despite the fact that there is a ban on the sale of turtles that are under 4 inches in length.

NEW CASES OF INFECTIONS FROM TURTLES

The 103 cases that Dr. Harris and colleagues reported in the CDC's *Morbidity and Mortality Weekly Report* represent just a fraction of the total number of salmonella infections from pet turtles, she said.

According to the report, cases were reported in all but 15 states, with most cases occurring in California, Illinois, Pennsylvania and Texas.

Two of the infected children included a 13-year-old girl and a 15-year-old girl who became stricken after swimming in an unchlorinated in-ground pool owned by the family of the older girl. Two pet turtles, purchased at a South Carolina pet store were allowed to swim in the pool, the CDC reported.

Dr. Harris said many people aren't aware of the risk of salmonella infections from pet turtles. "Only 20% of these cases [in the report] said they were aware there was a connection between salmonella infection and reptile exposure," she said.

HOW SALMONELLA IS SPREAD

Up to 90% of turtles carry salmonella, Dr. Harris said. "This is a very serious infection, especially for small children," she added.

The infection is spread from contact with the turtles, but the contact doesn't have to be direct. "We have one case where a baby was bathed in a sink that turtle waste was disposed in," Dr. Harris said.

In some cases, the children put the pets in their mouths. In other cases, children became sick from just living in the same house with a turtle or other infected family members. Salmonella can live on surfaces for weeks, Dr. Harris noted.

Adults can get sick from salmonella, Dr. Harris went on to say, but children get much sicker. Some can die. "Small children should not be allowed to come into contact with turtles. The outcome is too dangerous and the risk is too high," she said.

Gastrointestinal symptoms, such as vomiting and diarrhea, caused by the bacteria typically begin 12 to 36 hours after exposure and generally last for two to seven days.

HOW TO PROTECT YOURSELF

"Children tend to handle these turtles a great deal," said Pascal James Imperato, MD, MPH, the distinguished service professor and chair of the department of preventive medicine and community health and director of the master of public health program at the State University of New York Downstate Medical Center in New York City.

"Their fingers come into contact with all the material on the turtle and in the water. Then there is finger-to-mouth contact, and they acquire the infection," he said.

Dr. Imperato said that to protect themselves, people who handle these turtles should wash their hands thoroughly after touching the animals. They should also wash nearby surfaces, because the germ can also spread when salmonella-contaminated water gets splashed out of containers.

"The best strategy is not to purchase or touch these turtles," Dr. Imperato said.

info For more information on the salmonella –turtle connection, visit the Web site of the Centers for Disease Control at *www.cdc. gov* and type "turtles" into the search box.

Bunk Beds Dangerous For Both Kids and Young Adults

Nationwide Children's Hospital, news release.

Injuries related to use of bunk beds should be a concern for young adults, as well as small children, a new study shows.

Three-quarters of the children who sustain bunk bed-related injuries are age 10 or younger. Surprisingly, however, injuries among young people between the ages of 18 and 21 have risen, noted the study from the Center for Injury Research and Policy of The Research Institute at Nationwide Children's Hospital in Columbus, Ohio.

The study, which estimated that an average of 36,000 bunk bed-related injuries occurred annually over the 16-year period it analyzed, was published in the journal *Pediatrics*.

"Everyone wants to feel safe and secure while resting or sleeping, yet bunk beds are a common source of injury among children and adolescents," said study coauthor Lara McKenzie, PhD, principal investigator in the Center for Injury Research and Policy at Nationwide Children's. "Our study found that bunk bed-related injuries could be severe and require hospital admission. In addition to children less than six years of age, young adults have a significantly increased risk of injury from bunk beds in schools, recreational sports facilities and public properties."

STUDY RESULTS

The study found 18- to 21-year-olds experienced bunk-bed injuries at nearly double the rate of children in the 14- to 17-year-old age group. The researchers speculated this might be because the older age group may use bunk beds more frequently due to the greater likelihood these individuals are in institutional settings, such as college dormitories and the military. The chance of injury from bed malfunction was also significantly higher for older children, possibly because of their larger size and increased weight.

Children younger than age three were 40% more likely to suffer head injuries than older children, probably because their higher center of gravity tends to cause them to fall headfirst.

For all ages, cuts, bruises, scrapes and bone fractures were the most common injuries related to bunk beds. Fractures, while the third most common injury, were nearly six times more likely to require hospital admission, transfer to another hospital or overnight observation than all other injuries.

HOW TO PREVENT
BUNK BED-RELATED INJURIES

•**Use guardrails on both sides of the upper bunk.** The gap between guardrails should be 3.5 inches or less to prevent entrapment and strangulation.

•**Make sure the mattress foundation is secure** and the mattress is of proper size.

•**Do not allow children under age six** to sleep in the top bunk.

•**Use night lights** to help children see in a dark room.

•**Remove hazardous objects** from around the bed.

•**Place bunk beds a safe distance from ceiling fans** or other ceiling fixtures.

info For more information on bunk bed safety, visit the Web site of the Sleep Products Safety Council at *www.safesleep.org*. Click on "For Grown-Ups" and then "Bunk Bed Safety."

Get the Lead Out

Mark A. Stengler, ND, naturopathic physician in private practice, La Jolla, California...adjunct associate clinical professor at the National College of Natural Medicine, Portland, Oregon...author of many books, including *The Natural Physician's Healing Therapies* and coauthor of *Prescription for Natural Cures* (both from Bottom Line Books)...and author of the *Bottom Line/Natural Healing* newsletter.

The discovery last fall that toddlers' toys were causing lead toxicity called attention to a problem many people thought was behind us.

Reality: In the US, lead toxicity continues to be a serious health threat—and not just in children. I regularly see adult patients whose bodies harbor dangerous levels of lead.

Reason: Lead that entered the body decades earlier can linger indefinitely. Not too long ago, lead was part of everyday life, appearing in paints, gasoline, household pipes, tin can soldering, crystal goblets and glazed ceramic dishware.

Current laws have improved the situation, but lead is still associated with numerous industries and hobbies. Lead is found in some lipsticks...herbs from China and Japan...and soil contaminated by car exhaust and other pollutants. In up to 90% of currently occupied homes in the US built before 1940, residents are exposed to lead that leaches into tap water from plumbing. Paint manufactured before 1978 may produce dust or flakes that contain lead.

HOW LEAD AFFECTS US

Lead inhibits enzymes that affect brain chemicals and oxygen-carrying red blood cells, causing malfunctions in nerve signal transmission, muscle contraction and heartbeat. It depletes the liver's stores of *glutathione*, an amino acid vital to detoxification and liver cell regeneration. Lead may contribute to autoimmune disorders (in which the immune system attacks the body's own tissues), such as rheumatoid arthritis and multiple sclerosis.

Children are particularly at risk because they absorb lead more readily...and because their developing organs and nervous systems are more vulnerable to lead's damaging effects.

Symptoms of lead toxicity include...

- **Gastrointestinal problems**—abdominal pain, diarrhea, constipation.
- **Muscular weakness and fatigue.**
- **Impaired kidney and liver function.**
- **Neurological effects**—headache, dizziness, tremors, poor memory and possibly dementia.
- **Central nervous system problems**—mood disorders, sleep disorders, seizures, decreased libido.
- **Cardiovascular effects**—high blood pressure, hardening of the arteries.
- **Reproductive problems**—decreased sperm count, menstrual irregularities, increased risk of miscarriage and stillbirth.
- **Developmental and behavioral problems in children.**

TESTING TROUBLES

Blood tests can detect lead only if exposure was recent or extreme. Most adults do not meet these criteria. In adults, lead generally has been present for many years, so the body has had time to remove it from the blood and lock it away in the fat, nerves, kidneys and bones. Only 2% of the total lead in an adult body typically remains in the blood, making blood testing unreliable.

Urine-testing accuracy depends on how it is done. The best tests involve a *chelating agent*—a substance that binds to metal, pulling it out of the body's tissues and sending it into the blood, from which it can then be filtered through the liver and kidneys and eliminated via urine and stool. When an oral chelating agent is used, urine tests reveal higher-than-normal lead levels in about 75% of people tested—compared with a 25% positive rate when a chelating agent is not used.

Who should be tested: Request testing if you have been exposed to lead or exhibit any symptoms of toxicity. Parents who suspect lead exposure should have their children tested.

PREVENTION AND TREATMENT

Calcium competes with lead for absorption in the digestive tract and for storage sites in the bones. With adequate calcium, you retain less lead. As a general preventive measure, I recommend that all teens and adults take 500 mg to 600 mg of calcium twice daily...and that children ages three to 12 take 500 mg once daily.

Chelation treatment is needed to pull lead from tissues so that it can be excreted. The form used depends on the severity of toxicity. Options (from least to most aggressive) include oral medication taken five to seven days per week... rectal suppositories used every other night before bedtime...or intravenous (IV) therapy for one to three hours weekly.

Patients must have kidney and liver function tests done before starting chelation to ensure that treatment will not overtax the organs responsible for detoxification and elimination. Naturopathic physicians and holistic medical doctors administer all types of chelation...chiropractors provide oral chelation. Most people experience little or no discomfort, though side effects may include skin rash, digestive upset, fatigue, cloudy thinking and/or moodiness. Treatment typically takes from two to eight months, depending on symptom severity. Follow-up testing indicates when treatment is complete. Unfortunately, insurance rarely covers chelation.

To guard against mineral loss during treatment, supplement daily with a high-potency multivitamin/mineral plus an additional 1,200 mg of calcium and 600 mg of magnesium. I also recommend Heavy Metal Support from Thorne Research (800-228-1966, *www.thorne. com*), available on-line...or OptiCleanse GHI or OptiCleanse Plus by Xymogen (800-647-6100, *www.xymogen.com*), available through health care professionals.

If you have lead toxicity, ask your doctor for a blood test to measure iron levels. Iron-deficient people absorb two to three times more lead than those with adequate iron. If necessary, your doctor can prescribe iron supplements.

Caution: Do not take iron unless diagnosed with a deficiency—excess iron can damage the liver, heart, etc.

Smart: If you suspect that any portion of your home was last painted before 1978—when paint containing lead was banned—paint over it to minimize flakes or dust that might pose a threat. If your home was built before 1940, install a charcoal filter on each water tap.

Family History Raises Risk of Shingles

JAMA/Archives journals, news release.

People with a family history of shingles may have increased susceptibility to the disease, say researchers at the University of Texas Medical School at Houston.

BACKGROUND

Shingles, also known as herpes zoster, causes nerve pain that occurs when the chickenpox virus (varicella zoster) is reactivated in spinal nerves. Most adults carry the varicella zoster virus, but only 10% to 30% develop shingles, according to background information in the study.

There are a number of risk factors for shingles, including weakened immunity, older age and other illnesses. Stress, trauma, exposure to heavy metals and ethnicity may also play a role. Recent research has suggested genetic risk factors for shingles and other infectious diseases associated with a weakened immune system may also increase risk.

THE STUDY

Researchers compared 504 people treated for shingles between 1992 and 2005 to 523 people without shingles. Along with demographic data, both groups provided information about their personal and family history of shingles.

The study was published in the *Archives of Dermatology*.

THE RESULTS

"A significantly higher proportion of [those with shingles] reported having a family history of herpes zoster [39.3% vs. 10.5%]," according to study authors. They found shingles patients were 4.35 times more likely to have a first-degree relative and 4.27 times more likely to have another relative with a history of shingles than those in the control group.

IMPLICATIONS

"Our study suggests a strong association between the development of herpes zoster and having a blood relative with a history of zoster," said the authors. "Such patients may be at increased risk of developing herpes zoster and therefore have a greater need for vaccination. Therefore, targeting these at-risk individuals based on their family history may decrease both their chance of future herpes zoster infection and health care expenditures."

info For more information about shingles, visit the Web site of the National Institute of Allergy and Infectious Diseases, *www3.niaid.nih.gov* and type "shingles" into the search box.

Just Like Skin, Eyes Can "Burn" in Strong Sun

American Optometric Association, news release.

Don't overlook your eyes when you're thinking about ultraviolet (UV) protection while spending time outdoors, experts say.

Overexposure to the sun's UV rays has been linked to a number of eye problems, such as macular degeneration, age-related cataracts, pterygium (a benign growth of the tissue over the white part of the eye), photokeratitis (a burn of the cornea) and corneal degenerative changes, according to the American Optometric Association (AOA).

These conditions can cause blurred vision, irritation, redness, tearing, temporary vision loss and, in some cases, blindness.

"Just as skin is 'burned' by UV radiation, the eye can also suffer damage. The lesson—especially for young people—is that eyes need protection, too. Protection can be achieved by simple, safe and inexpensive methods such as wearing a brimmed hat and using eyewear that properly absorbs UV radiation," said Gregory Good, a member of AOA's commission on ophthalmic standards.

Children and teens are particularly susceptible to sun-related eye damage, because they typically spend more time outdoors than adults, and the lenses of their eyes are more transparent than those of adults, which means that more harmful light can reach the retina.

But it appears many people still don't fully understand the danger UV rays pose to eyes.

A recent AOA survey found that 40% of Americans don't think UV protection is an important factor to consider when buying sunglasses. The survey also found that 61% of Americans buy sunglasses for their children, but 23% don't check if the lenses provide protection against UV rays.

IMPORTANT ADVICE FOR PROTECTING EYES

• **Wear protective eyewear any time your eyes are exposed to UV radiation,** even on cloudy days and during the winter.

• **Purchase quality sunglasses** that block out 99% of UVA and UVB radiation and screen out 75% to 90% of visible light.

• **Make sure sunglass lenses are perfectly matched in color** and free of distortions or imperfections.

• **Make sure children and teens wear sunglasses.** They typically spend more time in the sun than adults.

info For more advice on protecting yourself from the sun, visit the SunProtection.net Web site at *www.sunprotection.net.*

How to Choose the Best Medical Treatments

Albert G. Mulley, MD, chief of the general medicine division and director of the Medical Practices Evaluation Center at Massachusetts General Hospital in Boston. Dr. Mulley is also associate professor of medicine and of health policy at Harvard Medical School and cofounder of the Foundation for Informed Medical Decision Making, *www.fimdm.org*, also in Boston.

For generations, people dutifully obeyed medical authority—the doctor was always right. Then, medical consumers were urged to take control of their own treatment—to scour the Internet for information and seek additional medical opinions.

But does this approach ensure the best possible medical care? Many patients engage in extensive fact-finding missions that can be overwhelming, expensive and confusing. What's more, some patients feel they are unintentionally turning their doctors into adversaries to be challenged at every step.

Latest development: Experts who conduct research on decision making say that it's more helpful to bring your own personal values and preferences to the medical process than to spend your time exhaustively gathering information and/or seeking multiple opinions.

Albert G. Mulley, MD, cofounder of the Foundation for Informed Medical Decision Making, a nonprofit organization dedicated to helping people understand their medical choices, answers question about this approach.

• **Why has the thinking changed on the best ways for patients to make medical decisions?** There is an increasing recognition that few medical decisions are clear-cut. Most of the time, doctors and patients work in a gray zone. Two or more treatment options may be consistent with medical evidence and good medical practice. For example, for some women with breast cancer, a mastectomy (removal of the entire breast) or a lumpectomy (removal of the tumor and surrounding tissue) with radiation will yield the same chances of survival. Women who strongly prefer to save the breast will choose lumpectomy. They figure that if the cancer returns, they'll undergo a mastectomy then—but at least they will have a few more years with the breast. Other women feel that if their cancer comes back, they will regret not having removed more tissue, so they opt for mastectomy. Both treatments are equally effective, but the "best" choice is largely dictated by personal preference.

Doctors who have studied patients' decision-making processes recommend cooperation between the doctor and patient, recognizing that while doctors have technical, objective information, patients have subjective knowledge of their life priorities.

Imagine that you buy an airline ticket. Who controls the flight—you or the pilot? You could say the pilot, because he/she has the technical know-how to fly a plane. But you chose a plane that was going where you wanted to go.

It's the same with medical decisions. If you have doctors you trust and respect, then you'll want to make great use of their technical medical expertise. Once you know all treatment options and possible outcomes, you need to do the hard work of thinking about what is important to you…what outcomes you hope for…and what consequences you are willing to live with.

•**How do I ensure that I will know what all the options are?** You ask. When faced with a new treatment option—whether it is surgery or a new prescription—you should always ask your doctor…

1. Why are you recommending this treatment? This will help you understand the doctor's reasoning.

2. What is the likely outcome of this treatment? Listen for the typical outcome as well as the best-case and worst-case scenarios.

3. What are the possible side effects or consequences, and what are the chances of these occurring? With this response, you will learn about the potentially negative physical and psychological effects of a proposed treatment.

4. What does the procedure involve? This will tell you what it feels like to experience a particular medical procedure or treatment.

5. What are my other options? For each option, ask why it wasn't the doctor's first choice. Keep asking about other options until the doctor has exhausted all possibilities.

6. What happens if I do nothing? This tells you the natural course of the disease. You always have the option to decline treatment.

The answers to these questions provide all the objective information you need—options, possible outcomes, risks and benefits.

•**Shouldn't I get a second opinion?** In some cases, another doctor might clearly have more expertise in one of the treatment options, and this may warrant getting a second opinion. But it doesn't make sense to go to one doctor, passively hear out his recommendation, then go to another doctor and get another recommendation. In general, it makes more sense to fully explore all the options with a well-trained doctor who is willing to work with you in sharing the decision-making responsibility. If you don't trust your doctor to give you all of your options, then you should look for another doctor.

•**How do I know that my doctor is telling me everything I need to know?** Although physicians may prefer one treatment over another, they usually know all of the possible options and are willing to share them with patients who ask. A doctor may have a bias toward treatments with which he is most familiar—patients should be mindful of this when deciding whether they have a balanced understanding of the options. If you are seeing a specialist, ask about his experience with each treatment option and whether it is advisable to speak to a different specialist.

•**Isn't there value in doing Internet searches to learn more about my disorder?** Of course, the Internet can be useful, but it often produces a lot of information that isn't necessarily relevant to your individual situation.

A good medical decision by a patient is not always based on knowing a lot of detail—it's often about knowing the gist of your problem, what your options are and what the outcomes may be. Then you can apply your own personal preferences.

Many people value data over feelings. But the subjective part of the decision-making process is at least as important as the objective information. If you don't factor in your needs and desires, you leave a lot to chance…and the stakes are too high to rely on textbook knowledge and statistics alone.

•**What is the best way to evaluate my needs so that I know I am making a sound decision?** For each treatment option, write down the reasons you might choose it (the benefits) and the reasons to avoid it (the risks). How much do those risks and benefits matter to you? How do you feel about the impact of each possible outcome?

If you find that you have unanswered questions or don't understand the possible outcomes, talk with your doctor again. Also, talk with other people who have been through similar treatments to discover how they feel about the experience. Ask your doctor if there is a support group you could attend or if there are counselors to consult.

There is an element of chance in any decision. You need to reduce uncertainty to its lowest possible point, then make a decision you can live with. That way, there can be no "wrong" decisions.

How to Get Top-Notch Medical Care—No Matter Where You Are

Karen Rheuban, MD, vice president of the American Telemedicine Association (*www.atmeda*.org) in Washington, DC, and senior associate dean for continuing medical education and external affairs, and medical director of the office of telemedicine at the University of Virginia Health Systems in Charlottesville.

Imagine this: On a Saturday night, a 70-year-old man who is vacationing in a small resort town feels weakness in his leg and starts slurring his speech. An ambulance rushes him to the nearest community hospital, where an emergency room doctor examines the man and concludes that he is probably suffering a stroke.

An hour has passed since the man's symptoms began, so the doctor must find out *quickly* whether the symptoms are due to a blood clot that is starving the brain of blood (ischemic stroke) or bleeding into or around the brain (hemorrhagic stroke). If a blood clot is to blame, the man must receive medication within three hours to dissolve the clot to prevent brain damage. But the very same drug could be deadly if there's a hemorrhage in the man's brain.

Since this is a small community hospital, there is no neurologist on staff who specializes in stroke care nor is there a radiologist on site to read a computed tomography (CT) scan of the man's brain. At one time, the doctor would have been forced to transfer the man to a facility where such specialists were available—a delay that would dramatically increase the patient's risk for irreversible brain damage or death.

Now: New technologies allow even the most remotely located patients to get state-of-the-art diagnoses, and perhaps even treatments, in

hospitals that are not staffed by the types of specialists who ordinarily administer such care.

WHAT IS TELEMEDICINE?

Telemedicine is an innovation in health care that allows doctors to exchange a patient's medical information, as well as X-rays, CT scans and magnetic resonance imaging (MRI) scans, through the use of advanced technologies, including broadband communication networks and high-speed Internet lines. With telemedicine, medical care and/or second opinions can be provided for people who live in areas where medical specialists—such as ophthalmologists (eye doctors)...endocrinologists (doctors who treat hormone-related disorders, such as diabetes)...cardiologists (heart doctors)...infectious disease specialists...and dermatologists (skin doctors)—are not always available.

Telemedicine can be lifesaving in cases such as that of the stroke victim described previously—the ER physician at the community hospital can quickly obtain a CT scan and transmit it via broadband communication services to specialists at another location, who can consult with the referring hospital to determine whether the patient should receive a clot-dissolving drug.

GET BETTER CARE

Approximately 3,500 medical centers throughout the US offer telemedicine services, such as...

• **Live, interactive videoconferencing.** This technology allows a patient, while at a hospital or doctor's office, to communicate live over a video monitor with a medical specialist in another location. Medical equipment, such as a digital stethoscope or dermatology camera, is operated by on-site medical staff so that the off-site specialist can "examine" the patient and talk to him/her via videoconferencing. The off-site doctor's recommendations are then implemented by the on-site doctor.

• **"Store-and-forward" technology.** A doctor can transmit medical records and diagnostic images to a specialist of the patient's choice for later viewing, interpretation and recommendations, using broadband networks or other communication services.

TELEMEDICINE AT HOME

People with chronic diseases, such as diabetes, heart disease, lung disease, kidney disease and high blood pressure, usually require regular monitoring. Rather than go to doctors' offices for routine tests, these patients often can benefit from home-monitoring technology, known as home "telehealth." An estimated 200,000 Americans now use telehealth services.

This technology allows patients to transmit their blood pressure, electrocardiogram (ECG) results, blood oxygen or blood sugar levels, for example, to a home-health agency or their own physicians. Home monitoring can help doctors identify subtle problems, such as elevations in blood sugar or blood pressure, allowing for prompt treatment. This may eliminate the need for hospitalization.

CAN TELEMEDICINE HELP YOU?

Telemedicine is available to diagnose and monitor more than 50 different medical conditions, including…

•**Cancer.** Telemedicine not only allows cancer patients to obtain timely consultations and/or second opinions with physicians who are not located nearby, but also facilitates access to clinical trials, which may be located in distant academic and/or research centers.

In these cases, telemedicine can be used to transmit medical information, including diagnostic images and patient data, to screen the patient for eligibility in a particular clinical trial. For more on clinical trials, go to the National Institutes of Health Web site (*www.clinicaltrials.gov*).

•**Diabetes.** People with diabetes are at increased risk for complications, such as diabetic retinopathy (a vision-robbing disorder of the retina). Every person with diabetes should have a regular retinal exam to look for signs of retinopathy, which often can be treated with surgery or medication to prevent or slow vision loss. With appropriate training and equipment, a health professional at a hospital or clinic can acquire images and transmit them to a retinal specialist for review.

•**Heart disease.** Home telehealth can be especially helpful for people with heart disease or heart failure—conditions that require monitoring of blood pressure and devices, such as pacemakers. This data can be sent to a home health care monitoring agency and shared with a cardiologist.

•**Mental disorders.** Mental health professionals, such as psychiatrists, psychologists and social workers, are in short supply in many rural areas of the US. With telemedicine, people who have mental disorders, such as depression and anxiety, can receive diagnostic evaluations, ongoing therapy and medication management via videoconferencing.

•**Skin conditions.** Nationwide, and particularly in rural areas, there is a shortage of dermatologists. Telemedicine can give patients access to a dermatologist, either through live, interactive consultations or store-and-forward technologies.

Research shows that primary care physicians cannot adequately treat all types of skin problems. For example, a patient who was mistakenly being treated for shingles was recently diagnosed via telemedicine with *necrotizing fasciitis*, or "flesh-eating strep," a potentially deadly skin infection that requires prompt, aggressive treatment with surgery and antibiotics. A remotely based skin cancer patient also can benefit from frequent telemedicine exams by a dermatologist.

FEES FOR TELEMEDICINE

Some health insurance plans cover certain fees associated with telemedicine. For example, Medicare pays for some telemedicine services, such as remote cardiac monitoring services and remote screening for diabetic retinopathy, if the patient lives in a federally designated underserved rural area or inner city. For more information contact the Medicare Rights Center, (800-333-4114, *www.medicarerights.org*).

If you have some other form of insurance and your primary care provider or a specialist has suggested that you get a medical service via telemedicine, check with your health plan provider to see whether the fees will be covered.

Some telemedicine providers have received grants from private foundations and the federal government to help offset the cost to patients, while others offer reduced fees for some patients who do not have insurance coverage for telemedicine services.

Telemedicine Better Than ER Visits

University of Rochester Medical Center, news release.

Telemedicine is a cost-effective way to replace more than a quarter of all visits to the pediatric emergency department, according to a community-wide study conducted in New York. In general, telemedicine is exchanging medical information via electronic communication, such as the telephone or Internet, to improve a patient's health.

Ailments, such as ear infections or sore throats, that virtually always prove manageable by telemedicine, made up almost 28% of all pediatric ER visits in Rochester, New York, during one year, according to investigators from the University of Rochester Medical Center.

Their findings were presented recently at the Pediatric Academic Societies annual meeting, in Honolulu.

"We learned that more than one in four local patients are using the pediatric emergency department for non-emergencies," said lead investigator Kenneth McConnochie, MD, a professor of pediatrics at the University of Rochester's Golisano Children's Hospital. "This mismatch of needs and resources is inefficient, costly and impersonal for everyone involved."

THE STUDY

Dr. McConnochie and his colleagues, who direct a Rochester-based telemedicine program that provides interactive, Internet-based pediatric health care service to the area, analyzed data for all pediatric visits to the largest emergency department in the city. Based on their experience, they determined at least 12,000 visits were ones they routinely treat with success via telemedicine.

The other visits were either problems that sometimes are treatable through telemedicine, such as asthma attacks; or ones beyond the scope of the technology, such as a serious wound or injury.

"This would've not only freed up emergency resources to people who needed them more, it would have afforded smaller co-pays for parents and more timely, personalized care," Dr. McConnochie said.

TELEMEDICINE REDUCES INSURANCE COSTS TOO

In related research presented at the meeting, Dr. McConnochie suggested that telemedicine could also help insurers and the community by providing better quality care at a lower price—saving insurers more than $14 per child per year in that local community.

The conclusion was reached by studying two groups of children that were almost identical, but one had access to their doctor's office, the emergency department and telemedicine technology for care, while the second had only the first two options.

"We found that the first group of families, which had access to telemedicine for their children, did in fact access care for illness overall nearly 23% more often than the second group," Dr. McConnochie said.

But since children with telemedicine access had 24% fewer ER visits, which cost about seven times the cost of a doctor office or telemedicine visit, the telemedicine group ultimately still cost insurers less per child over a year.

info For information on children's health, visit the Web site of the Nemours Foundation, *www.kidshealth.org*.

Not Telling Your Doctor The Whole Truth Can Be Deadly

Robert Klitzman, MD, associate professor of clinical psychiatry at Columbia University College of Physicians and Surgeons and Mailman School of Public Health and a faculty associate at the Center for Bioethics at Columbia University, all in New York City. He is coauthor of *Mortal Secrets: Truth and Lies in the Age of AIDS* (Johns Hopkins) and author of *When Doctors Become Patients* (Oxford University).

Did you tell any white lies at your last doctor visit? Maybe you were too embarrassed to mention a sexual problem or didn't want to be lectured about skipping your medication. Research reveals there's near- ly a 50-50 chance that a patient won't tell the whole truth during a medical checkup—but withholding even minor information from a physician can lead to needless suffering and misdiagnosis.

Robert Klitzman, MD, an expert on medical privacy and disclosure, talks about the lies pa- tients tell…

•**Why do patients lie so often to their doctors?** The Web site WebMD did a survey recently that found that half of all patients who lie do it because they don't want to be judged. About 30% say the truth is just too embarrassing to reveal. Others lie to avoid a lecture from the doctor…because they don't think the informa- tion they fail to disclose is important…because they don't want to appear stupid…or because they don't want the truth in their records.

Many patients don't consider it lying to leave out information. If the doctor fails to ask about a particular condition, these patients don't feel the need to bring it up. Patients may not even realize that they're failing to provide the entire truth. This is common with men who don't re- port to their doctors that they're feeling irritable or tired. They don't recognize that these could be symptoms of depression.

•**What do patients lie about most often?** The big one is adherence to treatment and med- ication. A patient doesn't do what his doctor directs, but he's afraid the doctor will get mad if he says so. Also, patients often lie about be- haviors that they perceive as taboo—smoking, alcohol and drug use, and sexual issues, such as impotence and infidelity.

•**Does telling "white lies" to your doc- tor really compromise your health care?** Let's say you are prescribed an antibiotic for a week. After three days, you feel better, so you don't bother finishing it. Your doctor asks, "Did you take the antibiotic?" You respond, "Yes." After all, you did take it for a while and you are feeling better. However, if the infection recurs, your doctor may now treat you with the un- derstanding that the antibiotic you took wasn't effective when, in fact, it may have been if you had finished the pills.

Also, "small" problems you ignore or conceal can lead to more serious ones. A man may have a persistent ache or pain but delays going to the doctor. Months later, the pain gets so intense that he can't delay any longer, only to learn that he has cancer or a heart problem that could have been caught earlier.

•**Is there ever a good reason to lie to your doctor?** This gets into a gray area. Say that one of your parents has Huntington's disease, a pro- gressive, degenerative brain disease for which there is no cure. You want to get a genetic test to determine if you have the gene associated with the disease. If the results are positive, do you really want that on your permanent medi- cal record? Legally, your doctor cannot divulge the contents of your chart without your permis- sion—but potential lapses in privacy are a le- gitimate concern. If you have insurance through work, someone in human resources might gos- sip, and then your employer could find out about your condition. While there are employ- ment laws that protect you from discrimination, all kinds of subtle discrimination do exist, such as getting passed over for a promotion.

I can see why patients sometimes feel the need to withhold sensitive information. What I would suggest instead is having a candid con- versation with your doctor. Say, "I'm interested in having genetic testing done. I'm concerned because I don't want the results added to my permanent record. Would you be comfortable with that?"

•**How can a patient get past his fears and inhibitions?** There are several strategies that can be effective. One is to discuss the un- derlying fear up front with your physician. Say, "Doctor, I have something I want to mention, but it's awkward." A doctor's reassurance— "There's nothing to be embarrassed about. I re- ally have heard it all before"—often can relax you enough to speak freely.

You also could send the doctor an E-mail be- fore your appointment or hand him a note in the exam room if you can't say what you need to out loud.

Or use a "surrogate approach." Ask your spouse or son or daughter to speak with the doctor. Lots of men come in for checkups with their wives. The husband doesn't want to admit he's in pain, so the wife tells the doctor.

Another way to bring up a sensitive topic is to do so with a different member of the medical team. If you have a good rapport with a nurse, say to him/her, "I feel badly that I haven't been taking my medication as I should. Could you please tell the doctor for me?"

It's very important to avoid compounding communication gaps. The longer you withhold information from a doctor, the more you compromise your chances of getting the best treatment possible. Say, "There are some things I need to mention that I'm afraid I haven't told you in the past."

When to Shop for a New Gynecologist

Joel M. Evans, MD, an obstetrician/gynecologist who is the founder and director of The Center for Women's Health (*www.centerforwomenshealth.com*), an integrative health care facility in Stamford, Connecticut. He is assistant clinical professor at Albert Einstein College of Medicine and Columbia University College of Physicians and Surgeons, both in New York City, and a founding diplomate of the American Board of Holistic Medicine. Dr. Evans is coauthor of *The Whole Pregnancy Handbook*. Gotham.

You're in the gynecologist's office, feeling vulnerable as can be—naked except for that flimsy gown...feet up in the stirrups...exposing yourself to the world. Your physician is going about her exam, and when you muster up the nerve to mention some weird cramps you had, she sighs and looks at her watch.

If this sounds all too familiar, it's time to ask yourself, *Does my gynecologist see me as a whole person?* For optimal wellness, you need to have at least one doctor who answers all of your questions and treats you with respect, acknowledging you as a collaborative member of your own health care team. After all, you know your body better than anyone else.

When you feel pressured, the levels of certain brain chemicals are altered, making it likely that you will forget some of the questions you

had planned to ask the doctor. This could be dangerous.

Example: Suppose that along with those weird abdominal cramps, you've had a few embarrassing incidents with incontinence. If you're too flustered to mention these or if your doctor brushes you off with, "Every woman has those problems occasionally," you've missed the opportunity to investigate these early warning signs of ovarian cancer.

SHOULD YOU SAY "SO LONG"?

Ideally, a gynecologist will invite you to share information about your whole self—your home environment, workplace, emotional concerns, social support systems, family history, overall health and energy, and personal approach to health care. This makes accurate diagnoses much more likely. For instance, after taking appropriate steps to rule out potentially serious health problems, the doctor can reassure you that your cramps are related to the stress of your new job, or that your occasional incontinence is caused by a pot-a-day coffee habit—but only if she knows about those aspects of your life.

I'm not saying that you should immediately leave your current gynecologist if she takes the hurry-up, waist-down approach. If you have an involved, caring internist or family physician as your primary care provider, you can stick with a gynecologist who focuses only on your reproductive organs if that feels right for you.

It's quite a different story if you lack confidence in the care you are receiving or feel objectified by a gynecologist who never looks beyond the speculum—especially if you use your gynecologist as your primary care physician, as many women do. In that case, try talking with the doctor about your needs. If that doesn't help, it is time to find a physician who is a better fit. Don't feel disloyal. You have a right to be cared for in a way that reflects who you are as a human being.

SHOPPING FOR A DOCTOR

The first step in finding a new gynecologist is to formulate a personal definition of the ideal doctor. To do this, make a list of what bothers you about your current doctor, as well as what you appreciate.

Examples: "He 'joked' that I was a hypochondriac"…"She gives only one-word answers to my questions"… "She's punctual." This clarifies that you want a doctor who takes your concerns seriously, answers questions completely and knows your time is valuable.

Next, get referrals from other doctors you respect—or from any nurses you know (they often have inside information about physicians). Ask friends for the names of their doctors.

Request a 30-minute consultation with any gynecologist you are considering switching to. For such a nonemergency visit, she should be able to accommodate you within a month or two. *During your initial consultation, ask the doctor…*

•**Where she was trained** and how long she has been in practice.

•**What certifications she holds.** She should be board-certified in gynecology, ideally with a subspecialty certificate in an area important to you, such as maternal/fetal medicine or gynecologic oncology.

•**What her philosophy on patient care is.** Beware of any response like, "I expect patients to trust in my expertise and comply with my instructions," which suggests a dogmatic approach that does not acknowledge patients' individual personalities and preferences.

•**How she would handle any specific concern you might have,** such as whether to get genetic testing for breast cancer. If you don't understand her response, ask for clarification. Discussing your particular health issues allows you to judge whether the doctor is right for you (and also increases the chances that insurance will pay for the visit).

If the doctor seems offended, recalcitrant, dismissive of your questions or eager for the consultation to be over, simply thank her for her time and leave.

THE INTEGRATIVE OPTION

In your deliberations, consider interviewing an integrative gynecologist—one who combines traditional gynecology with complementary and alternative medicine. The general philosophy of such physicians is that real health springs from prevention and involves an integration of the emotional, spiritual and physical. In other words, no one symptom is treated as a single event, but rather as a part of a larger picture.

For treatment, integrative gynecologists use numerous therapies, such as stress-reduction techniques, nutritional and herbal supplements, and diet and lifestyle changes to promote optimal health. The very nature of this approach to wellness—in which the patient is encouraged to be an active participant in her self-care—guarantees that an integrative gynecologist views a patient as a whole person, rather than a body part with a problem.

Like their conventional counterparts, integrative gynecologists graduate from a regular medical school and are board-certified in gynecology. In addition, they may be certified through the American Board of Holistic Medicine (509-886-3046, *www.holisticboard.org*), which requires specific additional training. At present, in the US, there are only about 200 integrative physicians specializing in women's health, but this number is growing. *To find out if there is one in your area, contact…*

•**The American Holistic Medical Association** (410-838-1010, *www.holisticmedicine.org*).

•**The Center for Mind-Body Medicine** (202-966-7338, *www.cmbm.org*).

•**The Institute for Functional Medicine** (800-228-0622, *www.functionalmedicine.org*).

Keep looking until you find a gynecologist who can provide the care and respect you deserve.

What Doctors Should Ask You— But Usually Don't

Lars Osterberg, MD, clinical assistant professor of medicine at Stanford University School of Medicine in Stanford, California, and chief of general internal medicine at VA Palo Alto Health Care System in Palo Alto, California. His article on medication compliance appeared in *The New England Journal of Medicine.*

Medication compliance means taking all your prescription drugs as directed by your doctor—at the right times…in the right dosages...every day you're supposed to, for as long as necessary. In other words, it means following the instructions precisely. Sounds easy, right?

Not necessarily.

Example: Longstanding research shows that about 125,000 Americans die each year because they don't take their heart medication properly.

Nearly one-third of people who are prescribed drugs don't even fill their original prescriptions. *Among those who do, compliance rates follow the "rule of sixths"...*

• **⅙ are perfect in their compliance.**

• **⅙ are pretty good,** but sometimes take the drug at the wrong time of day.

• **⅙ miss a day of medication every now and then.**

• **⅙ take "drug holidays"** (discontinuing medication for three or more days) three or four times per year.

• **⅙ take drug holidays once a month or more,** and frequently skip their medication for one to two days.

• **⅙ don't comply much at all...** but tell their doctors that they do.

WHY SO MUCH RESISTANCE?

There are a variety of reasons why people don't take their medication as prescribed. Unfortunately, many doctors don't ask about compliance, and patients usually don't bring up the topic on their own.

Important: Even if your doctor doesn't ask, be sure to discuss any problems you may be having adhering to the drug regimen you have been prescribed.

If you're having trouble sticking to your medication schedule, follow up with your doctor or his/her nurse by phone or E-mail between appointments.

Another option is to keep a medication log to take to the doctor—this will give you the feeling that you are preparing for an appointment every day. Make note of any side effects or problems you're having with adhering to the drug regimen.

The top nine reasons (listed alphabetically) that people don't take their medication and my advice for correcting the problem...

• **Apathy.** Some people lose interest in their health, so thus stop taking their medication.

Solution: Schedule an appointment with your doctor. Your apathy may be a sign of depression, a relatively common secondary disorder among people faced with a serious or painful illness. Your physician usually can prescribe an antidepressant, which may improve both your mental outlook and your medication compliance.

• **Conscious omission.** When a doctor prescribes medication, some people feel compelled to defy authority/assert their independence.

Solution: Rather than waging an emotional rebellion, remember who stands to gain from medication compliance—if you don't take the drug, only you will be hurt...not the doctor.

• **Cost.** The medication is too expensive.

Solutions: Ask your doctor if there is a generic version of your medication...or if another, less expensive medication could be substituted. Another option is pill splitting. For some medications, the cost is the same, regardless of the dose—for example, a 5-mg pill could cost the same as one that is 10 mg. By buying the higher dose and cutting the pills in half, you get twice the bang for your buck. Pill-splitting devices are available in drugstores for less than $10. Not all medications can be split—ask your pharmacist.

• **Denial.** When taking medications for a "silent" disease, such as high blood pressure, some people disregard the diagnosis, thinking that if they were really sick, they would feel bad.

Solution: Ask your doctor what the risks are in not taking the medication. For example, even if you know that a medication helps reduce blood pressure, you may need to be reminded that your risk for stroke and heart attack is increased if your blood pressure is not controlled.

• **Fear.** Some people think that all prescription drugs—or a particular prescription drug—will hurt them.

Solution: If you are concerned about potential side effects of prescription drugs and prefer "natural" or herbal treatments, discuss this with your doctor. He may be able to recommend a dietary supplement or to allay your fears concerning the medication.

•**Feeling better.** Once the immediate health problem improves, many people cut back or stop taking the prescribed medication.

Solution: Realize that doctors prescribe medication according to specific dosing schedules so that the medication builds up in the bloodstream. If you stop taking an antibiotic, for example, you may not eliminate all the bacteria causing an infection. "Drug holidays" should be avoided, because skipping days may cause fluctuations in the blood levels of medication, which can make the drug less effective.

•**Forgetfulness.** Memory problems, as well as having other priorities, cause many people to miss taking medication.

Solutions: Count doses in advance and store them in a compartmentalized pill storage box. One- or two-week containers are available at most supermarkets and drugstores.

It also helps to put medication in a place where you are most likely to see it. For example, if you take it in the morning, store the medication near your coffee mug or in the utensil drawer. If the medication must be refrigerated, place a reminder note near your mug or in the utensil drawer.

People who own cell phones, personal digital assistants or computers with an alarm feature can set these devices to ring at the same time every day. Pocket-sized alarms used solely as a reminder to take medication are available in drugstores for about $6 to $10.

•**Lifestyle.** Travel, inconsistent work or home hours, or a generally busy schedule can interfere with medication compliance.

Solution: Keep your medication stored in a pill box and leave it where you will be sure to see it—such as on a bedside table—whether you're at home or traveling.

•**Side effects.** Nausea, headache, drowsiness and upset stomach can occur with many medications.

Solution: Your doctor usually can change the prescription, give suggestions about other ways to take the medication—for example, with food—or prescribe an additional drug to counteract the side effects.

Electronic Pillbox Helps Seniors Take Meds Properly

David Flockhart, MD, PhD, director, division of clinical pharmacology, Indiana University School of Medicine, Indianapolis.
American Geriatric Society meeting, Washington, D.C.

Older adults following a medication regimen are less likely to miss doses when reminded by an electronic pillbox that both beeps at the appointed drug-taking time and announces the number of pills to take and how to take them, new research reveals.

The study, which was funded by the National Institute on Aging, was presented at the American Geriatric Society meeting in Washington, D.C., by co-authors Vesta Brue, founder and chairman of Lifetechniques Inc., of San Antonio, and Priscilla Ryder, of the Department of Pharmaceutical Health Services Research at the University of Maryland School of Pharmacy. Lifetechniques is the manufacturer of the particular electronic pillbox that was used in the study.

THE STUDY

The interactive pillbox was given to a group of patients between the ages of 65 and 84 who were each following a prescription regimen of at least four medications. All the patients were self-sufficient with respect to their ability to take their own medications.

Researchers tracked patients' natural pill-taking patterns for three weeks and then for three more weeks using "MedSignals"—a commercially available electronic pillbox.

The pillbox holds up to a month's supply of medications, with separate compartments for up to four drugs. As programmed, the box beeps at pill-taking times, indicates the appropriate compartment and displays the number of pills to take on a screen. When the compartment lid is lifted, a programmed audio message announces the number of pills to take, along with specific information about how to ingest the particular medication.

All the boxes were rigged to record, time-stamp and transmit via phone lines all lid openings, which the researchers equated with the taking of an actual medication. The researchers noted that the pillbox comes with such a phone-monitoring system, for patients and their caregivers to use as desired.

THE RESULTS

The researchers found that electronic pillboxes boosted drug adherence. With the boxes, patients prescribed more than a single dose per day of any particular drug took one pill more per day on average, the authors found. In addition, the number of days when patients accidentally skipped their drug regimen altogether dropped to just 6% when using an electronic pillbox—from 12% without the box.

Last, the proportion of doses taken at, or near, the time they should be taken went up with the electronic pillbox.

EXPERT REACTION

David Flockhart, MD, PhD, director of the division of clinical pharmacology at Indiana University's School of Medicine in Indianapolis, said the notion of an electronic pillbox draws critical attention to a major public health concern.

"Compliance with medications is a huge problem in general, and in particular among the elderly," he observed. "It is even more problematic among those who take a lot of medication, which is a lot of people, given that the majority of seniors who take medications take more than five prescriptions a day. So the value of something like this is potentially very large."

"However," Dr. Flockhart added, "the question always comes up as to whether these kinds of benefits seen in a clinical trial would really translate to the real world. Because the patients in a study like this know that they're being monitored, they might be remembering to do something when the box beeps that they might not actually remember in real life. So I would encourage the investigators to follow up this finding with a strictly observational study, rather than a clinical trial, to see how this will work in a natural setting."

KEEPING TRACK OF MEDICATIONS

To take control of their prescription medication regimen, the US Food and Drug Administration recommends that senior citizens use a calendar or a pillbox to help adhere to drug routines. They point out that pillboxes with multiple compartments are particularly helpful for older patients dealing with complex multi-pill regimens, as well as for those who have difficulty opening safety sealed drug containers.

The FDA also encourages seniors to undergo a yearly "Medicine Check-Up," as an opportunity to both toss out expired medicines and to discuss possible drug side effects and interactions with a pharmacist and/or doctor.

info For more information on safe prescription medication use for senior citizens, visit the Web site of the US Food and Drug Administration at *www.fda.gov*, and type "older adults" into the search box.

Saving Money on Medications

Marjory Abrams, publisher, *Bottom Line* newsletters, Boardroom Inc., 281 Tresser Blvd., Stamford, Connecticut 06901.

My eyebrows went up when I read recently about a North Carolina insurance program that saved $6.6 million over a three-year period through prescription drug "cost-control interventions." Individuals covered by the plan saved, too. Their average monthly drug expenditures dropped by about 11%, from $11.52 to $10.23 per prescription.

The study, published in *The American Journal of Managed Care*, was led by David P. Miller, Jr., MD, assistant professor at Wake Forest University School of Medicine in Winston-Salem, North Carolina. The study focused on the university medical center's own health insurance plan, which covers more than 22,000 people.

The bulk of the savings came from prescribing generic instead of branded drugs—an option that is becoming more widely available.